T0302024

Leading the Lean Healthcare Journey

Driving Culture Change to Increase Value

SECOND EDITION

Leading the Lean Healthcare Journey

Driving Culture Change to Increase Value

SECOND EDITION

Joan Wellman • Pat Hagan
Howard Jeffries • Cara Bailey

CRC Press is an imprint of the
Taylor & Francis Group, an **informa** business
A PRODUCTIVITY PRESS BOOK

CRC Press
Taylor & Francis Group
6000 Broken Sound Parkway NW, Suite 300
Boca Raton, FL 33487-2742

First issued in paperback 2021

ISBN-13: 978-1-03-209772-5 (pbk)
ISBN-13: 978-1-4987-3956-6 (hbk)

Publisher's Note
The publisher has gone to great lengths to ensure the quality of this reprint but points out that some imperfections in the original copies may be apparent.

Library of Congress Cataloging-in-Publication Data

Names: Wellman, Joan, editor. | Hagan, Pat (Patrick), editor. | Jeffries, Howard, editor. | Bailey, Cara (Cara Lee), editor.
Title: Leading the lean healthcare journey : driving culture change to increase value / [edited by] Joan Wellman, Pat Hagan, Howard Jeffries, and Cara Bailey.
Description: Second edition. | Boca Raton : Taylor & Francis, 2017. | Includes bibliographical references and index.
Identifiers: LCCN 2016008969 | ISBN 9781498739566 (hardcover : alk. paper)
Subjects: | MESH: Delivery of Health Care--organization & administration | Total Quality Management | Efficiency, Organizational | Organizational Culture
Classification: LCC RA971 | NLM W 84.1 | DDC 362.1068/1--dc23
LC record available at http://lccn.loc.gov/2016008969

Visit the Taylor & Francis Web site at
http://www.taylorandfrancis.com

and the CRC Press Web site at
http://www.crcpress.com

To leaders everywhere who are dedicating themselves to reducing waste and improving the reliability of healthcare.

Contents

Preface to the First Edition

Joan Wellman had invited Pat Hagan and Jerry Zimmerman to help her teach her weeklong Lean Leader Training to a group of physician and executive leaders at Children's Hospitals and Clinics of Minnesota. It was July 2008. During the course of the week, we talked a great deal with our "students" about the utility of applying continuous improvement principles to healthcare. After class each day, we took advantage of the long and warm Minnesota evenings to discuss the importance of an organization's leadership to a successful Lean transformation, and the different paths taken by different hospitals (and manufacturing companies) on their Lean journeys.

Joan noted her early 1990s involvement in the introduction of Lean principles to healthcare in the Northwest, citing Bellevue's Overlake Hospital as an example of an early adopter of Lean methodology due to the influence of their board chair from the Boeing Company. Later Peace Health, Virginia Mason Medical Center, Group Health, and Seattle Children's also began adapting continuous improvement to their organizations. Leaders at all of these organizations were taking the risk of applying "manufacturing methods" to healthcare practices. Each, however, took different approaches to implementation, some preferring a top-down approach and others a less philosophical "tools-only" path.

As we talked we discussed the Seattle Children's approach, what we called "continuous performance improvement" (CPI), and compared and contrasted it with those of others. At Seattle Children's, CPI was marked by guidance and direction from the top but grounded in the engagement and participation of clinical leadership, middle management, and staff, and we had embraced the philosophy of continuous improvement as well as the tools and methods. Not that we felt this approach was superior to others, but our results were pretty darn good and our people—faculty, management, and staff—were highly engaged in CPI.

As we talked we agreed we had a story to tell and, coincidentally, with the Lean Leader Training modules we were using that week, a structure with which to tell it. The training modules are based on the principles of continuous improvement, and we decided that our story should take the form of a series of chapters based on those principles. To highlight the leadership and involvement of clinicians, management, and staff, the chapters would be written by people who had applied Lean principles to improve their own processes, from 5S to load leveling to standard work....

So, two and a half years later, we're published. Most of the chapters that follow describe work at Seattle Children's, but to avoid an exclusive focus on any one organization and the possible concern that it is a "special" case, several other healthcare organizations with whom Joan has worked have also provided chapters.

We hope that readers both beginning and well on their way on their Lean journeys will find the stories within helpful as they seek to apply the philosophy and principles of continuous improvement to their work.

Preface to the Second Edition

The many authors of this excellent book are real pioneers in the Lean healthcare revolution. They bring years of experience and hard-learned insights in describing the issues and challenges of leading a Toyota-style Lean transformation. What makes this book unique is that the thirty-five-plus authors of the various chapters have a total of more than four hundred years experience of trying and learning the application of the Toyota System to the challenges they face in healthcare.

The second edition of *Leading the Lean Healthcare Journey* provides tremendous breadth. There are authors who are CEOs and presidents. There are nutritionists and business analysts. There are nurses and MDs. There are supply chain experts and psychiatrists. There are experts in Lean facility design and experts in running a superb pharmacy. There are experts in improving operating room operations and experts in improving laboratories.

These are not your usual suspects for authorship of a book on Lean healthcare transformation. These people have actually done it. I have the honor of knowing many of these people and they really believe any process can be improved! They subscribe to the notion that "every system is perfectly designed to get the results it gets."* And if they want different results, they need to change the design of the system.

Another truly special aspect of this book is the continuity to the case studies. Most of the original chapter authors of the first edition are the same in this edition. They bring with them the new insights that have been gained over the past five to six years. The chapters reflect what it means to become a "continuous learning organization" that is ever improving. I just hope that they write a third edition in another five years and share their continuing lessons learned. That would make a rarity by learning how a Lean healthcare system develops and unfolds over almost two decades.

Many of the chapters in the book are case studies from Seattle Children's, an early adopter in the application of the Toyota System to a healthcare system. Seattle

* Paul Batalden, MD, Dartmouth Medical School.

Children's has been at this for more than fifteen years and is one of the few organizations, healthcare or otherwise, that has sustained what Deming described as "constancy of purpose" for that long of time. There is much to learn from such organizations.

I highly recommend this second edition of *Leading the Lean Healthcare Journey* as required reading by healthcare CEOs, leaders at all levels, and Lean change agents. There are just too many insights and lessons learned to pass up.

Colin L. Fox Jr., PhD*
Member, Board of Trustees
Seattle Children's Hospital

* Colin Fox is retired from Terex Corporation where he was senior vice president of Terex Business Systems, responsible for Lean operations in Terex facilities around the globe.

Acknowledgments

We would like to thank Jill Post, this book's tireless project manager, for her hard work keeping us organized, reminding us of deadlines, and flogging us to the finish line. We couldn't have completed it without her.

We would also like to thank Katy Dowd for her many contributions and support for our team.

This second edition represents the hard work of many authors writing about how dedicated, smart people with great ideas are changing healthcare in America. We are privileged to present their stories in this book.

And we thank Productivity Press for its continued willingness to publish our work.

About the Authors

Joan Wellman, MS, MIM, is the founder and president of Joan Wellman & Associates (JWA Consulting) and executive vice president of Simpler®. She pioneered the application of Toyota principles to healthcare in 1995 and began more than a decade of Lean consultation to Seattle Children's Hospital in 1997. Today, JWA supports healthcare organizations as they implement the methods, management systems, and mind-set required for sustained Lean transformation. Previously, Joan was a partner at Deltapoint Corporation, consulting on implementation of Toyota Production System principles in the aerospace, telecommunications, high technology, pharmaceutical, and energy industries. She was director of Training and Leadership Development at Pacific Gas and Electric, and held key positions in organization development at Transamerica and 3Com Corporations.

Patrick Hagan, MHSA, is the former president and chief operating officer of Seattle Children's Hospital. A hospital executive for 25 years, he has held executive positions at children's hospitals in Ohio, Arizona, and Seattle. Pat helped develop and lead Seattle Children's continuous performance improvement (CPI) strategy. This multidimensional approach contributed to the hospital's success in improving its performance in service quality, clinical access, patient safety, staff engagement, and financial results. Pat has spoken at numerous national conferences about Seattle Children's successful application of its transformative CPI strategy and is currently an engagement leader at JWA Consulting.

Howard E. Jeffries, MD, MBA, is a cardiac intensive care physician and the chief medical officer of accountable care at Seattle Children's Hospital. He is a clinical professor of pediatrics at the University of Washington School of Medicine. He completed a residency in pediatrics at Children's Memorial Hospital and a fellowship in pediatric critical care at Children's Hospital Los Angeles. He has lectured and published peer-reviewed articles and book chapters with an emphasis on population health, cardiac intensive care, informatics, and quality improvement.

Cara Bailey, MBA, senior vice president of continuous performance improvement at Seattle Children's Hospital, joined the organization in 1998 and was involved in its earliest efforts to adopt the tools and philosophy of the Toyota Production System in healthcare. In her current leadership role at Seattle Children's, Cara is responsible for functions that support improvement throughout the organization, including Lean promotion, quality measurement and improvement, clinical effectiveness, patient safety, and project management. She has more than 25 years of broad administrative healthcare leadership experience.

Contributors

Robert C. Atkins
Pediatric Hospitalist
Hawaii Permanente Medical Group
Seattle, Washington

Jeffrey Avansino, MD
Department of Surgery
Division of Pediatric General and Thoracic Surgery
Seattle Children's Hospital
Seattle, Washington

Cara Bailey, MBA
Senior Vice President, Continuous Performance Improvement
Seattle Children's Hospital
Seattle, Washington

David J. Bailey, MD, MBA
President and Chief Executive Officer
Nemours Children's Health System
Jacksonville, Florida

Ruth Benfield, RN, MS, FACHE
Vice President, Medical Psycho-Social Services
Seattle Children's Hospital
Seattle, Washington

Michael D. Boyer, MBA, PhD
Joan Wellman & Associates (JWA Consulting)
Issaquah, Washington

Lisa Brandenburg, MBA, MPH
President
Seattle Children's Hospital
Seattle, Washington

Robert Bridges, CPA
Chief Executive of Nemours Florida Operations
Nemours Children's Health System
Jacksonville, Florida

Kristina H. Deeter, MD, FAAP
Fellow, Pediatric Critical Care Medicine
Seattle Children's Hospital
Seattle, Washington

Aaron Dipzinski, Esq, MHPA
Senior Director–Division Leader
Ambulatory Regional Services
Seattle Children's Hospital
Seattle, Washington

Sean H. Flack, MBChB, FCA
Acting Director, Clinical Anesthesia Services
Director, Regional Anesthesia Division
Seattle Children's Hospital
Seattle, Washington

Jeff Foti
Associate Medical Director/Consultant, Clinical Effectiveness, Hospitalist
Seattle Children's Hospital
and
Clinical Associate Professor
University of Washington
Seattle, Washington

Ken Gow, MD
Department of Surgery
Division of Pediatric General and Thoracic Surgery
Seattle Children's Hospital
Seattle, Washington

Debra Gumbardo, MS, RN, NE-BC
Chief, Psycho-Social Services
Seattle Children's Hospital
Seattle, Washington

Patrick Hagan, MHSA
Engagement Leader
Joan Wellman & Associates (JWA Consulting)
and
Former President and Chief Operating Officer
Seattle Children's Hospital
Mercer Island, Washington

Eric Harvey, PharmD, MBA
Pharmacy Quality Manager
Seattle Children's Hospital
Seattle, Washington

Charles Hodge, MBA
President and Chief Executive Officer
BlueBin, Inc.
Chicago, Illinois

Norm Hubbard, MBA
Executive Vice President
Seattle Cancer Care Alliance
Seattle, Washington

Bryan King, MD
Director, Psychiatry and Behavioral Medicine
Seattle Children's Hospital
Seattle, Washington

Janeen Lambert, CPC, CPC-H, CHC
Associate Administrator of Regulatory Compliance, Chief Compliance Officer
Everett Clinic
Everett, Washington

Polly Lenssen, MS, RDN, CD, FAND
Director, Clinical Nutrition
Cochair, Nutrition Subcommittee
Seattle Children's Hospital
Seattle, Washington

Barb Marquardt, RPh
Outpatient Pharmacy Operations Manager
Seattle Children's Hospital
Seattle, Washington

Lynn D. Martin, MD, FAAP, FCCM
Medical Director, Continuous Performance Improvement
Interim Director, Bellevue Surgery Center
Seattle Children's Hospital
Seattle, Washington

Darren Migita, MD
Medical Director, Clinical Standard Work
Seattle Children's Hospital
and
Clinical Associate Professor of Pediatrics
University of Washington School of Medicine
Seattle, Washington

Thérèse Mirisola, RN, MSN, CPON
Cancer Care Unit
Seattle Children's Hospital
Seattle, Washington

Kellie P. Olmstead, MBA
Continuous Improvement Manager
Nemours Children's Health System
Jacksonville, Florida

Iwalani Paquette
Director of Business Services
Everett Clinic
Everett, Washington

Elizabeth Poole
Associate, Continuous Performance Improvement Office
Seattle Cancer Care Alliance
Seattle, Washington

Xuan Qin, PhD
Department of Laboratories
Seattle Children's Hospital
and
Department of Laboratory Medicine
University of Washington School of Medicine
Seattle, Washington

Camille Rapacz
Director, Continuous Performance Improvement Office
Seattle Cancer Care Alliance
Seattle, Washington

Mark A. Reed, MD, MPPM
Medical Director
Joan Wellman & Associates (JWA Consulting)
Mercer Island, Washington

Karin Rogers, RN, BSN, CIC
Infection Prevention
Seattle Children's Hospital
Seattle, Washington

Joe C. Rutledge, MD
Department of Laboratories
Seattle Children's Hospital
and
Department of Laboratory Medicine
University of Washington School of Medicine
Seattle, Washington

David L. Suskind, MD
Cochair, Nutrition Subcommittee
Seattle Children's Hospital
Seattle, Washington

Glen Tamura, MD, PhD
Medical Director, Inpatient Medical Units
Seattle Children's Hospital
and
Associate Professor of Pediatrics
University of Washington School of Medicine
Seattle, Washington

Steven D. Wanaka, RPh
Director of Pharmacy
Seattle Children's Hospital
Seattle, Washington

Joan Wellman, MS, MIM
President
Joan Wellman & Associates (JWA Consulting)
and
Executive Vice President
Simpler®
Seattle, Washington

Jerry J. Zimmerman, MD, PhD, FCCM
Faculty, Pediatric Critical Care Medicine
Seattle Children's Hospital
Seattle, Washington

Chapter 1

Introduction

This book is about people who have implemented dramatic change in their organizations by applying the principles and methods of the Toyota Production System (TPS) to healthcare. In this second edition there are new chapters by people who have adopted a Lean strategy since we last published, epilogues to first-edition chapters by people who have been on this journey for many years, as well as chapters that remain as written from the first edition. Each chapter tells how determined men and women have applied the principles of TPS to their work, innovating and leading their organizations forward. These people are improving the patient experience by reducing waste and thereby reducing costs—vitally important to all of us, given that our healthcare system currently consumes almost 20 percent of U.S. gross domestic product.

Each of these stories started with a healthcare leader who was curious enough to read about TPS (or "Lean"), participate in training, and visit manufacturing companies that have proven Lean track records. Curiosity and exposure to new ways of thinking helped these leaders understand that much of what we do in healthcare is waste "cleverly disguised as real work." Curiosity also led them to understand that quality, cost, patient access, and safety are not mutually exclusive trade-offs but intersecting aims that can be improved concurrently if we are willing to learn from the likes of Toyota.

In our first edition of this book, we described the approach and lessons learned from some of the earliest healthcare organizations to apply TPS to their operations. Our focus, and theirs, was primarily on the "breakthrough" half of the Lean journey: the exciting initial forays in breakthrough improvements that often produce impressive results in waste reduction and staff engagement. However, we learned through experience that the gains that improvement teams struggle so hard to achieve can be easily lost. Five years later, chapters in this second edition address the need to couple breakthrough improvements with the other half of the Lean journey: the Lean management system (LMS). In 2010, we began organizing study trips to manufacturers steeped in LMS so that healthcare leaders could learn from the best. We observed leaders using LMS as a powerful means of focusing their organizations and achieving breakthrough levels of performance. We also observed a commitment to sustaining gains and ongoing, never-ending improvement through the rigor and discipline of LMS. These study trips made us realize that everyone in our organization, from executive leaders to those at the front lines of care, needed to embrace a new way of thinking and a new way of going about their work. No longer could Lean be a project-by-project activity with episodes of improvement. We had to all take on the responsibility for *continuous*, daily improvement, the cornerstone of LMS.

The stories that follow come from Seattle Children's Hospital (SCH) and other organizations that have engaged Joan Wellman & Associates (JWA Consulting) as consultants over the last 15 years: The Everett Clinic in Everett, Washington; Nemours Children's Health System in Florida and Delaware; and Seattle Cancer Care Alliance. These organizations vary widely in size and complexity from standalone hospitals (SCH) to multi-institutional systems (Nemours). These organizations also have very different physician models including a primarily academic model (Seattle Children's Hospital), an employed physician model (Nemours), and a physician-owned model (Everett Clinic).

The case studies demonstrate that organizations can effectively apply Lean principles regardless of their size, physician model, or structure. These organizations use different words to describe their version of the Lean approach, but their strategies are grounded in the same enduring philosophy around which everyone in the healthcare enterprise can rally: focus on the patient, support your people in their work, and take a strategic, long-term view. Lean is about reducing waste to achieve the goals that increase value for the patient. These goals, which we refer to in shorthand as QCDSE, are to improve quality, decrease cost, improve delivery (patient access), improve safety, and increase engagement of all organization members in continuous improvement. These stories demonstrate how Lean can drive and sustain improvement in QCDSE.

Furthermore, the variety of stories offered in the second edition demonstrate that Lean applies everywhere in the healthcare enterprise, with the engagement of everyone, every day. If the Lean effort in your organization has been pigeonholed to "only operations" or "only patient flow," with your colleagues thinking that Lean has little to do with the business office, or the work of caregivers or executives, take heart. This edition provides evidence that Lean is relevant everywhere in your institution. You'll learn, for example:

- How a cancer clinic overcame problems with inconsistent and unsustained results and achieved 100-percent improvement in on-time performance and 28-percent improvement in new slot utilization
- How a behavioral health clinic cut wait time for new appointments by almost 50 percent
- How clinical standard work can become the focus of collaborative, cross-disciplinary work that is continuously improved, reducing length of stay while improving resident teaching and patient outcomes

- How a health system improved productivity in its materials distribution process and improved productivity of materials management staff by 400 percent
- How clinical standard work in an intensive care unit (ICU) greatly reduced use of opiates, patient time on ventilators, and length of stay, but when those gains eroded over time a new understanding of the role of continuous improvement emerged
- How standard work for rounds resulted in higher patient satisfaction, less travel, fewer handoffs, and improved learning experience for residents
- How safety was improved and cost reduced for total parenteral nutrition (TPN) and, through continuous improvement, greatly reduced utilization of TPN overall
- How central line infection rates on a cancer unit were reduced after "plateauing out" for a number of years
- How nonoperative time in the operating room (OR) was reduced by 50 percent and with sustained gains
- How a business office saved millions of dollars by removing waste in the registration to cash value stream
- How a complex inpatient lab went beyond improvements in the core lab to reduce turnaround times by more than 50 percent for microbiology, autopsy testing, and cytogenetics
- How costs were reduced from $100 million to $70 million using Lean design and construction on an outpatient surgery and ambulatory center

Achieving outstanding results is anything but easy. You don't have to read between the lines of these stories to realize how hard it is to change deeply ingrained behaviors that embed waste and thwart the delivery of compassionate, safe, patient-centered care. You'll no doubt recognize the challenges as the authors describe their efforts to build and maintain a consensus for change in their organizations.

This book is not a "how to" improve healthcare book, or a recipe on how to run an operating room or intensive care unit more efficiently. It is a book about curiosity, humility, and the tenacity to challenge deeply held assumptions about how we deliver healthcare. Implicitly, the most fundamental assumption that this book challenges is that our country needs more money to operate an effective healthcare system. What we need most is great leaders who, like the chapter authors in this book, have the skill and tenacity to look critically at what they are doing and find better, less wasteful ways to provide safe, high-quality care.

Patrick Hagan
Amelia Island, Florida

Joan Wellman
Seattle, Washington

Chapter 2

The Continuous Performance Improvement (CPI) Journey: A Long and Winding Road

Patrick Hagan

Our continuous performance improvement (CPI) journey has been a long and winding road that has stretched out in front of us for more than a decade. We are always close to our destination, but we never quite get there. And that's how it should be. CPI keeps leading you down new paths that need attention, patching, and paving. It's an endless—but immensely satisfying—excursion that takes healthcare organizations and their people to new and never-before-imagined places that offer improved care, greater compassion, and heightened efficiencies that truly benefit patients, clinicians, and researchers.

We started down three separate trails in the late 1990s. The first one was cultural. We simply had to recognize and accept where we were in healthcare—and at Seattle Children's Hospital—10 to 15 years ago. Our people were bright and uniformly well intentioned, and so was leadership. But our "systems" were inefficient and at times unsafe. We simply weren't where we needed to be. Nowhere near where we needed to be. And that was OK—after all (with apologies to Tom Peters), we were no worse than anyone else. There were hundreds and hundreds of ways we could have been better as an organization, in the way we delivered patient care, and in the experience we offered our people—our doctors, nurses, and staff.

But we were generally complacent. We were a hospital where the sickest kids came for help, yet we were anything but welcoming for young patients and their families. At worst, our attitude was that people—patients and staff—were lucky to be here. But people had choices. They didn't have to come to Seattle Children's. So, if we wanted people to come to us for care, and if we wanted people to come to work, practice, teach, and study with us, we needed to change our culture.

We had traveled down the reengineering avenue, but it was an exclusively cost-focused and cold way to go, and it felt antithetical to our culture and values at Seattle Children's. In looking for other options, we started working with Joan Wellman, an organization change and process improvement consultant then with DeltaPoint. Joan challenged us with success stories of other organizations—stellar enterprises outside of healthcare. She told us we could learn from these companies and how they focused on customers and removed waste that got in the way of their people and their customers.

At first, we found it a bit off-putting to hear of Boeing and jet airplane manufacturing or Toyota and automobile production in the same breath as neonatal care or pediatric cancer. But that eventually led us to an even more important conversation in which we asked ourselves, "Why do we really want to improve?" We started talking about becoming the best children's hospital, not in an immodest way, but as the rationale for striving to continuously improve our performance. We began to talk about wanting to improve every year, continuously, so that we provided the best possible experience for our patients and the best possible environment for our faculty and staff to work and practice. We didn't want to be the "above average" children's hospital, and we certainly didn't want to be the "we're no worse than anyone else" children's hospital. We wanted to be the best children's hospital.

That meant we weren't interested in changing at the margins; we were determined to make fundamental, long-lasting, and long-term changes. But we also believed that a "big bang" approach would be counterproductive, and indeed the best way to generate resistance and opposition. Instead, we proceeded iteratively and incrementally, gradually improving our processes and how we functioned on behalf of the patients, clinicians, and researchers in our world. Using that approach, we gave ourselves time to "prove the concept"—and we did.

We learned from the companies we observed that to achieve this kind of change would require substantive and sustained leadership commitment. Leadership would have to go beyond talking the talk to walking the walk of performance improvement. What we've learned from our experience is that leaders need to be present with their people in observing and supporting their work, and in noting their performance improvement efforts. Leaders need to be trained and knowledgeable in the principles, methods, and tools of CPI, and they need to participate in improvement events. And leaders need to be tenacious and patient: tenacious because there will be resistance to this effort and because that's what's required to keep CPI from becoming the next "flavor of the month," and patient because it will be hard, difficult work; some events will fail; and fundamental improvement takes time.

The second trail we found ourselves on was all about events and circumstances. In the late 1990s and early 2000s, Joan, with Seattle Children's employees Barb Bouche and Margaret Dunphy, had led Rapid Process Improvement Workshops (RPIWs) to help us improve our emergency, pharmacy, and supply departments; our lab had employed this methodology as well, working with a different consultant. Initial results were enlightening. But, as we headed down this route, we were routinely, if infrequently, reminded that we really weren't all that great. Our errors and defects caused injury and even death in our hospital, and, worse, we came to the sobering conclusion that we weren't learning from our mistakes. We weren't seizing the opportunities to improve. We had serious systemic issues that absolutely had to be addressed in the name of patient safety.

After a particularly tragic error caused by communication failures between clinical teams, we decided to use the RPIW tool to improve our clinical care processes. Our approach was "simple"—give the clinical teams most affected by the mistakes the opportunity to improve the way they cared for patients. We pulled together the medical director, the chief of nursing, the chairman of pediatrics, and the clinical teams, and we began in earnest the process of continuously improving our performance by giving our people the tools and resources to do so. This was a seminal moment for us. It was the true beginning of directing "from the top"; and we would use this method, which enabled the real work of improvement to occur on the front line. It was 2002.

We asked members of the clinical teams (faculty, nurses, residents, coordinators, et al.) to participate in an RPIW to improve communication among the teams and to consider changes in the way we were conducting patient rounds. The RPIW team identified multiple flaws in the rounding process, not least of which were a remarkable absence of reliable physician-to-nurse communication and a profound lack of involvement with patient families. The RPIW team pointed out that rounds had become an esoteric conference room process that needed to be redirected to the patient bedside. The team recommended changes in the way rounds are conducted, and this began a journey of continuous improvement in our rounding process that has endured to this day.

Over time, we labeled our work "continuous performance improvement." We framed our work as a CPI "house" representing the elements of quality, cost, delivery, safety, and engagement (see Figure 2.1). Patients and families would "come first" and be the roof of the house, the engagement of our people would be the foundation of the house and of our success, and quality, cost, delivery, and safety would be the pillars supporting the roof of the house, our patients.

We gradually expanded our CPI focus. In addition to the RPIWs we were running, we started using the Five Ss of CPI: sorting, simplifying, sweeping, standardizing, and sustaining. Importantly, we decided to invest in our own performance improvement infrastructure. We trained our own people (with Joan's able leadership) and hired others to form a cadre of internal performance improvement

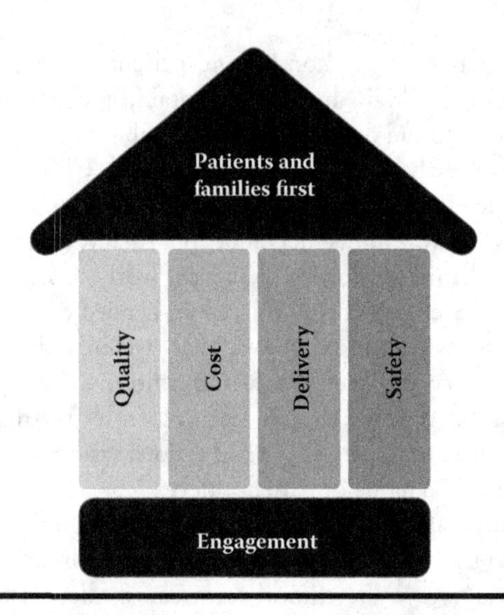

Figure 2.1 The Seattle Children's House. Seattle Children's uses a house to show how we think about evaluating and improving healthcare. Patients and families are our primary customer, as illustrated by the roof. Patients and families are supported by pillars that indicate areas where we strive for continuous improvement: quality, cost, delivery, and safety. The pillars rest on a foundation of engagement: employees, faculty, and referring physicians who are engaged and committed to the care of our patients.

consultants to help spread the methodology throughout the organization. Today, we have over 30 people in our CPI Department.

Our third trail—after the cultural and circumstantial ones—was intellectual. I finally sat down and read *The Toyota Way*. It was a definite capstone for my thinking about continuous improvement. It woke me up to the kind of overarching philosophy of leadership and management necessary for our hospital to become the best. It was now clear to me that it wasn't *what* Toyota did that was important; it was *how* they did it.

There were several other crystal clear learnings from Toyota: first, our prime focus should be on our customer, the patient; second, we always need to support our people in their work; and, third, we must take a long-term view and be relentless in performance improvement, never abandoning our goals of continuous improvement in response to short-term issues.

This translated into several important principles at Seattle Children's Hospital: we involve patients and families directly in our improvement efforts; physicians and staff are partners to be engaged, not customers to be served; and our goals are multiyear initiatives, not flavors of the month.

By 2007, we had had good—not great—success after several years of incremental CPI development. Having observed and learned from various American manufacturing companies, it became apparent that we needed to experience more sophisticated continuous improvement environments if we were to accelerate the pace of our cultural transformation. We knew other organizations that had traveled to Japan for that experience and recommended it highly. Generally speaking, they had done so to "shock" their culture and jump-start their transformation. Early on, we had consciously decided *not* to invest in Japan trips because we had chosen a more gradual, incremental approach to cultural transformation. But, after several years of experience, the timing to go to Japan seemed right. The trip to Japan wasn't needed to shock our people into CPI awareness, but rather to accelerate our transformation and truly set the wheels in motion for a long-term generational effort.

The decision to take 25 of our people to Japan for a two-week "CPI immersion" was a step we had to take. We were ready for it, but it was a high-risk move nevertheless. Right off the bat, there was the fact that none of us had done this before; it was a completely new experience. We had a new CEO and medical director at the hospital; both were only just getting started with CPI and beginning to appreciate what it could do. We also took two board members, and the rest of the group was composed of executive, faculty, and CPI leaders.

The trip went very well—beyond our wildest dreams and expectations. The trip's theme was "learning to see"—and we were focused on observing flow in sophisticated companies and applying their lessons to our work. We learned a huge amount by observing these companies and the way they used the philosophies and tools of continuous improvement. Each successive company we visited had ever-increasing time investments in continuous improvement, from 20 years to Toyota's 50 years of commitment. Each company was therefore more accomplished than the last.

That yielded another profound truth for us—that it takes time and patience to implement CPI, and it truly is a generational effort.

And, finally, we saw something in Japan that stuck with us: the leaders of CPI organizations are teachers and coaches, not bureaucrats; these leaders personally embody the change and transformation of their company.

So far, we've made six trips in all to Japan, and we learn more each time we go.

For example, on the second trip, we visited a piano factory and came to the realization that the art and craft of building these wonderful instruments—with wood, strings, and wires—was very much akin to the craft and art of medicine. We saw pianos being built on a moving line to takt time. It was eye-opening for our physicians as they concluded that it's possible—and desirable—to pursue the craft of medicine to the rhythm of takt time. And as with each of our trips, this experience highlighted the importance and value of standard work for clinical practice. On each trip, our clinicians have learned how standard work is not constraining but in fact frees one to focus more attention on the patient or, as in this case, the piano.

The third trip taught me about the language of CPI. The bottom line is that these Japanese companies do not use shorthand or catchphrases to convey and communicate the generational changes of continuous improvement. You don't hear the word "lean" in Japan. But you do hear about the focus on the customer; the commitment to, and support of, the people; and the long-term view.

Our most recent trip took place in late 2008, just after the financial meltdown hit. This visit was also instructive. We immediately saw and felt the Japanese companies' commitment to waste reduction as the means to cost reduction. They redeployed or further trained their people instead of laying them off. This breeds a true sense of engagement and participation among all staff; everyone in the companies we saw was pulling in the same direction. We were impressed with the concept of "scarcity drives improvement." It wasn't about taking resources away, but about providing workers with the tools to eliminate waste so that work can be done with fewer resources. This makes a big difference. In the toughest times, CPI tools and processes help drive meaningful change.

After each of our Japan trips, our teams were very excited about what they had learned and they were eager to apply it. But we were also very cautious and careful. We didn't want the hospital to become divided between those who had been to Japan and those who hadn't, so we always cautioned against being too "evangelical" upon our return. It was, however, definitely difficult to restrain ourselves.

The lessons from the American and Japanese companies that we visited were many, but high on the list was learning how important it was to "steal shamelessly" from others—their improvements, innovations, and ideas, regardless of where you find them. We had reached the point where all of us—physician and nurse leaders, staff, and executives—were willing and able to apply the lessons of others to our work.

So where are we now, and how did we get here? Looking back on a decade of development, we got here through a series of successive waves of improvement. Not that we consciously proceeded in this fashion; but armed with the clarity that's achieved by peering through the retrospective lens, it's now apparent that there were four overlapping waves of organizational transformation, and we're working on number five.

Our first wave was borne of caution. We began our improvement efforts behind the scenes, without much clinical involvement, let alone clinical leadership. The best example of the first wave was the 5S project in our loading dock–receiving area. Very "offstage" and a classic place for good "before-and-after" 5S photos, it was also an excellent example of a "point" improvement, where the project focuses only on the process at hand and does not take into account the related processes or departments.

Success in our first wave bred the second wave, where we continued with point improvements and began to see more clinician involvement, but without explicit clinical leadership. Projects occurred in places like the laboratory and pharmacy, and began to come to the attention of more folks in the organization. It was at this point, too, that we learned the important lesson that removing waste from our processes not only improved process performance (e.g., lab and pharmacy turnaround times) but also reduced cost. Indeed, improved pharmacy turnaround times directly led to reduced IV wastage, which saved $350,000 per year.

The beauty of this achievement was that, unlike reengineering, we did not focus on cost as a target. We asked our people to help us improve the quality of our service, the access to our services, and the safety of our care. And we demonstrated that when we did these things by removing waste, we inevitably reduced our cost per patient (by 3.6 percent in 2006–2007 and by 6 percent in 2008–2009).

Our third wave saw the emergence of physician and nursing leaders not only heading up point improvement projects but also driving the organization's embrace of continuous improvement. Faculty leaders saw that the core principle of CPI is to apply the scientific method to clinical and operational practices, and they were eager to see this approach applied in their areas.

During this wave, we had point improvement efforts throughout the hospital, and even in our research institute. The General Medicine Rounding RPIW occurred in this wave, as did projects in operative services, the emergency department, and the clinical laboratory; we also instituted multisystem projects like Total Parenteral Nutrition. In research, we improved processes for the institutional review board and the vivarium.

These projects helped us become comfortable with two significant cultural changes—the application of learnings from other companies in other industries, and the routine involvement of patients and families in our improvement workshops. Joan was very helpful with the former, and she motivated us to literally leave the comfort of our conference rooms for the factory floor to advance our learning.

Our ongoing focus on family-centered care helped us with the latter cultural change. We were quite concerned that inviting patients and families into our workshops would reveal our "dirty laundry," and that no good would come of this, but our family support leaders assured us that we needn't worry because our patients and families knew better than anyone else what our shortcomings were. Indeed, we quickly learned the folly of believing that we could "imagine" what our customers wanted, and we found that having them directly involved in our improvement work is invaluable.

The fourth wave was the most distinct, in terms of time and type of improvement activity. It began with the development of our new strategic plan in 2006 and the implementation of "value stream mapping" in our CPI efforts. Our strategic plan identified six specialty "focus" programs (cancer, orthopedics, general surgery, cardiac, neonatology, and transplant) and called for improvements in quality and safety and for growth in patient activity. Over time, each specialty's "value stream" (i.e., the specialty's activity from the patient's perspective)—from referral to outpatient visit to procedures to admission to discharge home—was mapped.

The mapping process is time intensive and involves dozens of people, including parents and patients; it ultimately yields a description of the specialty's work, waste and all, from the beginning of the patient experience to the end. It also yields innumerable opportunities for improvement as well as projects for growth, and it enables those dozens of people (physicians, nurses, management, and staff) to reach alignment on the projects in a way previously not possible. Several of the focus programs have sent teams to Japan to hone their maps and project plans.

Our work is progressing through a fifth wave of CPI activity and organizational improvement as we embrace the concepts of integrated facility design (IFD) and strategy deployment. IFD adapts Toyota's Production Preparation Process model for designing and building new car factories to healthcare building design and construction. As with all CPI efforts, IFD is a multidisciplinary approach, in this case involving architects, general contractors, hospital facility executives, physicians, nurses, other frontline staff, and patients and families. Using this approach with a new ambulatory building and surgery center, we reduced conventionally derived space estimates by 30,000 square feet with a new design applauded by all—and saved $20 million. We are now applying IFD to a new inpatient facility and expect similar results with excellent design, optimal square footage, and reduced costs.

Strategy deployment is the next iteration of CPI for Seattle Children's. It will involve explicitly connecting staff-level improvement objectives and daily work with our strategic goals. This will require the development and implementation of leader standard work and daily management systems throughout the organization, and will help us continue to spread CPI thinking—everyday improvement—to all of our people in all areas of Seattle Children's. Very challenging and very exciting!

In view of the recent financial meltdown and the surprising difficulties of Toyota, one might ask how we've fared and whether our direction has changed in light of these events. The answer is that we believe that CPI is critical to our success, quite literally now more than ever. As we move forward, we will learn from Toyota's mistakes as we have learned from its great successes. As we grow we will strive to grow responsibly, building quality and safety into our improved processes and our new designs. We will continue to focus on our patients and families first, and support our people in their work; and, at the same time, we will take the long-term view in our leadership and in the management of our organization.

In these difficult economic times, we have focused more intently on translating waste reduction to cost reduction, and we have emphasized cost reduction more than we have in the past. Yet, at the same time, we have made the commitment of "no layoffs" and instead repurpose and redeploy our people as our work changes. Our efforts now are directed at preparing for the recovery, and we continue to see improvements and great results in the quality, cost effectiveness, and delivery of our services; the safety of our care; and the engagement of our people.

Naturally—and of course—our journey continues.

Epilogue

Five years on, our understanding of Lean and the critical role of leadership continues to develop. Though still small in scale in national terms, the number of healthcare organizations embracing continuous improvement is cause for (some) optimism about the industry's future. Happily, the continuing development and growth of CPI at Seattle Children's Hospital has been impressive, incorporating as it has clinical standard work, integrated facility design, and a rigorous daily management system. Significantly, Seattle Children's has continued to prosper and grow its CPI effort in spite of the departure of certain executive and physician leaders throughout the past five years.

For some of us, the Lean journey has led to new professional endeavors as we have become teachers and coaches for other organizations, or if you prefer, consultants. My experience, both at Seattle Children's and with several other healthcare organizations, has helped me immeasurably in furthering my understanding of three key elements of Lean thinking and particularly Lean leadership.

The first is the deep importance of continuous learning to the practice of continuous improvement. One of the reasons we are writing this second edition is to highlight this truism and to document what we know now that we didn't understand or appreciate five years ago.

The second element is the interrelationship between strategy deployment, breakthrough improvement, and daily management, the integral parts of any Lean management system. Strategy deployment, linking the goals of the organization from executive leadership all the way to the front line, enables clear choices about what people throughout the organization should be working on. It is wonderfully clarifying, and if done well accelerates the pace of strategic plan implementation and operational process improvement.

Event-based breakthrough improvement is what initially sold many people, myself included, on the value (and excitement) of Lean methodology. But it eventually becomes apparent, even to a plodder like me, that without rigorous daily management the ability to sustain breakthrough gains, let alone improve upon them, is next to impossible. Daily management is the engine of continuous improvement—identifying, surfacing, and escalating problems. It is the source of feedback for leadership and the beginning of problem solving for staff. Done well, rigorous daily management provides operational stability and enables the possibility of not just stable but capable processes. It is the first and necessary step to everyday and breakthrough improvements.

The third element is committed and engaged leadership. Leadership sets the tone for continuous learning by virtue of its visibility and presence in gemba, its willingness to experiment, and its humility in the quest for new knowledge and in the face of occasional but inevitable failure. Leadership must drive strategy deployment and daily management, and sponsor and support breakthrough improvements and everyday problem solving. Without it, organizations cannot be successful in implementing and sustaining continuous improvement over time.

An observation: It is certainly important that the CEO, with the full support of the board, embraces this philosophy and methodology and ensures that it is *the* approach taken by the organization to improve its performance. But it does not go without saying that the denizens of the C-suite—the Chief Operating Officer (COO),

Chief Nurse Executive (CNO), Chief Medical Officer (CMO), and Chief Financial Officer (CFO)—must be aligned and pulling in the same direction in this effort. If that is not the case, then the continuous improvement journey will be hampered by fits and starts in the short run and will have no chance of success over the long term. Continuous improvement is hard work; it requires cultural transformation, and it can only be accomplished with unity of purpose at the C-level.

Chapter 3

Creating High-Powered Healthcare Improvement Engines

Joan Wellman

It is now well known that the United States spends as much as two times more per capita on healthcare than other developed nations. This fact begs the question: what additional value do consumers in the United States receive for the extraordinary financial commitment made to healthcare? It does not appear that we are healthier than our industrialized peers. In fact, a 2008 Commonwealth Fund Report ranked the United States last in quality of healthcare among 19 comparative, developed nations. Not a stellar track record for a society paying top dollar.

There are plenty of candidates for the root cause of the U.S. healthcare system's woes, including a complex network of third-party payers that do not "add value," public policy that drives patients to emergency rooms rather than to appropriate and safe care in less expensive settings, physicians practicing "defensive medicine" over concern about medical liability, and the list goes on. Many of these root causes are related to public policy and the structure of our healthcare delivery system, factors not controlled by healthcare administrators and physician leaders.

Brutally Honest Leadership

There are an increasing number of U.S. healthcare leaders who, despite the systemic causes of poor performance mentioned earlier, are demonstrating that they can, in fact, achieve dramatic improvement of healthcare quality, cost, safety, and patient access to services. These leaders are brutally honest about the tremendous amount of work conducted in their organizations that is actually waste cleverly disguised as "real work." Their definition of waste is expansive and includes things that are easy to see such as excessive transportation, patients waiting, and the human cost and financial burdens caused by defects, as well as things that are more difficult to see such as complexity. For the purposes of this chapter, the leaders who are actively removing waste in healthcare are called "Lean leaders."

Lean leaders are, at their heart, people developers. They know that their ability to drive out waste depends on using the brainpower of all organizational members. If you ask Lean leaders what the most important element of their improvement strategy is, they will tell you, "Developing and respecting people." They actively engage staff, physicians, patients, payers, families, educators, researchers, and suppliers as problem solvers, getting out of the conference room and going to "gemba," or the workplace, to observe and support problem solving.

If you hang out with Lean leaders, you will find that they are some of the most dissatisfied people you have ever met. While they are never short of praise and recognition for achievements, what they value most is the reflection that leads to even further improvement. They are constantly learning, constantly experimenting, and not shy about trying things that may not pan out.

Lean leaders do not rout out waste or solve problems in their spare time; they see improvement as central to their job. When a critical mass of these people converges in one organization, the organization can become a "healthcare improvement engine."

Imagining a Different Approach to Defects and Waste

I once told a group of healthcare executives that if they saw high reliability in action in organizations that measure all defects in "parts per million," rather than "parts per thousand" as is often done in healthcare, they would recognize such an extraordinary gap that they would weep. Recently, I took a group of them to see just this kind of organization. Our host company supplies Honda, Toyota, and other auto manufacturers with safety equipment. The visiting group got invited to the plant for a daily 5 a.m. "abnormality escalation meeting," starting with production team leaders and supervisors meeting to discuss quality and production problems that occurred on the previous shift. This meeting was followed by the supervisors meeting with production managers and finally the managers meeting with the plant manager. At each level, the managers worked on issues that required action on their part. By 8:30 a.m., everyone who needed to know that they had an issue to resolve was on point to do just that. All of these meetings were held on the factory floor with the plant manager's meeting on loudspeaker at one end of the factory, visible to all.

While the visiting healthcare group did not exactly "weep," they got the point. Their visit debrief described the gulf between what they had seen that morning and their healthcare organizations. They contrasted their world, in which deviation from standards is a daily event and staff feels the need to "protect" patients from safety and quality hazards or apologize to patients and families for long wait times, poor communication, and "everyday" errors. In their organizations, staff has learned to cope with a far from perfect world, with problems so frequent that they go unreported and unaddressed.

The trip to the automotive supplier gave the healthcare visitors the ability to imagine what it would be like if deviation from safety and quality standards and barriers to patient flow were considered defects worthy of "stopping the line for immediate attention." For example, a nurse who notices that the wrong medication has been delivered to a drawer in a medication room would not only correct the problem to protect patients from the defect (which is what nurses spend a good deal of time doing today) but also STOP and NOTIFY someone IMMEDIATELY that a defect worthy of attention has occurred (as opposed to writing up the event and sending it to the quality department later in the shift … if time permits). Most important, the nurse would have confidence that when a defect signal is sent, the organization's problem-solving prowess would swing into action.

In this environment, problems would be seen as "treasures" that provide the raw material for improvement. Staff would feel valued for using critical and creative thinking to solve problems. Problem identification and problem solving would be accelerated to the point that the healthcare organization is a "learning and improvement engine."

Imagine further that if you ask the executive team to not limit the description of its organization's mission to the "what" (i.e., the delivery of healthcare), they would also tell you that their mission is to *improve how patient care is delivered*, and that the *how* is central to ensuring sustainable high-quality care to their community.

Beginning to Build the Engine

Most healthcare organizations have begun their improvement journeys, and over the last decade there have been hopeful advances in the application of improvement tools and methods to some tough problems. These advances, sometimes aided by lessons from other industries, are the topics of great interest at national conferences with titles such as "improving access in ambulatory operations" or "reducing length of stay for heart failure patients." At various points during the year, improvement projects go before the board quality committee or the process improvement steering team with well-deserved congratulations all around.

So what's the problem? It lies in the episodic approach to improvement, that is, improvement as a series of unconnected "projects" rather than a way of organizational life. It also lies in the pace and intensity of improvement. Our current rate of improvement simply will not close the gap between what we are paying for healthcare in the United States and the value we receive. Finally, the problem lies in the focus on tools and methods rather than on the mind-set of organizational leaders and the management systems that create the "improvement engine" (see Figure 3.1).

Figure 3.1 Gears of the healthcare improvement engine. When everyone shares the same frame of reference, the wheels of progress can turn faster.

It's Not about the Tools and Methods

Unfortunately, many healthcare organizations suffer from "methodology incongruence," where frontline managers are confused by the various specialized departments requesting adherence to initiatives led by that department. Clinical education wants to use storyboards, finance wants to use cost reduction methods, quality wants to deploy e-feedback, compliance wants tracer rounds, process improvement wants to engage people in Six Sigma, and the list goes on. This incongruence can make for an improvement technology alphabet soup that confounds some of the most sophisticated change agents.

There are really only two critical "must haves" regarding improvement methods and tools.

1. Whether using Rapid Process Improvement Workshops (RPIWs), Six Sigma tools, value stream mapping, tracer rounds, or root cause analysis, any method worth engaging must drive rigorous, rapid, and frequent plan, do, check, and act (PDCA) cycles (see Figure 3.2). The PDCA cycle is not a method or tool per se; it is a way of thinking. By completing the entire cycle, and not leaving the check and act parts of the cycle to chance, organization learning can be accelerated.
2. Improvement methods must be accessible to organization members. Too much variety or complexity distracts rather than enhances progress.

This is not to say that tools and methods are not necessary. The organizations with case studies in this book all use Lean tools and methods with a common vocabulary and set of tools. A standard set of improvement tools and a commonly shared vocabulary of improvement are critical, but they are not sufficient to achieve the results described in this book.

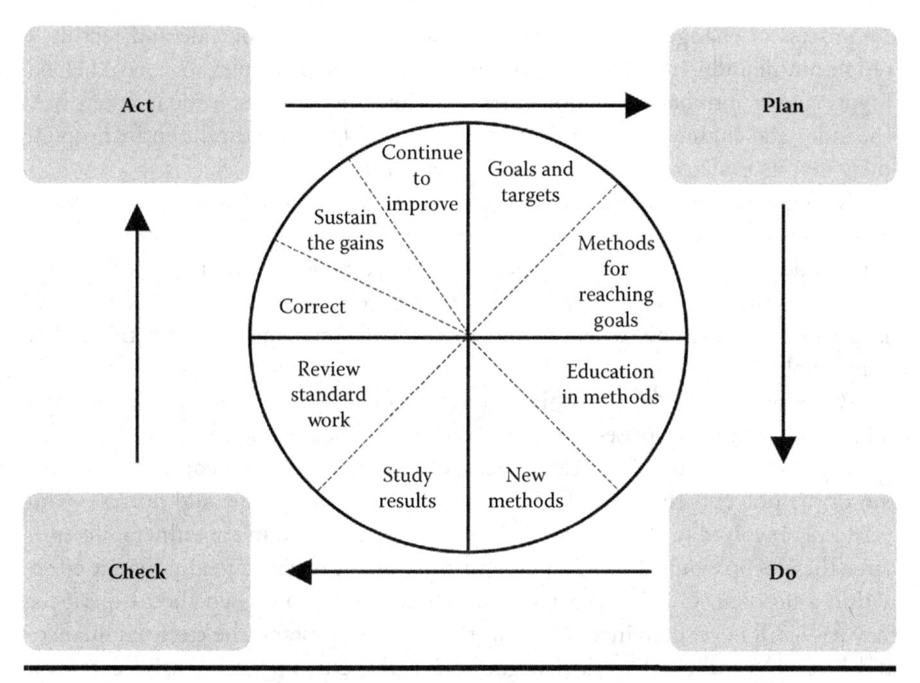

Figure 3.2 The PDCA cycle. The PDCA cycle is not a method but a way of thinking. (Adapted from Kaoru Ishikawa, *What Is Total Quality Control? The Japanese Way*, Englewood Cliffs, NJ: Prentice Hall, 1991.)

It Takes a Leadership Mind-Set

So if it's not about the tools and methods, what drives the improvement engine of the healthcare improvement engine? Most important is a leadership mind-set that expects everyone in the healthcare organization, including executives, to actively apply scientific thinking (PDCA) to remove waste and variation. Managers in these organizations are not willing to accept organizational silos, which create hardship for their patients as "a fact of life." They are not complacent about the fact that defects are occurring hourly in their organizations or that waste is making their services more expensive and less safe for patients. They are curious and constantly learning. They treat problems raised by patients, staff, and physicians as "gems" to be solved rather than irritations. Most important, they are willing to become students, then practitioners, and finally teachers and coaches of the methods and principles that will remove waste and defects.

To illustrate the difference that mind-set, management systems, and methods can make, let's take a look at two hospitals and explore the differences in the mind-sets of Hospital A and Hospital B when it comes to improvement.

The CEO of Hospital A was introduced to the concept of a Lean enterprise, and he liked the idea a lot. But he didn't want to engage his senior managers in the process of change because they were busy. So, he went outside and recruited a high-profile industrial engineer who understood the principles that have helped Toyota and a number of manufacturing organizations improve their enterprise. The industrial engineer reported directly to the CEO; as a result, the entire hospital knew that its leader was serious about implementing change.

The new recruit's first assignment was the operating room (OR). And he went ahead and did solid engineering work. He mapped the process, did time observation studies, and zeroed in on ways that the OR could run more smoothly. But several months later, he left the hospital, frustrated and with little to show for his hard work. Most of his recommendations weren't implemented, and those that were simply weren't sustained.

What happened? Why did this experienced outside expert fail to help Hospital A become a Lean enterprise—or even move toward becoming a Lean enterprise?

The first reason for this lack of success has to do with the people at the sharp end of the process. These are the frontline players—the doctors and nurses—who are deeply involved in the hazards and constantly immersed in the vulnerabilities of care. These people must be intricately and emotionally engaged in any change effort within a hospital. Outside experts—no matter how deep or rich their experience may be—will never convince clinicians that they understand the essential nuances and lifesaving technical work that goes on in the OR, in the intensive care unit (ICU), and at a patient's bedside. Hospital A failed to realize that Lean healthcare organizations must, therefore, make those at the "sharp end," the content experts in the work, their greatest source of finding and solving problems. This requires a significant change in management mind-set and investment strategy: Lean organizations invest significant time and money in the development of people.

The second factor behind the failure is that many hospital CEOs want quick and big fixes, so they turn to compelling outside experts—but they do so without considering how difficult, time-consuming, and expensive it is to integrate these new hires into the actual cultural and technical fabric of the healthcare organization. While outside experts may be critical to success, their best role is as coaches and mentors of content experts, not as the primary "change agents."

The third variable that contributed to Hospital A's misstep revolves around the CEO's assumption that if he brought in the industrial engineer, it would be helpful to his leadership team, who were "too busy" to be involved. What the CEO of Hospital A did not realize is that without executives and managers changing the way they manage, how they spend their time, and what gets their attention, improvement progress would be slow and episodic.

Hospital A obviously went down the wrong path and ended up in an organizational cul-de-sac that did very little—if anything—to advance the cause of continuous improvement.

Now let's talk about the mind-set at Hospital B, which is starkly different from that of Hospital A. The best way to understand what went on in Hospital B is by looking at its pharmacy, which changed dramatically over a four-year period.

On one visit, the pharmacy staff had implemented sort, simplify, sweep, standardize, and sustain (5S). By the next visit, it had standardized the workflow and balanced the work to meet demand and achieve shorter lead times. And, when it came time to designing a new physical space, the team laid out a U-shaped work cell and limited the work-in-process inventory. The pharmacy also demonstrated its new and improved inventory-ordering signals and work-leveling tool.

The key takeaway here is that the process of improvement within Hospital B's pharmacy just didn't stop. The team constantly upgraded safety, steadily cut waste, and consistently reduced lead times. And, over time, it became clear that the staff was redefining what it called "good." That new definition didn't come from a healthcare industry average for order turnaround times and medication safety; it came from the team's vision—operating a waste-free process with zero defects in a Lean enterprise.

The pharmacy director at Hospital B said it all when he was asked how, with all the competing demands on his team, he was able to develop a learning-focused mind-set in his organization.

"The hospital leaders have told me that improvement is what my job is," said the pharmacy director. "At first, I was the sponsor, process owner, and the person making sure that the follow-up was done. Now, we've developed our staff, and they do what I used to do, so we can address projects concurrently. We've spread the wealth of knowledge … it's permeated the organization."

That's a far cry from Hospital A, which went out and tried to buy the change management talent it needed to solve its problems.

Hospital B mobilized its leaders and transformed them into coaches, teachers, and role models who helped inspire and motivate managers like the pharmacy director with a "Lean state of mind." Hospital B's pharmacy director understood that change was his job, because his boss helped him see that; and the pharmacy director's boss got his Lean education and mandate from *his* boss. The point here is that with the right mind-set, all managers can become dynamic change agents in a hospital and do what they've never done before—what they might think is impossible.

The moral of this story is that the more educated senior people are about Lean principles, the greater the opportunity for a hospital to achieve continuous improvement. When leaders—all the way up to the board—share a mind-set about improvement, the work goes faster because everyone in the organization is on the same page.

The Management System Provides the Dance Steps

On Seattle's Broadway Avenue, dance step instructions to the tango, waltz, fox trot, and other ballroom dances are laid as brass footsteps in the concrete sidewalk. These dance steps are reminiscent of the next ingredient of a healthcare improvement engine: standard "dance steps" for managers that ensure success is not left to the chance that managers and leaders will have that "certain something it takes to lead." In high-velocity improvement organizations, the dance steps are clear and form the basis for not only continuous improvement of processes but also continuous improvement of the organization's management.

The dance steps are laid out in three basic management systems, all based on the PDCA cycle.

1. **Strategy deployment:** This is a method for ensuring that strategic initiatives are developed with high levels of intelligence of what is happening at the "ground level." Strategy deployment establishes a learning system that ensures continuous improvement in the organization's bandwidth to achieve strategic results. This is the PDCA of senior management. This is also referred to as "hoshin planning" or "policy deployment."

   One of the most rewarding parts of our consulting work is watching clients reflect on how much they have learned after their first and subsequent years of using strategy deployment. The check and act phases of executive PDCA drive thoughtful, frank reflection, leading to better and better execution versus a "blame game" that can easily take center stage when goals are not reached.
2. **Cross-functional management:** Sometimes referred to fondly as the system that ensures that the fact that we are a complex, multidepartmental, multisite organization with complex organizational relationships is *not* our patients' problem. Cross-functional management uses value stream management methods to ensure that patients experience ever-improving results in quality, cost, access, and safety as they move throughout their continuum of care (see Figure 3.3).
3. **Daily management or the daily engagement system:** Everyday problem solving, checking, and coaching on standard work, work balance, staff huddles, visibility walls, and metrics are all ingredients of daily management. This is the glue that ensures reliability, holds improvement gains, and provides insights for "what needs work" (see Figure 3.4).

Let's imagine what it would be like to have all three of these management systems in full working order. Strategic goals would be clearly set, articulated, prioritized, and deployed. And there would be lots of discussion throughout the organization at every level—not just about the goals themselves but also about the means to actually achieve them. Just as important, frontline supervisors and managers would be released from the tyranny of putting out daily fires, and instead they would spend much more of their time actively engaging, coaching, and huddling with staff members. This would enable a host of staff-inspired ideas to surface and be put to constructive use.

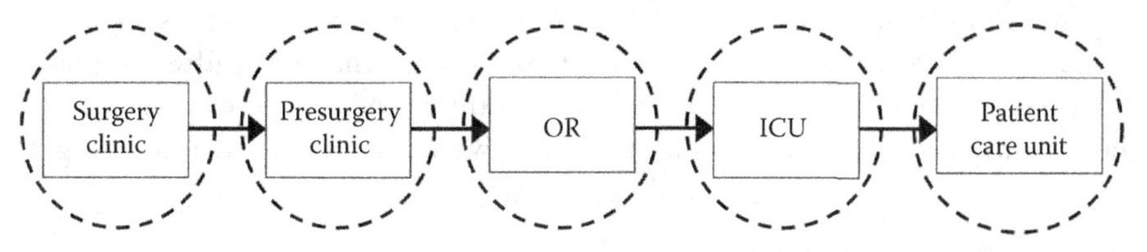

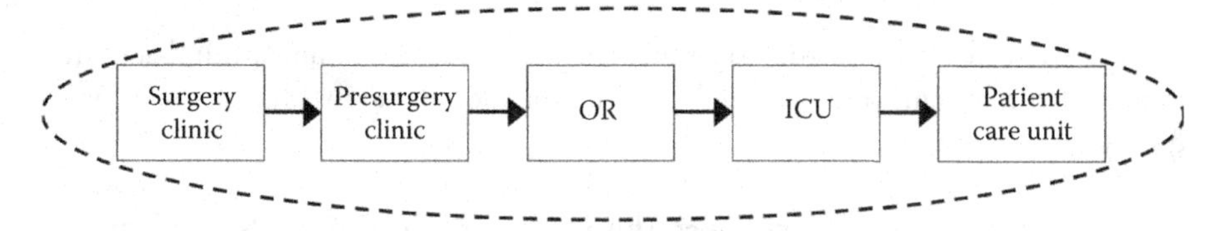

Figure 3.3 A cross-functional management system. Cross-functional management focuses on loyalty to the customer rather than loyalty to functional silos.

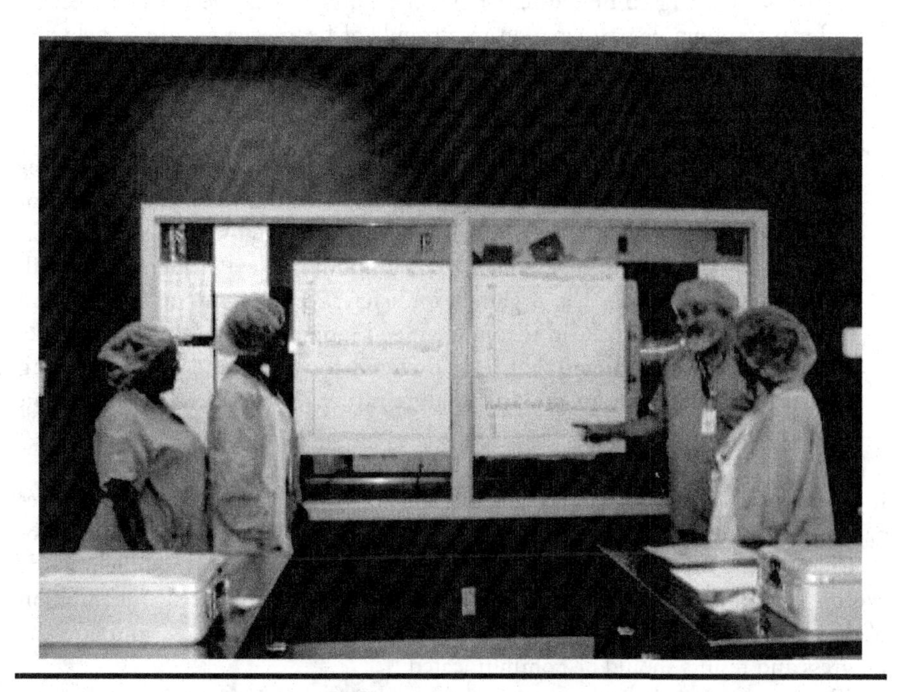

Figure 3.4 The daily management huddle. Getting on the same page. Daily management huddles provide teams a chance to "check in," verify expectations, and more.

Prior to implementing daily management, the typical supervising nurse spent 90 percent of any given shift in meetings, in the office answering e-mails, or on the phone; once daily management was adopted, however, the ratio shifted dramatically, and the supervising nurse now spends nearly 50 percent of the time on the floor, auditing, coaching, engaging, balancing workloads with demand, and getting and implementing ideas from the staff.

How to Get Started

Healthcare leaders who realize that this journey involves methods, mind-set, and management systems, and are ready to embark should start with a series of hard questions.

- **Are we serious about change?** This is not a trick question. "Serious" means that hospital executives want their organization to become the best it can possibly be and are willing to spend the time and resources required. "Change" refers not only to processes and people, but also to how leaders spend their time and attention.
- **Are we willing to be students?** An afternoon of Lean lectures, a week of Lean training, or participation in a couple of Lean events will not help any hospital reach the tipping point for lasting change. The baseline investment here is three to four years of learning through application, reflection, and the coaching of others.
- **Do we have the patience, tenacity, and focus to see this through over the long term?** This may be the toughest question of all. The type of change outlined in this chapter isn't just about joyful case studies that yield 50-percent improvement. It's also about the experiments that fail, which usually bring the organization's naysayers out in full force. And it's about learning to lead through rugged moments, a willingness to take on intractable problems that have lingered for years, and active learning that engages people in making change rather than merely talking about change.

If the answers to these three thoughtful and thought-provoking questions are yes or reasonably close to yes, then senior leaders should begin a frank assessment of their healthcare organization's current situation. This self-analysis will help guide executives as they contemplate the scope and plan of work, the speed and ambition of the change plan, the people who should be involved in the process, and how the progress and results should be communicated.

To get going in this assessment of the current situation, it will help to frame the discussion around these eight questions:

1. **What is our organization's sense of urgency?** Organizations that have taken a deep dive quickly have a high sense of urgency, often based on financial, quality, access, or safety concerns. Leaders in these organizations hold a strong conviction that a new way of managing and an all-out effort are required.
2. **Is our leadership team convinced that healthcare must look for models from other industries?** Leadership conviction varies widely when it comes to the need for disruptive change, both in the technologies of improvement and in the content of the improvement. This is particularly true if the change models are coming from progressive and successful companies like Toyota, which are outside of healthcare.
3. **What is our organization's appetite for risk taking?** Any new approach or direction involves risk. As more healthcare organizations embrace learning from Lean and achieve sustainable results, the perceived risk of using this business approach is decreasing, but anxiety is usually high on issues such as physician buy-in, the teaching mission, and time and resource demands in order to generate lasting change.
4. **How much willingness is there to invest resources?** It takes resources to improve. Organizations vary widely in their ability and willingness to invest in improvement. Most of this investment is in the time and energy of people.
5. **How are the roles of leaders perceived?** One of the toughest pills to swallow is the deep involvement of leaders in the change process. Not only must leaders become educated in the content, thought process, and technologies of Lean, but also they must become practitioners and coaches. This is a far cry from the typical delegation of improvement to the process improvement department, and it has profound implications for leaders, including how they spend their time.
6. **How do our frontline managers currently spend their time?** It is not unusual for nursing managers to have 60 to 100 direct reports and spend much of their day struggling with human resource issues. In a Lean enterprise, just as there is standard work for processes, there is standard work for managers. This work includes using a daily management system to make work progress transparent and enable engagement in proactive process control versus reactive firefighting. This may not be something that comes naturally to healthcare, but it is a critical element of sustainable improvement.
7. **What stories exist about the successes or failures associated with past improvement initiatives?** Some organizations are still talking about what happened during the days of reengineering or any improvement technology that has come and gone. The degree of healthy—or not so healthy—skepticism will make a real difference in how an organization launches and proceeds on its Lean journey.
8. **What is the current level of staff and physician engagement?** "Engagement" in this sense refers to the psychological commitment to an organization's

mission and the commitment to advance the work of the organization itself. Organizations that have high levels of cynicism and disengagement need to chart a more gradual course than those with high levels of engagement.

These questions helped shape strategies adopted by the three organizations described next. In each case, executives used the understanding of their current situation to shape how they would introduce Lean to their organizations and what they would emphasize in the first years of work.

Pat Hagan, for example, adopted an evolutionary strategy in order to bring Lean principles to his organization. At the outset, Hagan was aware that process improvement in his organization was directly tied to the highly unpopular reengineering work done by Seattle Children's in the mid-1990s. The reengineering work had sparked widespread cynicism that hospital administrators were focused primarily on cost reduction at the expense of clinical work. It took slow and steady progress to prove that this time around there would be a balanced approach.

"At the beginning of the journey, we were in the aftermath of the reengineering era," explains Hagan, "and that made us gun shy about addressing any process improvement activity, particularly with cost as a focus. We knew, however, that there were safety, service, and process improvement issues that needed to be addressed and we were looking for ways to do that. We began with point improvements in nonclinical areas, and we discovered that this approach worked. By improving quality and safety, we could and did reduce cost. We also found that we could learn a lot from other industries. We took our time to prove the concept, and, in doing so, we engaged our faculty and staff in the work to a degree that became our strength."

Seattle Children's conducted its first proof of concept Rapid Process Improvement Workshop in 1998. Six years later, Hagan went to the board of directors for support of an all-out Lean effort. And several years after that, when Seattle Children's reached a plateau in its learning, it began to send physician and operations leaders to study in Japan. At Seattle Children's, the steady and balanced approach went a long way in developing the leadership mind-set and cultural changes, which are foundational to many of the case studies described in this book. Their Lean mind-set permeates everything they do today from the design and construction of their facilities, to supply chain management, to their research mission. There isn't a part of their enterprise that doesn't think in terms of "continuous performance improvement."

Jim Hereford, the executive vice president of strategic services and quality at Group Health Cooperative, adopted a different strategy, focusing early on transforming the management system. As he puts it, "Anyone can improve a process; that isn't hard. It's getting it to persist and to demonstrate it at scale that is difficult. It won't work to use old-style management. You have to change the management system."

Like Seattle Children's, Group Health began with point improvements. But after some early struggles and successes, Group Health expanded its efforts in 2005. Executives at the organization realized that it wasn't enough to change processes; they also had to translate strategy into action and transform the work of managers at all levels.

"After our initial comfort level with point improvement, we knew we had to bring this to scale," recalls Hereford. "In order to be truly successful, managers needed to have a different mental model of who they were and what their role was. We became convinced that our vision would be limited if we didn't change our management system."

Today, Group Health incorporates the three elements of a Lean management system into its work: strategy deployment (hoshin kanri), cross-functional management, and daily management.

Tammie Brailsford, the COO of MemorialCare, a large hospital system in Southern California, took yet another path when MemorialCare began its Lean journey in 2007. MemorialCare had a healthy sense of urgency and a leadership team that was willing to take on some risks when they began. The first year, MemorialCare completed 17 point improvement projects, launched its Lean office, launched a value stream, engaged 245 employees in Lean events, and realized an economic benefit of $700,000. In its second year, MemorialCare completed 47 improvement projects, launched four more value streams, and engaged 1,823 employees in its Lean efforts. While this may seem to be a rapid start-up strategy, Brailsford and her colleagues were careful to position Lean as part of an ongoing organization change, called MC21, that was in place prior to the time that executives were trained in Lean principles. MC21 represents the MemorialCare of the future and, with the incorporation of a Lean mind-set, methods, and management systems, is on track to deliver $3.4 million in savings by the end of 2010. MemorialCare's goal is to have its costs at or below Medicare reimbursement rates by 2014, a $2,800 reduction per discharge over today's rates.

Whether Seattle Children's evolutionary strategy, Group Health's management system-focused strategy, or MemorialCare's aggressive cost reduction strategy, each of these organizations has thought carefully about the organization's integrated plan to achieve the transformation it is hoping to achieve.

After a strategy is selected, it's essential that a master plan be crafted and adopted. A master plan details how Lean technologies will be learned and deployed as well as how the necessary management systems, philosophy, and leadership competencies will be developed—from frontline supervisors to senior executives.

Ultimately, the master plan drives the transformation of a Lean enterprise from a "proof of concept" phase to Lean as a "management system." With thanks to Malcom Gladwell for his characterization of *the tipping point*, the Lean transformation tipping point is shown in Figure 3.5.

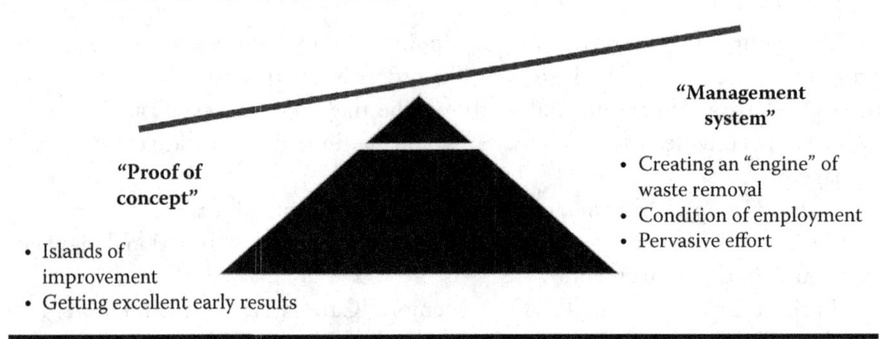

Figure 3.5 The tipping point. Three phases of change characterize the transformation to a Lean enterprise. Early learning in the "proof of concept" phase captures people's attention to start the journey. The second phase begins the hard work of deeper change with work deep into value streams. In the third phase, "management system," there is no doubt in anyone's mind that this is the "way we run this place."

The following list emphasizes the systemic nature of this journey and describes each element once the organization has reached the tipping point.

- **Leadership engagement** (executive, upper, and middle management). Lean leadership is a condition of employment and promotion, and incentives are tied to value stream improvement. QCDSE is targeted and tracked for every value stream. Lean is seen as the "right thing to do" for patients, families, staff, and the community.
- **Leadership development.** Lean expertise is central to leadership development, and hospital leaders are required to demonstrate the technical, cultural, and political aspects of change. Succession planning candidates are expected to demonstrate Lean leadership and may be asked to rotate into the department supporting Lean, often referred to as the "Lean resource office."
- **Human resource (HR) system.** Recruitment, orientation, succession planning, performance appraisal, and development are all integrated into Lean initiatives.
- **Financial system.** Accounting is linked to value streams, and all major capital expenditures are subject to Lean analysis and improvement prior to authorization. Capital building projects are subject to Integrated Facility Design (see Chapter 19).

- **Operating system.** Daily management and cross-functional management are practiced once the tipping point has been reached. Organization metrics should also reflect flow, including patient routing.
- **Methods and tool integration.** Lean tools and methods are used for virtually all processes and projects within the healthcare organization, and leaders should have well-developed skills that enable them to choose the right tools and methods for the right projects and processes.
- **Infrastructure and Lean resource office.** A dedicated team of internal experts is well-established, primarily internal hires and succession-planning candidates, who rotate into the Lean office for 18 to 24 months. Each of these professionals operate with a common training and framework.
- **Physician engagement.** Physicians see Lean as directly tied to long-term clinical and financial success; physician leaders are promoted, in part, on the basis of their Lean engagement and success.
- **Board engagement.** The board attends Lean training, engages in Lean events, and has a long-term view of the importance of continuous improvement work. Directors evaluate CEO candidates for their ability to lead a Lean healthcare organization.
- **Patient and family focus.** Patients are involved as full-time participants in Lean events and are an important voice in the change process.
- **Supply chain and supplier development.** Suppliers are involved in value stream work throughout the organization. The right supply in the right amount in the right place at the right time is a reality.
- **Pace and intensity of Lean effort.** During the "management system" stage, there should usually be four to eight Lean events per month with daily problem solving everywhere.
- **Visual systems.** There are visual systems for all value streams that tie directly to the daily management system.

Implementing Lean using a 13-component master plan can certainly pave the way for a healthcare organization as it tries to reach the tipping point and transform itself into an improvement engine.

The first sign of progress will be the contagion or attraction to change among staff members. This usually occurs during the "proof of concept" phase, when the work yields initial results. In the end, it's very hard to argue with a 50-percent reduction in waste in project after project.

The next eye-opener takes place when there's a basic understanding of what actually constitutes waste. The resulting mobilization of talent, expertise, and energy leads to an even greater removal of waste. This frequently happens during the "cautious learners" stage and leads to serious learning.

Lean healthcare organizations ultimately reach a point of no return, when they can't turn back and the mind-set of staff members has been radically changed. At this juncture, the operational process and principles that drive waste reduction are in place and the hospitals are deep into the management systems phase.

So many challenges, so much complexity, and a vast amount of ongoing hard work surround this quest for continuous improvement. But, after watching healthcare organizations apply Lean principles over the last 15 years, one realization is fairly clear, and it's simple: leadership in the healthcare industry today can't be effective, and can't help patients, if it's not focused on building high-powered improvement engines.

Epilogue

The application in Lean in healthcare has become widespread since the first writing of this chapter in 2010. Healthcare leaders' questions have shifted from "What is Lean and why should I do it?" to "Are we doing this well? And how do we get better faster?"

While there are many excellent examples of Lean healthcare in action at this point, there are still too many organizations where Lean is a "middle-up" strategy owned by the process improvement department, where short-term project activity is prioritized over continuous improvement with sustained gains over time, where executive leaders do not own the Lean management system, and Lean does not extend deeply into the clinical enterprise through engagement of clinicians of all stripes.

Furthermore, we continue to overburden frontline and middle managers with competing improvement methods, assuming they can respond to the disparate demands of functional staff representing patient experience, finance, safety and quality, regulatory … and the list goes on. This is not a recipe for increasing the velocity of improvement in healthcare.

The healthcare leaders who are getting this right understand Lean simply as "the way we manage": how we plan, how we execute, and how we improve through the respect and engagement of our people. Continuous improvement is replacing firefighting as the most valuable managerial activity. Everyone in the organization understands True North and is able to activate a standard set of processes and skills to achieve improved performance. There is alignment and continuity to this effort regardless of who is in charge. It comes from the top including the board, who is ultimately responsible for the quality and continuity of Lean thinking and acting.

This was a bold idea in 2002 when Seattle Children's, ThedaCare, and Virginia Mason all launched their Lean efforts. It's still a big idea today. These three institutions have had significant influence on Lean healthcare thinkers throughout the world. But while visitors to these institutions marvel at the technical solutions they observe (for example, standard rounding at Seattle Children's, collaborative care units at ThedaCare, flow stations in Virginia Mason's clinics), the most profound takeaway should be how these three organizations have avoided getting distracted and achieved continuity to their efforts for more than a decade, even in light of CEO and COO transitions. Moreover, these three institutions can demonstrate to visitors how to embed the skill set and processes to respond to environmental changes be it Ebola, value-based pricing, or nursing shortages. A middle-up effort owned by the performance improvement department would simply not be this durable, adaptable, and innovative.

In retrospect, a more appropriate metaphor for a high velocity improvement organization is a *living system* rather than an *engine.* While an engine, as a nonliving system, is subject to greater disorder over time (entropy), a living system tends to evolve to higher levels of order through feedback loops. Building the highly interdependent elements of such a living system cannot be done without continuity of effort and executive leadership.

Chapter 4

Leadership and Culture Change: What We Need Most We Can't Buy

Patrick Hagan and Cara Bailey

> "We tried this 12 years ago."
> "Sounds just like reengineering to me."
> "It's a scheme to cut jobs."
> "I'm waiting this one out."
> "Another flavor of the month …"
> "This, too, shall pass."

How often do you hear those remarks whispered in your organization? These are not just the utterances of a skeptical workforce; they are the voices of your culture.

Organizational culture, the way things are done "around here," is the context in which improvement occurs. Culture includes the commonly held beliefs and assumptions about the organization's mission, its hierarchy and power structure, and its tolerance for differences of opinion. It includes stories that are told about its history, its triumphs, and especially how its leaders have behaved in tough times.

It has been widely acknowledged that *culture eats strategy for lunch.* No matter how carefully crafted an organizational strategy is, its culture will enable or hinder the execution of that plan. This is particularly true in the implementation of the management system and philosophy of continuous performance improvement

(CPI). Regardless of the state of an organization's culture, it is critical to begin the journey to continuous improvement with a realistic understanding of the beliefs and assumptions defining that culture.

At Seattle Children's Hospital (SCH) we began the quest to understand our culture in 2003, when we engaged the Bard Group, a consulting organization specializing in physician and hospital relations, to help uncover the unwritten "simple rules" that informally define the way things get done at Seattle Children's. After a series of interviews and discussions with faculty physicians and administrative leaders throughout the organization, we uncovered the simple rules at the heart of the culture. The top seven unwritten simple rules identified at Seattle Children's are as follows:

- You're only accountable to your boss or silo—not the institution.
- Value peace: avoid confrontation. Challenging an issue is a personal attack.
- Don't set priorities—everything is a priority.
- New ideas must be fully developed to be considered.
- "Plan–do" is more valued than "check–act."
- Get buy-in for all decisions—participation is required for commitment.
- Add new initiatives without reorganizing the systems and processes upon which they are based.

Imagine the implications of these simple rules on the ability to implement and sustain a continuous improvement strategy! Importantly, once we identified these rules we didn't set out to "break" them. But we did publicize and openly discuss them, and made it clear that they could not be tolerated if we were to be successful.

Changing a Culture

If continuous performance improvement is to create meaningful and sustainable change in an organization, it must be much more than a set of analytical and process improvement tools. CPI must become integrated into the culture of the organization—it must become the new "way we do things around here." It must become the philosophy and management system that guides the short- and long-term management strategy. This means leaders must intentionally take action that will, over time, change the culture.

As described in Chapter 2 and depicted in the Seattle Children's CPI "house," staff engagement is the foundation of continuous performance improvement. The roof of the house represents the ultimate focus of all improvement efforts, patients, and their families. These two concepts—engagement and patient- and family-centered care—shape the work of leaders in crafting a culture capable of meaningful and sustainable improvement.

As leaders at Seattle Children's, we recognized we had cultural challenges to both concepts. Although staff engagement was generally high, as measured by the Gallup Organization's workplace survey, memories of a "reengineering" effort in the early 1990s that resulted in staff layoffs were still strong in the cultural lore of the organization. And although Seattle Children's had been a leader in efforts to understand patient- and family-centered care, feedback from families indicated that there were major service deficiencies. This dissatisfaction was echoed by referring physicians who described significant problems in access, communication, follow-up, and confusing systems and processes. Although they acknowledged Seattle Children's as the quality leader for pediatric care, survey results demonstrated that access and communication were more important than quality in their decisions on where to refer their patients.

The service culture at Seattle Children's Hospital was accepting of these circumstances—in fact, many families described a staff attitude of "You're lucky to be here; we're well worth the wait." Our quest was to change that to "We're happy to serve you—how soon can you get here?"

Critical Success Factors for Cultural Transformation

Intentionally changing the culture of an organization requires more than leadership commitment—it requires a relentless and unwavering focus on the desired outcomes. Several elements are critical to this cultural transformation, including the following.

Executive and Faculty Leadership

It was the Hospital Steering Committee—the executive and faculty leadership group—that determined the need to uncover the unspoken assumptions (i.e., the simple rules) in Seattle Children's culture that were hindering its progress. This same group studied the philosophy and methodology of continuous performance improvement, and came to understand the leadership rigor and discipline that would be required for its successful development and implementation. And it continues to be executives and faculty leaders together who spearhead the improvement efforts, acting as sponsors and management guidance team members for our improvement work.

Community Physician Participation

As the primary referrers to Seattle Children's Hospital's specialty services and as members of the medical staff, community physicians cannot be left out of the cultural transformation process. Community physicians provide a critical perspective on the opportunities for improvement, the competitive environment, and the experience of their patients with the care provided. Community physicians should be engaged directly in improvement projects on processes that are important to them, and should be compensated appropriately for their time and effort.

Patient and Family Participation

Hearing the perspective of patients and their families directly during CPI events is the most powerful element in overcoming staff resistance to process change. At first we worried about revealing our "dirty laundry" to patients and families in improvement workshops, but we soon realized they lived with and knew our foibles quite well. We learned not to imagine what our patient and families thought, but to directly ask them. In fact, without the direct involvement of patients and families, a team makes assumptions about what is important to the customer—assumptions that are often misguided if not simply wrong. (See Sidebar 4.1.) We have many examples at Seattle Children's of family involvement that has changed the outcome of a process improvement effort. Appropriately recruiting and preparing patients and families for this role are key to a successful experience. (See Sidebar 4.2.)

Sidebar 4.1: Don't Assume You Know What Families Want

In 2007, a team from the cancer value stream was working on improving chemotherapy start times for patients. The process for admission was lengthy, beginning with patients' visit to the outpatient clinic for blood tests necessary to determine whether their lab values were appropriate to be admitted to the hospital for chemotherapy. Patients who met the appropriate clinical criteria were then admitted to the inpatient cancer unit. During this process, families waited for hours while lab tests were run, reported, and confirmed; chemotherapy orders were written; the inpatient bed was prepared; and medications were prepared and dispensed by pharmacy. Many hours later, and often in the middle of the night, patients received their first dose of chemotherapy. The process had been purposefully designed so that families, particularly those coming from long distances, could accomplish the lab test and then begin the inpatient stay in one visit. The assumption was that families would not want to do the outpatient testing one day, and then return the next day for their inpatient admission. During the improvement workshop, however, families told the team that the one-day process was not as important to them as the ability to predict when they would be admitted and to reduce the total time spent waiting around the hospital for the next decision to be made. This led the team to develop a two-day process as an alternative: patients could have their lab work and clinical evaluation done one day, then return at an assigned time the next day for admission with their meds made and ready to be administered if they met the clinical criteria. The newly designed process reduced total wait time for families, improved the reliability of chemotherapy start times, and has become the option of choice for families.

Sidebar 4.2: Patients and Families Know What's Important—Just Ask Them

Getting an appointment in a timely manner with Seattle Children's specialty providers had been a long-standing problem, due to the limited supply of pediatric specialists and clinic-specific requirements for preappointment screening and patient preparation. In an effort to address this issue, ambulatory service leaders began a series of scheduling improvement workshops to address process barriers to access. One of the first events was to address orthopedics clinic scheduling. One of this team's assumptions was that each patient needed to be carefully screened and matched with the particular subspecialist who might best address the unique patient needs—and that families would want the "perfect appointment," even if they had to wait many weeks to get in to see that provider. However, when families were interviewed during the improvement event, they had a different perspective. They told the team that their first priority was getting into the orthopedics clinic to be seen by a clinician; they wanted to get the cycle of care started and were more than willing to return to see a specific physician if that was determined to be necessary. This insight led the team to think differently about what constituted the "perfect appointment," enabling them to simplify scheduling rules and open up more appointment slots with a wider variety of providers. Along with other process improvements in the clinic, this change has improved clinic access from 27 to 28 days.

Staff and Faculty Engagement

Staff and faculty are often initially skeptical of the power of continuous performance improvement to change their work lives for the better. They've experienced many organizational initiatives over the years, very few of which they remember as being ultimately successful. It is not until they actually participate in a CPI event, working on a process or outcome that is important to them and to their patients, that they begin to believe that CPI can be effective. "Proving the concept" through workshop participation is incredibly compelling and highly effective. It is these staff and faculty members who ultimately and more credibly speak to their colleagues about the benefits of the CPI philosophy and approach. These are the people who begin to change the culture and indeed begin to clamor for increased use of CPI methodology.

Board Support

If continuous performance improvement is to become the philosophy and management system for the organization, the board must be engaged at many levels. First, they must be educated about what CPI is, what the benefits are, and the investment that will be required in terms of organizational infrastructure to support it. Involving board members in workshops and other CPI events is an effective way of showing them firsthand what CPI is about, and gives them a chance to witness the focus on the patient and enthusiasm of the staff. Ultimately, involving the board in its own CPI effort is most powerful, as demonstrated in a governance CPI project at Seattle Children's. (See Sidebar 4.3.)

Sidebar 4.3: The Hospital Board Applies Continuous Performance Improvement (CPI) to Governance

In late 2004, the Governing Board of Seattle Children's realized that its structure and processes were no longer effective in meeting the governance needs of a growing health system. Through a series of retreats, board members concluded that they needed to make some radical changes to enable them to be more efficient and effective in their work, to focus on "value-added" governance work, and to recruit and retain a broader diversity of trustees.

The board members were familiar with the continuous performance improvement philosophy and tools being applied in hospital operations; they had approved the resources to support CPI infrastructure in the organization, and had seen the initial success of the CPI program. Therefore, they wanted to apply the concepts to their own process redesign project, and a governance team was formed to evaluate committee structure, process, and outcomes. Facilitated by Joan Wellman, the group agreed upon design principles that included focusing on governance responsibilities and reducing waste in their processes. The result was a reduction in the number of board committees from 42 to 15, and the average number of committee assignments per trustee from eight to three. Using the quality, cost, delivery, safety, and staff and physician engagement (QCDSE) framework, they added a quality committee, defined consistent staff roles for board support, and implemented clear roles and training for committee chairs. Board member satisfaction with governance effectiveness improved by 84 percent in one year, and they were successful in recruiting a more diverse trustee membership. They continue to plan, do, check, and act (PDCA) their design through ongoing assessments of governance effectiveness.

Financial Investment

Leaders who are committed to transforming the organization into a continuous improvement culture must recognize that the transition will require a substantial financial investment. Initially this means utilizing external consultants, but to be enduring CPI requires the development of internal expertise—one must "learn to fish." Therefore, investing in in-house CPI resources and providing education and training for all leaders and staff are of paramount importance. The investment also includes ensuring that financial incentives throughout the organization are aligned to support CPI. For example, this may mean budgeting for "backfill" costs of staff who are participating in workshops so that individual departments aren't penalized for labor cost variances, as well as ensuring that community physicians and faculty are appropriately compensated for their time spent in CPI activities. The investment is substantial—our board originally approved a $10 million budget over three to five years, and we now invest $6 million per annum (≈1% of our operating budget) in CPI.

Infrastructure Support

Continuous performance improvement requires well-trained internal experts who can guide the work at the local level and ensure adherence to the methodology of improvement. In the hospital setting, it also means aligning traditional quality improvement, patient safety, customer service, and staff and leadership development resources with CPI. Our $6 million annual CPI budget encompasses all of these functions and includes a 30-person CPI department. The long-term goal of these internal experts is to build expertise and improvement capability at the local level, so that this philosophy and methodology is fully integrated into the organization.

Values

Most organizations have an articulated set of values that guide their work, and leaders must tie the continuous improvement philosophy to these core values. This anchors the CPI efforts in something that is familiar and enduring to staff. At Seattle Children's, these values and the behavioral expectations that define them are embodied in an acronym called ART—Accountability, Respect, and Teamwork. Seattle Children's leaders and staff refer to ART-ful behavior, in terms of both how they treat each other and how they interact with patients and families. CPI supports their ability to demonstrate these core values in their daily work.

Revealing the Simple Rules

As noted in the first section of this chapter, understanding the current state of your organizational culture is crucial to intentionally transforming it. Making the "simple rules" that describe individual and group behavior enables leaders and staff to hold each other accountable for breaking out of the old patterns.

Stealing Shamelessly

Good ideas come from everywhere, inside or outside the industry, and leaders in continuous improvement should be quick to seek new ways to approach old problems. In most organizations, however, using ideas from outside one's company, let alone outside one's industry, is very difficult. Part of the leadership and then broader cultural transformation of a company is the growing appreciation for the power and value of ideas from "outside." The degree an organization has moved from "not invented here" (i.e., don't learn from others) to a willingness to "steal shamelessly" (i.e., learn from others) is a good measure of the depth of its cultural transformation.

Methods for Cultural Transformation

Beyond these critical success factors at SCH, there have been three key methods important to the success of CPI. Our leaders fit these methods together to create what we call continuous performance improvement.

Learning from Toyota: The Philosophy of Continuous Improvement

As Seattle Children's leaders began to study the Toyota Production System (TPS), and to see the adoption of TPS at local manufacturing sites such as Genie Industries and the Boeing Company, we came to understand that the transformative power of TPS was in the philosophy and system, not just its tools. As Jeffrey Liker articulates in *The Toyota Way*,[1] Toyota's success is rooted in its business philosophy and approach. Liker has categorized the principles that Toyota embodies into four categories: philosophy, process, people and partners, and problem solving. Unless all of these concepts are addressed systemically, CPI will fulfill the prophecy of the skeptical employee as a "flavor of the month." We have adapted Toyota's thinking into our CPI philosophy, the elements of which are as follows:

- Focus on the patient and family.
- Support our people in their work.
- Take the long-term view.

Learning from the Gallup Organization: Engagement Matters

Seattle Children's began using the Gallup Organization's workplace survey tool and concept of engagement in 2001. Key to this approach is an understanding of the difference between employee satisfaction and employee engagement. Employee satisfaction connotes whether the person is "happy" with a job and the working conditions, whereas engagement is a much richer concept. According to the Gallup Organization's research, engagement is the degree to which the employee is psychologically committed to the organization and its mission, and the overall staff engagement in an organization is predictive of important business outcomes, such as customer satisfaction, profitability, and safety. This concept ties directly to the fundamental principle in the Toyota Production System of supporting the people who are doing the work.

Such support requires leadership commitment to deeply understand the problems that workers encounter in their daily work lives. This means leaders must be visible in the workplace and constantly asking what they can do to remove barriers for staff. The focus remains on the patient and family as the "customer," but acknowledges that the care and service provided are direct reflections of the ability of the staff and physicians to get their work done without unnecessary hassle (i.e., waste) in the organization's systems and processes.

Learning from the Studer Group: Hardwiring Matters

Beginning in the late 1990s, Seattle Children's leaders took steps to address the service deficiencies identified by patients, families, and referring physicians, but found sustained success elusive. In 2004, as our continuous performance improvement philosophy was taking shape, we discovered the work of Quint Studer and his colleagues.[2] As senior vice president and COO of Holy Cross Hospital in Chicago, Studer successfully transformed the culture of service from one that was producing patient satisfaction scores in the fifth percentile to one that was achieving satisfaction scores in the 94th percentile. He then replicated these results as administrator at Baptist Hospital in Pensacola, Florida. Success in service improvement was also reflected in stronger clinical and financial results. Along the way, he discovered several key actions (the Nine Principles℠) that, if done consistently, can lead to this kind of organizational transformation. Fundamental to achieving and sustaining these principles and the specific interventions he prescribes is a concept Studer calls "hardwiring." This requires that leadership implement the key concepts in a standard way, and that adherence to these interventions is audited and reported to leadership on an ongoing basis. Only by hardwiring such behaviors does the organizational culture change in a way that will transcend the tenure of a specific leadership team.

At Seattle Children's, we used our learning from the Studer Group to continue building our continuous performance improvement philosophy, leadership expectations, and tools. The principles and actions supported by Studer's research and experience integrate well with the Toyota Production System's focus on the customer, supporting the staff, and creating the standard work and expectations for leadership. The link to the concepts of engagement, as articulated by the Gallup Organization, is also very strong. By integrating these three methods, we have created a robust leadership philosophy that has helped transform our organizational culture.

Tools for Cultural Transformation

Changing the culture to support continuous performance improvement requires the buy-in of a critical mass of those working within the organization. The belief that the CPI philosophy and management system works requires experiencing it at the individual and work-group levels—something that can be achieved only through direct involvement in continuous performance improvement initiatives and education.

Participating in CPI Activities and Experiencing Results

There is no substitute for direct involvement in CPI activities, such as rapid process improvement workshops, process design events, value stream mapping, A3 problem solving, and 5S events. Well-designed CPI initiatives address issues that are important to the staff working within the process, are well scoped, and have measurable targets. Participants represent all roles in the process, and management supports their active involvement in the improvement effort. In these activities, a didactic review of concepts is integrated with process walks and analysis, and enables integration of theory and practice for participants. Most important, well-scoped and executed events enable participants to achieve the targets and experience success in a time frame not possible without CPI methodology.

Participating in CPI activities enables staff and physicians to directly experience the power of the rapid improvement methodology. However, even those in the work area who are not directly involved in workshops are engaged in the improvement activity and given the opportunity for input into process design during the course of the CPI event through tie-in meetings and feedback sessions during implementation. Following CPI principles, the targets and outcomes for events should be visible to all staff working in the area. A successful event is noticeable to staff and physicians because it produces a visible improvement for patients and/or makes the work easier or less complex for staff. Experiencing results that matter to patients, families, and staff engenders support for the CPI philosophy and its role in the organization.

Learning Strategies

Although direct participation in CPI activities is the best way to engage people throughout the organization in the methodology, events must be supported by the overall learning strategy. Continuous performance improvement concepts are new to most people in healthcare, and specific learning experiences that cover these topics build the foundation for spreading the knowledge throughout the organization. These strategies should include both didactic and experiential elements, and should be designed in accordance with adult learning principles.

Human Resource Systems

Human resource systems must be designed to support CPI as the organizational philosophy and management system. This means that CPI should be integrated into recruitment, orientation, development, and performance management within the organization. Becoming proficient with CPI concepts and embracing the philosophy are key to advancement, and leadership development tracks are designed with CPI at the core.

At Seattle Children's, there are several examples of how CPI is being incorporated into human resource systems. Willingness to embrace the CPI philosophy has become an integral part of faculty recruitment; all leaders are expected to participate in CPI leader training, and CPI is an explicit part of leader performance evaluations.

Leadership in a Continuous Performance Improvement Culture

Organizational culture is always evolving; whether that evolution is positive or negative is dependent on the actions of its leaders. To truly transform organizational culture and embrace continuous performance improvement, leaders must intentionally behave in ways that support the philosophy of focusing on the patient and family, engaging staff and physicians as partners, and taking a long-term view. The most important leadership behaviors are described next.

Leadership Presence

Two tenets of the CPI philosophy relate to leadership presence: (1) improvement occurs not in the conference room but where the work is being done; and (2) supporting staff doing the work is essential to improving the care experience for patients and families. In order to support these tenets, leaders must regularly go to the place the work is being done, observe the key processes, and engage staff in understanding the barriers and enablers within the processes. Leaders can't develop this understanding by sitting in their offices, or merely hearing reports about progress and challenges. They must be visible, interactive, and supportive. Leadership presence in a work unit is not, however, about micromanagement. It is about setting clear expectations at all levels, and then supporting the next level of leadership and staff to achieve the goals.

Knowledge

Leaders become teachers of the continuous performance improvement philosophy and concepts, and in order to do that, they must first become students. CPI concepts are both elegantly simple and, at the same time, difficult to integrate into the fabric of the organization. Therefore, CPI leaders are on a long-term path to develop and deepen their understanding of the CPI philosophy and methodology.

Leadership Participation

Leaders in an organization that embraces CPI must actively participate in improvement activities, serving as sponsors, management guidance team members, or participants. This participation serves several purposes. First, it reinforces the CPI concepts of support for those doing the work and understanding the work through direct involvement and observation. As important, direct participation in CPI activities is the best way to deepen the leaders' understanding of the CPI concepts and their application within the processes for which they are responsible. And it demonstrates clearly that "we're all in this together."

Tenacity

Intentionally changing organizational culture is very hard work and takes many years to accomplish. Resistance to this change comes in many forms—some blatant, most much more subtle. Leaders who commit to the demands of a CPI philosophy must be prepared to continually recognize, confront, and overcome that resistance. To those who say, "This too shall pass," leaders must reply, "Resistance is futile."

Patience

Adopting the continuous performance improvement philosophy and management system is long-term, generational work. One of the counterintuitive aspects of this philosophy is that it must be based on a sense of urgency to drive improvement, every day, at all levels of the organization. Yet that urgency must be tempered with the understanding that dysfunctional processes, systems, and culture did not evolve overnight, and that sustainable improvement will, likewise, take time. It will be the ongoing work of leadership. Therefore, the tenacity to push through resistance must be coupled with patience, and the conviction that transformational change is only evident over the long term. Studying companies that have been implementing continuous performance improvement for many years, indeed generations, bears this out.

Implications for Leadership Development

Successfully transforming organizational culture to support a continuous performance improvement philosophy depends on effective leadership. As described earlier, many of the required leadership competencies and behaviors in a CPI management system are quite different than those required in a more traditional work setting. The leadership development strategy, therefore, must also be tailored to foster, model, and reward the new behaviors. The leadership learning should be intentionally designed and cascaded throughout the organization.

At Seattle Children's, CPI learning activities began with the executive and faculty leadership group, and included reading, lecture, discussion, and experiences at local manufacturing sites that had successfully implemented CPI. Through dialogue with leaders from these manufacturing sites, we learned not only key concepts but also what it takes to truly lead in an organization that embraces CPI. We learned firsthand about the importance of our presence, participation, knowledge, tenacity, and patience. These experiences served to provide us with the information we needed to commit to the cultural transformation it would take to make CPI the organizational philosophy.

The long-term leadership development strategy at Seattle Children's is to build CPI capability at all levels of the organization. Our leadership development strategy includes a mix of experiential and didactic activities designed to deepen understanding of CPI concepts. Over time, leaders are expected to develop the skills necessary to engage in basic problem solving using these concepts. As the leaders progress in their skill development, they are able to coach others and to lead more complex CPI activities. (See Figure 4.1.)

As we continue to build our CPI management system, leadership competencies necessary for success in our transformed organization will be iteratively redefined to reflect the role of leader as teacher, coach, and mentor. Integrated into leader

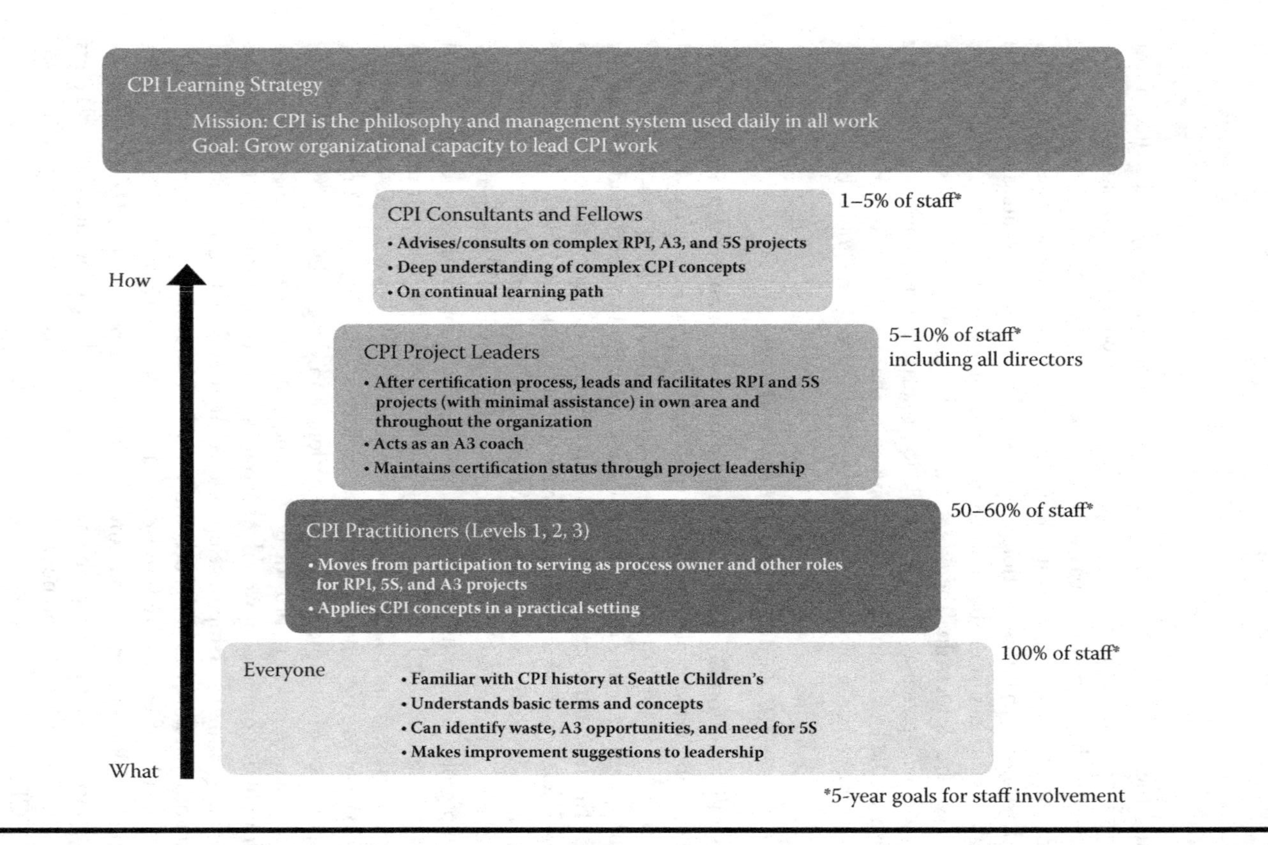

Figure 4.1 CPI Learning Strategy. Continuous performance improvement for all levels of the organization—a look at the core competencies at every level. RPI, rapid process improvement.

recruitment, selection, development, and succession planning, these competencies will form the basis for leadership expectations at SCH as over time we become incrementally more sophisticated at continuously improving our performance.

Conclusion

The continuous performance improvement philosophy requires taking a long-term view, and nowhere is this more evident than in the work needed to shape organizational culture. The good news is that culture is constantly evolving; the work of leadership in an organization committed to CPI, then, is to take action to *intentionally* shape that culture. We've learned at Seattle Children's that, by getting clinical and executive leadership buy-in, understanding and building on our current culture, and holding a vision of what it needs to look like, we are truly beginning to transform the "way things are done around here."

Notes

1. J. Liker, *The Toyota Way*, New York: McGraw-Hill, 2003, 6.
2. Q. Studer, *Hardwiring Excellence: Purpose, Worthwhile Work, Making a Difference*, Gulf Breeze, FL: Fire Starter Publishing, 2004.

Epilogue

Cara Bailey

In the five years since this chapter was written, fundamental changes have occurred, both inside the organization and in the external environment in which we operate. From executive and middle management retirements to shifts in customer expectations and the evolution of new financial models, our need to stay focused on the long term while adapting to the environment has never been stronger. The continuous performance improvement philosophy is now well rooted in the culture, yet we are constantly humbled by how much more we have to learn about effectively applying those principles in our organization. Ironically, as CPI has become the "way things are done around here," adaptations to our CPI methodology are sometimes interpreted as rogue attacks on our bedrock values. Go figure!

We now realize that our CPI practice must continually evolve as our understanding matures and the environment changes. We've learned the importance of explicitly tying new ideas, concepts, and behaviors within our CPI framework so that our people know we haven't abandoned the CPI philosophy; indeed we are strengthening it. One example is in the work we've done to reinforce our safety culture and to embed the principles and tools of high reliability science into our daily management system. As we've partnered with a consulting firm that supports hospitals in their work to eliminate preventable harm, we have "translated" the language of safety and reliability into the terminology with which our staff are already familiar from their CPI work. For example, "rounding to influence" is embedded in the leader standard work and tiered accountability structures of the management system. The error prevention tools we are teaching our staff reinforce principles of mistake-proofing and supporting people to do the right thing. The Daily Safety Brief is the culmination of the series of morning huddles that begin our daily management cycle. Our ongoing mantra as we roll out each concept is, "This is *not* different! It is an enhancement to our CPI toolbox." Connecting the dots between CPI and emerging concepts and structures has become a major role of our executive leaders. As we introduce new methods and tools for improvement, we remain true to the philosophical approach and mind-set of CPI.

When we originally wrote this book, much of our CPI work, be it point improvement or value-stream based, consisted of large-scale improvement projects requiring rapid improvement workshops. Over the years, we have come to appreciate the power of iterative daily improvement, and its primacy in engaging and developing our people. However, this new emphasis has proven difficult to catch on in our organization. We gravitate toward the dramatic, breakthrough improvement projects, and the skepticism that small improvements can add up to something meaningful seems to be deeply ingrained in our culture. Once again, we've discovered a new area of leadership development that we must address and nurture through executive leadership modeling, explicit coaching, and tools to help document the value of these improvements.

It has been said that the only sustainable advantage is a company's ability to improve more quickly than the competition. This means that executive leaders must evolve in their own understanding and appreciation of what comes next in the CPI journey, and must demonstrate the constancy of purpose Deming articulated as the first key to sustainable improvement. Although we have been pursuing a CPI philosophy and methodology for over 15 years, we cannot count on a continuity of this commitment without intentional and long-term board and executive development plans. Our board members became involved in our CPI activities early on, participating directly in improvement activities and study trips. Today, we continue to tailor appropriate learning experiences for board members and executives, whether they are new to the organization or long-tenured. We anchor the developmental experiences in the strength of what already exists in the organization, while challenging leaders to look ahead to what the organization needs to thrive five to ten years in the future.

Chapter 5

Strategy Deployment and Daily Management: Implementing a Lean Management System at Nemours

David J. Bailey and Kellie P. Olmstead

Implementing a Lean Management System to Sustain Gains

Imagine that a healthcare organization musters the will and the resources to implement continuous improvement (CI). Executives are on board and have been trained in Lean philosophy and strategies. Leaders have successfully engaged managers and frontline staff in rapid process improvement (RPI) workshops. All involved are encouraged by the removal of waste from the system and the improvements in care delivery that they have observed. Everyone is gratified to see clear evidence of positive change, for example, reduced length of stay, shorter operating room (OR) turnaround time, and increased supply chain reliability.

Now imagine everyone's dismay several months later when the hard-won improvements begin to slip: length of stay trends upward, OR turnaround time increases again, and frontline staff notices the reappearance of empty bins in the stock room. After such widespread enthusiasm for continuous improvement and such focused effort, how could the gains slip away?

RPI workshops, 5S (sort, simplify, sweep, standardize, and sustain) events, demand flow, and clinical standard work are elements of breakthrough improvement that can fire up the Lean transformation within an organization. However, the Lean Management System (LMS) is the foundation of continuous improvement. LMS enables and helps sustain the gains an organization achieves through the other elements of CI. LMS embodies the plan, do, check, act (PDCA) cycle and is critically important to an organization's long-term success with CI.

Daily management and strategy deployment are two essential components of LMS. *Daily management* is a tool that includes four elements to ensure ongoing monitoring of an improvement process: visual controls (e.g., visibility boards), daily accountability (e.g., tiered huddles), leadership discipline (e.g., audits), and leader standard work (e.g., standard tasks and responsibilities). *Strategy deployment*, which is also known by the Japanese term *hoshin kanri*, is a top-down and bottom-up ongoing dialogue between senior managers and project teams about the resources and time needed to achieve targets. The dialogue is often called "catchball," because ideas are tossed back and forth like a ball in a game of catch.

This chapter will illustrate how an integrated hospital system, Nemours Children's Health System, implemented and continues to use LMS to sustain improvement on a daily basis.

The origin of Nemours Children's Health System was an endowment in the will of a wealthy Delawarean and began with The Alfred I. duPont Hospital for Children in Wilmington, Delaware, founded in 1940. Nemours also developed a clinical presence in Florida, consisting of pediatric specialty clinics, and opened its second hospital, Nemours Children's Hospital (NCH) in Orlando in October 2012. The organization has taken steps to create enterprise-wide integration, despite the geographic distance between the Delaware Valley and Florida sites.

Reading the Writing on the Wall

In the fall of 2011, we came to the difficult conclusion that the enterprise would not be able to execute its strategy without some substantial changes. Like other peer organizations, Nemours was feeling significant financial stresses caused by the economic downturn of 2008. To continue providing the highest quality pediatric care, we needed to address the inefficiencies that were using precious resources without adding significant value. We also realized that we needed an effective way to address apparently competing concerns: containing costs, given the current financial reality and future predictions, and improving the care experience for children and their families.

We began a series of "come to Jesus" meetings about the economic realities we were facing. Eventually, the entire executive team agreed to implement the Toyota

Production System (TPS). In addition to dealing with the economic issues facing Nemours, we wanted to ensure complete integration of all care sites and departments as one enterprise with shared goals.

We also realized that the entire process of goal execution would need to be revamped. In the past, we were successful in creating enterprise goals but not in translating those goals into action steps for clinicians and support staff at the front lines of care. Similarly, we felt we were not receiving sufficient feedback from the frontline staff (referred to as associates at Nemours) and were aware that at times executive leaders and managers were left with a sense of frustration from participating in meeting after meeting but not seeing effective follow-up action and results.

Beginning Our Journey

Over the following year, we implemented TPS across the entire Nemours enterprise, referring to the work as Nemours' Continuous Improvement. The executive team participated in intensive classroom training in Lean and took several week-long trips to visit other healthcare institutions and manufacturing sites that were applying the principles of TPS. In the recent past we had successfully implemented a "balanced scorecard for strategy." These experiences paved the way for our adoption of CI, which went relatively smoothly.

Not long after beginning our CI work, we realized that without an ongoing management system, the many gains we had achieved were likely to slip away over time. We began implementing in earnest two key elements of LMS: daily management and strategy deployment.

Monitoring Gains with Daily Management

Leaders across the enterprise facilitated the implementation of the four elements of daily management: visual controls, daily accountability, leadership discipline, and leader standard work. These daily management tools have helped us promote readiness for the day's activities, identify gaps, and address the problems or barriers that contribute to those gaps.

Visual Controls

Our leaders have ensured that daily management visibility boards are posted in every department. Initially the boards had two sections: readiness (a quick assessment of how ready we are for our day's work) and problems (divided into quick hits and complex problems). Every day, teams in each department use the board to identify immediate problems. Leaders use the boards to monitor progress, understanding, and engagement, and to audit each site's status. The area owner, most often the department leader, supervises use of the board. Once we had successfully launched strategy deployment, we added a third section to the boards for True North Goals.

Daily Accountability

To apply the daily accountability component of daily management, we implemented a tiered huddle process throughout the entire Nemours enterprise. Our executive leaders began the huddle process at the Orlando campus just prior to moving into the new hospital. Key representatives of the various clinical and operational functions met every day to check in about readiness as it related to the hospital opening.

We then replicated the tiered huddle process in Delaware and at our other clinical sites in Florida. The tiered huddle structure gives us a regular, standardized forum for escalating problems from the front line up to leadership, and for disseminating direction and providing resources to address those problems. (See Figure 5.1.)

Every weekday, each unit gathers at a specified time to have a concise, action-oriented briefing. For example, the OR teams gather at 6:45 a.m., the nurse managers at 9 a.m., the registration and finance departments both gather in the afternoon, and the emergency department (ED) holds a huddle for every shift. Information gathered at huddles from associates is communicated up the chain to the middle management huddles (e.g., the huddle for managers of all ambulatory care sites),

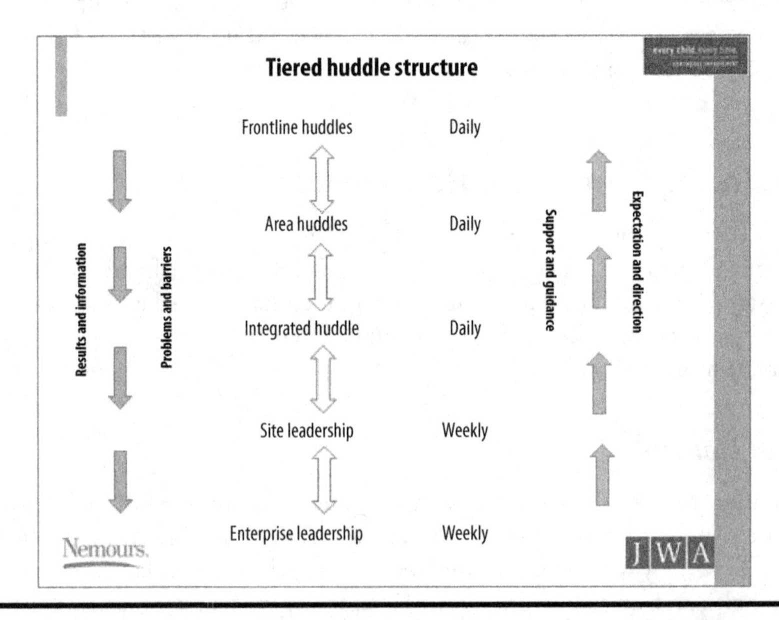

Figure 5.1 The tiered huddle structure allows Nemours to ensure regular communication between associates at the front line of care and enterprise leadership.

Figure 5.2 A team huddles at the visibility wall, which displays the visual controls used for daily management.

and from the middle management huddles to the integrated huddles, held every weekday morning at each clinical site.

Our integrated huddles are open to all associates at each site, and generally about 50 people attend the integrated huddles at our hospital locations, including managers, physicians, and executives. Teams hold similar, smaller huddles at our other clinical locations. These huddles have a facilitator and a scribe and are timed to ensure they are brief and highly efficient, and like the integrated huddles, generally last for just 15 minutes. (See Figure 5.2.)

From the beginning, the huddles have followed a standard agenda: daily readiness reports, then reporting on problems associated with methods, equipment, supplies, and associates (MESA), with issues categorized as either quick hits or complex problems. Associates and managers present issues from the past 24 hours with a short (i.e., one-to-two sentence) explanation and propose potential solutions. The team creates a high-level action plan and assigns an owner to ensure accountability for related action steps and countermeasures. At the subsequent integrated huddles, the owner reports on the status of the countermeasures. The huddles are not arenas for discussion. Rather, they are a forum for quickly giving attention to issues as a group and identifying ownership and support for addressing them.

In addition, top enterprise leaders hold an executive team huddle once a week. At this huddle, leaders recognize trends across sites, identify system-level problems and share information across the entire Nemours system. These huddles follow the same agenda as the other huddles. Leaders use the huddles to collect data on problems (e.g., frequency of events) and to ensure compliance with new processes.

Leadership Discipline

Auditing and gemba walks are two examples of how we have applied the leadership discipline component of daily management. When we are implementing a new process or procedure, we use a simple auditing process to ensure that we are moving in the direction of improvement and sustaining previous gains. Associates develop a small set of questions to assess the daily status of the novel practice. We purposely identify no more than five questions to keep the auditing process as simple as possible. The results of these audits are displayed on the daily management board and reviewed by leaders at our huddles.

For example, Orlando associates uncovered an issue related to the proper labeling of lab specimens. Associates brought the issue to light at a daily huddle, and the team worked together to determine how often it was happening and why. They used the following auditing questions to track improper labeling: Was proper labeling of lab specimens completed, yes or no? If not, what barriers prevented proper labeling?

Based on the frequency and impact, the team decided to convene a work group, consisting of bedside nurses, lab associates, and nursing education associates, to focus on solutions. The group created a set of clear, reliable techniques for proper specimen labeling and trained all associates in the new process. When the training was complete, nursing leaders began auditing the process every day and displaying the results on the daily management board. By the following month, the number of errors had dropped to zero.

Gemba walks are another important part of leadership discipline. Our executives conduct walking rounds at the units of each site. They meet with managers and associates to review the data on the daily management board. They ask about barriers to achieving the identified department goals, and they free up needed resources to address these barriers. Leaders include two of their direct reports in each gemba walk, which allows for coaching at multiple levels and learning across departments (i.e., both horizontal and vertical coaching) in each session.

Leader Standard Work

We implemented the leader standard work component of daily management by developing descriptions of standard tasks and responsibilities for each level of administration and management at Nemours. These descriptions include a specified time frame for each task. For example, at the Jacksonville site, the practice administrator completes at least three gemba walks with teams each week. Operations managers at the site are expected to complete gemba walks at least once a week. We use a visible tracker to confirm participation.

Addressing Barriers to Daily Management

We experienced two main barriers as we implemented daily management: the geographic distance between our campuses and the need for effective champions of new practices. We dealt with the geographic distance by facilitating frequent travel of leaders between the two locations and by convening the weekly executive team huddle with leaders from all sites.

We knew that identifying champions was essential—these individuals modeled to others "this is how we work now." We addressed the challenge of finding effective champions by casting a larger net when considering individuals for these leadership roles. We found no correlation between an individual's job title and their effectiveness as a champion. We also found that enlisting some frontline associates as champions was a key to success.

Reaping the Rewards of Daily Management

Implementing daily management at Nemours has had a number of positive effects. As an organization, we are much more appreciative of identifying problems and feel greater urgency about rooting out defects and solving problems. To put it bluntly, the messenger of bad news is no longer "shot."

The new process for communicating problems quickly to the executive team and sharing them at the enterprise-wide weekly executive huddle helps us when we identify problems at one campus to prevent them from occurring at the other. For example, nurses and nurse managers at the Orlando campus noticed that the medication identification system was not reporting narcotic waste correctly; the reports were not making it clear that narcotics were being properly wasted, which meant that we could not verify a lack of drug diversion. The software developer denied there was a technical problem with the device, saying, "You're the only organization with the issue." Orlando executives presented the issue at the enterprise-wide executive huddle; the Delaware executives and frontline nurses initially did not think there was a problem at their site, but when they investigated, they found the same issue. When presented with evidence of problems at both sites, the vendor reevaluated the system and found a glitch on all of the machines with the newest version of software—and created a fix.

Similarly, executives at the Orlando campus learned that the preadmission testing clinic was falling behind, resulting in some tests being completed on the day of procedure instead of 72 hours prior, which led to some procedure cancellations. When the leaders presented the issue at the executive huddle, they learned that the nursing staff at the Delaware campus had some time availability. The Delaware nurses were able to help the Orlando staff virtually by taking on some of the charts for preadmission processing, which alleviated the backup.

Due to daily management, leaders spend less time discussing problems and more time eliminating them. As one administrator stated, "Since we started using this approach, problems are being surfaced in huddles. I'm not attending as many meetings related to problems—probably 50 percent fewer—so I have more time freed up to *solve* problems."

Using these daily management tools helped us improve at identifying and solving problems related to readiness for the day's activities, but we recognized that we had to tie our daily management activities to the larger goals of the organization. Connecting our enterprise goals to the goals of frontline associates required strategy deployment.

Strategy Deployment: Cascading Enterprise Goals and Soliciting Feedback

To apply the strategy deployment component of TPS, we began "cascading" enterprise goals. When assessing the past honestly, we had to admit we had not been very successful at modifying the enterprise goals to take into account the problems of the frontline workers and to make them actionable and relevant at the front lines.

With strategy deployment we began working with managers and associates in an iterative process to translate the organization's True North Goals (see Figure 5.3) into actionable daily goals.

Catchball was the solution for cascading our goals and providing a feedback process to move ideas back and forth between leadership, management, and the frontline staff. The process started when we identified the specific enterprise goals based on the Nemours' True North Goals. We then reviewed these goals and metrics with each site, asking for feedback and making adjustments based on that input. When these goals were solidified, leaders at each site created site goals, which they reviewed with their departments and adjusted based on feedback. Department leaders then developed department goals, which they adapted based on input from frontline care providers. See Figure 5.4 for an example of the cascading goal process for a specific enterprise goal.

"Help me receive exactly the care I need and want, how and when I need and want it."

Child and family experience	
Quality and safety	Error free; zero defects; perfect care
Delivery	No delays
Cost	Achieve greatest value at lowest cost
People	100 percent engagement

Nemours. Children's Health System

Figure 5.3 The organization's True North Goals translated into actionable daily goals.

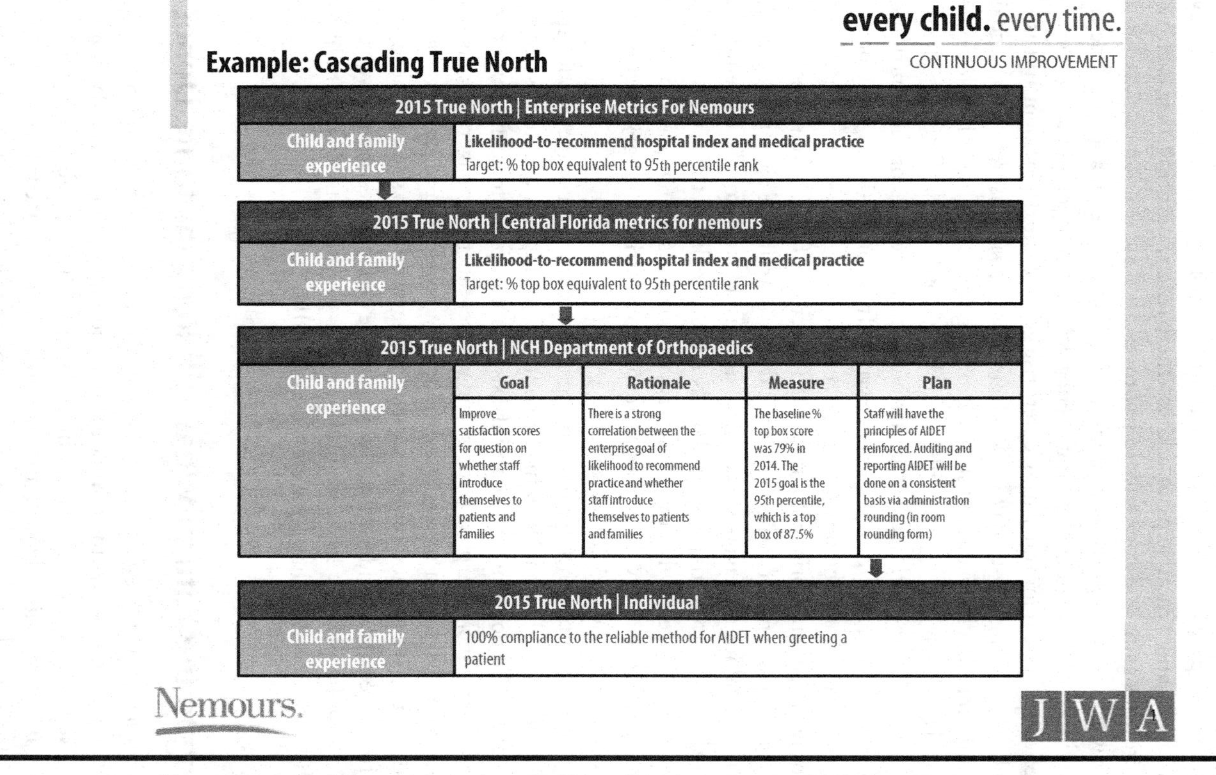

Figure 5.4 Cascading a True North Enterprise Goal. The cascade process involves taking an enterprise goal and its associated metric and translating it to a goal and metric at the site, department, and individual level. AIDET = Acknowledge, Introduce, Duration, Explanation, and Thank You.

We use the visibility boards in each department to facilitate strategy deployment. Each board lists the True North Goals of the site and those of the department, which tie directly to the site goals. For example, one of the goals for the med-surg units this year was "delivering medication correctly," which tied to the site goal of reducing medication errors by 30 percent. The visibility boards provide a central common space for ongoing communication about goals, barriers to achieving these goals, and action steps to address the barriers, ensuring that each site sustains previous gains and continues to improve.

We now have a clear line of sight between the executive team and frontline clinicians and staff in terms of goal setting, feedback, and resolution of issues. We also have an effective system for translating enterprise goals to the department and associate level. Connecting day-to-day work to our overall goals ensures that the goals are meaningful to all clinicians and staff. According to a CI manager for Nemours, "Now associates know and can articulate our True North Goals. For example, the medical assistant in the orthopedics department knows how he or she contributes to our overall patient and family experience goals. That connection is really powerful now, in a way it wasn't before."

Not only are our enterprise goals translated effectively for the front lines, but all our goals are in place much earlier in the fiscal year than in the past. In past years, it was not unusual for managers to receive their goals in April for the current fiscal year, and then need to readjust their plans based on goals for the several months already passed. Last year, which was our first with the cascading goal process, we distributed goals in January. This year, we expect to distribute all goals across the Nemours system by the end of December.

Applying the components of Lean management, daily management, and strategy deployment has allowed Nemours to continue to improve and to sustain the gains achieved. We now have a strong infrastructure in place for communication between the front line, enterprise leaders, and all the leaders, managers, and associates in between. We have a reliable way to identify problems and quickly address them and an effective method for translating high-level goals to specific ones applicable to frontline care providers. Finally, despite the capital investment involved in opening a new hospital in 2014, we find ourselves on solid financial standing—quite a different situation than we were facing in 2011.

Looking to the Future: What Still Remains to Be Done?

One of the foundational tenets of Lean is that it is an unceasing endeavor of continuously searching for ways to eliminate waste and improve processes. Two of the key areas Nemours will be addressing in the near future are stabilizing costs and communicating more quickly with associates who raise a problem.

Our adoption of LMS has engaged leaders, managers and associates at all levels of our organization. Individuals are engaged not only in daily readiness—being truly prepared for the day's work—but also in reaching our True North Goals. CI has created a direct line of sight between our executives and our frontline associates, has helped us translate our True North Goals into meaningful action steps for our clinicians, and has provided an open channel for conveying existing and potential problems at the front lines to our leaders. And we have an effective means for rapidly addressing these problems.

The effectiveness of CI is evident in the experience of the director of pharmacy at our Orlando hospital. She had been working to address the issue of duplicate medical orders in the electronic medical record since the hospital's opening two years before. Initially skeptical of CI, she had raised the issue several times in traditional forums but had seen little appreciation for the problem or means for addressing it. Finally, after seeing the effectiveness of CI in problem solving, she decided to bring the issue to the integrated huddle.

She presented the problem on a Wednesday and returned with supportive data the following day. The chief operating officer, who was running the integrated huddle that day, immediately convened a cross-functional work group to address the concern. Within 36 hours the group had developed and vetted new ordering, dispensing and administration methods, trained associates and physicians, and conducted audits on the new process. The experience left the pharmacy director with a deep appreciation for being part of an organization that reacts to problems rapidly and effectively. As she remarked, "It's pretty amazing to work in a hospital where broken doesn't have to be the norm."

Chapter 6

Leadership and Lean Transformation at Seattle Cancer Care Alliance: If We Knew Then What We Know Now

Michael D. Boyer, Norm Hubbard,
Camille Rapacz, and Elizabeth Poole

As Seattle Cancer Care Alliance advances its thinking and understanding of improvement through its Lean transformation, cultural barriers to change continue to be revealed. In fact, the more the organization learns, the more what is left to learn is revealed, and chasing that revelation requires greater active participation of leadership. In hindsight, the organization's evolution was essential for the development of a strong continuous performance improvement (CPI) mind-set and lasting change.

Introduction

Seattle Cancer Care Alliance (SCCA) is a beacon of hope to patients diagnosed with cancer. Seattle Cancer Care Alliance is the only National Cancer Institute (NCI) Comprehensive Cancer Center in the Pacific Northwest and *U.S. News & World*

Report's highest-ranked institution west of the Rockies. Patients diagnosed with any cancer type consistently have higher five-year survival rates if treated at SCCA.[1]

While SCCA is an institution of the highest standard of care, it has not been immune to its own aches and pains. The tale is familiar among many U.S. healthcare organizations; rapid changes in the political and economic environment coupled with an internal management system inconsistent with continuous process improvement principles cause leaders to seek a better way of operating. While the case for change has been a common story, SCCA's path has been anything but. This chapter is a reflection on Seattle Cancer Care Alliance's improvement journey.

The Case for Change

The "Alliance" of Seattle Cancer Care Alliance is the namesake reminder of the organization's complex structural and cultural conditions. In the mid-1970s, E. Donnall Thomas, the head of the University of Washington's oncology program, found himself butting up against the chair of the University of Washington Medical Center (UWMC). The institution sought to limit Dr. Thomas's authority and ability to conduct research on an experimental treatment for leukemia patients, the bone marrow transplant (for which Dr. Thomas would later go on to win the Nobel Prize). Dr. Thomas sought to continue his research regardless of the location. In the same time frame, Dr. Bill Hutchinson, spurred by the death of his brother and famed Seattle Rainers' pitcher, Fred Hutchinson, opened the Fred Hutchinson Cancer Research Center (FHCRC) on Seattle's First Hill. Dr. Thomas quickly moved himself and his staff to the center. The group retained their University of Washington status and left a trail of ambiguities in the relationship between UWMC and FHCRC that would not be hashed out until the 1990s.

By 1992, FHCRC had outgrown its original home. The need to expand pushed FHCRC, UWMC, and local pediatric center, Seattle Children's Hospital, together in common interest. The benefits were clear: joining together could create a world-class cancer care, research, and education program. Yet the mutual recognition of common good did not mean that the affiliation agreements were smooth. FHCRC's rugged individualism had been a constant clash with the institutionalism of UWMC and the agreements were a tumultuous affair. Despite this, the tense negotiation period ended in 1998 when the three organizations set pen to paper on the affiliation agreement. As the dust settled, the terms of the "Cancer Care Alliance" included: (1) Seattle Children's, Fred Hutchinson, and University of Washington would give equal contributions; (2) SCCA would have a "hospital within a hospital" model and lease 20 beds from UWMC; (3) the Alliance of Dedicated Cancer Center Membership would be transferred from FHCRC to

SCCA; and (4) physicians would be UWMC employees and FHCRC research faculty (later joint services agreements would refine financial details).

SCCA grew quickly in reputation and profits, yet this initial success shrouded institutional factors that would pose ongoing management challenges. On the one hand, the coming together of the greatest scientific and medical minds in a world-class facility has been the foundation and source of the institution's excellent outcomes. On the other, three culturally disparate organizations coming together under a single roof resulted in several hospitals within a hospital, each with its own personality and practices. As the wide variety of clinic and service lines opened (shown in Figure 6.1), external and internal pressures exacerbated these differences.

The Patient Protection and Affordable Care Act (PPACA) coupled with mounting competition made it clear that survival would be dependent on organizational improvement. Although PPACA would expand Medicaid and private insurance coverage to millions, many of the exchange plans would not cover the SCCA charges. Those that did were marked by low reimbursement caps and visit type restrictions, severe limitations to cancer patients. PPACA also mandated that Medicare payments would now be partially dependent on measures of quality and efficiency. Meanwhile, local Seattle medical centers were aggressively pursuing the cancer market. SCCA not only needed to grow, it needed to grow efficiently while keeping the highest quality of care.

Internally, the organization's structural and affiliation design posed significant operational challenges. Structurally, SCCA was designed in a classic model: shared services such as intake, lab, pharmacy, and infusion were grouped into large departments while physician clinics were grouped by specialty services. When the organization was small, the flow of patients from patient intake, through diagnostic services, consultation and examination, and to treatment and care was dedicated and disease centric. As volume grew, the disease-specific flows were diluted and the once highly focused treatment pathways and processes melded into large departments and shared services (e.g., infusion and lab).

Furthermore, as determined by the original affiliation agreements, physicians that held clinic at SCCA were not SCCA employees, but instead UWMC, and sometimes FHCRC faculty. Although this model was excellent for the progression of the cancer care, it created many operational issues. Physicians traveling between two or three institutions found it more efficient to group their SCCA patients on a few select days rather than across a week. Physicians would also rotate in and out of specialty clinics, operating independently during their time there. This physician model created three problems at SCCA: specialty clinic volumes swung from feast to famine across the week; providers varied wildly in practice; and, as a result of the former two, the remainder of SCCA operations would scramble to adjust. Shared clinical departments, such as Lab, Imaging, and Infusion, struggled with the impact of wild volume variations and attempts to serve many competing demands.

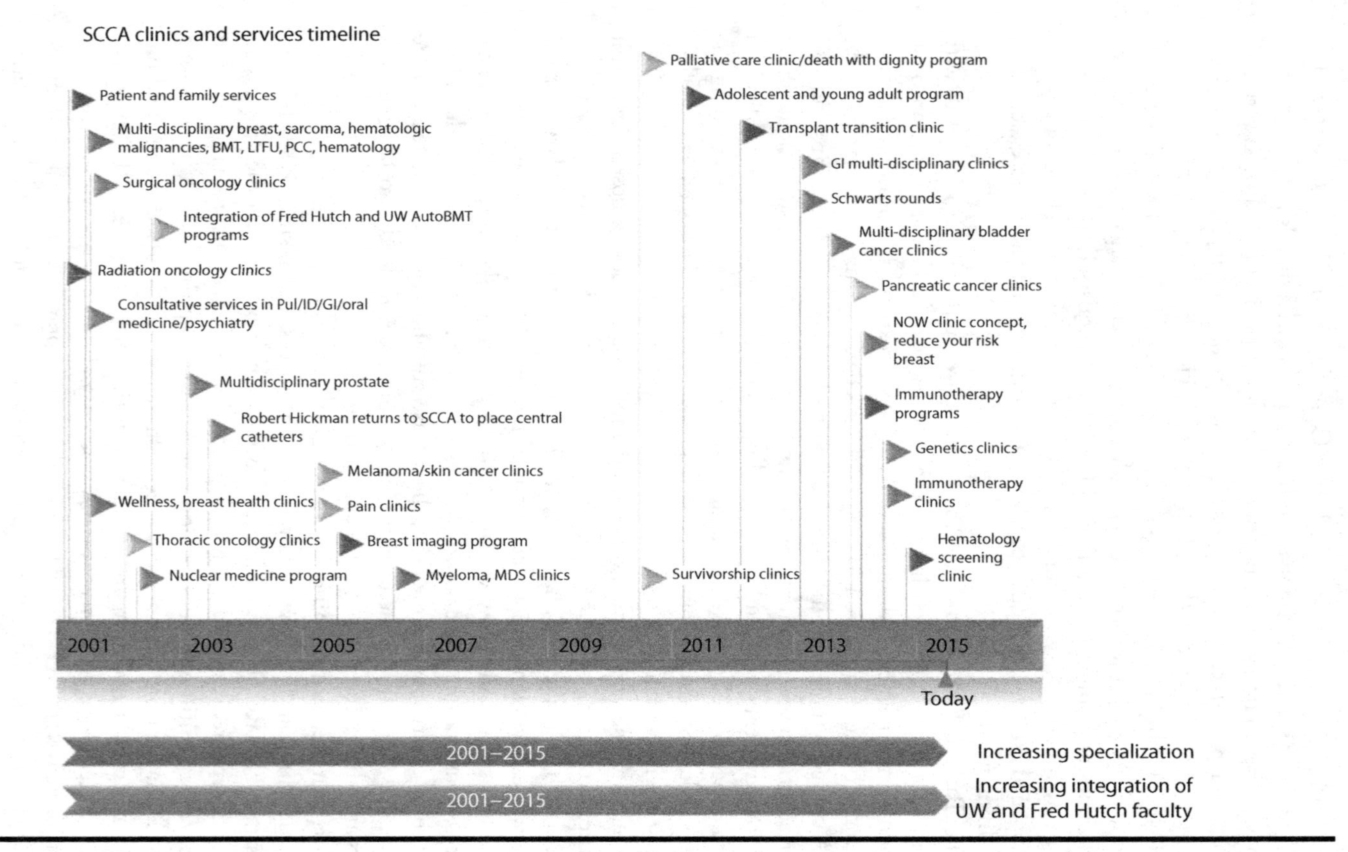

Figure 6.1 Clinic and service line openings. BMT, Bone Marrow Transplant; LTFU, Long Term Follow Up; PCC, Patient Care Coordination.

These external and internal issues did not quell SCCA's success in the cancer care market. By 2011, volumes were on a steep rise and SCCA executives were increasingly concerned about the organization's ability to keep up. During strategy meetings that year, leadership voiced their belief that SCCA did not have the capabilities to solve internal issues and that services would become too expensive and threaten the organization's ability to survive. One executive captured this concern by stating, "We can hardly standardize a simple patient form, let alone a care process."

SCCA leaned on the outside community to provide a counterpoint to its current management practices and face its operational challenges. Leadership looked first to its affiliate partner, Seattle Children's Hospital (SCH). SCH had been using operational methodologies adopted from the Toyota Company in Japan and seeing exciting results. At Seattle Children's "CPI Showcase Tour," SCCA executives witnessed what Toyota's manufacturing principles applied to clinical operations could do. Seeking greater immersion, SCCA leaders attended a North American Study Tour. Participants traveled to Lean organizations, including Herman Miller, Steelcase, Autoliv, and Group Health Cooperative, to observe continuous improvement and supporting management systems in action. SCCA leaders witnessed stark contrasts to their current conditions back home. These Lean organizations evidenced a clear linkage of organizational goals to operations, top-down support for improvement work, leaders who "walked the talk" of their commitment to educating all levels of the organization, and real improvement results. SCCA attendees were inspired by these different systems of operating.

Over the years, SCCA executives had participated in many unsuccessful improvement programs that seemed to fail more often than succeed. What the leaders witnessed at these Lean organizations seemed different and worth investigation. After returning to home, SCCA executives instituted a formal continuous performance improvement program with the intent to behaviorally and culturally immerse key leaders in this different way of operating. As a reference, Figure 6.2 shows the CPI timeline beginning in 2010.

Realization: The decision to adopt CPI Principles and pursue a CPI path was a strategic leap of faith rather than business case or quantitative based.

Bias for Action: Misapplications and Mishaps

Seattle Cancer Care Alliance had always been an expert at everything they had tried. They cured rare and difficult diseases and had forged an alliance where others had failed. What could stop them from immediate mastery of continuous process improvement? SCCA, like many high-achieving organizations, set out to

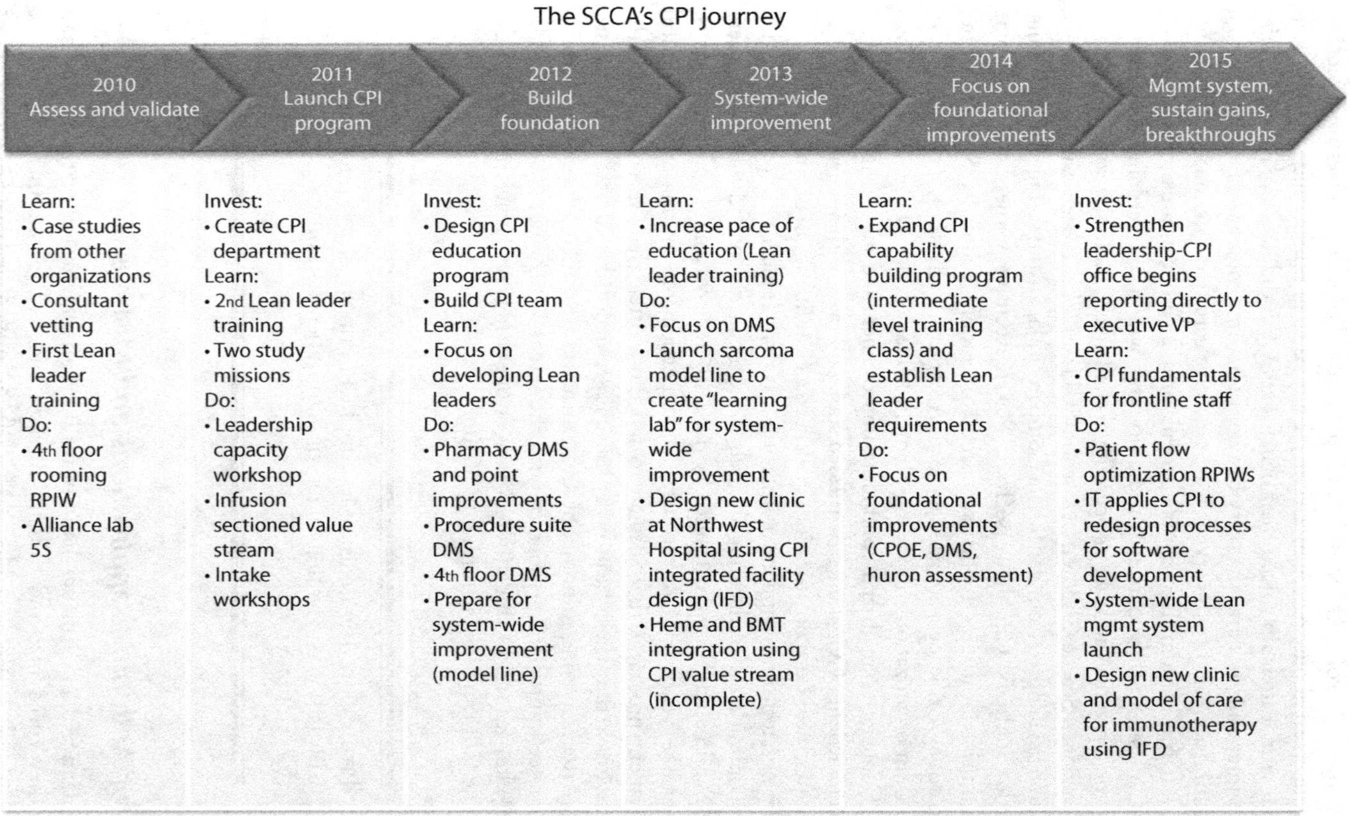

The SCCA's CPI journey

2010 Assess and validate	2011 Launch CPI program	2012 Build foundation	2013 System-wide improvement	2014 Focus on foundational improvements	2015 Mgmt system, sustain gains, breakthroughs
Learn: • Case studies from other organizations • Consultant vetting • First Lean leader training Do: • 4th floor rooming RPIW • Alliance lab 5S	Invest: • Create CPI department Learn: • 2nd Lean leader training • Two study missions Do: • Leadership capacity workshop • Infusion sectioned value stream • Intake workshops	Invest: • Design CPI education program • Build CPI team Learn: • Focus on developing Lean leaders Do: • Pharmacy DMS and point improvements • Procedure suite DMS • 4th floor DMS • Prepare for system-wide improvement (model line)	Learn: • Increase pace of education (Lean leader training) Do: • Focus on DMS • Launch sarcoma model line to create "learning lab" for system-wide improvement • Design new clinic at Northwest Hospital using CPI integrated facility design (IFD) • Heme and BMT integration using CPI value stream (incomplete)	Learn: • Expand CPI capability building program (intermediate level training class) and establish Lean leader requirements Do: • Focus on foundational improvements (CPOE, DMS, huron assessment)	Invest: • Strengthen leadership-CPI office begins reporting directly to executive VP Learn: • CPI fundamentals for frontline staff Do: • Patient flow optimization RPIWs • IT applies CPI to redesign processes for software development • System-wide Lean mgmt system launch • Design new clinic and model of care for immunotherapy using IFD

Figure 6.2 CPI timeline. RPIW, Rapid Process Improvement Workshop; DMS, Daily Management System.

implement continuous improvement in one fell swoop and initiated a value stream mapping activity for the entire clinic.

SCCA spent the early months of 2011 developing a value stream map, a map so enormous and complicated that it soon consumed the largest conference room in the organization. This value stream mapping activity, intended to generate improvement activities and engage the organization in change, failed to produce leaders' desired results. Reflecting back, SCCA leaders now recognize that this failure was due to a few key factors: SCCA had not built a foundation of principled thinking among their leaders, did not yet have the muscle memory to sustain operational change, did not define value from the perspective of their patients, and attempted to conduct value stream improvement without first questioning the validity of their departmental structure. This latter factor resulted in the inaccurate definition of many support and treatment areas, like the Infusion Department, as "value streams." The resulting work at the close of the mapping activity was frenetic and expansive, yet failed to leave SCCA leaders with a clear picture of what to do systemically. The organization agreed to pursue problems in areas that were already perceived to be problematic prior to the mapping activity, initiating value stream projects in the Infusion and Intake Departments, an improvement workshop with the 4th Floor clinical spaces, and 5S work in Apheresis and Laboratory Services.

In the absence of a strong supporting foundation, a solid understanding of the principles, a method to sustain, or a systems approach, most of the improvement efforts identified by the value stream activity struggled or dissolved between 2011 and 2012. The infusion value stream was a square peg in a round hole, the equivalent of initiating a value stream project in an automotive assembly line where only door installation or body weld is considered in isolation independent of the remainder of the vehicle. The misapplication never left the ground and was eventually abandoned. Intake, attempting to mirror factory cell design, reorganized into pods of cancer specialties. However, much like the Infusion effort, the application of value stream thinking to a functional department in the absence of a systems perspective showed limited local gains. Intake was plagued by provider dissatisfaction and many key individuals in the department left during the implementation. The rapid process improvement workshop in the 4th Floor Clinics attacked severe issues (59 percent on-time starts, each of the 33 rooms were only turned three times a day on average). While the improvement workshop provided some gains in reducing wasteful activity, it missed the foundational components of process standard work and a Daily Management System to hold the gains, and the clinic quickly fell back to its original condition. Workplace organization through a 5S methodology seemed to have more staying power and is still in active use and visible today in Apheresis and the Laboratory Services.

SCCA's frantic start quickly dissipated due to inconsistent, disconnected, and non-sustainable results. SCCA was missing an experimenter's mind-set and its early applications of Lean were fraught with implementation errors common to the inexperienced and unguided organization. The organization still lacked the basic understanding of

Lean principles, did not use value stream thinking, or see the flow of patients as a system. SCCA had been conditioned for success, but the normal struggle of initiating a Lean program shook their confidence in the methodology. By mid-2011, the leadership team hit their first fork in the road and had to decide whether to stay the course.

> Realization: During this early stage, the pursuit of a "proof of concept approach" instead of conducting multiple, rapid, well-designed experiments caused the organization to mistakenly question the efficacy of Lean principles.

Time for Reflection: Mixing Mind-Set with Methods

At a crossroads, SCCA executive leadership paused and reflected on the activities of the past year. Why had they failed where others had succeeded? Did the principles of continuous improvement just not work for Seattle Cancer Care Alliance? Was leadership not committed? Was it the internal implementation choices? To answer these questions, SCCA leaders took a hard look at the circumstances surrounding their CPI activities and drew the following conclusions.

First, in their impulsive start and drive for immediate results, SCCA had quickly dropped the *plan*, *study*, and *adjust* components of W. Edwards Deming's cycle and had instead driven their energy into *do*. SCCA had not planned their first improvement activities as experiments, starting small and using the lessons to lead them to their next experiment. They had also not studied the perceived issues with a scientific mind or a systems perspective. While Infusion was indeed wrought with inefficiencies and delays, many of the problems appearing in Infusion actually originated upstream in the system. Infusion relied on laboratory results, physician orders, and pharmacy delivery to be complete, accurate, and on time when a patient was ready for treatment. If there were any defects or delays upstream, Infusion's schedule would be thrown off and the delays would compound throughout the day. Furthermore, improvement activity was executed with an eye on immediate resolution rather than on researching and understanding the underlying causes. Without purposeful plan and study, the adjustments were not meaningful and the organization would simply apply the next Lean tool and do it again.

Second, SCCA had picked up the tools and methods of continuous process improvement and applied them before developing the mind-set of local leaders and staff. Even objectively successful efforts like the 5S work in Apheresis hit cultural snags. The Apheresis staff, while energetic at first, soon perceived the methodology was "authoritarian." If newly implemented standards started to lag, local leaders would take a disciplinary approach with staff. They would reinforce the standards dutifully and blindly, instead of asking the staff questions or learning if the process was capable. While local leaders quickly understood that process discipline would be essential for sustainment, SCCA had not yet adopted a learner's mind-set, relying instead on command-and-control techniques.

After these reflections, SCCA leaders came to the conclusion that it was not the methodology or principles of continuous improvement that had failed, but the organization's application of methods in the absence of the correct mind-set and culture. By late 2011, SCCA leaders chose to continue the course of continuous improvement and made the following decisions: (1) they would create a long-term strategy for improvement that would counterbalance tools and methods with a culture of scientific thinking and continuous improvement; and (2) they would invest internally by creating a department dedicated to the tenets of CPI.

Realization: Clarity of purpose and a supporting mind-set must lead activity and action.

Master Plan: An Unconventional Strategy Emerges

SCCA's long-term strategy for continuous improvement was quickly dubbed the "master plan." In December of 2011, the vice presidents held their first master planning session, facilitated by the newly assigned director of CPI. Initially, SCCA's leaders sought a continuous improvement recipe—the right combination of workshops and activities that would mechanically and predictably produce positive results. External counsel challenged the team to instead build a plan that focused on investing in the organization's capabilities, culture, and ability to foster change.

SCCA's pursuit of the master plan began to surface a deeper concern. Leaders began to ask what was the purpose of the master plan and recalled the *True North*, or an "ideal way things should be," at other Lean organizations. Although a strong strategic plan had always existed, there was a nagging perception of goal misalignment and SCCA leaders latched onto this idea of True North as the missing element to their current strategic condition. True North became a kind of trope or stand-in for the master plan, without which the SCCA could not continue on the path of continuous improvement. Leadership's attempts at constructing the precise language for SCCA's True North proved challenging, and the issue was left simmering.

The plan that emerged, while still somewhat mechanistic and project-driven, began to structure SCCA's approach in terms of methods, mind-set, and management system—a balanced and systemic view. For *methods*, the organization would lean heavily on its internal Continuous Performance Improvement Office to canonize and stabilize the methodology in a way that was a cultural fit for SCCA. Early decisions in the CPI Office included the hiring of a small team of experienced practitioners, standardizing the lexicon (i.e., removing Japanese phrases in order to make the methods more accessible), and identifying a broad set of standard methodologies for improvement work. For *mind-set*, the organization began to document its cultural tenets of continuous improvement unique to SCCA's culture. SCCA rewrote the five-day "Lean Leader Training" program inherited from its consulting firm to specifically address current cultural and management issues of the clinic. The organization also created the SCCA CPI values and beliefs, an aspirational cultural touchstone (see Figure 6.3). For *management system*, the organization recognized the need to implement a structure that would sustain improvements, control processes, and promote daily continuous improvement. This became the focus of the SCCA's early work in Infusion, Intake, and the 4th Floor Clinics.

The master plan fostered forward motion in a number of organizational areas. For example, the Infusion Department began to collect process information on issues that had long affected patient satisfaction (e.g., patient rooming time, medication turnaround, chart completion, and visit duration variability). The infusion process metric performance is shown in Figure 6.4. Infusion now had real-time data and leading indicators, and was able to use process controls to make decisions rather than taking action from anecdotes or outdated reports.

In addition to clarifying local issues, the Infusion Daily Management System allowed SCCA to study the clinic as an interconnected system. Infusion's data showed that 30 percent of patient late check-ins were due to SCCA system issues including lab delays, late physician appointments, or internal scheduling

Values and beliefs

- Value is defined by our current and future patients
- Our employees' expertise and imagination are our most valuable resource
- Problems are opportunities for improvement
- We collaborate with humility and respect
- We are an organization replete with keen problem solvers
- Transparency and visibility are the norm
- Every action every day is done with the utmost attention to the quality of care and service our patients deserve
- We will never accept the current state
- Every employee is relentless about the pursuit and elimination of all forms of waste
- We implement performance improvement ideas everywhere, every day.

Every action is performed with the desire to improve the current condition, learn from the experience, share the discovery, and build the organization's capabilities.

Figure 6.3 CPI values and principles.

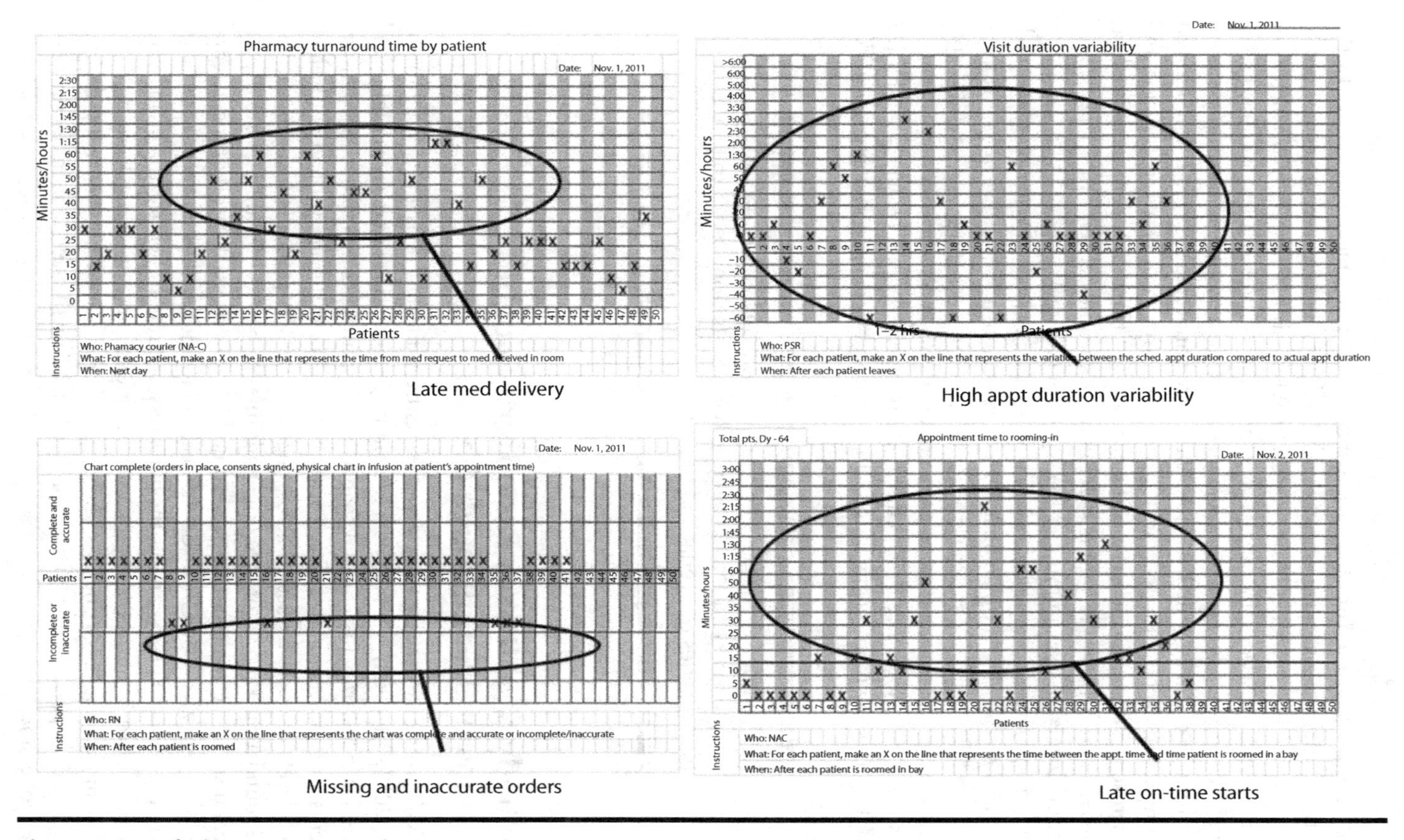

Figure 6.4 Infusion process metrics.

communication errors. Pharmacy's chemotherapy mix delay times, an issue that had long-plagued the Infusion Department, were now tracked real-time. In the past, mix delay issues were addressed through random interdepartmental phone calls and ad hoc complaints between staff. Using Infusion's Daily Management System data, the two departments were now able to pursue a synchronized solution. This infusion work led to a Daily Management System in Pharmacy during the summer of 2012 to further stabilize the interconnected system. This reinforced the new approach to improvement. From this early work between Infusion and Pharmacy, medication delivery performance went from 75.6 percent of medications delivered in over 15 minutes (zero orders on time delivery) to 4.1 percent of meds delivered in over 15 minutes (85.5 percent on time).

With progress underway, the debate of whether to have a master plan subsided. Rather than focusing the plan on a series of workshops and events as in its first iteration, the SCCA decided to focus the master plan on developing internal CPI capabilities and competencies, that is, problem solving and scientific thinking. The sense was that True North needed to emerge from experience and leaders recommitted to CPI, investing more deeply in the CPI Office and in the people doing the work.

Realization: A master plan focused on building capability of people, processes, and the system is a better long-term strategy than a series of events and projects.

Nobody Said It Was Easy: Hard-Fought Lessons of Breakthrough Change

SCCA leaders saw increased positive results from local or departmental efforts by late 2012. The Daily Management System implementations were encouraging and effective in fostering incremental change (e.g., Pharmacy turnaround time improvements and a reduction in missing order data within Infusion), yet had not yielded high levels of waste reduction across the larger SCCA clinical system or affected the foundational model of care. The fault lines or barriers within SCCA's departmental structure could not be patched up by local process controls or incremental improvement alone. SCCA made the decision to address flow and efficiency issues from the patient's perspective as they progressed through their treatment and care. If approached in an integrated manner, solutions and subsequent learning could affect more areas faster due to a likely multiplier effect. SCCA leadership decided to test this hypothesis using a concept they had originally seen in manufacturing—the model line.

The purpose of a model line is to make a tenfold improvement in a 90-day period via a structured implementation approach, apply value stream thinking, and demonstrate Lean principles in an "inch wide and mile deep" fashion. The selection criteria of the experimental line required (1) a complete value stream, (2) a core component of the business' success and an area seen as high-value investment, (3) a small but meaningful clinic size where change could occur quickly, (4) a high probability of success, (5) a cut that would go deep across all business functions, and, most important, (6) physician leadership. The goal of the line was to establish a focused, safe, and predictable test bed for process design and experimentation from which to learn. Many of the disease groups met the criteria but Sarcoma had physician leadership that was eager and ready to make a difference. At Seattle Cancer Care Alliance, the Sarcoma Clinic fit the bill.

SCCA formed the Sarcoma Model Line as an experiment to create a patient workflow and a care delivery model unmatched to that of any healthcare institution. In this ultimate model of care, patient flow would be unidirectional, seamless in its connection of activities, and void of all idle time or delay; research would be inseparable from clinical care; and the best possible patient outcomes would be delivered. This experiment radically challenged the existing model of care ubiquitous within the SCCA clinic. Instead of calling the General Intake Department, new patients would contact an Intake team member on the floor of the Sarcoma Clinic. Instead of traveling from floor to floor to the Lab and Infusion Departments, patients would have their labs drawn and infusions administered in the same room that they would see their provider. Instead of packing their clinic schedule into one "Super Tuesday," Sarcoma providers would balance their patient schedules over the week. Instead of reacting to each day as it came, the Sarcoma Clinic medical director and manager would lead a Daily Management System to sustain the design and promote continued improvement. These ideas were designed as a compact system of interconnected processes that brought services to the patient rather than the patient traveling to a department where the services were delivered. The left panel of Figure 6.5 illustrates the "pre-improvement" Sarcoma model line with the patient moving throughout the building. The right panel of Figure 6.5 represents the "post-improvement" view with the services coming to the patient in the clinic.

The Sarcoma Model Line met its purpose of teaching the organization about the challenges of implementing Lean principles in clinical operations, but unexpectedly, it demonstrated other organizational weaknesses. In addition to testing the limits of value stream redesign, the Sarcoma Model Line tested SCCA's capacity for change and perseverance in challenging conventional wisdom. Key elements of the Sarcoma Model Line design proved too challenging for the team and the complete vision was never realized. As in baking, the omission of a few vital ingredients can lead to surprising and sometimes unappetizing results. First, the design element of drawing and processing labs on the floor of the Sarcoma Clinic required a certified lab tech on staff, which was never filled. Sarcoma labs were instead transported to the General Lab Department for analysis, a step that increased lab flow time.

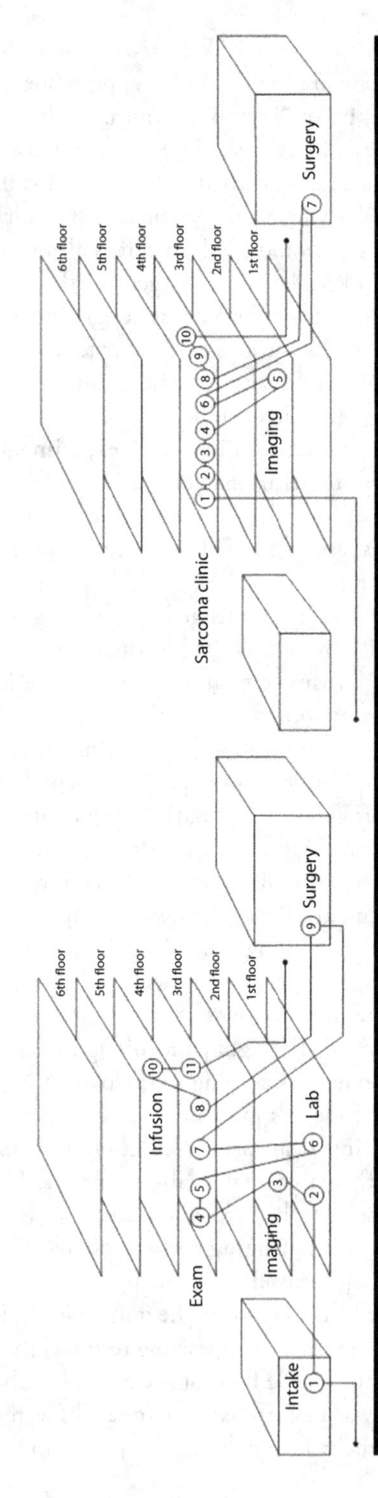

Figure 6.5 Pre-Sarcoma Model Line (left) and Post-Sarcoma Model Line (right).

Second, labor was never made available for infusion treatments in the multifunctional room. Initially, the Infusion Department would loan nurses for short periods of time but soon stopped. Third, and most important, the organization did not assign crucial roles for the Daily Management System. Daily Management was implemented in the Sarcoma Clinic but not sustained.

Unexpected events following the Model Line's launch worsened this rocky start. The Sarcoma physician leader, a leader who had held the Model Line together through positive spirit and tireless energy, left the organization to share his talent with others. Without this internal champion and the Daily Management System to hold the model together, the original design slowly disintegrated. At the same time, patient volumes rose (30 percent in a three-month period when the initial growth projections were planned at 2 percent per year over five years) and caused the system to overload. The Sarcoma Clinic abandoned its standard work, operational controls slowly fell into disuse, and essential roles were moved out of close proximity from direct patient care. Leadership struggled to maintain performance and the 90-day rapid test and adjust approach stretched to a 259-day experiment.

Although the Sarcoma Model Line upset the status quo, challenged long-held beliefs, and created discomfort for most every department, the results were positive and are shown in Table 6.1. Most important, the Model Line served its purpose as a test bed for process design and experimentation, and ideas first tested in the Sarcoma Clinic began to appear in other areas of the organization.

Despite relative successes, SCCA did not see the dramatic reduction of waste that they had initially hoped for. Operational expenses were rising 9 percent each year and SCCA's primary payers were capping reimbursement rates for expensive treatments. The Sarcoma work was hard, slow, and agonizing as the 90-day model line seemed to never end. Leadership reflected and wondered if there was a better way. Was improvement occurring fast enough to survive external pressures? To

Table 6.1 Sarcoma Model Line Results

Performance Metric	*Results*
On-time performance	100% increased from baseline
Scheduled time to roomed time	78.2% decrease
Provider productivity	60.6% increase
Staff productivity	43.3% increase
Growth in new patient volume	30.2% increase from baseline
Growth in return visit volume	19.0% Increase from baseline
Staff satisfaction	Tier 3 to tier 1
Space	47% reduction in required space

explore an alternative, leadership turned to an outside consulting group specializing in "turnarounds," who promised immediate improvement and the ability to quickly cut organizational costs. This outside consulting group proposed sweeping changes to the organization, many of which were in opposition to the continuous improvement principles the organization had been seeking to adopt.

A large number of the consultant group's recommendations had already been made by internal area leaders including standardizing clinical processes, linking the flow between departments, and staffing to demand. While the recommendations were generally aligned with the organization, the consulting firm's approach stood in stark contrast to the organization's master plan of methods, mind-set, and management system. An army of outside consultants would implement sweeping changes, leaving no management system or support structure in their wake. A minority of leaders pushed back and believed that long-term sustainable change is best achieved when supported internally. Having a plan imposed on the organization and delivered by others was in sharp contrast to the principle of supporting organization members to accept responsibility for their own improvement. After months of assessment and subsequent deliberation, the executives decide to double down on continuous process improvement and declined the services of the external experts. This turning point in SCCA's journey was invigorating and at the same time frightening as the organization, more than ever, held its future in its own hands.

> Realization: The change journey is not for the faint of heart especially when painful experimentation causes doubt and despair. Perseverance took on a new meaning for leadership and the organization.

Perseverance Understood: Failure Is Part of the Equation

While the Sarcoma Model Line captured much of the clinic's attention in early to mid-2013, the methods, mind-set, and management approach to continuous improvement still hummed in the background. The organization had formalized its CPI Capability Building Program and by October of 2013, 138 students had graduated from the customized Lean Leader Training course, 56 students had attended a North American Study Tour, and the organization was launching smaller methodology-based courses called (just as the title implies) "Learn-Dos." SCCA had also been creating pockets of cultural change through large sharing events. Monthly CPI *Report Outs,* which had been standard practice for over a year, gave engaged leaders and employees a platform to share their improvement work. The leadership team continued to advance SCCA's structure for operational control by implementing Daily Management in the Intake Department and introducing the concept to the 4th Floor Clinics, Procedure Suite, and the Investigational Drug Studies Pharmacy. The organization was not only picking up momentum with improvement work, but it was also beginning to see returns on its investment in mind-set. Lean leaders began to independently connect CPI to their work and pull on the CPI Office for help in improvement efforts.

During this time, SCCA was expanding its reach outside of the downtown Seattle location and into the surrounding communities. SCCA, in affiliation with Evergreen Health, opened a medical oncology clinic in the neighboring suburb of Kirkland as well as, in affiliation with the University of Washington's Northwest Hospital (UW-NWH), a radiation oncology clinic in the suburb of Northgate. Later at the Northwest Hospital location when a cancer provider group adjacent to SCCA's existing radiation oncology clinic exited the site, SCCA jumped at the opportunity to implement the model of care first tested in Sarcoma. To effectively design the clinic, SCCA employed a design methodology called Integrated Facilities Design (IFD). This process and value-stream-driven approach flips classic facility design on its head by using the knowledge of the people providing the services to create the space they will soon inhabit. Before designing a space, the specific sequence of activities is designed around continuous patient flow and process capability to ensure that form follows function. In seizing this opportunity, the UW-NWH Medical Oncology Clinic design team further advanced the ideas developed in the Sarcoma Model Line.

SCCA's NWH Medical Oncology Clinic went from concept design, to a full-scale cardboard mockup in a local warehouse, to construction and occupancy within a year. The 13-room Medical Oncology opened with most of the Sarcoma Model Line inadequacies resolved and lessons learned applied. The clinic flow included all parts of medical oncology value stream within a single area and department; from initial patient contact and intake, to consultation, examination, internal sample collection, internal pharmacy, and treatment (infusion), to continuing care. Additionally, the Northwest Hospital design was defined by a patient-centric flow, universal rooms, standard work, point of care testing, right-sized service, level-loaded provider time, the blending of traditional roles, line of sight design, and Daily Management System control. This design yielded an increase in appointment access, high employee engagement, increased referrals, and eliminated patient wait time.

The Northwest Hospital effort accelerated SCCA's organizational learning for a few key reasons. First, having services like blood draw and infusion travel to the patient rather than the other way around was radical when initially proposed in the Sarcoma Model Line but elementary to care once tested at Northwest Hospital. Second, Northwest Hospital was a satellite, a 20-minute drive and world away from the centralized SCCA campus. This closed system provided SCCA a unique opportunity to set up a controlled experiment, watch, and learn.

The success of SCCA's Northwest Hospital Clinic was another positive step in support of the organization's CPI journey. In light of this success, more leaders began to incorporate CPI principles into their daily work, including SCCA's electronic medical record implementation, the resolution of cross-functional patient care problems and various IT development projects. This improvement mind-set caught on as the experience and knowledge of individuals grew and many former skeptics became advocates. Throughout the organization, there was an increasing belief that leadership was serious, committed, and believed in CPI. Those who were waiting out this change saw a new level of leadership perseverance in the face of repeated challenges. Uncomfortable but rigorous experimentation was seen as necessary if improvement was to occur. Yet new concerns arrived in the form of sustaining, informing, and training the organization in CPI. Finding the time to improve with limited resources was the next hurdle.

Realization: Remaining principle-based and persistent when resistance seems relentless is possible through accepting and understanding the role of experimentation and keeping your compass focused on the experience of the patient.

Spinning Many Plates in the Air: We Can Do It All

Inspired by the growing foundational CPI work, lessons of Sarcoma, and successes at NWH, SCCA felt confident in its abilities to flex its continuous process improvement muscles. The organization set its sights on improving the Hematology and Transplant services. The Bone Marrow Transplant (BMT) and Hematology (HHM) programs at SCCA are core to the organization's service offerings. SCCA has performed more than 14,000 bone marrow transplants, more than any other institution in the world. These two programs accounted for 40 percent of SCCA's total charges, 54 percent of all infusion hours, and 38 percent of discharges. Culturally and operationally, the BMT and HHM programs were diametrically opposed. Owing to its FHCRC origins, the BMT program was still run by some of the staff that had migrated from the original First Hill Campus in 2001. In contrast, the Hematology program shared the same space on the fourth floor with many other oncology programs. The general perception was that BMT was a well-oiled machine, whereas Hematology was erratic and fragmented, and starved for resources and a support infrastructure.

The SCCA BMT and HHM physician groups saw the value in integrating the services to leverage their collective strengths and connect the programs for patient benefit. The argument was that if these two highly related services could be evaluated for overlapping value, cooperative operation might yield even better results from two already outstanding yet independent programs. The scope of this improvement effort went well beyond the "inch wide, mile deep" approach of prior endeavors and included the clinical operations, research, and academics of both the BMT and HHM programs.

In addition to deciding to improve the largest and most complex segment of the clinic, the SCCA continued to pursue and implement a number of initiatives such as a new digital electronic medical records and clinical orders system, a brand strategy, clinical pathways, ICD-10 implementation, new business develop activities, and the growth of an aging infrastructure. With scarce resources already committed to previously launched improvement efforts (e.g., Intake, DMS, Sarcoma, NWH), SCCA staff soon began to feel overwhelmed and overworked. SCCA began to lose grip on its earlier gains and stopped attending to small wins, sequencing priorities, and finishing what was started.

At the same time, the organization was in the final year of implementing its computerized physician order entry (CPOE) system. Due to this initiative's large impact on every aspect of the business, SCCA made the decision to pull back on all CPI efforts and make space for a smooth and effective CPOE implementation. SCCA leadership recognized early that an unsuccessful implementation would have an unacceptable impact on the organization and made an all-hands-on-deck call. The organization redirected resources from continuous process improvement efforts to CPOE workflow development. While this represented a step back for improvement momentum within the clinic, CPOE implementation also marked a step forward in SCCA's Lean thinking. It was the first time SCCA had integrated Lean methodology in a major technology project. Leadership's mind-set was beginning to shift from thinking of continuous improvement as an independent or additional effort to thinking of continuous improvement integrated into all organizational actions.

By the fall of 2014, CPOE implementation was on track to completion and the SCCA leadership began to revive its other improvement efforts. The BMT/HHM integration effort, however, fell victim to overreach and unpreparedness, stalled, then shrank to a small portion of the original scope. This disappointing setback gave rise to voices that proposed further pause or break in all new CPI efforts so that stability could be achieved. Counteradvice cautioned that reducing CPI efforts would result in the loss of organizational momentum and give ammunition to local skeptics. SCCA soon came to the sobering realization that it had an overload of priorities and attempted too much in the BMT/HHM integration effort. This realization drove leadership to recenter and reconsider the organization's capacity. This pause in improvement efforts promoted SCCA leadership's future promise to focus on a few things and to do them well.

Realization: Honoring the reality of a complex world, entropy, and multiple priorities, and responding with Lean thinking and focus is better than delaying or, worse, abandoning Lean principles.

Storytelling: A Deeper Connection than Data

Storytelling is ubiquitous in all organizations and, early in its continuous improvement journey, SCCA recognized the power of storytelling to foment or inhibit change. Storytelling can engage an organization in a way data cannot. It can appeal to both logic and emotion while creating a shared narrative of hope for an improved future. Storytelling can also disassemble change and reinforce the status quo. SCCA has experienced both sides of storytelling and has actively sought to create spaces where stories of continuous improvement can be told transparently, evenly, and in the spirit of learning and improvement.

Seattle Cancer Care Alliance's breakthrough improvements demonstrated the power of both sides of storytelling. Through the implementation of both the Sarcoma Clinic and Northwest Hospital design, statements like "Sarcoma was a failure" and "NWH would never work at main campus" made the rounds and reinforced the opinions of skeptics. While some SCCA members actively sought failure of continuous improvement, others repeated such stories because the compartmentalized nature of the organization only provided a shallow view of the work. For example, early in the stages of the Sarcoma redesign, the Infusion Department was swaying under high peaks in volume. Infusion nurses had been told that the intent of the model line was to alleviate Infusion capacity issues by infusing Sarcoma patients directly in clinic rooms. When in-room infusion failed to be instituted in the Sarcoma Clinic, Infusion nurses assumed that the entire effort had been a failure because the only story they had been told about the effort was the element that had failed. After this and similar misunderstandings, SCCA leaders realized that CPI would have a story no matter what and that leaders needed to create opportunities for an even and fair telling of that story in order to foster organization learning.

SCCA worked to create spaces devoted to the holistic storytelling of improvement work to counter misunderstandings and address inaccuracies. The organization emphasized the monthly CPI Report Outs, events similar to Seattle Children's Hospital's "Show Case," initiated topic specific *Brown Bag* lunches, formalized *Out Briefs* from events, and invited graduates of quarterly Lean Leader Trainings to attend monthly *Lean Leader Forums* and share stories. These learning spaces provided a place for SCCA leadership to practice new behaviors. At the first Report Outs, executive leaders would listen from the back of the room. Today, they stand in the front, open the events, and lead group discussions at the close.

SCCA could openly discuss the good, the bad, and the ugly side of continuous improvement in these learning spaces. In addition to the stories outlined in this chapter, these events hosted stories such as:

- How the Intake Department was able to increase its new slot utilization by 28 percent in two years of DMS
- How the Materials Management Department became a leader in inventory reduction through 5S

- How members of the Integrity, Billing, Intake, Patient Financial Services, and Clinical Immunogenetics Laboratory used the A3 methodology to reduce the human leukocyte antigen (HLA) typing patient intake process by 24 days
- How the Information Technology team applied Lean principles to standardize its project methodology, completing a project that was originally expected to take nine months in two

These wins, some quantitatively and others culturally large, were essential in setting organizational cultural norms. At SCCA, storytelling was used to reinforce the experience and affect behavior, not act as a replacement for personal experience, experimentation, and individual learning. Reflection and storytelling caused a different level of evaluation and meaningful discussion that was unlikely without the larger context.

Realization: Leaders are able to promote, engage, and inspire through the skilled delivery of stories that promote meaningful discussion and organizational learning.

Delays, Distractions, and Dilemmas

Four years into SCCA's journey, one might have assumed that the path of continuous improvement was clear, that process stability and capability were increasing, and leadership was set on a known and clear path for the organization to execute perfectly. Over time, it became apparent that the sense of progress and calm would always be subject to distractions and diversions. SCCA leaders were continually tempted by quick fixes and appealing but shallow answers. Organizational leadership had avoided the temptation of the army of consultants back in 2012, but that near miss did not mean the organization was permanently immune to the lure of solutions that were too good to be true.

SCCA leaders still wondered, even after multiple positive experiences with the scientific method and productive events, if there was a faster, better alternative to continuous process improvement. This pondering was different than their CPI of "never accept the current state." It was marked by a desire to go faster by skipping experimental steps. SCCA members would ask for shortcuts such as "an abbreviated A3" or ask to skip the step of collecting data before implementing an already-desired solution. Possibly motivated by overconfidence or, worse, by incompetence, this questioning of the previously accepted continuous improvement principles and rigorously proven methods was surfacing.

Externally, many experts were eager to step in and provide performance improvement guidance, infusion optimization schedules, information technology (IT) solutions, level-loading designs, and workforce management counsel. Internally it was no different. The organization would sometimes be host to no less than ten disparate and competing approaches to address capacity constraints. Leadership's challenge at this stage was quite different than at the start. In the beginning, organizational questions were more what, when, and why to do improvement work. Over time, after experiencing the sometimes difficult and tedious path of improvement, the organization shifted to questioning methodology over purpose. Leadership contemplated whether there was a better way, if others found a better way, and if they could take a shortcut by copying other Lean organizations. To ensure a stable and capable path, the organization adopted a transformation model with six basic elements: (1) purpose, (2) process, (3) capability, (4) management system and leader behaviors, and (5) basic assumptions and mind-set, as seen in Table 6.2. The progress from left to right utilized the Toyota routine of understanding current state, the target condition, the ideal condition, and subsequent actions. This structure clarified a path for leadership recognizing that principled vigilance was essential.

Realization: In times of fatigue, disappointment, discouragement, and setback, magic antidotes or cure-alls seem more appealing than hard work, tedious detail, and persistence. Staying true to purpose is essential.

Becoming the Leader the Organization Requires

If the heart of CPI is learning and the soul is the appreciation and development of others, the servant leader has proven to be the best leadership style in navigating the thrill and disappointments of a transformation. If scientific thinking and principled behavior is the expected natural way of being for all members in the organization, the requisite leader is a servant first, contributes to the well-being of people and community, looks to the needs of the people, and places their main focus on people. This servant leader understands that only content and motivated people are able to reach their targets and to fulfill the set expectations. SCCA has adopted this archetype of this servant leader as the style most suited for managing performance improvement. The characteristics SCCA values in leading CPI are shown in Table 6.3.

Leading by example means to demonstrate the characteristics of servant leadership in good times as well as in bad. At Northwest Hospital, the care team was empowered to create its own patient care environment. In the Infusion Department, the team used the accountability inherent in its Daily Management System to improve performance. SCCA's leaders faced humility head-on as they pulled back improvement during the electronic medical record (EMR)/CPOE implementation, realizing that the organization

Table 6.2 Transformation Model: Reviewed and Adjusted Monthly

Transformation Dimensions	*What Is Our Current Situation?*	*What Is an Ideal "Lean" Condition?*	*What Is Our Specific Target Condition to Achieve in the Next Year?*	*What Are Our Next Steps?*
Purpose: What is the purpose, what value is being provided, or what problem are we trying to solve?				
Process: Is the value-creating work defined and being continually improved? Do we have capable processes?				
Capability: Are necessary capabilities defined and being developed effectively?				
Management system and leader behaviors: Are the management system and leader behaviors established that support desired ways of working?				
Basic thinking and underlying assumptions: What basic assumptions or mind-set exists? How do we need to change?				

Table 6.3 Leadership Characteristics

Empowerment	A motivational concept focused on enabling people and encouraging personal development. The leader's belief in the intrinsic value of each individual is the central issue in empowerment and the realization of each person's abilities and what the person can still learn.
Accountability	Holding people accountable for performance they can control. It is a powerful tool to show confidence in one's followers; it provides boundaries within which one is free to achieve one's goals.
Humility	The ability to put one's own accomplishments and talents in a proper perspective. Humility in leadership focuses on daring to admit that one is not infallible and does make mistakes.
Authenticity	Is closely related to expressing the "true self," expressing oneself in ways that are consistent with inner thoughts and feelings. Authenticity is about being true to oneself, accurately representing—privately and publicly—internal states, intentions, and commitments.
Courage	Daring to take risks and trying out new approaches to old problems. Within the organizational context, courage is about challenging conventional models of working behaviors and is essential for innovation and creativity.
Interpersonal acceptance	The ability to understand and experience the feelings of others, understand where people come from, and the ability to let go of perceived wrongdoings and not carry a grudge into other situations. It is important to create an atmosphere of trust where people feel accepted, are free to make mistakes, and know that they will not be rejected.
Stewardship	The willingness to take responsibility for the larger institution and go for service instead of control and self-interest. Leaders should not only act as caretakers but also act as role models. By setting the right example, leaders can stimulate others to act in the common interest.

could not do everything at once. Leadership demonstrated authenticity when openly discussing the organization's poor readiness and failure to launch the Hematology/Transplant integration effort. The Sarcoma Model Line design work required early adopters to display an incredible amount of courage and continue when circumstances said they should retreat. Early in their journey, after multiple failed attempts were made to imbue value stream thinking in the Infusion Department, SCCA leaders displayed interpersonal acceptance by owning a faulty approach rather than blaming others. And finally, organizational leaders model stewardship each day by coaching individuals and teams through difficult problems without compromising principles or proven methods.

Realization: Respect for people is at the core of the Lean transformation. Leading by example is the challenge; people will follow if led.

Conclusion: The Journey Continues

Today, as SCCA's journey continues, continuous improvement advocates are still an organizational minority, engagement has not reached the tipping point, and many still struggle with living the basic principles every day. The organization struggles to effectively measure improvement and to collect the data needed to accurately understand performance.

Yet there is hope. SCCA leadership has made their commitment to continuous improvement clear, placing the CPI Department directly under the Executive Vice President's Office. This commitment means direct ownership, consistent and constant involvement, and an unyielding dedication to the principles. The organization is again poised to advance its care delivery model and realize a new level of research and operational integration by using CPI principles to develop a new Immunotherapy Clinic. Leadership, recognizing that improvement cannot occur by merely optimizing a poor system, is sponsoring a patient flow optimization effort designed to cut across departments and minimize patient wait and idle time. And from a strategic vantage point, SCCA is implementing a patient-centric structure to link strategy to action. This SCCA Management System is dedicated to learning and people development, driven by strategic intent, and focused on goal alignment, effective metrics, and standard work rather than on local needs.

For 2015, *U.S. News & World Report* ranked SCCA/UM Medical Center as number 5 out of 902 cancer hospitals in the nation. SCCA's CPI journey has certainly contributed to that distinguished standing. The organization's pursuit of a target condition of a self-organizing system of self-improving individuals and teams started with a leap of faith. Reaching for this aspirational target requires the organization to constantly learn and confront conventional wisdom. As evidence of this learning, SCCA scores itself worse on every new organizational assessment, not because it is objectively worse, but because it is developing a greater understanding and a shrewder appraisal of the continuous process improvement methods, management system, and mind-set. The more leadership learns, the more humble their self-assessment, knowing that continuous improvement is essential in their effort to remain a beacon of hope to the patients they serve.

Realization: Accelerants for learning are the key—the more that is revealed, the brighter the future will be. As the journey has no ending, neither does the learning.

Note

1. This statement refers to outcomes of 18 different cancer types at varying stages.
   Both rare and common cancers in patients diagnosed or receiving their first treatment at SCCA.
   Higher five-year survival compared to all National Cancer Data Base (NCDB) cases (diagnosis years 2003–2006).
   For all that had a statistical difference, SCCA rates are higher than NCDB.
   Data limitations:
   No risk adjustment.
   All causes of deaths included.

Chapter 7

Transforming Doctors into Change Agents

Jeffrey Avansino, Ken Gow, and Darren Migita

Dr. P is a new intern on the pediatric hematology-oncology service. It is his third day on this service and only his second month as a resident. Dr. P is thus still learning the ins and outs of the hospital. Having just finished rounds, he is trying to prioritize the many tasks he has to complete in the next few hours prior to evening sign-out.

One of Dr. P's patients is a new admission for leukemia. During rounds, Dr. P was asked by his attending to make sure the patient received a central line in the next 24–48 hours so that therapy could be initiated without delay. With little guidance, Dr. P set out to accomplish this task.

After talking with the scheduler, the surgical resident informed Dr. P that the patient would not receive the line for a full week. Dr. P related this scheduling delay to the team the following day on rounds. Despite a call from the attending, the line still could not be placed sooner due to scheduling in the operating room (OR).

Dr. P was now sent on a second mission, when he tried to obtain a peripherally inserted central venous catheter (PICC) line. This task was even more daunting and confusing than the first. A nurse was available to place the line, and an interventional radiologist was able to do the procedure, but a general anesthetic was required.

Dr. P called the line nurse to evaluate the patient; the nurse, in turn, felt that the line placement would be an appropriate task for the interventional radiologist, who was willing to put the line in the next day.

Circuitously, then, the patient finally received a PICC line—a full two days after the decision for PICC insertion was made. And five days later, the general surgery team was able to find the patient a time slot on the OR schedule, and a tunneled central venous catheter was placed.

Within a week, the patient had two procedures and received two anesthetics, ultimately receiving the definitive procedure a whole week after it was initially requested. These system, communication, and scheduling challenges are unfortunately all too common in clinical scenarios.

Providers, especially those who have been practicing a while, typically know how to navigate the convoluted system by circumventing the roadblocks and using back doors to get things accomplished. Obviously, this process for getting things done is disturbingly variable and unreliable, and it's highly dependent on the people, services, expertise, and circumstances involved. Such variability inevitably leads to inconsistent, unpredictable results with frustration ensuing all around. In the wake of this shaky process, teamwork too often dissolves, and providers find themselves losing their focus on patient care.

Clearly, this confusing process begged for change and improvement. And our response to this challenge demonstrates how the impetus behind our continuous performance improvement (CPI) efforts has been to enrich the lives of our patients, enhance the efficiency of delivery of care, and ensure quality and safety.

In 2005, Seattle Children's Hospital decided to map out the line placement process, or value stream. A group of general pediatric physicians, nurses, residents, surgeons, and anesthesiologists gathered together for three days to review the current state of this process and lay out a plan of action. Not surprisingly, each discipline had its "story" about how difficult it was to get this work done. The conversations were emotional and often difficult, but no one ever lost sight of the fact that patients deserved better and that physicians and staff needed relief from the stress exemplified by Dr. P's story.

An analysis of the current process conducted by this team found that, at most, only 15 percent of the time staff and physicians were spending trying to get lines placed for patients was "value added" to the patient; the rest was wasted time and resources that did nothing to advance patients' care. In response to these findings, the team outlined their "ideal state" for vascular access and went to work chartering projects that would become the improvement roadmap for line placement at Seattle Children's.

Two of the many projects completed are discussed later. Both projects began with Rapid Process Improvement Workshops (RPIWs), five-day events with full-time participation of physicians, nurses, and administrative managers.

Many physicians will say that they are just too busy to get involved. In an academic institution, the division of time among clinical, research, and academic duties makes physicians reluctant to add more to their overloaded plates. Others have been practicing medicine "their way" for decades, and change represents a threat to their tried-and-true method of delivering care. In addition, the very physicians who have the actual power to make change are likely far removed from the daily challenges faced by our intern, Dr. P, in the earlier example. As a result, these physicians might not recognize the need or urgency to change existing processes.

So how does a provider take up the reins and surmount these obstacles to deliver effective change?

The following examples illustrate two change processes surrounding the governance of PICCs and a reduction of lead time in the scheduling of surgically placed tunneled central venous catheters. Both of these stories encompass many of the CPI principles described elsewhere in this book. What this narrative is really about is creating, implementing, and embedding change in the intrinsic fabric of our healthcare institution.

Case Study 1

A PICC is a type of central venous catheter (CVC) that was developed in 1975 to provide a secure method of administering intravenous medications to patients in both inpatient and outpatient settings. PICCs differ from peripheral IVs (PIVs) in that they are longer and terminate in the large vessels close to the heart. Due to their "central" location, these catheters are more secure and, oftentimes, obviate the need for repeated needle sticks for blood draws or frequent replacement that commonly occurs when more ephemeral PIVs are used. Additionally, total parenteral nutrition (TPN), which takes place when the patient is fed intravenously and no food is given by other routes, can be administered in higher concentrations when a catheter is located centrally. PICCs can be placed at the patient's bedside with less need for sedation than more invasive surgically placed catheters.

The convenience of PICCs led to a dramatic increase in their usage soon after their introduction. However, as the medical community gained more experience with these devices, we learned that PICCs are not without significant complications. Up to 50 percent of PICCs require radiological guided insertion techniques requiring anesthesia, 0.7 percent experience fracture of the line, 7 percent become occluded, and 58 percent migrate 20 mm or more from their original placement. Other complications include deep venous thrombosis, vessel rupture, and catheter-associated bloodstream infections (CABSIs). Between 30 and 46 percent of all PICCs are removed due to a complication prior to the completion of therapy.[1]

Given that nearly 80,000 CVC-associated bloodstream infections (BSIs) occur in intensive care units each year in the United States, that the reported mortality from a CABSI may be as high as 12–25 percent, and that central line infections are far more likely than PIV infections (2 percent versus 0.04 percent), placing a PICC can no longer be considered a benign procedural intervention.[1]

At Seattle Children's Hospital, we were faced with three major issues surrounding PICC lines: infection, overutilization, and confusion regarding the PICC-ordering process. These problems were all rooted in the same fundamental issue—failure to standardize work methods.

In order to eliminate wasted time and energy, increase the margin of safety for our patients, and establish a new baseline for continued improvement, we needed to draw upon the principles of standardization, error proofing, waste reduction, and andons, which are lights that serve as visual signals.

Keeping these principles in mind, this endeavor was subdivided into four key projects:[1]

- Six questions to ask each day for patients who have a CVC
- PICC clinical criteria—the creation of insertion standards for PICCs (see Table 7.1)
- Creation of a vascular access service (VAS) from preexisting staff
- Creation of a PICC order set

Completion of these projects resulted in a sustained 33.4-percent reduction in PICC placements, as well as improved provider satisfaction with the ordering process as measured on a Likert scale (see Figure 7.1). The data also show that overall provider satisfaction scores increased from 2.68 out of 5 to 3.55 out of 5 over a nine-month period.[1]

Central catheters require day-to-day management; if this does not occur, they may be retained for longer than necessary, thus increasing patient risk. Moreover, opening the line to administer intermittent medications or to draw blood further increases the potential for infection. Since each day that a patient has a central catheter represents a day of risk, our mission was to standardize the daily attention paid to central catheters.

To support this process, six questions were reproduced on daily progress notes in the intensive care units (ICUs) in a checklist format. In addition, medical unit registered nurses (RNs) were required to give a synopsis of their patients' central lines on intake forms as well as on daily progress notes. The six key daily questions were as follows:[1]

1. Can the line be removed?
2. Can we change intravenous medications to oral?
3. Can the patient be fed enterally (i.e., no TPN)?
4. Can we decrease blood draws?
5. Can we bundle tubing changes with blood draws?
6. What does the dressing look like today?

Prior to this work, PICCs were an unregulated procedural intervention. There were no standards for their placement and it was not uncommon for a PICC to be placed—only to be removed a few days later. In these cases, the patient was exposed to all the aforementioned risks of a central catheter when a simple PIV would have sufficed. This, in itself, was viewed as an error of clinical management.

Table 7.1 Peripherally Inserted Central Venous Catheter (PICC) Criteria

Indication for Placement	*Criteria*	*Rationale*
General	Use peripheral IVs (PIVs) whenever possible. Medically complex patient requiring central venous access—decide on PICC placement early. Patient requires home IV therapy. Documentation of long-term vascular access plan required.	Central venous catheters (CVCs) increase the risk of bloodstream infections (BSIs). An infected PIV is easier to identify than an infected CVC. An infected CVC carries a greater risk of complication than an infected PIV. Documentation of long-term vascular access plan facilitates site preservation.
Total parenteral nutrition (TPN)	Anticipated duration of TPN use >3 days.	TPN is an independent risk for infection.
Antibiotics	Antibiotic therapy ≥7 days from placement of PICC.	The risk of CVC infection outweighs the benefits of short-term PICC usage for antibiotics.
Chemotherapy	Selected standard risk acute lymphocytic leukemia (ALL). Oncology patients: Unable to schedule a surgical central line.	Multiple infusions and blood draws during chemotherapy. Avoidance of surgical line placement, especially during steroid dosing.
Vasopressors	Acceptable for unstable patients in intensive care unit (ICU) settings.	Intermittent temporary need for central venous access.
Anticipated need for hemodialysis.		

(*Continued*)

Table 7.1 (Continued) Peripherally Inserted Central Venous Catheter (PICC) Criteria

Contraindications to PICC Placement
Do not place PICC for TPN if the patient can be fed enterally or if peripheral parenteral nutrition can be used. Do not use PICC for antibiotics that have a good oral availability (e.g., Clindamycin, Rifampin, Flagyl, or Cipro). Documented bacteremia or high suspicion of bacteremia requires 72 hours of negative cultures (2 separate complications, 24 hours apart, and at least 24 hours of maturity in the lab) prior to PICC placement. (For selected populations, this may not be possible.)

Source: D. Migita, K. Gow, and J. Avansino, "Transforming Doctors into Change Agents," *American Academy of Pediatrics* (April 1, 2009): 1155–61. Reproduced with permission from *Pediatrics* 123:1157–61. Copyright © 2009 by the AAP.

By convening a panel of local experts, we were able to achieve consensus on specific criteria for PICC placement. Members of this team included interventional radiologists, general surgeons, infectious disease experts, nurses, and pediatric hospitalists. Specific contraindications for PICCs, based on the best available medical evidence, were also identified and compiled. Although achieving consensus was a somewhat arduous process, gaining general agreement proved to be a critical factor

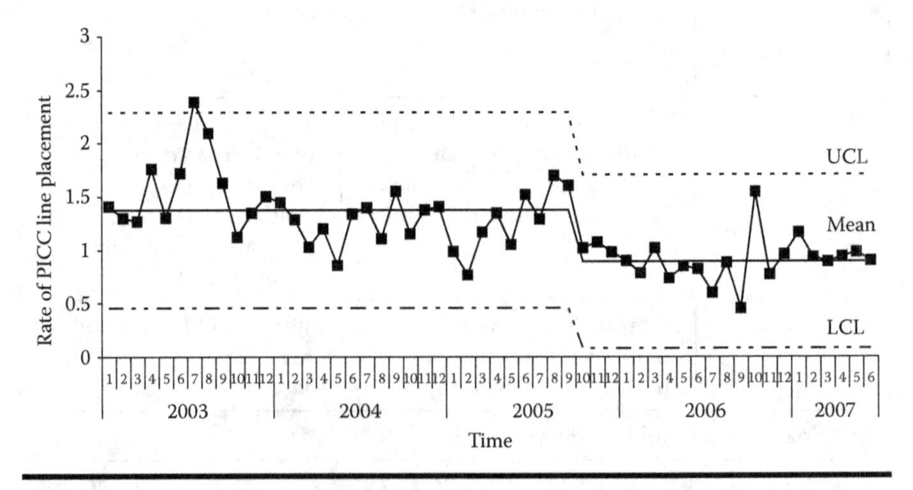

Figure 7.1 Peripherally inserted central venous catheter (PICC) volumes. Rate of PICC line placement per 100 census days. (From D. Migita, K. Gow, and J. Avansino, "Transforming Doctors into Change Agents," *American Academy of Pediatrics* (April 1, 2009): 1155–61. Reproduced with permission from *Pediatrics* 123:1157–61. Copyright © 2009 by the AAP.)

during the implementation stage of these criteria. In creating consensus, the vital groundwork for change was established, and the substance of change in this case was the implementation of a new reliable work standard.

From a patient's perspective, the PICC clinical criteria were constructed to help ensure that PICCs were placed when the benefits outweighed the risks. Patients who did not meet these criteria would instead be candidates for PIVs.

Prior to this work, PICCs were ordered via computerized physician order entry (CPOE) and placed by either interventional radiology (IR) or an RN-staffed "IV team." The ordering provider was responsible for determining the mode of insertion (IR versus bedside), contacting the proceduralist, coordinating PICC placement with other procedures requiring anesthesia, and coordinating care directly with the patient's primary nurse.

Significant dissatisfaction with the protracted PICC-ordering process resulted. Moreover, given that Seattle Children's is a busy teaching hospital, completion of this multitude of tasks in a timely manner was often difficult. Trainees might be unfamiliar with navigating a complex system, which, in turn, would lead to delays, errors, and dissatisfaction. In short, waste abounded in the forms of rework, waiting, and complexity.[1]

To target these problems, we created a vascular access service (VAS) composed of seven RNs whose function was to place PICCs and coordinate the aforementioned maze of tasks. These nurses were previously part of the RN-staffed IV team, and the creation of the VAS did not require adding new people.[1]

The VAS is now automatically notified by pager once an order has been placed via CPOE, thus ensuring that the process begins in a timely fashion. By centralizing this work within a small group, individual variation was markedly reduced, and the maintenance of the new standard work method was preserved. The VAS fulfills the requirements of a reliable method—the PICC placement process was consciously developed, always followed, and clearly owned, and had a strong foundation for continued future improvement.

The CPOE-based PICC order set (see Figure 7.2) unifies the work of the aforementioned projects. The order set contains the data the VAS needs to verify that placement meets criteria, to ensure there are no contraindications to placement, to avoid placement in certain extremities, and to coordinate PICC placement with other procedures requiring anesthesia. This computerized order set cannot be signed unless all required fields are completed—a vital error-proofing measure.

Because the VAS reviews each PICC request and proceeds to placement only if criteria are met and no contraindications are present, the order set serves as an andon that warns of a potential clinical error. The VAS also has the authority to hold a PICC placement by "stopping the line," thereby preventing an error from becoming a more serious and entrenched defect. The response to the andon is graded, too. And if the VAS staff member cannot resolve the issue by inserting a PIV rather than a PICC, the case is escalated to either the medical director of line management or to the RN director of VAS, one of whom is available at all times.[1]

Non-Surgical Vascular Access Profile - PCOTEST, JOANNE

*Performed on: 07/18/2006 1537 By: Anderso

Consent and Ind
Contraindications

Consent and Indications

Approved by attending ○ Yes ○ No

If parent requests PICC, Informed consent regarding the risks of central line placement is needed

Consent signed (must be obtained by ordering provider) ○ Yes ○ No Date/time consent signed

Current venous access ☐ No intravenous access ☐ Arterial line ☐ PIV ☑ Central line ☐ PICC ☐ Port-a-cath

PICC Indications
- ☐ Anticipated duration of TPN >3 days
- ☐ Antibiotics for >7 days from PICC placement
- ☐ Patient requires vasopressor or inotropic support
- ☐ Anticipate multiple problems requiring central access
- ☐ Standard risk acute lymphocytic leukemia (ALL)
- ☐ Unable to schedule a surgical central line
- ☐ Patient will require PICC for home care
- ☐ Patient comfort
- ☐ Other indication

Other PICC indications

Long term vascular access plan (length of therapy)

Do NOT place PICC:

for IV antibiotics when required for <7 days

for TPN if patient can be fed enterally or if parenteral nutrition is needed for <3 days

for bacteremic patients until there has ben 72 hours of negative cultures (2 separata cultures, 24 hours apart and at least 24 hours of maturity in lab)

for frequent blood draws; consider placing large bore peripheral IV and maximizing comfort measures (Elamax, J-tip, distraction, biofeedback)

for antibiotics that have good bioavailability (Clindamycin, Rifamoin, Flagyl or Ciprofloxacin) and patient can take oral medications

Non-Surgical Vascular Access Profile - PCOTEST, JOANNE

*Performed on: 07/18/2006 1537

Consent and Ind
Contraindications

Contraindications and Procedure Planning

Potential contraindications
- ☐ No contraindications
- ☐ Anticipated need for hemodialysis
- ☐ Documented bacteremia within previous 72 hrs
- ☐ High suspicion of bacteremia
- ☐ PICC used for TPN and patient ca be fed enterally
- ☐ Patient on Clindamycin, Rifamoin, Flagyl or Ciprofloxacin
- ☐ Other contraindications

Other potential contraindications

Contraindicated placement sites
- ☐ No contraindicated sites
- ☐ Right upper extremity
- ☐ Right lower extremity
- ☐ Left upper extremity
- ☐ Left lower extremity
- ☐ Scalp
- ☐ Tunneled femoral PICC line

Attending approves patient for potential deep sedation or anesthesia ○ Yes ○ No

Planned procedures requiring anesthesia (potential to be at same time of PICC placement) ○ Yes ○ No

Document planned procedures (include date/time if known)

Figure 7.2 PICC order set. The PICC placement order set directs the physician to provide the minimal necessary information the vascular access service (VAS) requires to place the PICC. (From D. Migita, K. Gow, and J. Avansino, "Transforming Doctors into Change Agents," *American Academy of Pediatrics* (April 1, 2009): 1155–61. Reproduced with permission from *Pediatrics* 123:1157–61. Copyright © 2009 by the AAP.)

Case Study 2

One of the problems that arose at Seattle Children's was that services referring patients to general surgery felt that the lead time for inserting a tunneled central line was too long. As a result, an unnecessary number of patients were having PICCs placed so that therapy could be initiated as quickly as possible. However, since PICCs are not meant for long-term access, this process routinely led to a second procedure that inserted a more permanent form of IV access—again exposing the patient to infection and catheter-site issues.

The general surgery division saw this as an opportunity to address longstanding issues related to scheduling tunneled central lines; it was also an opportunity to provide a better level of service to the referral groups and, ultimately, to our patients.

In reviewing the salient data, we noted that the average lead time from central catheter order to central catheter placement was eight days. After identifying the processes that resulted in the current eight-day lead time, we created a guiding coalition of various representatives involved with the catheter placement process (referring services, schedulers, surgeons, and nurses). Together, we were able to distinguish steps in the process that were crucial and provided value for the patient from those that were redundant and/or did not provide value. We then brainstormed and explored strategies to improve the process with the explicit goal of reducing lead time.

We agreed to revise the line order sheet, to improve the mechanisms for request handling, and to broaden access for line insertion in the operating room schedule. For example, we asked the referring service to specify the type of line that would be needed on the order sheet. This would prevent placement of the incorrect type of line, which could result in a second procedure.

Once the new process was delineated, it was rapidly implemented with a concomitant period of observation to assess for positive change. This postimplementation assessment is critical to measuring success and fine-tuning the new process.

Fortunately, after the changes were implemented, the lead time to insertion of a central venous catheter was reduced from an average of eight days to six days over the next year. This was studied the following year and, as the next few pages will explain, significant improvement was made (see Figure 7.3).

Also, as a likely result of the improved process for scheduling surgically placed central venous catheters, the percentage of PICC lines placed in patients was strikingly reduced from 78 percent to 15 percent. And, equally important, the referral services considered the changes an important improvement for their patients. In fact, everyone involved in the CPI work agreed that these changes were a marked improvement over the original process. Finally, because a diverse coalition was involved in designing and implementing the new process, all participants felt invested.

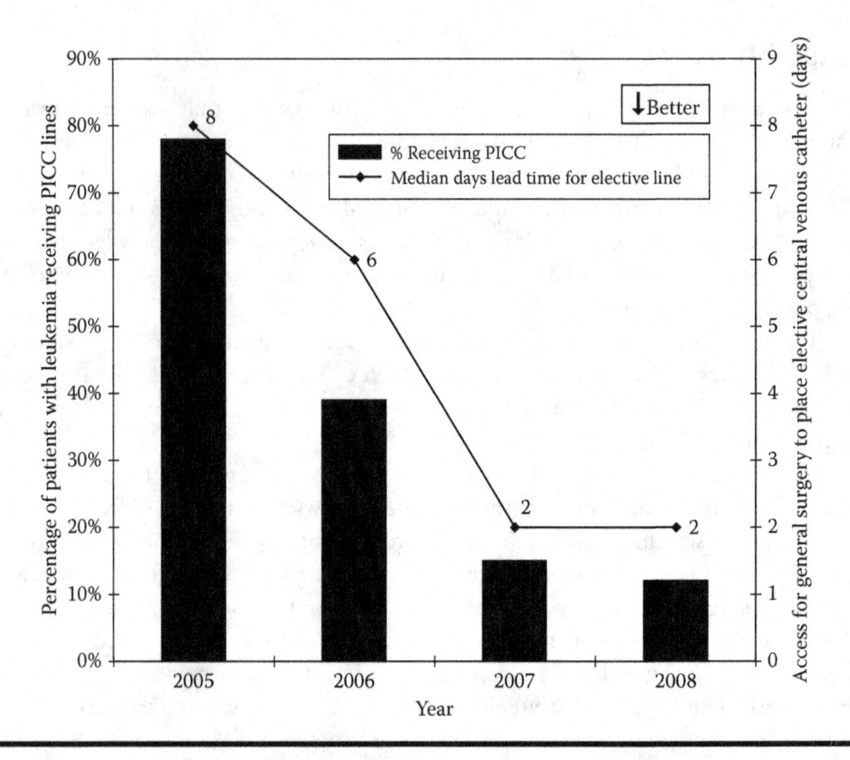

Figure 7.3 Reduction in percentage of patients receiving PICC lines, and reduced lead times for placement of tunneled central venous line. An improved process for scheduling surgically placed central venous catheters is the leading influence of the reduction in PICC lines placed in patients. (From D. Migita, K. Gow, and J. Avansino, "Transforming Doctors into Change Agents," *American Academy of Pediatrics* (April 1, 2009): 1155–61. Reproduced with permission from *Pediatrics* 123:1157–61. Copyright © 2009 by the AAP.)

Easier access to the OR for catheter insertions was considered a success, but this also increased pressure to find extra time within an already crowded OR schedule. Also, with a more urgent need for catheters, a concern arose that the necessary operative information for the attending surgeon would be lost in the flurry. But there is no need to choose between rapid delivery of services and providing quality care. By developing a system that works for everyone, we can have the best of both worlds.

In addition, we originally thought that the degree of need for line insertion could be ascertained in a speedy consult-type fashion. But standard consults require patients to be seen in clinic or in the hospital by either the surgeon or a physician extender, so we agreed that this step would add unnecessary lead time.

This provided an opportunity to eliminate waste by shifting the responsibility for a patient's preoperative management (such as transfusions of platelets or packed red blood cell levels and addressing neutropenia) to the referring team. Structured this way, the patient continues to be cared for by the original team with the most intimate knowledge about him or her. This also means that parents don't receive mixed messages—something that often happens when pediatric patients are handed off to another team.

Another working group was brought together to respond to scheduling issues that were hindering the placement of surgical central lines in the operating room. Ideally, an increase in operating room time would solve this problem, but this wasn't possible because of limitations in available operating rooms and time allocated in the OR to individual surgeons (block time). So the challenge was to try to do more with the same amount of time. Many of these issues came to light in our discussions.

First, in looking at the average number of central venous line requests in a week, we saw that this matched up with the number of block times available to the surgeons. This provided the surgical team with the option to "level load" central line insertions so that each surgeon would be performing a similar number of line placements (and so that one surgeon was not placing all of the lines), while the number of line placements would be evenly distributed over the course of a week.

This even distribution is essential because central line insertion always requires additional components that must be available, including fluoroscopy, a radiology technologist, and appropriate operating room staff. As a result, we established that each block time in the operating room would reliably reserve one slot for possible line insertions, effectively planning for the unplanned.

Second, the line insertion requests had always been held up by the need to schedule this with the family. While most of the contact numbers were correct, this was not always the case. Also, many parents were non-English speaking, so time was routinely required to secure appropriate translators. In addition, some families had to be called several times before a date for surgery could be established.

All of these areas of delay were identified as waste that needed to be eliminated.

In discussing how to reduce this lead time, it was agreed that an online calendar should be created to indicate "open" OR time for central venous procedures (either insertion or removals). The referral services would be granted permission a priori by the surgery division to schedule patients at the precise date that the line was deemed necessary. This improvement quickly reduced lead time for scheduling. And families knew the date of the surgery right away, before leaving the referral service's offices. Also, by placing the scheduling responsibility back with the referral services—the providers who knew the patients best—they were empowered to decide which patient had priority when more than one patient was initially assigned to the same date. This removed the attending surgeon from the awkward role of "referee" for patient priority. The net result is that each of these improvements successfully leads to greater overall satisfaction for every player: the referral services, families, schedulers, and surgeons.

Third, by bringing together everyone involved in scheduling a case, the group discovered that much of the scheduling communication that typically occurred was, in fact, redundant. For example, the attending surgeon received information from two different sources: a central venous access device (CVAD) sheet and a separate form that one of the divisions was also using for requesting lines. In tracking this second form, the group found that it was not providing additional value-added information, and that it might lead to confusion if it didn't fully match the information on the other form. By eliminating this redundancy, the CVAD emerged as the only form that was necessary. The unique information on the second form was added to the CVAD form to augment and optimize it. The form was then finalized and placed in a central online site for universally easy access. The form, completed by the requesting team, was sent to the surgeon so it could be viewed prior to the scheduled date of procedure, thereby allowing time to sort out any issues that might need clarification.

In summary, we were able to solve several catheter-scheduling issues very quickly and effectively by looking at areas of waste and choosing to focus on opportunities. By providing the referral services with the ability to schedule cases for their own patients, we provided them with an increased sense of empowerment. Also, because they were able to choose dates for surgery, they were better able to coordinate overall patient care (timing of chemotherapy, timing of radiotherapy, timing for diagnostic imaging, stem cell harvest, and optimizing surgery to time based on blood levels).

This empowerment created a sense of ownership by the referral services. It also highlighted the power of flexibility since the referral services were being asked to perform several steps of scheduling that had been previously performed by surgery scheduling. In addition, because the cases were more "level loaded," schedulers had a much-reduced need to ration resources for the procedures. For the patients, referral services, and operative services, all of these changes were perceived as a resounding "win–win–win." And, as a demonstration of this success, we found that after implementing the new process, the overall satisfaction rate among referral services rose impressively from 49 percent to 71 percent.

The ability to implement or embed change like this is inevitably the result of a committed team that is involved in the process. And paramount to successful outcomes are the people who lead that team in the change process.

The physician leaders in the case studies followed a series of process steps and successfully generated change. The first step was the creation of a sense of urgency. The scenario involving our intern, Dr. P, was not uncommon. The long lead times in placement of tunneled central lines resulted in aggravating and alarming delays in patient care. These delays were responsible for causing the placement of three times as many PICC lines as were actually needed. Deleterious issues surrounding PICC lines were also indentified and included infection, overutilization, and confusion regarding PICC line orders. These problems all stemmed from a lack of standard work; together, they provided the urgent motivation for the change process.

The second step was forging a group that has the power to create change, and that is supported and championed all the way up the chain of command. Equally important is the involvement of the people closest to the process being changed. In both examples, the group is composed of local experts involved in the process being changed.

Once this group is formed, it must create the vision of change and develop a strategic path. That is step three. In case study 2, the vision of the division of pediatric general and thoracic surgery was to reduce the lead time for scheduling tunneled CVCs. The guiding coalition mapped out a strategic plan that included creating a single new line request form, transferring the scheduling of catheter placement to the referring services, identifying and reserving a fixed number of OR blocks for catheter placement scheduling, and developing an easily accessible online calendar.

The fourth step in the process was to communicate the vision of change that has been established. In our case, this was successfully done by examining PICC utilization. A PICC checklist was incorporated in the providers' daily rounds, and this promoted and ensured increased awareness among users of the system. Eventually, a computer-based order set for PICC line requests was created, which served as both an education and communication tool.

Once the desired change is outlined and the vision communicated, the fifth step involved amending the current system to eliminate any barriers to change. The division of pediatric general and thoracic surgery, for example, allowed patients in need of central lines to bypass the typical surgical consult in clinic or in the hospital prior to scheduling the procedure. This systems revision opened the way for achieving the ultimate goal of reducing lead time. Yet the goal of reducing lead time is never-ending; every improvement requires even greater improvement on the journey toward best practices.

Thus, the sixth step encouraged the team to design short-term wins that reassure larger audiences that the change process is, in fact, working. This fuels momentum and keeps the team engaged in the process. For example, after the creation of a line order sheet to request a surgically placed line, lead time was reduced 25 percent over the first year. With additional changes, a 75-percent reduction was achieved the following year (see Figure 7.3).

In addition to building credibility and drawing more people into the process, these short-term wins provide stepping-stones for further projects and greater refinement. And, as the sixth step made clear, the short-term gains also act as a springboard for change on a larger scale. For instance, the creation of a sixth vital sign (discussing central line status) in the pediatric intensive care unit (PICU) eventually evolved into a hospital-wide, consensus-based pathway embedded into the daily workflow of all providers.

As more people are brought into the improvement process, they are empowered through involvement. They come to realize that each team member offers something valuable and unique to the change process. Using this bottom-up approach, people who might otherwise not have a chance to provide input become leaders in their group. They gain confidence in their abilities to lead change and, ultimately, to teach it to others. Eventually, a self-perpetuating cycle is created in which processes are improved and new leadership is developed.

This cycle of energetic change—the seventh step—will gain robust momentum, making it nearly impossible to derail. And it is at this point that continuous performance improvement is successfully anchored in the culture of the organization.

Note

1. D. Migita, K. Gow, and J. Avansino, "Transforming Doctors into Change Agents," *American Academy of Pediatrics* (April 1, 2009): 1155–61. Reproduced with permission from *Pediatrics* 123:1157–61. Copyright © 2009 by the AAP.

Epilogue

The success that we achieved by having everyone on board had the side effect of adding more patients into the system. The higher numbers that were added to the queue revealed issues that required refinement of the process. Indeed, this refinement fits well with the concept of continuous performance improvement. Specifically, issues included the variability in the quality of the electronic consult, the lack of timely feedback by the ordering providers, and a limit to the ability to handle a higher numbers of patients. Each solution that arose demonstrated how working with all those invested in the process leads to delivering timely and safe care for patients.

Stopping Errors Early

In a large tertiary care and teaching hospital, the number of ordering providers is vast. Each has a varying degree of experience in ordering central line insertions. While the central line ordering process was working well, the schedulers who were handling the orders began to notice some issues that often resulted in "stopping the line" until a question could be answered, for example, incorrect lines being requested, requested dates not matching on the order, and missing information. This generated a lot of rework with the schedulers, who needed to page and/or call providers to clarify the orders. Further, at times, some patients would get to the OR with these errors in tow, thereby resulting in some patients requiring changes at the last minute. It became clear that a clinical "check" would be helpful in identifying issues early on to avoid those errors from being passed down the line toward the patient. Because all the orders were generated electronically and the system was already designed to send this out as an e-mail to our schedulers, another iterative change was made to send it to a reviewer who could catch some of these issues early on. This review would occur in the background and not delay scheduling. With the addition of this new early step of e-mail (Figure 7.4), there have been

From: Discern_Expert@seattlechildrens.org
Subject: Central Venous Access Device Consult
Date: July 24, 2015 at 9:04 AM
To: kenneth.gow@seattlechildrens.org

Central Venous Access Device Consult Alert

Order entered for:

Patient Name: TEST, MEDRECO
Patient MRN: 5111378
Patient Date of Birth: January 01, 2010

Ordering Provider: Dr. Jane Doe
Date/Time Ordered: June 05, 2015 09:04:48 PDT

Requesting Service: Pediatric Oncology
Attending Provider: Test, Dr. John Smith
Attending Pager Number: 206-555-0000

Diagnosis: Wilms Tumor

Order Placed: Central Venous Access Device Consult
- INSERT central venous access device –
Subcutaneous Port - ACCESS with needle
Other Venous Access Device: NONE

Procedures required while sedated - NONE

Platelet Support Required: No
Patient Receiving Anticoagulants: No

Elective: No
Preferred date – July 25, 2015
Schedule In - Current Admission
Timing - Urgent less than 48hrs page surg on call

Surgeon Contacted: Dr. Kenneth Gow

Special Instructions: Patient has allergy to penicillin

BMI: 18 kg/m^2 July 23, 2015 06:58:00 PDT

Figure 7.4 Sample email for the central line ordering process that is generated and sent to a reviewer.

multiple issues fixed before they were passed on: lines being corrected to appropriate type, surgeons on call alerted to help facilitate scheduling; anesthesia consults generated, surgical house staff alerted to in-house patients so they can be preoperatively prepared, and identification of patients in whom a port may not be possible (by adding the body mass index [BMI] in the e-mail message). This concept of central review with rapid, real-time results was based on a process validated by the Children's Oncology Group, which properly stages patients with solid tumors so they may be correctly slotted into the appropriate open study. This early check has been extremely successful as about 5 to 10 percent of orders have some issues, and, by addressing these early, a great deal of wasted effort and rework has been avoided. Most important, however, this avoids errors from potentially reaching the patient. And for the ordering providers, having timely feedback teaches them quickly so that good habits can be learned.

Immediate and One-Stop Information

To provide documentation for clinical and billing purposes, all surgical procedures need to be documented with an operative report. The traditional method was to do this through dictation, but this method was open to variability in the content. Further, trying to find that content later on was difficult because there was no standardization in how one dictated and where the information was placed. To create a standard method, it was decided to have online documentation (Figure 7.5) where all of the pertinent information would be standardized, with standard options available in a drop-down menu. By adding information such as packing information (lot number, code), the tracking of potential issues such as "bad lots" became much easier. The nurses on the floor needed to know the line length in order to assist in determining the volume of the catheters and without a standard home for this information, floor nurses were often left trying to figure this out. By building this information into the online documentation (Figure 7.6), this information was easily notated immediately after the procedure and could be found by anyone caring for the patient. This has made care for patients easier and smoother as well as tracking lots for review if there are any issues about the catheters. This method has been readily accepted and has also saved time for all the providers involved.

Leveraging Your Options

Finally, it was noted that the scheduling of port removals had become very easy—so much so that parents were able to select the date of the removal to coincide with their visits. Unfortunately, with the continued limited OR availability, it was also noted that while the removals were being scheduled several weeks ahead, these were filling up valuable OR slots that were then not available for central line insertions. The result was the more urgent line insertions—needed for initiation of therapy—were being delayed to later in the day or potentially to another day while elective port removals were being done. This led to further exploration of options that might alleviate this bottleneck. During the time that we were implementing all of the changes outlined, the hospital had created an offsite outpatient surgery center.

P Central Line Insertion - TEST, MEDRECO

*Performed on: 07/25/2015 1019

✓ Infection Control Elements

Central Line Insertion

Central Line Insertion

Lot Number **Reference Number** **Manufacturer** **Catheter Material**

○ Silicone ○ Polyurethane ○ Unknown

Location of Procedure **Proceduralist** **Assistant**

Primary Indication

○ Chemotherapy
○ Dialysis/Apheresis
○ Infusion therapy
○ Long term antibiotics
○ Nutritional Support
○ Poor peripheral venous access
○ Central venous pressure monitoring
○ Continuous arterial pressure monitoring
○ Other:

Sedation/Analgesia

☐ None
☐ Local anesthesia
☐ Minimal sedation
☐ Moderate sedation
☐ Deep sedation
☐ General anesthesia

Local Anesthesia Type

Local Anesthesia Concentration

Local Anesthesia Volume

mL

Catheter Placed

○ Central line uncuffed (temporary)
○ Hemodialysis/apheresis temporary
○ Hemodialysis/apheresis permanent
○ Hickman/Broviac/Leonard
○ PICC
○ Port
○ Pulmonary artery/Swan Ganz
○ Umbilical

Insertion Site

○ Temporal
○ Facial vein
○ Internal jugular vein
○ External jugular vein
○ Subclavian vein
○ Antecubital vein
○ Axillary
○ Umbilical artery
○ Umbilical vein
○ Femoral vein
○ Leg/saphenous, above knee
○ Leg/below knee
○ Other:

Side

○ Right
○ Left
○ Umbilical

Antibiotic Prophylaxis

○ None
○ Cefazolin
○ Vancomycin
○ Clindamycin
○ Other:

Technique

☐ Percutaneous
☐ Percutaneous with ultrasound guidance
☐ Percutaneous with micropuncture
☐ Open cut down
☐ Guide wire exchange with dilator
☐ Guide wire exchange without dilator
☐ Patent vessel was engaged under ultrasound guidance, image retained and recorded
☐ Patent vessel was engaged under ultrasound guidance, image not retained or recorded
☐ Fluoroscopic guided placement confirmed final catheter tip location
☐ Trans umbilical
☐ Peel away sheath

Final Catheter Tip Location

○ Internal jugular vein
○ External jugular vein
○ Subclavian vein
○ Innominate
○ Cephalic
○ Aorta
○ Superior Vena Cava
○ Cavoatrial junction
○ Right atrium
○ Inferior Vena Cava
○ Common iliac
○ Femoral vein
○ Pulmonary artery
○ Other:

Location Confirmation

☐ C-Arm Fluoroscopy image capture
☐ Chest X-ray
☐ Abdominal X-ray
☐ No imaging

Number of Lumens

○ Single
○ Double
○ Triple

Catheter Size/Gauge

Depth of Insertion

cm

Original Catheter Length

cm

Estimated Blood Loss

○ None
○ Less than 10 mL
○ Other:

Amount of Catheter Cut

cm

Post-Placement Catheter Lenc

Additional Procedural Elements

☐ Demonstrated blood return in all ports
☐ Catheter flushed
☐ Catheter caps placed and heparinized
☐ Catheter secured at exit site with monofilament suture (nylon or prolene)
☐ Catheter secured at exit site with silk suture
☐ Port accessed with needle
☐ Stat Lock securement placed

Port Needle Gauge

Port Needle Length (in)

inch(es)

Total Number of Wires Used During Procedure and Accounted for After Procedure

Was an existing catheter removed?

○ Yes
○ No

Catheter Type Removed

○ Central line uncuffed (temporary)
○ Hemodialysis/apheresis temporary
○ Hemodialysis/apheresis permanent
○ Hickman/Broviac/Leonard
○ PICC
○ Port
○ Pulmonary artery/Swan Ganz
○ Umbilical

Post-Procedure Patient Disposition

Complications

☐ None
☐ Air embolism
☐ Arrhythmia
☐ Broken wire
☐ Catheter embolization
☐ Fractured catheter
☐ Hematoma
☐ Inadvertant arterial stick
☐ Lost wire
☐ Pneumothorax
☐ Other:

If child was < 4 kg or if the case was technically difficult, please document details.

Additional Information

Attending Present

○ Yes
○ No

Attending Attestation

☐ I was present for or performed the entire procedure
☐ I was present for or performed at least the key elements of the procedure
☐ I was immediately available for the remainder of the case
☐ Another teaching physician was immediately available for the remainder of the case

Name of Teaching Physician Available

For Interventional Radiology only, refer to Radiology exam report for confirmation of exam details by provider.

Figure 7.5 Standardized online documentation for surgical procedures utilizing drop-down menus.

Seattle Children's Hospital
206-987-2000

Central Line Insertion Note TEST, MEDRECO - 5111378

Result Type:	Central Line Insertion Note
Result Date:	25 July 2015 10:19
Result Status:	Auth (Verified)
Result Title:	Central Line Insertion
Performed By:	Gow, Kenneth W, MD on 25 July 2015 10:19
Verified By:	Gow, Kenneth W, MD on 25 July 2015 10:19
Encounter info:	30140765, PRIMARY CARE, Outpatient, 7/24/2015 -

Central Line Insertion Entered On: 7/25/2015 10:25
Performed On: 7/25/2015 10:19 by Gow, Kenneth W, MD

Infection Control Elements
Infection Control Before Procedure : All participants used alcohol-based hand hygiene, Central line cart utilized and covered with sterile drape, Full field barrier draped over patient
Antiseptic Use : Chloroprep (2% Chlorhexidine + 70% Isopropyl Alcohol) - Corrected gestational age GREATER THAN 34 weeks
Infection Control During Procedure : Provider performing procedure wears gloves, gown, hat, and mask. Eye protection is strongly recommended but not required., All people in room wear masks (including patient for upper lines, exclude intubated and LMA patients), Sterile technique maintained throughout, including dressing placement, Date labeled on dressing, BioPatch placed at exit site (except umbilical lines or documented Chlorhexidine allergy) - Corrected gestational age GREATER THAN 34 weeks
Infection Control Universal Protocol : Universal Protocol, Procedural Checklist, and/or Timeout completed prior to procedure

Gow, Kenneth W, MD - 7/25/2015 10:19

Central Line Insertion
Lot Number : LOT NUMBER HERE
Reference Number : REFERENCE NO.
Manufacturer : MANUFACTURER
Catheter Material : Silicone
Location of Procedure : OR
Proceduralist : Gow, Kenneth W, MD
Primary Indication : Chemotherapy
Sedation/Analgesia : Local anesthesia, General anesthesia
Local Anesthesia Type : Bupivicaine
Local Anesthesia Concentration : 0.25 %
Local Anesthesia Volume : 5 mL
Catheter Placed : Port
Site Insertion : Internal jugular vein
Side : Right
Antibiotic Prophylaxis : None
Technique for Line Placement : Percutaneous with ultrasound guidance, Percutaneous with micropuncture, Guide wire exchange with dilator, Patent vessel was engaged under ultrasound guidance, image retained and recorded, Peel away sheath
Final Catheter Tip Location : Cavoatrial junction
Location Confirmation : C-Arm Fluoroscopy image capture
Number of Lumens : Single
Catheter Size/Gauge : 6.5
Original Catheter Length : 76 cm
Amount of Catheter Cut : 36 cm
Estimated Blood Loss : Less than 10 mL
Post Plcemnt Catheter Length : 40 cm
Additional Procedural Elements : Demonstrated blood return in all ports, Catheter flushed, Catheter caps placed and heparinized, Port accessed with needle
Port Needle Gauge : 20
Port Needle Length : 0.75 inch(es)
Number Of Wires Used During Procedure : 2
Existing Catheter Removed : No
Post Procedure Patient Disposition : PACU
Complications : None
Attending Attestation : I was present for or performed the entire procedure
Attending Present : Yes

Gow, Kenneth W, MD - 7/25/2015 10:19

Completed Action List:
```
* VERIFY by Gow, Kenneth W, MD on 25 July 2015 10:19
* Sign by Gow, Kenneth W, MD on 25 July 2015 10:19
* Perform by Gow, Kenneth W, MD on 25 July 2015 10:19
```

Figure 7.6 Documentation for surgical procedures is easily notated using the online documentation immediately following the procedure.

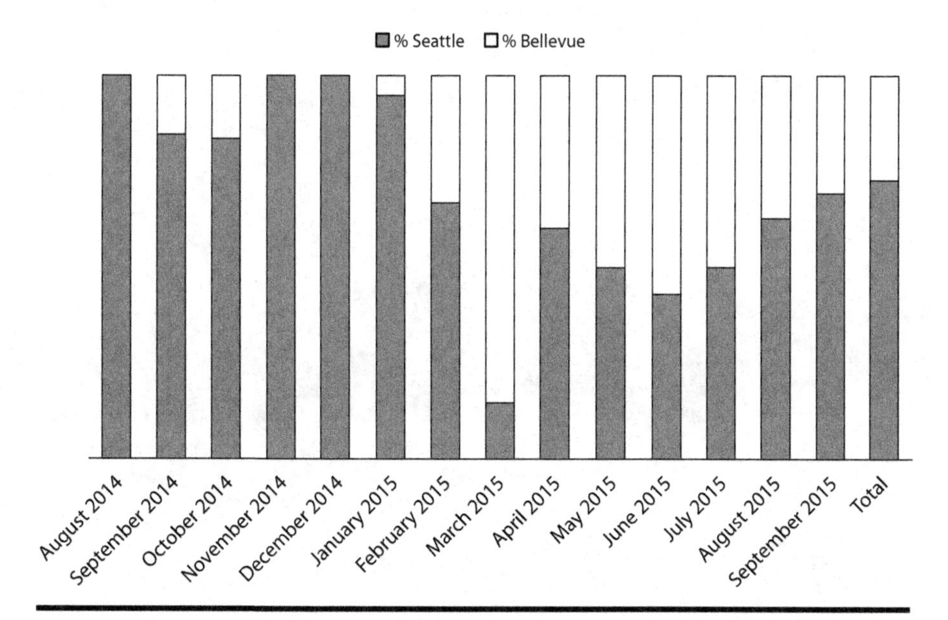

Figure 7.7 Level loading that occurred by utilizing the outpatient center for elective port removal procedures.

Because central line insertions required the main operating room there had been no interest in using the outpatient surgery center. However, as we started to explore options, it became obvious that elective port removals *could* be done primarily in the outpatient center. There was some initial concern that families would be impacted, as they had received all of their care at the main campus. To ensure success in this transition, it was important to work closely with the ordering providers to make sure that they knew we were making these changes so that the messaging to the families could be unified from the onset of surgical planning. The anticipated and realized outcome of this iterative change was that this has facilitated level loading by allowing more urgent lines to be done in the main OR and more elective removals to be done in a center designed for those rapid turnover procedures (Figure 7.7).

Conclusion

In conclusion, as a leader of change, one must realize that while there are often successes achieved with a new process, change often reveals new challenges. It is important to embrace this and strive toward continued improvement. This methodology demonstrates to all that are involved that the leader is also involved and is accountable for all aspects of change—the successes and the challenges. And if the focus is always on providing the best care to the patient as the central mission, the motives of the leader will not be in question.

Chapter 8

Clinician Engagement: Continuous Performance Improvement (CPI) Applied in a Not-So-Touchy-Feely Environment

Bryan King, Ruth Benfield, and Debra Gumbardo

It is shocking but true: In some parts of the United States, parents have felt compelled to make the devastating decision to abandon their children in an emergency room in order to access mental healthcare.

The "mental health void," as described by *New York Times* writer Judith Warner, is characterized by a dearth of mental health providers, significant gaps in inpatient and residential capacity, and poor service integration. These factors converge to create a perfect storm in which children suffering from hallucinations, uncontrolled aggression, and suicidal impulses are languishing on waiting lists for services.

That's why, when Nebraska passed a "safe-haven" law to provide an alternative to the rare—but tragic—cases where an infant might be abandoned and sometimes left for dead by an overwhelmed and frightened new parent, officials were surprised to see nearly 40 young teenagers, most with serious mental illness, turned over to the state.

The Pacific Northwest is no different than America's Heartland when it comes to the frustration and painful experiences that families are forced to endure as their children wait to access mental healthcare. Estimates, based upon a conservative utilization rate of 2.5 per 1,000 youths, yield a current shortage of 200 psychiatric hospital beds for children in the State of Washington. And, indeed, over the course of the past year in our emergency department at Seattle Children's Hospital, we have had to divert 140 children in need of psychiatric hospitalization to other facilities or situations. The list of children waiting to access outpatient services is longer still.

Obviously, we must find ways to extend our mental health resources to support these families. At the same time, in an environment where there is seemingly an endless to-do list—always another patient or family that could be seen—there is little energy or enthusiasm for focusing on process or systems issues. It's sad, but it's just a given that things are broken.

Early Struggles

To begin to fix this huge problem, our starting point with continuous performance improvement (CPI) was simple: How could we see more patients within our own system—without creating more work for our faculty and clinical staff?

This was easier said than done. The conventional wisdom is that mental health professionals are more receptive than other clinicians to out-of-the-box thinking. But this isn't necessarily the case. And our experience in the psychiatry department at Seattle Children's as we tried to embrace CPI demonstrates this clearly.

The Department of Child Psychiatry and Behavioral Medicine is composed of care providers and support staff at all levels of training across multiple disciplines—including psychiatry, psychology, nursing, and social work. The University of Washington (UW) largely employs the psychologists and psychiatrists, although not exclusively so. Both Seattle Children's and UW faculty leaders serve as administrators for the department. The bottom line is that this is an inherently difficult environment in which to introduce significant change.

It is even more difficult because the director of the department is a skeptic who is wary of the ways that "pop psychology" repackages or relabels common human experiences to seemingly confer more significance or to suggest unique expertise. The department director's "psychobabble radar" is thus very well tuned, and his initial exposure to Lean transformation, CPI, and the Toyota Production System set off that radar like a screaming siren. As a result, our department was more than happy to explore process improvements, but we had no interest in cloaking our efforts in kaizen or in referring to waste as "muda."

The big challenge, then, was getting faculty and staff to commit to a methodology that smacks of psychobabble but that, in fact, acknowledges waste in our system and instills a willingness to help eliminate it. The honest truth is that we have yet to fully meet this challenge in our department, and CPI is still a work in progress for us. But we have moved forward, and this is well worth noting.

An Organization Mandate

Taking a step back: The organization as a whole had previously developed an executive leadership group that included department medical directors and operations administrators who oversee the day-to-day workings of the hospital. The group had addressed multiple issues specifically focused on safety and quality improvement. With the guidance and commitment of a facilitator who was an expert in this methodology, as well as leadership from the president of the hospital, the executive group learned about Lean together and committed to adopting this methodology throughout the organization. The top medical and administrative leadership from our department was part of this team and was involved in all the educational efforts and mandates to move forward.

Despite this engagement, however, our department wasn't truly willing to take a leap of faith for CPI. It seemed obvious that operating room (OR) scheduling was rife with waste and unneeded complexity that arose from the demanding schedule of surgery. But the complexity and waste in scheduling a 50-minute psychology or psychiatry session with a patient were far less apparent to us.

Nonetheless, the senior leaders in our department participated in several additional trainings that exposed them to CPI principles in theory and practice. Indeed, we were among the first to participate in the "Wash Your Hands" practicum, a weeklong "kaizen" or improvement event at a local manufacturing facility that applied Lean principles.

In addition, we participated in the first Japan Super Flow trip, which allowed us to immerse ourselves in factories that had been using the Toyota Production System for many years. The trip to Japan cemented the real value of this work because we finally saw for ourselves the cumulative outcomes that resulted from decades of CPI effort.

But our department leaders still walked away wondering how they would apply these CPI principles to their work and get others on board; we knew we had a long and bumpy road ahead.

"Our Department Is Different"

Some of those bumps were due to the fact that people in our department wanted empirical proof about CPI. And, because most people see fairly significant incompatibilities between the medical and manufacturing cultures, it's critical that academic leaders are out in front in terms of embracing, adopting, and implementing Lean methodologies. One of the accelerators in this process—from our experience, at least—was helping faculty leaders become fluent in Lean processing principles and giving them the opportunity to work in the lab (i.e., to directly experiment with CPI and observe its potential). These experiences are critical in getting people to authentically advocate change in the face of potent resistance and doubt. The embrace of CPI may have the appearance of a statement of faith, but we found that in our department it had to be anchored in experience and fact.

We also learned how important it is to focus, not only on the improvements that lead to a more reliable and consistent product, but also on the impact that this has on the worker's experience. This notion was displayed in an exhibit that chronicled the evolution of the loom at the Toyota Commemorative Museum of Industry and Technology in Nagoya, Japan (see Figure 8.1). Indeed, in thinking about the earliest modifications to the loom—for example, the introduction of a foot pull to separate vertical threads—Toyota recognized the interdependence of the worker and the machine, the artist and his or her creation.

Figure 8.1 The evolution of the loom at the Toyota Commemorative Museum of Industry and Technology.

And, after seeing the incremental gains that come from process improvements, we were also led to the inescapable conclusion that "standard work" and "reliable methods" actually free up workers so they can lavish more attention on the art and craft of their jobs. In the case of the loom, the simple addition of the foot pull eliminated some of the worker's burden; in the case of pediatric medicine, it means more focus on patient care.

After our trip to Japan, we extended our commitment to CPI and included more of our leaders in an effort to offset the perception that we were simply taking a wild leap of faith with CPI. The hospital selected projects that clearly showed that our current process was taking clinicians or staff away from direct patient care or keeping patients from being seen. We then recruited department members to participate in hospital-wide CPI events such as a Rapid Process Improvement Workshop (RPIW) to revise handoff communications. During these events, our staff was exposed to didactic material and had the opportunity to apply CPI principles over the course of a week. These were wonderful opportunities to see how the process worked and to contribute to the success of areas outside of our own department.

It was helpful that early successes were celebrated throughout the organization, but there were—and remain—challenges in getting the uninitiated in our department to recognize parallels between their work and the improvements in OR scheduling or the labeling of lab specimens. Staff members who were naturally interested and motivated to seek better ways to provide care were intrigued by the successes in other areas. Others continued to believe that "we are different," and that while standard work could be applied to cars and perhaps even the OR, the same did not hold true for us in psychiatry and behavioral medicine.

Creating Some Initial "Wins"

Despite the departmental doubts, we pushed ahead. And point improvement work in centralized scheduling offered us a start as well as key lessons.

We have several outpatient clinics that collectively receive more than 350 referrals each month. The small group of staff members who process these referrals recognized that they were spending more time investigating, correcting, or rerouting referrals than actually scheduling patients to be seen. Our wait list was growing, and we had unfilled capacity among our providers. Consequently, the department's initial CPI event focused on shaping demand and the quality of the referral information received—a daunting task, because it involved changing the behavior of providers outside our organization. The results of this effort, which reduced appointment lead time by over 50 percent and the number of referral requests returned to providers for additional information by a staggering 95 percent, are shown in Table 8.1.

Table 8.1 Psychiatry Clinic Intake Workshop Results

	Pre-Workshop 2006	*60-Day Follow-Up*	*40-Month Follow-Up*	*% Change between Pre-Workshop and 60-Day Follow-Up*
Lead time (days)	77	27	37	–52%
Percentage of referrals returned to provider for additional information	37	2	N/A	–95%

Departmental Training

With this success under our belts, we ultimately decided that all staff in the department would attend CPI Fundamentals—a full-day course introducing the basics of this philosophy. As we undertook this phase of our CPI journey, it was important that a direct applicability to our psychiatry systems be demonstrated. Having our department leadership, rather than CPI consultants, provide the training helped ensure that this would occur. We also made a strategic effort to have all of our department's staff exposed to CPI as a separate and unified group, rather than among a group of providers or staff from the hospital at large. In this way, we could focus on examples and class exercises on topics that were directly meaningful to those in the class—psychiatry and behavioral medicine.

Several challenges that emerged from these initial trainings are worth noting:

- Many providers in the department, like others in academic centers, had trouble balancing the importance of patient-centric clinical care and success in teaching and research.
- Many clinicians and staff had difficulty accepting the fact that aspects of their work might be seen as "waste" or "non-value added" (see Figure 8.2).
- We discovered that CPI is not for those with thin skin. We urged staff to rise above their own personal interest and investment in keeping the status quo.
- Many staff members could not accept 50-percent improvement targets; iterative change and improvement over time were not "good enough" for a number of our highly successful colleagues.

The department-focused trainings only went so far to solidify staff commitment to CPI and Lean approaches. They did, however, contribute to the use of a common language, which gradually helped many of us get on the same page. It is not uncommon now to hear senior faculty leaders in our department speak about

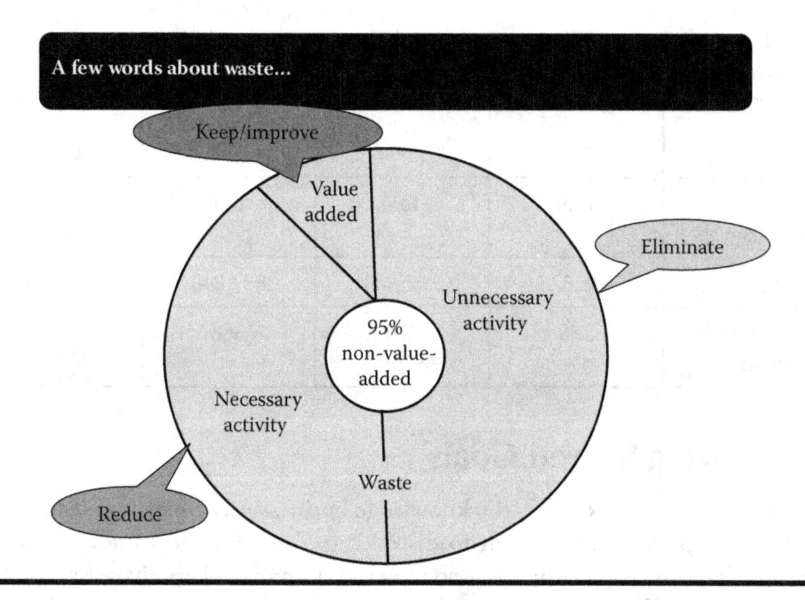

Figure 8.2 Focus on waste versus value-added steps. Results from analyzing value-added steps, non-value-added steps, and waste in a process. Identifying non-value-added steps leads to difficult but necessary conversations with staff.

reducing "lead time" for scheduling or "waste" as it relates to searching for equipment or supplies.

Building Momentum

As a result of the training, our neuropsychology service recognized several variables that were contributing to long lead times. Working with one of our quality specialists who had received the foundational CPI training, we mapped our outpatient neuropsych testing process from initial visit to discharge and identified several areas of focus. Thereafter, the average cycle time for selecting and preparing a test decreased from 20.4 minutes to 9.2 minutes.

To further extend our knowledge and application of CPI principles, we invited clinical leads and operation managers in our department to participate in the formal weeklong training that was initially offered to hospital leaders. After attending this training, the clinical director of the inpatient psychiatric unit (IPU) commented on the value of seeing the integration of CPI principles in practice. She was later instrumental in implementing reliable methods in the IPU. This ultimately led to a cost savings of more than $10,000 per hospital stay (2007–2009), despite an increase in costs during this same time period (see Table 8.2). These numbers helped advance CPI within our department.

Table 8.2 Inpatient Psychiatric Unit (IPU) Outcomes following Implementation of Care Guidelines and Daily "Huddle"

	2007	*2008*	*Annualized 2009*	*% Change*
Length of stay (days)	16.9	13.4	11.4	–33%
Cost per stay	$48,672	$41,808	$37,840	–22%
Patients served	376	473	568	51%

Recognizing Shared Goals

The fact that professors are in the knowledge business was a plus, too. Most of us choose this scholarly career path to discover and to apply new findings, and to integrate and disseminate these developments to improve others' lives. As we found out during our CPI experiences, medicine doesn't have a monopoly on improving people's lives and wanting to make the world a better place. Recognizing these shared goals helped to overcome initial resistance from staff who were apprehensive about looking to manufacturing for solutions in healthcare. For example, we are committed to the notion of "engagement" as a true reflection of how one invests in his or her work. Supporting staff in being able to do their best each day and using people in their fullest capacity is consistent with the concept of eliminating waste associated with over- or underutilizing workers. We also made it clear that staff opinions count and that in the end staff members are the ones who must identify the CPI-based changes that need to take place.

Coming to Grips with Standard Work

Our department continues to wrestle with the idea that CPI means that we must determine a standard approach to care. Standard care means changes, and changes take time to implement; they don't generate benefits or results overnight. We saw this with the use of online order entry and electronic documentation templates. It cropped up again when we implemented daily "huddles" and team rounding. At first, it appeared that the huddles and team rounding would require more of our psychiatrists' time. But the exact opposite occurred. Indeed, devoting time to the rounding process reduced the amount of ad hoc questions and requests that came to our attending physicians via phone calls and e-mails.

CPI is science in action. And this registers squarely with our clinicians, who can see that CPI embodies the scientific method of hypothesis generation and testing. By recognizing the scientific basis of CPI, many have come to appreciate that by eliminating unnecessary variation with a protocol (or standard work), we can effectively free up more time for psychiatry and behavioral medicine.

Specifically, clinicians understand that once a decision is made to initiate treatment with a particular therapy, the implementation of that decision should be uniform and predictable. A psychiatrist shouldn't need to decide which rating scale to use to monitor change associated with the introduction of a medication, calibrate the starting dose of that medicine, or calculate the rate at which the medication is increased. These dosages should be per protocol. In the end, all of these potential variations simply divert energy from the most important thing: choosing which medication is most appropriate for a given patient.

We saw the benefits of standard care in other ways, too.

Improving the Quality and Consistency of Inpatient Stays

Our IPU struggled for many years to improve access so that no child who needed a bed would be turned away. A decade ago, admissions of up to four to six weeks were the norm and focused primarily on diagnostic evaluation. Managed care companies gradually limited the lengths of stay and challenged inpatient leaders to redefine the role of inpatient care in this changing environment. However, our efforts to improve access by further reducing lengths of stay were unsuccessful. Many argued that the community was not ready to maintain high-acuity patients, given the limited resources. Community programs that touted good results were not readily available in all areas, and parents and providers believed extended stays were valuable. Consequently, the urgent platform for change did not exist, and there was little effort, beyond raising awareness, to support reductions in lengths of stay.

More recently, the inpatient unit redefined its purpose; it now provides behavior stabilization and focused intervention in order to address the immediate precipitants that lead to the need for hospitalization. To improve reliability and quality, the unit developed and implemented guidelines of care for various diagnostic groups and developmental ages. But this strategy alone did not ensure change. A reliable method is only "reliable" when it is consistently utilized. We also adjusted rounding processes so that rounds were used to check progress along a pathway to discharge and ensure adherence to clinical guidelines.

While the intent of these guidelines was to improve the quality and consistency of care, an unintended consequence was further reductions in lengths of stay. Indeed, lengths of stay and costs for patients served were reduced by 33 percent and 22 percent, respectively; at the same time, the number of patients served per year nearly doubled (see Table 8.2).

It is worth noting that simply looking at length of stay, or even suggesting it as a target for improvement year after year, did not yield any traction; but efforts to improve treatment quality and consistency reduced both cost and length of stay dramatically.

An Ongoing Journey

Though our didactic experiences were helpful in mobilizing faculty and staff, experience in practice has proven to be the most critical engine for change in our department. Over time, we have learned that identifying relatively small, but significant, opportunities for process improvement helps "pilot" new approaches while making sure we challenge people to do work they are actually capable of performing. And our experiences, both on the IPU and in our neuropsychology service, underscore the fact that the cultural transition to a CPI environment in a medical setting is an incremental and iterative process.

This evolutionary element of CPI is embodied by Toyota in many ways. When you watch the Toyota assembly line in action after decades of Lean processing, for example, you are looking at efficiency and consistency that make error proofing seem like a well-choreographed ballet.

Our department isn't quite at that level yet—it runs more like a rugby match. But our trainings have provided an opportunity to reemphasize our goals for CPI, and we're moving the ball downfield. To be sure, CPI has helped us recommit to our priorities: quality and safety through the use of standard clinical protocols, improving access to care through the elimination of waste, and greater staff engagement.

While we haven't come close to solving the void in children's mental health services that exists locally and nationally, we believe that CPI gives us the tools to do the most with what we have and to reach more families than we ever have in the past. And it's now safe to say that CPI is no longer considered "psychobabble" in our department; on the contrary, it's seen as a critical element in our work, and an effective way for us to provide better care for patients.

Epilogue

Debra Gumbardo and Bryan King

CPI Growth over Time

Over the past five years, the external forces affecting pediatric behavioral health services have intensified. The prevalence of mental illness in children in the United States has increased.[1] And the number of referral requests to Seattle Children's Hospital for behavioral health services has grown dramatically. At the same time, we have experienced increased pressure from payers to reduce costs, intensified utilization review efforts, and a narrowing of provider networks. The ultimate result of these forces is that access to services within the Seattle area and across the country remains a significant problem for children and their families.

By continuing to embrace CPI at Seattle Children's in the face of these challenges, we have actually improved access to our behavioral health services. The average wait for the next new appointment has fallen from 37 days in 2008 to 20 days in 2015. This almost 50-percent reduction translates directly into value for our patients and their families. Our approach has been to expand service where we can, and recognize that we must not only sustain but intensify our CPI efforts to keep up with the growing demand.

Expanding Access

Over the past five years we have expanded services in several major ways. We opened a specialized autism center in 2009. The center now services a large number of children, over 7,000 to date, with more than 17,000 clinic visits per year. Unfortunately, even with the expanded resources, the center maintains a waiting list for virtually all of the services provided.

In an effort to improve our access, we have maintained our focus on CPI principles and have placed the spotlight of that focus on improving value (as mutually defined by patients, families, and care providers). One of the most engaging and revealing exercises in this regard was using a center-wide retreat to capture and prioritize our collective values. To facilitate this process, we employed an analytic hierarchy process in which everyone, regardless of his or her role in the center (i.e., clinical or nonclinical, professor or student), was asked to contribute to a list of values and goals.

To further assist in identifying these values, we asked people to list the pros and cons of what we do or what we might like to do if the sky was the limit. For example, one of the pros associated with doing diagnostic assessments is that these types of evaluations are comprehensive and state of the art. Conversely, the downside of offering this service is reduced access to providers and longer lead times to diagnosis. The "pro" might be subsumed under the value of being leaders in state-of-the-art and comprehensive service. The "con" might reflect values of being efficient or ensuring timely access for all patients and families who need us.

When we completed head-to-head ratings of these values and identified top priorities, some values seem in direct conflict. Can comprehensive care be efficient? If we were a fancy restaurant, would it make sense to offer only window seating and to make everyone wait in long lines for those seats? Or is there room for good food to be served to more people overall by expanding capacity with interior seats? Many of our families said via focus groups and interviews that they would overwhelmingly prefer to trade the wonderfully comprehensive window experience for a more streamlined approach to address their hunger for answers.

An unexpected outcome of our value-defining exercise was that it highlighted the differences in priority of different specialists in our center. Schedulers and frontline medical providers prioritized access, while our psychologists and speech and language pathologists prioritized comprehensiveness. Other priorities that rose to the top included the provision of coordinated and efficient care, family-centered care, staff development and satisfaction, the availability of targeted treatments, financial viability, innovation and research, training and outreach, and collaborative community relations.

Our working collective values provided an opportunity for alignment and created a shared understanding of our challenge to balance multiple and sometimes conflicting priorities. One of the more exciting improvements that emerged involves a more efficient "one-piece flow" diagnostic assessment in which medical providers and psychologists are paired up on the same day to complete an evaluation. Previous practices necessitated a series of visits involving testing and other assessments over time that would result in confirmation of a diagnosis. Many payers require a confirmation of an autism diagnosis before authorizing additional services. Long lead times to diagnosis result in a delay of care for this population for whom early intervention is critical. "Blitz week" is an event in which over 100 *new* evaluations are completed in five days, an increase of upward of 400 percent in our new-visit productivity for that week and a reduction of lead time to receive the diagnosis. Families no longer need to wait to access therapeutic services due to long lead times for diagnosis.

Creating a CPI Learning Community

One still hears a healthy skepticism from faculty and staff, particularly the uninitiated whose cultural embrace of CPI is less established. "Believers" come across as blindly accepting the approach to improvement. And perhaps because the use of CPI terminology and methods are now such a part of our cultural fabric that people unapologetically include them when we think about how to move through our challenges, believers may come across as even more cult-like than they did five years ago.

Nevertheless, as a measure of our embrace of CPI, it is remarkable that program directors have incorporated a daylong seminar on the topic into the formal didactic schedule for all of our psychology and psychiatry trainees. At a time when competition for space in the curriculum has never been greater, with seemingly daily advances in our knowledge base and no increase in the time available for training, CPI is getting an extraordinary amount of airtime. Moreover, it is our faculty and directors of the training program who are engaged in developing this curriculum and leading the day's events. It is a testament to our culture that CPI is identified as their pathway forward to eliminate waste from the training program, enhance value, and improve quality. We've learned the value of engaging faculty and providers as champions of improvement work that most closely aligns with their academic and clinical interests. Corroborating these observations, our scores for staff engagement have steadily improved over the past five years, from 4.11 (on a 5-point scale) in 2010 to 4.45 in 2015.

While the intrinsic improvements may be enough to propel interest in CPI, we have uncovered other strategies to help maintain engagement in this work. Improved efficiency and clinical productivity have provided a buffer that allows some providers to diversify their work effort, perhaps initiating a project that sparks their interest. Staff is active in the decisions about how to reinvest the gains that have come from CPI. In addition, we recognize the fatigue inherent in the pace of change and working in a field where demand exceeds capacity. As a team we actively discuss the need to keep true to our values and take steps to achieve our goals, while balancing these pursuits with the need to avoid overburdening staff and providers.

As part of our CPI training, we are intentional about offering learning opportunities for staff and managers, which involve mutual sharing with other organizations, both inside and outside healthcare. We see these "road trips" as a way to give people space in their day to recharge with a different kind of activity and to go learn more about CPI. We have learned that it is very important to make CPI lessons specific to the behavioral health topics in the beginning but less so over time. It seems to be easier for the uninitiated and skeptical if we clearly make the connections between manufacturing and behavioral health services. As we have matured in our CPI culture, it is less critical to make those connections for staff. We all have a greater appreciation for the fact that we can learn very important lessons by watching cars get built and applying what we learn to behavioral health.

Outcomes Tracking

Improving access and engaging staff in CPI are notable accomplishments but ultimately only important in the service of our goal to improve outcomes for patients and families. Routine outcomes measurement emphasizes our focus on recovery and demonstrates for patients and families that their symptoms are improving. We will also use aggregated measures as a critical metric for all future improvement work.

That said, being deep in CPI has not ensured a smooth path for staff and faculty to examine whether we were actually providing effective treatment. Deciding which measures to use to track outcomes has proven to be challenging. For example, it is not unusual for staff to assume that outcomes measurement reflects on them as individuals. How do we agree on a set of measures, how frequently can or should we measure symptoms, and from whom are we collecting these data? If we had tried to select a single set of metrics a decade ago, we're pretty sure each clinician would have nominated his or her personal favorite, resulting in 27 different sets of metrics. Today we have a measures committee and specialty clinic work teams making the decisions about standard work for groups of patients.

Although support from clinical supervisors, made possible with resources reallocated from previous improvement efforts, helped in addressing concerns about outcomes measurement, it remains a challenge.

Looking Forward

CPI has enabled us to keep evolving, even as the challenges to provide access to high-quality behavioral healthcare intensify. And although we certainly haven't solved all the problems, CPI has given us the philosophy and shared mental model to keep striving, day after day, to improve both care and access to care for our patients and their families.

Note

1. R. Perou, R. H. Bitsko, S. J. Blumberg, P. Pastor, R. M. Ghandour, J. C. Gfroerer, S. L. Hedden et al., Mental health surveillance among children—United States, 2005–2011, *Morbidity and Mortality Weekly Report Surveillance Summary* 62, suppl. 2 (2013, May 17): 1–35.

Chapter 9

Asthma: Continuous Improvement (Kaizen) of Clinical Standard Work

Jeff Foti and Robert C. Atkins

The Case for Standardizing Care

The standardization of care processes is a critical first step toward improvement in clinical care. At Seattle Children's, the initial standard work created to manage hospitalized patients with asthma was a resounding success with the development of a standardized respiratory scoring tool used by nurses and respiratory therapists that promoted weaning of respiratory treatments independent of providers. This resulted in a decreased length of stay without any associated increase in readmissions.

The argument for initiating standards is based on three significant changes that are occurring in the way that care is provided. First, it is no longer the standard of care to value individual decision-making over medical evidence. Care providers must know how to apply this evidence in their management of patients. Second, the age of physician paternalism has passed. We now work with teams of nurses, nurse practitioners, pharmacists, nutritionists, and many others. All of these members of the medical team bring a particular expertise that needs to be integrated into care processes, which results in a higher level of care than could be offered by a single decision maker. The third element that has changed is that clinical information systems are actively collecting data with which to make real-time decisions. The existence of this information mandates examination and response. All of these changes have effectively increased the value of care delivery. It should be noted, however, that successful standardization of care takes time, dedicated personnel, consensus building, and a culture amendable to change.

With standard processes in medicine, interdisciplinary teams can collaborate to improve the standard over time. Groups of care providers can meet regularly to discuss where improvements should be made based on the review of data and feedback from other care providers. The CPI term for this style of improvement is *kaizen*. This Japanese term is synonymous with improvement, that is, frontline workers making "small tests of change" in processes with which they are intimately involved. It was by this method that asthma care has been improved at Seattle Children's. We will use this example to demonstrate how care providers can collaborate through kaizen to make small changes leading to improved outcomes, while simultaneously making patients safer and improving the engagement of our care providers involved in the actual work.

First Wave of Change

Our original efforts to standardize asthma care began over a decade ago. Pathways were developed in the emergency department as well as the inpatient units. Small teams of leaders collaborated to implement a shared mental model concerning how medications were to be administered. Medical evidence was reviewed but not comprehensively. Readmit rates and length of stay were measured, but data were not available in a way to make real-time response possible.

In order to convince everyone that this initial pilot was plausible, the group had the foresight to design a study to build engagement. The study addressed a shared concern about whether various members of the care team assessed asthma severity differently and evaluated how the various groups applied a score to the patient's asthma severity. When the results came in, everyone was surprised to see that scoring tended to be within a single point of one another on a 12-point scale.[1] With this data in hand, the asthma team had a much easier time engaging staff in its pilot.

Despite this being an early effort, the process was wildly successful. The Emergency Department (ED) created a low and high acuity pathway that was embraced broadly by its staff. The inpatient group created a tool that allowed nurses and respiratory therapists to advance therapy independent of the physicians. This was initially viewed with skepticism by physicians but came to be widely appreciated by all once the change was piloted. Providers found that they could rely on the clinical skills of the nurses and respiratory therapists. Consequently, the staff was invested with a greater degree of responsibility for medical decision making. It was a test of change that proved successful and became the model for many further tests in the future.

Once this work was established and running for several years, the group set out to evaluate outcomes associated with the change. The results were remarkable. Patient length of stay for asthma exacerbations trended downward over a period of several years and rested at 1.2 days, which was well below the averages of peer institutions. Other conditions by comparison showed no such trend during that time. The readmission rate for asthma was far below the national average as well. On the surface, it was a "mission accomplished" moment. These numbers reflected that we were doing well. Despite this, there was a widespread feeling that there was always room for improvement. We turned ours eyes to other metrics associated with asthma care in an effort to figure out what our next step should be.

Second Wave of Change

By 2010, Seattle Children's had been developing its Lean culture for many years at this point and the organization was applying it more broadly in clinical settings. A five-year strategic hospital goal was set with a target of having 50 percent of inpatients on a clinical standard work pathway. This initiative was instrumental to the expansion of Seattle Children's Clinical Effectiveness Team and created a structure and resourcing for consultants, project leaders, project coordinators, and analytics involvement. The overall stage was set for an opportunity to reexamine progress with asthma. A new working group was put together led by a pediatric hospitalist. Hospitalists, at the time a relatively recent addition to the physician landscape at Seattle, are generalists who are experts in inpatient care. As frontline workers who work on a daily basis with nursing and respiratory therapist partners, hospitalists are ideal provider representatives for this work. Another change in the group makeup was the inclusion of other frontline representatives. Respiratory therapy and nursing leaders thought that it was vital to include the people who do the work everyday as part of the team that was making the decisions. As a result, the new group was comprised of a broad array of people from different backgrounds and experience levels who were heavily invested in seeing improvement in asthma care. This was an essential step toward transforming our change management culture to "be more kaizen."

The next step was to create a way for the group to receive actionable data with which to make decisions. This came from several sources. The clinical nurse specialists in the ED and inpatient units were in many ways the most essential members of the team since safety and quality issues were already being reliably reported to them. We supplemented their abilities with hospital-wide metrics that were updated anywhere from daily to monthly depending on the source. Any member of the team could access this data through an easy-to-use dashboard interface.

The final tool was the comprehensive and systematic literature search. Specific questions were designed to ensure that the search results properly informed any change that might be made to the pathways. With the help of our medical librarians, a literature search strategy was developed that would allow the group to revisit the clinical questions periodically to ensure that information is up to date.

The asthma committee made the decision early on to start from scratch with many of its previous assumptions. This was difficult at first because it was not clear if there was really a problem to solve or any significant gap to close. The metrics looked good. There was a general sense that the pathway was working well. So why change something that works or worse, start from the ground up? One reason was that it had never been done this way before. The literature search for the original pathway had not been comprehensive. The previous metrics were based on a national standard that did not include many of the potentially confounding asthma patients. As a result, we were not sure our results were as good as our numbers indicated. Another reason to start over was that we were working with a new group and the process of all of us building de novo was likely to be much more engaging. With those benefits in mind, the group made the decision right out of the gate to combine the ED and inpatient pathways into one common asthma care continuum. It was also thought that the ED and inpatient units were more likely to collaborate well if they were working off the same document. Despite the fact that the original charter was just to work on the inpatient process, the Clinical Effectiveness leadership team agreed to the change in direction and allowed the working group to include everything together. It was this decision that began a yearlong process that ended in September 2011 with the rollout of the asthma pathway (see Figure 9.1).

In order to understand how this was successful, we will examine a handful of the issues that we tackled with this work. The first was addressing an unintended consequence of the improvements that we made in our first wave of change. In discussions with many of the frontline people involved, it became clear that the tool that allowed the respiratory therapists and nurses to drive care independently of the physicians required some fine-tuning. In expediting patients through their hospital stay, families and residents were no longer receiving the same amount of asthma education during their stay. Another side effect was that the residents and attendings felt less engaged in the asthma care process. They seemed to be taking less ownership for patient care. Why wouldn't they when the process worked without them? In group sessions, they reflected that while they appreciated that the work was getting done in a high-quality fashion, they weren't learning from this. There was also the infrequent situation in which the patient was not doing well on the pathway and the providers were unaware of this. All of these consequences cried for some change management, but it was unclear how to proceed given the fact that the overall care and processes had been improved with the original pathway.

Could we find a compromise in which families would move through the system safely and receive the highest quality of care while allowing the residents to learn from the process? The answer was yes, but it did not come right away nor is the story fully written. Some of the changes that were trialed seemed successful and so were implemented. The respiratory therapists structured their asthma teaching process and began documenting more carefully to ensure that families left with the information they needed. The residents were encouraged to be actively involved with the patients even when they were not driving the process. We also added the ability for the residents to select patients who they thought were at high risk so that they could be involved with the respiratory therapists and nurse in the weaning of

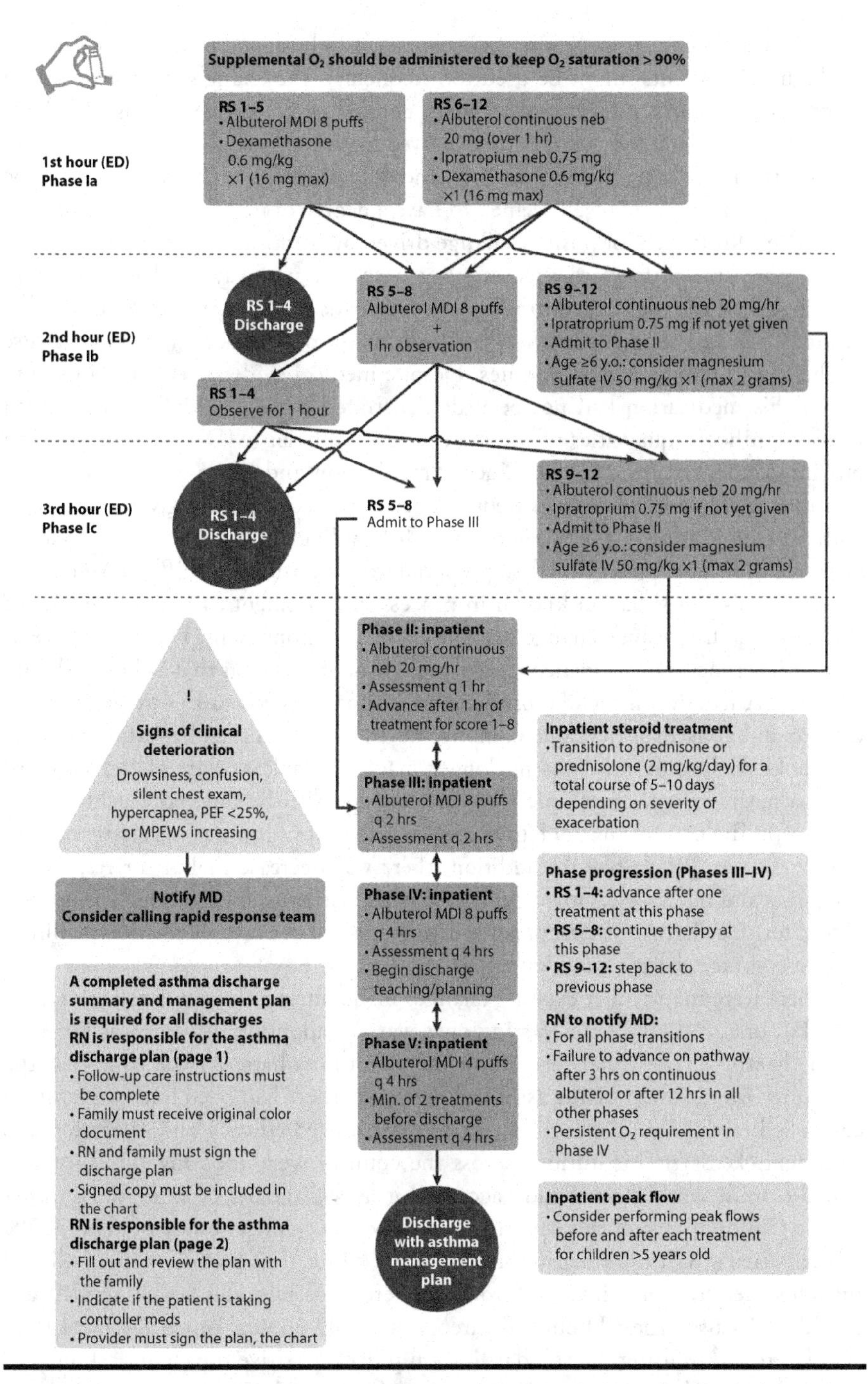

Figure 9.1 Asthma pathway. (Please see the following link for further information: http://www.seattlechildrens.org/healthcare-professionals/gateway/pathways/.)

their patient's medication. While there continues to be concern that this exception for high-risk patients might be used too frequently, the change has not increased length of stay and is used in only 5 to 10 percent of the patients. This will likely evolve over time, but the changes were derived from and agreed upon by the respective groups: respiratory therapy, nursing, and the residents. As a result, not everyone was happy but most involved seemed to have a degree of investment in the process that allows for kaizen, or positive change driven by frontline workers.

A more straightforward success story with our pathway implementation in 2011 involved the use of ipratropium bromide. This medication was built into the original ED and inpatient pathways due to medical evidence supporting its use in the ED to reduce admission rates. Despite medical evidence that the inpatient use of this medication had not been demonstrated to be effective, we continued to use significant quantities of the metered-dose inhaler (MDI) preparation with our inpatients, resulting in a significant medication and labor cost impact. Each treatment that could be given as frequently as every six hours was given eight times with 30-second intervals between puffs. While individual providers knew that the evidence did not support this therapy, standardization made it difficult to change practice. This is a situation known in process improvement as a "monument." In this case, the first wave's change became the next's monument. During the literature review process the evidence was presented and it was clear that a change should be made. A new recommendation that limited ipratropium to ED usage only was drafted and consensus developed among the asthma team members and other key stakeholders. Ipratropium was no longer made available as part of the standard asthma pathway computer order set (but it could still be ordered outside of the order set). The cost savings due to decreased use of ipratropium were estimated to be $75,000 in 2012 alone. In addition, there was decreased labor for respiratory therapists and nurses who no longer had to administer this medication. The process metric for this change is an impressive demonstration of our organization's willingness to embrace change (see Figure 9.2).

There were many other exciting changes made during the standardization process, but one of the most interesting ones was the adoption of what was largely a novel therapy at the time: intravenous magnesium sulfate. At the time that the literature was reviewed by the asthma committee, there had been four randomized controlled trials in pediatric populations that showed efficacy and safety for this treatment. Pediatric institutions across the country were adopting this approach and the adult world had already accepted it as a standard of care. Why wasn't Seattle Children's using this as well? Well, it was but only at a rate of about 4.7% of the patients. On examination, there were a handful of providers that believed that this therapy worked. Other providers were uncertain and largely recalcitrant regarding its use. The ED clinical director and ED clinical nurse specialist were very interested in using the standardization process to drive the change. They presented the intended change to their group and discussed what some of the barriers might be to adopting the new approach. In order to address some of the concerns,

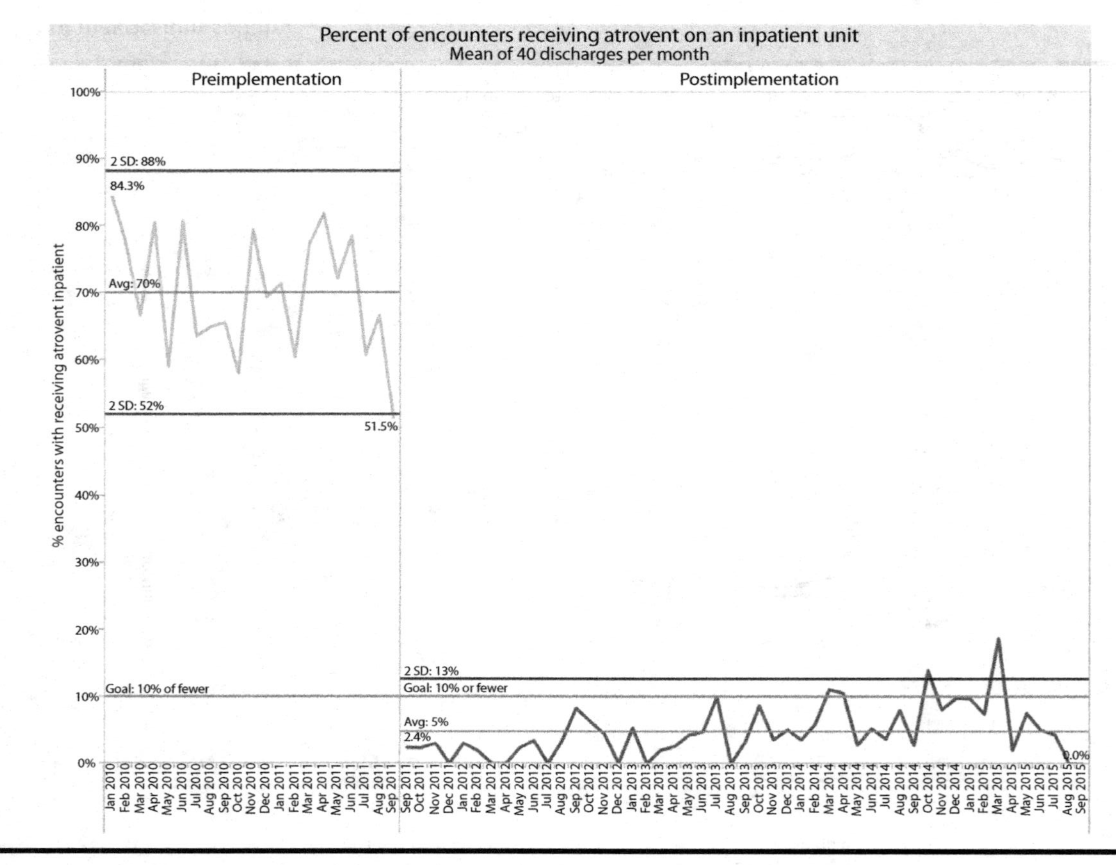

Figure 9.2 Dashboard data showing pre- and postipratropium (Atrovent) use around 2011.

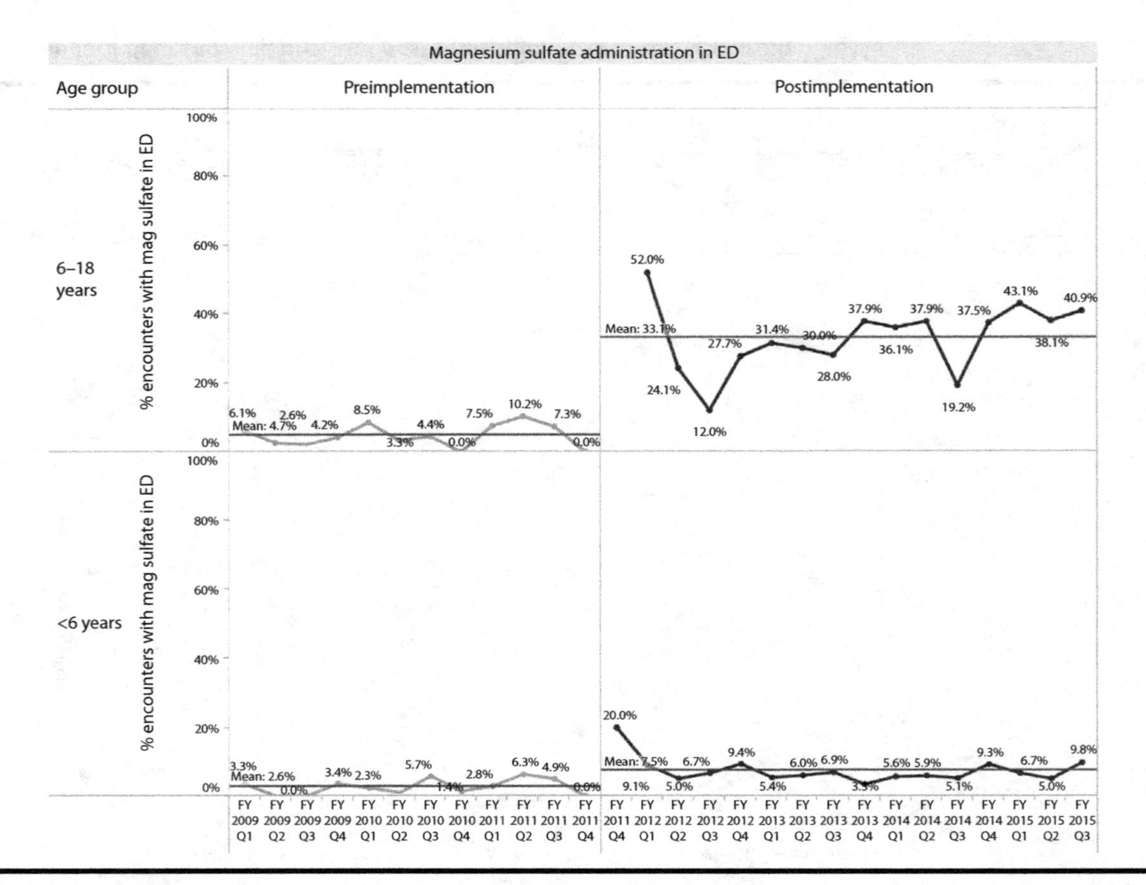

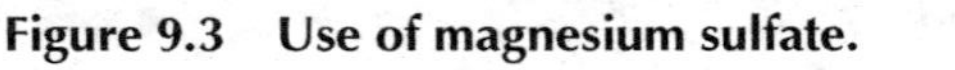

Figure 9.3 Use of magnesium sulfate.

intravenous fluids were included as part of how the medication was to be given and we chose age six as the lower limit, as all of the patients in the studies were six or older. The literature itself did not recommend either of these changes, but we thought that it was an important step toward getting broader acceptance of the management change. After more than three years, the use of intravenous magnesium sulfate increased to 33.1% in the patient population for which it was recommended (see Figure 9.3). Not all of the providers were won over but that is often the case in the improvement world.

Third Wave of Change

The efforts that were put in place with the asthma pathway in 2011 were very successful and widely appreciated by the staff. More important, the pathway continued to evolve in response to frontline workers and family feedback. Finally in 2015, the asthma committee decided to bundle a series of changes that it had been waiting to implement into a yearlong improvement cycle. This was a chance to methodically review the literature again, update findings, and capitalize on the learnings of the previous four years to improve care. The group had struggled to implement learnings into shorter plan, do, check, act (PDCA) cycles, and the culture of the hospital was not ready, in some ways, to move at a rapid pace. As a result, the changes that needed to be made were ready to be included in this process. The institution had come to accept the pace of a year long cycle through the efforts of the Clinical Effectiveness (CE) team, thus creating a built-in advantage with respect to engagement with the process. As moving too fast made people nervous, the CE team had programmed in a four-year cycle for reviewing literature, which lined up perfectly with the opportunity to bring the whole group together and enact some more changes.

At the time of writing, we are in the process of implementing a new series of changes; the details of these changes are not as important as the way in which we continue to carry them out. The members of the asthma committee are collaborating on an everyday basis on our "shop floor" to figure out how to make things better. The literature review was updated leading to an ipratropium dosing trial in the ED. Intravenous magnesium sulfate will be used in younger children as there is now more literature validating this use and our institutional experience has made us more comfortable with this therapy. The review included extensive discussions with several pediatric intensivists that were recently added to our working group to improve how patients who are not responding to therapy should be managed. A change trialed in the fall was unsuccessful but ultimately led to an important policy change for the management of very sick asthmatic patients who need to be admitted to the intensive care unit. All of these changes are the result of successes as well as failures that we are learning from as a group. We have learned that the perfect solution for a problem in 2011 might no longer be the ideal answer in 2015. More important than the changes themselves is the foundation of an actively engaged group of care providers who are committed to the cause. If we can persevere, then the kaizen, or "positive change," will continue.

Note

1. L. L. Liu, M. M. Gallaher, R. L. Davis et al., "Use of a Respiratory Clinical Score among Different Providers." *Pedatr Pulmonol.* 37(3) (2004 Mar): 243–8.

Chapter 10

Supply Chain: Ensuring Clinical Staff Have What They Need

Robert Bridges and Charles Hodge

Imagine you're a nurse in the pediatric intensive care unit (PICU) of an academic tertiary care hospital. You're caring for a child with severe, ongoing seizures, refractory to the short-acting intravenous drugs he's been receiving. He needs a nasogastric (NG) tube for long-acting oral meds. Leaving the pediatric resident with the patient, you rush to the supply closet. The child needs a 14-french sized NG tube, but the bin is empty. You hurry down the hall to the general pediatric units and look through their supplies—none the right size. Materials management is closed so you call the emergency department (ED) and are put on hold. You page the nursing supervisor, but need to go help with the patient before you receive a call back. The child starts vomiting. The NG tube is now urgently needed to prevent aspiration pneumonia. In desperation, the resident leaves the bedside and runs down to the ED to get the tube. The entire escapade has meant lost time for direct patient care and delays in care delivery with potentially serious consequences.

Materials management departments are traditionally only responsible for the low-cost, high-volume supplies used in general inpatient services, leaving the clinical staff to manage the higher-cost, specialty supplies. This approach partially explains the fact that supply chain costs are the second highest expense after salary for most healthcare organizations. Yet despite the high cost of the supply chain, most healthcare organizations fail to measure the waste and unnecessary costs associated with equipment and supplies. By bringing accountability to materials management, organizations can reap the benefits of removing unidentified waste from the supply chain. An optimized supply system is the secret treasure of a healthcare organization.

The foundation of an optimized supply chain is a single, unified supply management process that provides complete visibility and control over every medical supply used in all areas of patient care—inpatient, ambulatory, and other. Such a system improves quality and reduces waste by identifying and eliminating non-value-added activities. It allows organizations to reduce par levels (i.e., quantity of an item that is needed to support daily operation) and minimizes excess and hoarded supplies. It also minimizes or eliminates the time that clinical staff and other users are involved with activities related to the supply chain. Simply put, when executed successfully, an optimized supply system ensures that when clinical staff reaches for an item, it is available in its specified location for immediate use.

This chapter will describe how Nemours Children's Health System applied the principles of Lean to remove waste and improve efficiency in the supply chain across the Nemours enterprise: a new hospital in Orlando; an existing hospital in Wilmington, Delaware; and outpatient clinical sites in both locations.

Our Burning Platform for Change in Supply Chain Management

As continuous improvement (CI) was rolled out at Nemours in 2012, our executive team realized it was critically important to address the supply chain, because of its impact on all business units and activities of the enterprise. (For more information on Nemours, see Chapter 5.) In addition, a "buffer inventory" existed on many clinical units—extra supplies set aside by staff as a means for dealing with inadequate supplies, or "stock-outs."

In our existing hospital in Delaware we had been using a hybrid supply chain system in all of our inpatient units. The materials management department handled the higher volume supplies, while clinical associates managed the specialty and other supplies that were not stocked in our materials warehouse. Because of this fragmentation of supply management duties and the lack of an effective method for monitoring the frequency of stock-outs, clinical associates (at Nemours we refer to all staff as associates) did not trust the system to supply the items they needed for patient care. The lack of system reliability led to ordering excess supply and hoarding.

In addition to the fragmentation of duties in the areas that the materials department managed, the larger issue was the fact that the department did not manage many areas at all. The department serviced only 20 of the 136 clinical units within the existing hospital and only provided service five days a week, despite the fact that the hospital was a 24/7 operation. Nemours needed a program capable of supporting all clinical areas every day of the week, without requiring a fourfold increase in materials management staffing.

Our executive team was keenly aware that the current system pulled clinical associates away from their work with patients. When faced with the lack of an item, clinicians would call the materials management technicians at our warehouse—non-value-added work that meant time away from clinical activities. The urgent calls also represented rework for the materials management associates. On average a "call down" required 15 minutes to fulfill, a quarter hour of pure redundancy for the materials management department. We estimated that every year the clinical associates spent about 28,000 hours in work related to the supply chain instead of direct patient care. One of our primary objectives in reworking the supply chain process was giving clinicians back this time for direct care.

We saw that the productivity of the materials department was less than optimal. The materials management associates spent a significant amount of time handling one-off orders placed by clinical associates as well as call downs. Under the existing process, the associates spent between 20 and 60 minutes restocking inventory in each department in the clinical areas serviced by the materials management department. In all, the process of servicing 20 clinical departments in our existing hospital five days per week required six materials management technicians.

Our executive team also realized that the current supply chain process was wasting revenue that could be better used to support improved patient care. The materials management department did not manage the majority of clinical units, leaving clinicians to order supplies directly, often more frequently than needed, which resulted in a stockpile of excess supplies. We found that when the clinicians directly managed their own supplies, it was difficult to maintain supply standards. The special orders made contract compliance more difficult. Plus, we were paying a premium of up to 15 percent for these special orders. By our estimate, the lack of supply standardization was costing our organization an additional $1 million to $2 million per year.

When we looked across the entire enterprise, we saw that end users were managing 100 percent of the medical supplies in the surgical services areas of our hospital and in the laboratories and other ancillary areas in which expensive supplies are used. We became convinced that the process had to change. We also realized that removing waste from the supply change would require our leadership to develop the "will to corral variability."

Implementing a Reliable Process for Managing Supplies

Initially, our executive team was interested in implementing the new system in our existing hospital but reluctant to begin the process in a green field hospital. The new hospital in Orlando was an entirely new facility in a new market for Nemours. It was staffed with an entirely new workforce and led by new leaders. It was served by new physicians who came from different parts of the country, had different processes for decision making, and were trained in different organizational cultures. In addition, we committed to making hiring decisions and shaping service lines based on clinical need, rather than predetermining clinical areas and recruiting physicians for those areas. Uncertainty in the service lines meant great uncertainty regarding stocking shelves and predicting the type and volume of supplies our clinical associates would need. When we considered the highly unpredictable environment for planning and optimizing the supply chain, we were hesitant to throw a new approach to supply chain management into the mix.

After looking at the pros and cons, our executive team chose to take a long-term perspective, deciding that the benefits of implementing the new system in a green field hospital outweighed the disadvantages. While we knew it would be challenging to implement the system in an unpredictable environment, the alternative was unappealing. We considered it a matter of "pay me now or pay me later." Besides, implementing the new system in the green field hospital had the benefit of educating associates about the process from the hospital's opening.

Early on, our executive team realized that the replacement system had to have high reliability and credibility with frontline clinical associates or it would never work. We also recognized that we needed a really successful launch of the new system with the first model lines, because they would demonstrate success to the rest of the organization. With this in mind, we committed the necessary people and resources needed for an intense effort. Specifically, over a six-month period, we invested a substantial amount of resources and leadership time, going "all in" to execute the new process. We brought top leaders and future leaders together to work on the project at the new hospital in Orlando.

In April 2012, we brought together more than 20 leaders and associates for a two-day meeting to learn about the new system and their new responsibilities. The following month, a group of executive leaders participated in a one-week trip to Seattle, Chicago, and Ogden, Utah, for orientation and training in the new system and critical success factors. We convened a multidisciplinary team to make sure that key stakeholders from all relevant groups were engaged in the new process, including the leaders from pharmacy, analytics, administration, and materials management, plus physician leaders. We used a structured process to ensure that the team made decisions promptly, that implementation proceeded as designed, and that leaders addressed any problems or barriers to a smooth implementation.

To ensure consistency across the enterprise, we brought together the procurement associates and managers for both locations with the team from Orlando;

these individuals completed orientation and training together in May 2012 and worked collaboratively on the implementation of the new system in Orlando. After the orientation, leaders began weekly team meetings and status checks to facilitate communication and collaboration among the team members.

Using a Kanban Inventory Control Process

With the help of a consultant who specializes in supply chain optimization, we decided to implement a two-bin "kanban" (visual signal) system (see Figure 10.1). The two-bin system seeks to match supply to customer demand (or "pull"), while continuously reducing waste and improving quality. The primary objective is reducing the waste inherent in the supply replenishment process. A core element of the system is the use of product runs specifically designed to meet current customer

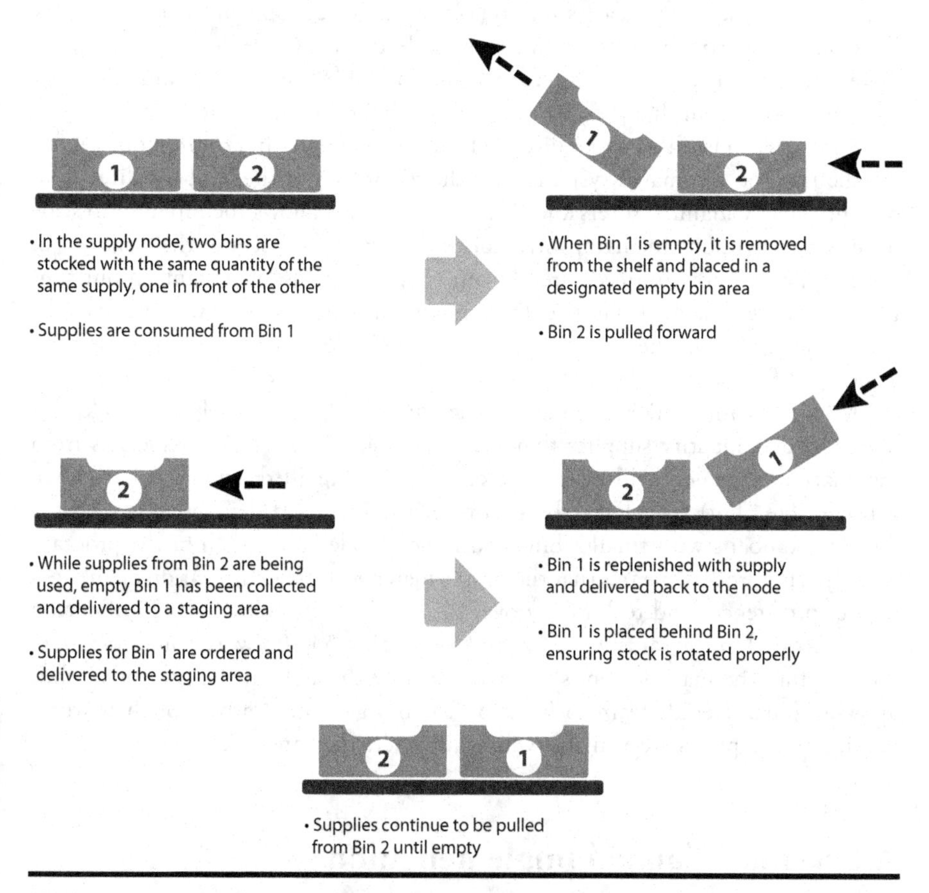

Figure 10.1 The two-bin kanban system. The two-bin system uses visual cues to signal the need for more supplies. (Courtesy of BlueBin, Inc.)

demand, in contrast to a "push" system in which batches of product are delivered and stored for later anticipated demand.

About 95 percent of supplies are distributed in these bins; stocking of items too large for bins is triggered via kanban cards. In most nodes (i.e., the unit's supply storage area) the bins are sized to hold a three-day supply. Other bins are sized to hold a larger supply, depending on the lead time of the item from the manufacturer. When an associate takes the last of an item in a bin, he or she places the empty bin in the designated holding area, which triggers the replenishment of supplies in the first bin. The associate pulls supplies from the second bin, which holds an equal quantity of the item.

Materials management associates retrieve the empty bins and return them to a staging area, which is located in our central warehouse. Associates there scan the bins; the scanning triggers an order to the supplier to deliver the supplies required to fill the empty bins. In most cases, the bins are filled within 24 hours of the scan. (Some bins require a longer replenishment time, because of a longer lead time from the supplier.) The kanbans are sized to hold a sufficient supply of the item to carry the clinical department through this external lead time. Once the bin is filled, the materials department associates return the restocked bin to the clinical node, placing it behind the bin that the clinical associates are currently using.

Kanbans can be filled either directly from the manufacturer or from our central warehouse. The automated system sends the fill orders for the kanbans directly to our third-party manufacturers and distributors, which allows the program to scale up or down without incurring inventory holding costs. Because the majority of our supplies are now sourced directly, our supply chain is less reliant on our central warehouse. The distributors deliver the supplies ready to use, with most of the packaging removed. The automated system, which does not require any specialty knowledge for use, records the frequency with which each kanban is refilled.

A "dashboard," which is linked to the automated system, helps us track supply usage and identify supplies that are "hot," "slow," or "stale." Associates from materials management will switch out kanbans that are filled more frequently than expected (i.e., hot) with larger bins to meet the increased demand. They switch out slow kanbans with smaller bins and remove stale kanbans from the program entirely. This process ensures that the supply matches shifts in utilization or changes in user preferences and technology over time. A kanban holding $0.25 of cotton balls is treated in the same way as a kanban holding $3,000 worth of an orthopedic implant. The management system is the same throughout the enterprise, thus allowing our materials team to focus on the most essential aspect of their work: making sure supplies are available when and where they are needed.

A Carefully Planned Implementation

We used a six-step process for implementation of the new system: (1) collecting data, (2) planning supply lead time and source availability, (3) building an initial mock node, (4) hosting a mock event, (5) building final nodes, and (6) installing the nodes. Our implementation team began by collecting data. We assessed all the items we planned to use and created a forecast of supplies. For example, the team went to the emergency department to identify the supplies and equipment that had been special ordered in the past and to interview every nurse on every shift to learn which supplies they had "scavenged" from other units. We used these data to plan the total supplies needed by the emergency department, including both high-volume and specialty supplies. Using additional data pulled from the hospital's enterprise resourcing planning (ERP) system, the team assessed the demand (i.e., par level) and lead time from the manufacturer for every item included in the plan for the department.

Next, we built an initial mock node. The mock node included all needed supplies organized in the two-bin system for a clinical unit. We then hosted a mock event. The implementation team invited all the physicians and nurses from all three shifts in the clinical department to give feedback on the mock node, including additional items needed, naming of items, and ideal locations for the items. They also gave feedback on the numbers of each item needed to validate the estimated par levels. The mock event helped to identify potential gaps, ensured that the program was built with the end-user in mind, and provided training on the kanban system.

The event also helped to engage clinical associates and encourage their adoption of the new system. We knew that the engagement of clinical associates was critical, because succeeding with the new process would require that they use common names for supplies, use a common set of supplies wherever possible, and minimize the use of individual clinician preference items. In short, we saw the importance of driving supply standards.

The team used the data gathered from the mock event to work with vendors to ensure that the required items could be procured at the price and units of measure targeted by the new program. After confirming the availability of the external supply chain, the team built the final kanban system (see Figure 10.2, which included the final rack configuration (i.e., the one that best supported the clinical work flow), barcode labels on the individual kanbans, and other final features.

Once the final node was ready, the team installed the node in the first clinical unit in Orlando, trained and certified all associates in the new system, and quickly began planning for the next implementation.

Our intense effort to support an effective launch was rewarded, and we were able to go live with the new supply chain system in Orlando on time. In addition, because we had involved leaders and associates from both hospitals in training and implementation, when we launched the new process in Delaware, procurement associates were experienced and understood the complexity of launching the system, and leaders knew what to look for to prevent issues in Delaware. As a result, implementation in Delaware went smooth and according to plan.

Figure 10.2 A completed node. The final node contains all needed supplies in an organized, two-bin system. (Courtesy of BlueBin, Inc.)

Maintaining the Gains: Daily Management of the Supply Chain

With the nodes in place, we implemented a daily management system that would allow Nemours to maintain a successful pull system. The system includes a data component and a leadership component. The first component is software that extracts data daily from the hospital ERP about the fill level of the bins. The software creates a signal when bins are overstocked or understocked, reflecting the consumption of an item that is slower or faster than estimated by par level. The software indicates when an item is in danger of stocking out, which has helped us move from a reactive to a proactive approach to replenishment.

As noted earlier, the software also generates online dashboards that refresh daily. These dashboards provide materials management associates and leaders with critical data on the current stocking level of all bins. Materials management associates use the data to identify the bins that need to be replenished or examined each day (e.g., "These 13 pars in these three specific nodes need to be addressed today"). The dashboard provides leaders with fill rates and other metrics and creates sourcing reports that indicate supplier performance, such as how often the external supply chain procurement was on time and how much of the spend was off-contract.

We came to appreciate the complexity of the data and analytics functionality required to support the daily standard work of the materials management associates. We have learned that the two-bin system can be intuitively understood at the node, but for the entire system of more than 40,000 bins to work, the process must also have an aggressive analytics application.

The second daily management component is leader standard work. The team defined these daily activities to include regular rounding, gemba walks, standard work audits, and management huddles. These elements enable the new supply chain process to be successful.

Engaging Associates and Addressing Barriers

Our leaders engaged associates and managers in the new supply chain process in several ways. Nemours executive leaders engaged the entire executive team by communicating a burning platform for change, then holding workshops with the clinical champions of each department, and finally by conducting gemba rounds. Leaders then made sure that all constituents who touched the supply chain (e.g., data analysts, respiratory therapists, frontline nurses) were involved in the implementation and invited to give feedback and problem-solve during the mock events. We found that after the first three departments had held workshops on the new process, associates and managers in other departments began requesting it. Recognizing the importance of the involvement of frontline nurses, leaders promoted some nurses into performance improvement positions to directly support implementation.

Leaders throughout Nemours then worked to focus all constituents on a common goal: safety for patients. This singular focus was the key to effective collaboration. Care providers wanted safety for the children and thus wanted supplies to be available when needed and easy to locate; they also wanted to spend their time on clinical duties and direct care, rather than on supply chain activities. The materials management team wanted care providers to have the supplies and equipment they needed to ensure patient safety.

Leaders also took on the task of having the difficult conversations necessary to bridge conflicts and achieve collaboration. During implementation, materials management associates and leaders were integrated with clinical associates. Initially, conflicts arose between the two groups. The executive team, especially the chief financial and chief operating officers, negotiated many conflicts to ensure that the clinical and supply teams could collaborate, getting on the phone with other leaders to work through conflicts to keep the two groups working together. Over time the teams developed a close working relationship, which eventually blurred the lines between the care and supply teams. The culture shifted and the two groups began acting as a single team.

Executive leaders also had difficult conversations with clinical department leaders who had traditionally managed their own supplies; the executives made it clear that everyone needed to adopt the new process (i.e., "there would be no sacred cows") and trust that the new system would reliably deliver the supplies they needed. According to one executive leader, the key to making the collaboration work was "the willingness to put the elephant out on the table and talk about it."

Leaders also committed sufficient staffing resources for the new supply chain process to be a success. We learned that it was critical to hire associates with a high level of proficiency in materials management to conduct the daily auditing and other activities related to the new process. We responded to this need by increasing the expected level of proficiency for these positions and changing our recruitment strategy. Leaders empowered frontline associates and managers to perform the work related to the new supply chain process by allocating protected time for these tasks.

During the planning and implementation phases we encountered several barriers. First was the matter of establishing the new process in a green field hospital where the type and volume of needed supplies was unknown. We addressed this issue with intense training in Lean and by bringing in top leaders to work on implementation. Second, we were working with two geographically separate sites. We found that by training leaders and materials management associates from both sites as a single team, we were able to create a cohesive system across the entire enterprise and leverage lessons learned for the second implementation. Third, our existing medical supply distributor was unable to provide the service requirements needed for the new kanban delivery system. Specifically, the distributor was not able to deliver in a low unit of measure, a capability that is not currently industry standard. We addressed this problem by changing distributors to one that was able to deliver supplies in this way.

The After State: A Highly Reliable, Efficient Supply Chain

How does our supply chain perform today? It is reliable, efficient, and requires minimal clinician time. Most important, our new supply chain process has freed up time for direct care and is supporting the safety of our pediatric patients. Clinical associates no longer need to order their own supplies. The new process has virtually eliminated stock-outs, back orders, and urgent supply calls from clinical associates. Currently, 85 percent of supply orders enterprise-wide are processed through the new program, thus requiring no time for clinicians. (In the near future, we hope to see 100 percent of supply orders routed through the process.)

Our new system has removed waste from our supply chain, greatly increasing its efficiency. Materials management associates spend just a few minutes each day restocking nodes, much less time than previously. Prior to implementing the new system, Nemours employed four technicians to service 21 nodes, five days per week, during the first shift only. Now the team consists of five or six technicians who service 101 nodes, seven days per week. (We keep a total staff of nine to accommodate for weekend coverage.) As we move forward, we will be able to service an additional 80 nodes on weekdays (a 400-percent increase over our old system) with the addition of just three more full time equivalents (FTEs).

With the new supply chain process in place, nearly all supply purchases are easily monitored, which has helped us to work toward product standardization and contract compliance. Today, all stock-outs for items on the program are identified and most are managed on the same day. If they cannot be handled on the same day, materials management associates place a cone in the bin notifying the clinical associates of the situation and adjust par levels as needed. With our new process, special-order items are loaded in the ERP. When an item is removed and the kanban is triggered, it is ordered as a contracted inventory item or a non-stock item. The new process makes it much simpler to place the order and to ensure that the order is on contract.

What We've Learned

Over the course of our implementation of the new process, we have learned that the supply chain must be highly reliable, standardized, and actively managed. To be successful, it must deliver high credibility and reliability; if our associates do not trust the system, they will stock up to safeguard patient care, creating an expensive, space-consuming buffer inventory. It seemed clear to us that we had only one chance to do this right. Being convinced of the need to get the process right from the beginning, we dedicated significant resources (both people and financial) to implementation. Both selecting a reliable system and committing sufficient resources were essential to our success. As one leader put it, "Had we not created a highly reliable system and put the resources to creating it, we would not have been able to pull it off." We needed to have every member of the executive team invested in the project; we needed to ensure that they had no competing priorities during the launch of the new process.

As we suspected, it was easier to implement the process in a predictable, stable environment than in a new facility in a new market. However, we learned that with adequate leadership, training, and resources, the process can be successfully launched in a green field facility. We observed firsthand that the new supply chain process only functions when integrated with robust analytics and strong system support (i.e., a rigorous management process with regular auditing). These audits must become part of daily standard work for the process to work. Finally, we learned that the supply chain and clinical activities should not be separate pursuits. Integration of the two is critically important to creating an efficient, reliable system that ultimately supports patient safety.

Chapter 11

Intensive Care Unit: Developing and Implementing Pull Systems

Kristina H. Deeter and Jerry J. Zimmerman

Ensuring Comfort during Critical Illness: A Question of Balance

In providing care for critically ill children, probably the most common and arguably the most important intervention involves alleviating pain and anxiety. Continuous infusions of analgesic and sedative agents are frequently used in intensive care units (ICUs) as a means to provide a constant level of comfort. This approach has been proven to decrease the discomfort associated with mechanical ventilation, traumatic and surgical wounds, invasive devices, and procedures. Besides this basic humanitarian benefit, analgesics and sedatives also decrease oxygen consumption, modulate intensity of the stress response, foster patient safety in a potentially dangerous ICU environment by reducing risks of falls from the bed and the dislodgement of critical invasive devices, and facilitate bedside nursing care.[1] For children, adequate sedation is particularly critical and based on patients' developmental level and ability to communicate and understand what is happening to them.

On the other hand, continuous infusions of analgesics and sedatives have been identified as independent predictors of longer duration of mechanical ventilation as well as extended ICU and hospital length of stay.[2] Prolonged sedation has also been associated with increased procedures, acquired neuromuscular disorders, delirium, and posttraumatic stress disorder. Patients may become tolerant of sedatives, prompting dose escalation and ultimately resulting in delays in the restoration of normal mental status and drive to breathe, delaying the patient's ability to liberate from the ventilator. Sedation may limit clinicians' conduct of thorough physical examinations. Accordingly, evolving neurological injury may be missed. Excessive and/or prolonged administration of analgesics and sedatives can lead to drug tolerance and even dependency, increasing the risk for serious, even life-threatening withdrawal disease if these medications are discontinued too abruptly.[3] Long-term consequences of analgesics and sedatives on the developing brains of children are largely not understood.

In trying to balance comfort (both pain and anxiety) needs for the individual patient a multitude of variables are operative, and it is easy to swing between oversedation and undersedation, particularly in the absence of a standard approach. Administration of sedative infusions and boluses is highly variable, and historically has been based on individual physician preference and nurses' subjective assessment of pain and anxiety. In general, practice variation based on physician preference has been associated with both poorer outcomes as well as higher costs. Objective scoring systems for pain and anxiety have recently been developed. But even these assessments inherently vary depending on the scoring system used, nursing experience and bias, and even time of day.[4]

Providers strive to keep patients comfortable and pain-free. However, many end up oversedated or receive levels of sedative infusions that later make weaning of ventilator support complicated and may also result in drug withdrawal issues. Most care providers are comfortable with increasing levels of sedation for patients receiving mechanical ventilation. Conversely, providers have not had as much success decreasing sedative infusions while avoiding signs of drug withdrawal.

Weaning from sedation can take from days to months and may prolong the duration of hospitalization. Children are often sent home on prolonged oral analgesic and sedative medication-weaning protocols that create risks for patient and family safety (e.g., accidental overdose, ingestion by another family member, and the inexperienced ability of the parent to monitor for signs of drug withdrawal).

Due to these and many other concerns about the detrimental effects of continuous sedation, comfort protocols are being developed and trialed worldwide in both adult and pediatric ICUs in an attempt to minimize these complications. Recent randomized trials summarized in peer-reviewed publications have demonstrated that such protocols decrease the length of mechanical ventilation and hospital length of stay.[5,6] This in turn may lead to decreases in other complications such as ventilator-associated pneumonia, ventilator-associated lung injury, hospital-acquired infection, and venous thrombotic disease.

Love, Medicine, and Chaos

Prior to the development of Seattle Children's Hospital's ICU Comfort Protocol, everyone had the right intention, and approaches to analgesia and sedation were based on training, experience, and the personal preference of individuals. No reliable method was in place as a guideline of care. Patients were frequently oversedated, and the need for prolonged sedative weaning utilizing oral methadone and diazepam was common. Many classes of sedatives were being utilized, frequently simultaneously. No controls were placed on drug escalation. Immediacy of patient comfort, with less regard for the subsequent consequences, was the norm. Many felt that our patients were receiving a tremendous amount of analgesic and sedative medication. Survey data relative to analgesia and sedation administration in ICUs internationally have similarly demonstrated wide intrahospital and interhospital variability in clinical practice.[7,8]

Homeostasis as a Pull System

In 1878 the renowned physiologist Claude Bernard noted that "all of the vital mechanisms, varied as they are, have only one object: that of preserving constant the conditions of life in the milieu interieur." Later, this concept was further developed by Walter Cannon and termed "homeostasis."[9] This framework largely provides the rationale for care of critically ill patients, who typically lose their ability to maintain homeostasis. In actuality, the provision of critical care involves iterative plan, do, check, and act (PDCA) cycles; attempting to restore some aspect of homeostasis; and employing continuous titration of various therapies in response to changes in patient status.

Interestingly, this describes a classic pull system that is customer (patient) driven and that responds only when the customer (patient) needs it. Whereas a push system might attempt to force changes in patient status at a time that might increase risk to the patient, a pull system continuously responds to changes in patient status, whether subtle or overt. PDCA cycles define titration of therapy based on feedback of changes in patient status. This logic is widely used in delivery of care in ICUs, and we felt that an ICU Comfort Protocol (a reliable method) could be successfully applied for the administration of analgesics and sedatives (see Figure 11.1).

On the Bus along a Yellow Brick Road

So began an enthusiastic journey of continuous performance improvement (CPI). First, a thorough review of existing Seattle Children's ICU analgesic and sedative practice, diverse as it was, followed by a review of the current evidence provided by the practice of other leading children's hospitals were conducted. Not surprisingly,

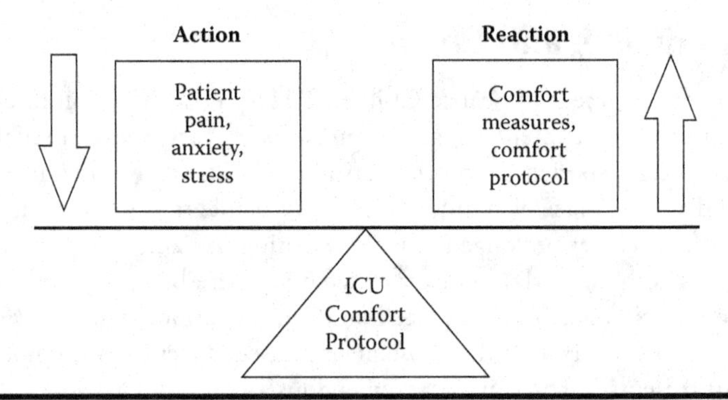

Figure 11.1 Facilitated patient comfort homeostasis utilizing the ICU Comfort Protocol. Critically ill patients experience a variety of pain, anxiety, and stress insults that vary in intensity over time. These "actions" represent the primary inputs affecting patient comfort. The ICU Comfort Protocol is a patient-demand pull system based on continuous quantitative assessment of the patient by the bedside nurse utilizing the ICU Comfort Score, with resultant measured reactions by escalating or weaning various comfort measures, including the titration of infusions of analgesic and sedative medications. This approach to comfort homeostasis is governed by reliable methods for patient comfort assessment and drug administration, and ensures that the patient receives adequate but not excessive medications to ensure comfort.

successful models of pediatric sedation protocols were almost nonexistent, and there were almost no examples of such protocols that had been thoroughly researched and published. As part of the ICU value stream mapping process, the need for development of an ICU Comfort Protocol was identified as a priority.

With support from hospital administration, a multidisciplinary team was assembled to develop and implement an ICU Comfort Protocol. From the onset, the primary goal was to improve the comfort and safety of critically ill children. It was reasoned that if this overall objective was realized, it seemed logical that decreased overall analgesic and sedative drug use, improved ICU staff satisfaction surrounding the issue of patient comfort, enhanced patient flow through the ICU (realized as shorter duration of mechanical ventilation and ICU stay), and reduced overall cost per ICU patient would also be achievable.

Rain, Mud, and Potholes

In the development of a new protocol for sedation and analgesia for the ICU, the implementation team faced many challenges and obstacles. In pediatric medicine, the patient population ranges from newborn babies with immature nervous systems and metabolism to full-grown young adults and everything in between. Pediatric critical care practitioners notably provide care for a substantial population of children with chronic special healthcare needs. Provision of appropriate analgesia and sedation is especially challenging for these vulnerable children.

Creating a protocol for the administration of medication to such a range of sizes and developmental levels was daunting. It was necessary to think critically about the sedative agents involved, the timing of administration, the peak and duration of effects, the quantitative assessment of appropriate analgesia and sedation, opportunities to minimize drug administration, and the weaning of the medications.

The implementation team sought to identify the most effective and safe sedatives and analgesics that allowed for escalation and weaning while minimizing withdrawal effects. Choosing intravenous agents with dosing that could be easily converted for oral administration was also deemed to be important to decrease hospital length of stay.

The next challenge came in the selection of a sedation scale, as the entire proposed protocol revolved around nursing responses to a patient's "comfort score." A sedation scale provides a target around which the patient's needs are matched with medication administration or withdrawal.

Ideally, a reliable sedation scale

1. Reflects the presence and intensity of clinical conditions requiring analgesia or sedation;
2. Targets an optimal level of sedation;
3. Defines clearly discrete, ideally nonoverlapping, comfort strata;
4. Identifies a sufficient number of strata to permit drug titration;
5. Exhibits reliability and validity;
6. Demonstrates ease of education and implementation; and
7. Responds to longitudinal changes in comfort level.

In the current discussion, the sedation scale reflects the "check" step in repetitive PDCA cycles attempting to restore patient comfort homeostasis. While there are many reliable scales available for adults, there are few designed for pediatric care, and certainly no gold standard exists.

To simplify the education process, the implementation team decided to continue to use the same comfort and sedation scale that had been used in the ICU over the past few years. This ICU Comfort Score was developed and validated within the Seattle Children's Hospital ICU, meets most of the criteria for an effective sedation scale, and demonstrates excellent interrater reliability. It should be appreciated that other ICUs have demonstrated success using alternative scales such as the Comfort Scale and Richmond Agitation-Sedation Scale (RASS). Astutely, the team recognized that it was important to not introduce another change into the system, as the other aspects of the protocol represented a significant departure from the status quo.

Another acknowledged challenge in delivering effective and safe sedation for patients receiving mechanical ventilation is providing training and education for all ICU providers. Medical staff caring for these fragile patients would need education regarding the medications being used, anticipated side effects, pharmacokinetics, and the treatment of complications. Teaching would need to include standard doses, peak effect time, and the metabolic elimination of these drugs. Ultimately, such education would improve provider knowledge of and skill in the administration of analgesic or sedative infusion and bolus dosing in the ICU.

All ICU service providers were stakeholders that would need to be involved in the rollout of an ICU Comfort Protocol, as patient safety and work flow would be compromised if different services utilized different protocols. Designing standard work for a common ICU intervention would undoubtedly be beneficial to ICU patients, but convincing anesthesia, surgery, and specialty service colleagues of this assertion was another story. Encouraging participation by these groups was essential to create consensus for and ultimately compliance with an ICU Comfort Protocol.

The Importance of Multidisciplinary Leadership

With clear goals in mind, and recognition of the many challenges to be faced, a multidisciplinary implementation team began work on designing a protocol. Key team members and their respective roles included the following.

Physician Leader

It was important to identify someone from the ICU staff who was respected clinically, had an ICU administrative role, and was knowledgeable about continuous performance improvement. This leader was knowledgeable about ICU sedation practices and helped to shape the ICU Comfort Protocol. Additionally, this person was also involved with ICU strategic planning and facilitated inclusion of the protocol into ongoing ICU CPI work.

A formidable challenge for this role was the development of consensus among physicians, with focus on the importance of relinquishing autonomy (i.e., to the bedside nurse) while simultaneously enthusiastically embracing accountability for the ICU Comfort Protocol team model. The generation of clinically meaningful data would be particularly important for this group of largely skeptical stakeholders. For this transition, the director of critical care medicine served as the physician leader.

Process Owner

Identification of a single person to champion the need for standardization and to be responsible for the process was essential. This person assumed principal ownership for all aspects of development and implementation of the ICU Comfort Protocol. Responsibilities of this individual included conducting individual and team meetings to provide education and promote consensus, overseeing construction and "just do it" PDCA revision of the algorithm, supervising physician and nursing education, and organizing objective data collection to compare effects of the intervention. The process owner was a pediatric critical care medicine fellow.

Clinical Nurse Specialist

An energetic nursing leader was an integral component of the team. She championed the need for the proposed change, and encouraged and educated the nursing staff. The clinical nurse specialist had outstanding bedside, administrative, and people skills that were critical in both development and implementation of the protocol. She was respected by the nursing staff, a characteristic that was instrumental in facilitating change in practice.

This individual managed the grassroots education phase of implementation, oversaw the auditing portion of compliance analysis, and fostered protocol sustainability. A particular challenge for this leadership role included recognition of a differential approach to experienced nurses versus more junior nurses. The former nurses were definitely more suspicious of the process due to lingering nightmares of previous failed "reengineering promises." On the other hand, new graduate nurses viewed ICU Comfort Protocol implementation as another interesting facet of orientation education. The nurse manager employed the "dangling carrot" of empowering bedside nursing practice (essentially independent serial and continuous PDCA cycles) as the key element of the ICU Comfort Protocol (see Figure 11.2).

ICU Pharmacist

Pharmacy staff must be involved in the creation of any clinical protocol that involves the administration of medications. For the ICU Comfort Protocol, the lead pharmacist was instrumental in providing nursing and physician education and information about the sedative medications that were considered for the algorithm and comparing agents routinely used at other institutions. Based on research linking delirium to the use of benzodiazepines, she played an important role in creating a protocol that minimized the use of this class of sedatives. The pharmacy staff became responsible for bedside auditing of compliance and ongoing, real-time education of staff on rounds and at the bedside.

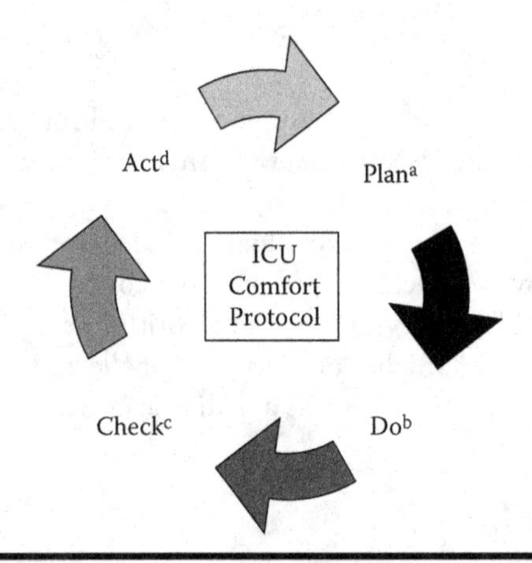

Figure 11.2 Nursing bedside interaction with the ICU Comfort Protocol. In this scheme, the titration of ICU comfort is portrayed as a continuous series of PDCA cycles that characterize delivery of critical care in general. (a) Planning involves implementation of the comfort plan derived during daily interdisciplinary rounds. Depending on the patient status, this target may involve anything on a spectrum from very light or no sedation to heavy sedation where the patient exhibits minimal spontaneous movement. This target will usually change over time. (b) Doing reflects administration of the prescribed standard concentration analgesic and/or sedative infusion. (c) Checking refers to real-time, dynamic bedside nursing assessment of the patient's ICU Comfort Score, based on quantifiable symptoms reflecting status of pain and anxiety. (d) Acting characterizes the empowered bedside nurse titrating the analgesic and sedative infusions based on the target comfort goal (a, stated above) and the patient's current status (c, stated above). Because the ICU Comfort Protocol prescribes a scheduled assessment every four hours, the process functions as standard work and not just a reliable method. Protocol forcing function of the scheduled assessments provides the pull in this methodology.

Designing and Marketing the Standard Work Product

After gathering similar protocols from both adult and pediatric institutions and reviewing the existing literature, development of a general framework and theory of what the implementation team considered to be an optimal approach to comfort began. Protocols based primarily on continuous infusions as well as those based solely on bolus medications were both considered. Ultimately, the team concluded that a hybrid of these two approaches would be most effective and created an algorithm in which bolus medication doses were given to achieve a specific acute effect with a low rate of medication infusion provided for background effect. The protocol suggested frequent bolus doses to maximize speed of effect, while the continuous infusions were titrated slowly based on the number of boluses required over a specified time interval to reach a targeted level of comfort.

Morphine was selected as the primary protocol medication due to its well-known safety and efficacy profile among children. As beneficial synergistic effects between opioids and benzodiazepines are well described, the team opted to include a benzodiazepine (lorazepam) as an adjuvant medication for use when comfort was difficult to obtain with morphine alone, thereby allowing individualization within a standard protocol.

Even though surgical patients (admitted following surgery or invasive procedures) and medical patients (admitted for pneumonia or seizures, for example) might have very different sedative and analgesic needs, the team decided to proceed with the development of a single ICU Comfort Protocol. With the benefit of hindsight, this was the obvious correct standard decision.

Education Phase

Educating over 200 nurses, as well as a multitude of physicians and other care providers interfacing with the ICU over a short period of time, was only possible with thorough preparation and planning. Initially, the team scheduled a month of preparation time, followed by two months of focused education prior to the planned implementation date. Practically, this proved too lofty a goal, as implementation was delayed by almost two months. However, setting a deadline forced focus on the task. A preparation phase consisted of development of in-service sessions, production of laminated bedside cards and posters to place around the ICU, and training of the nursing governance team, a group of influential nurses who are elected by their peers to guide ICU nursing policy. This leadership group was involved in the early development of the protocol (see "Creating Consensus ('Buy-In')" section), and was trained as "super users" to answer common implementation questions.

The clinical nurse specialist and the process owner created a PowerPoint presentation that outlined the need for an ICU Comfort Protocol, reasons for moving forward with protocol implementation, a description and discussion of the actual standard work, and a case-based quiz at the end. Twenty separate sessions were led by the nursing governance team and involved small groups of ten nurses over a one-hour period usually scheduled during their regular shift. Two additional resource nurses were employed during the weeks of training in order to facilitate patient care while bedside nurses received training. A computer-based module was also created in order to provide bedside continuing education training for new staff during their orientation.

In addition to the nursing staff training, a training session was held with the ICU attending staff and fellows. Each month four new residents begin their rotations in the ICU. These individuals ultimately are responsible for transcribing the majority of orders for ICU patients (including ICU Comfort Protocol orders). Understanding that it would be almost impossible to teach the protocol to nearly 100 residents at one time in one place, a decision instead was made to provide just-in-time training about the protocol during their ICU orientation. They were also provided pocket cards with a figure outlining the algorithm on one side and tips and ordering assistance along with the ICU Comfort Scale printed on the other side.

Creating Consensus ("Buy-In")

Hospital administration agreed that an ICU Comfort Protocol should be implemented, and that it was essential that the ICU attending physicians were engaged and receptive to the protocol. These individuals were met with early in the protocol's development and frequently one-on-one to discuss concerns and suggestions. These ICU physicians were reassured that protocol-driven care (standard work) need not stifle individual decision creativity or clinical judgment. The success in treatment of acute lymphocytic leukemia (ALL) over the last 50 years was provided as a relevant example. In the 1950s, a diagnosis of leukemia in a child was essentially a death sentence; however, due to iterative therapeutic PDCA clinical research cycles and rigorous standardization of care, over 90 percent of children routinely now survive.

Understanding individual case exceptions was emphasized, as this information would inform future adjustment of the protocol. Accordingly, ICU staff were told that they would be able to identify exceptions from the protocol whenever they felt it was clinically necessary, but that the team would be carefully tracking these exceptions. Needless to say, not everyone was happy prior to implementation. However, with patience, listening, addressing concerns, and providing data collected along the way, feelings began to change. Eventually, the protocol took care of itself with its own success as the staunchest opponents soon became allies as they watched the ICU Comfort Protocol work and clinical care improve.

The nursing staff initially felt burdened by the need to learn a new protocol and change their clinical practice. They soon realized that they had gained autonomy within the structure of the protocol and were no longer dependent on calling a physician to obtain orders for analgesic and sedative infusion rate changes to maintain patient comfort. They were provided new tools to deliver analgesia and sedation and were able to take pride in how well they maintained comfort with minimal medication.

The process owner also met with physicians representing medical, anesthesia, and surgical services. By including them prior to protocol implementation, we were able to make them partners in the development of the protocol, thereby increasing buy-in and trust.

A Remarkable Story

Implementation of the ICU Comfort Protocol is a remarkable story (see Figure 11.3). In less than two years, introduction of this standard work has significantly

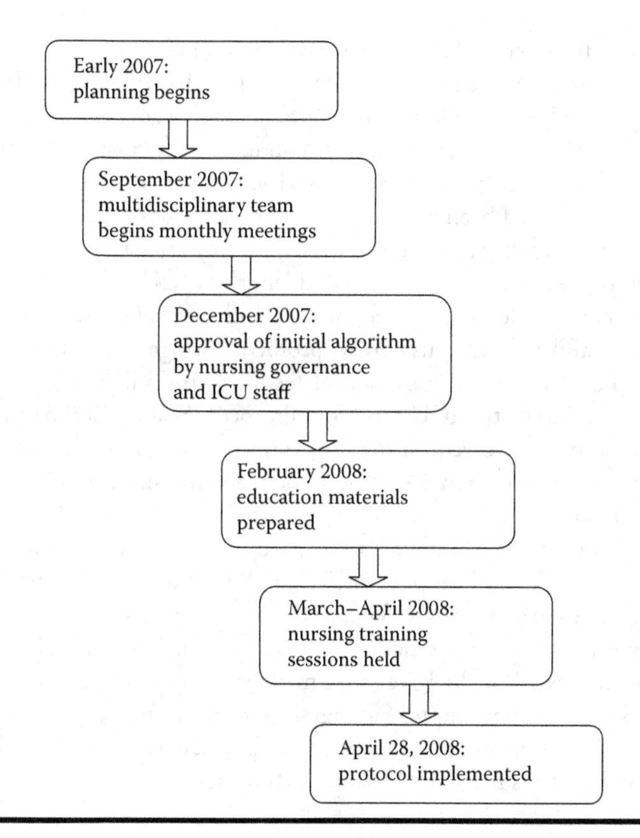

Figure 11.3 ICU Comfort Protocol implementation timeline. The high-level milestones to implement the ICU Comfort Protocol.

improved patient care and patient flow through the ICU. We have seen a dramatic reduction in overall benzodiazepine use. The team tracked compliance, provided bedside education and feedback on daily rounds, and prospectively gathered data for a human subjects institutional review board-approved study examining the first three months of protocol introduction. By February 2009, initial data and experience were presented and favorably received at a national critical care meeting. By the summer of 2010, a publication comparing the year before and the year after protocol implementation was drafted. Data from this study show that the protocol has markedly decreased the duration of both benzodiazepine and morphine infusions.[10] As larger groups of patients are followed over time, statistically significant decreased days of mechanical ventilation and ICU length of stay are also expected.

Most performance improvement experts would identify implementation of the reliable ICU Comfort Protocol method as a continuous performance improvement success. Seattle Children's ICU experienced profound culture change around providing continuous comfort to critically ill children in a little over a year. Patient comfort is now discussed daily on medical rounds and plays a major role in nursing shift sign-outs. Subjective survey results demonstrate that the ICU staff is more satisfied with how analgesia and sedation are provided now as compared to before the change. ICU respiratory therapy staff now conducts daily readiness trials assessing suitability for discontinuation of mechanical ventilation on all relevant patients. Though this routine had been previously attempted without success, it is now part of the daily care of each patient and represents a key aspect of the overall goal to decrease days of mechanical ventilation and length of ICU stay.

Improved communication with anesthesia and surgical colleagues has encouraged continued and expanded use of the protocol with good results. This ongoing attention to the protocol and provision of feedback and support to the ICU staff has helped to maintain the ICU Comfort Protocol. Seattle Children's pharmacy staff remains actively involved on medical rounds tracking levels of sedation and the need for bolus medication dosing, and occasionally surveys for ICU Comfort Protocol compliance.

Online materials and computer-based modules allow new nursing graduates, newly hired care staff, and float pool nurses quick and easy access to protocol training. Seattle Children's electronic feedback system permits any staff member to comment, praise, or challenge sedation practices. All such feedback is immediately reviewed and addressed by the ICU nurse manager, and is utilized to drive iterative PDCA cycles to revise and improve analgesia and sedation practice as appropriate. On the suggestion of the nursing staff, a related protocol designed for nonmechanically ventilated patients has also been successfully adopted.

Other ICU Pull Systems

1. Traditionally, medical rounding once or twice a day is focused on the creation of a daily care plan. This approach results in stuttered patient flow through the ICU, as opposed to an ideal model where continuous bedside rounding would again mimic iterative PDCA cycles and provide more at-the-moment, patient-driven escalation or weaning of therapy in synchrony with the natural course of the illness. In this latter ideal state, rounding becomes an exercise of determining where the patient is positioned relative to an expected natural course trajectory for a given diagnosis or disease. Work in the ICU becomes 24/7/365.
2. A variety of visual cues is now commonplace in ICUs to ensure the adequacy of a myriad of supplies needed to provide critical care. A less utilized tool, a patient status board or trajectory andon, summarizes the state of a number of variables that relate to pull of the patient toward ICU discharge.

   These variables might include the absence of hemodynamic instability, the resolution of pulmonary failure, the tolerance of enteral nutrition, the discontinuation of nonessential invasive catheters, the provision of transfer education to the family, the identification of a receiving care team, the composition of transfer orders, the completion of respiratory therapy, and nursing and physician communication with respective ward counterparts.

Each activity is coded as red (not finished), yellow (in progress), or green (completed). This visual tool allows all care providers to assess the dynamics of overall patient flow in the ICU, the trajectory for an individual patient, and what needs to occur next to pull a particular patient toward discharge from the pediatric intensive care unit (PICU). Empty ICU rooms are similarly coded as red (dirty), yellow (being cleaned), or green (ready for admission) (see Figure 11.4).

3. Standard work or clinical pathways for individual diseases should identify expected patient trajectories and hence facilitate patient flow. This information delineates specific discharge criteria at the time of admission as well as expected patient status at various times following ICU admission. In addition, the clinical pathway suggests specific interventions as well as laboratory and imaging studies along the way. It is designed to standardize the overall approach to a patient, such that the effect of altering this approach can actually be measured. It is not designed to stifle care-provider creativity. Reasons for not following clinical pathway standard work are documented and summarized to iteratively improve the standard work algorithm.
4. A number of critical care standard work and decision support tools that provide adequately explicit algorithms to promote pull therapy to continuously reestablish physiologic and biochemical homeostasis are under investigation. All of these tools employ the concept of iterative PDCA cycles with scheduled serial assessments and actions based on an overriding care plan and results of the assessments.

   Although still controversial, a multitude of studies indicate that high blood sugar among critically ill adults and children is associated with increased morbidity and mortality. Ongoing clinical investigations are attempting to define both the benefits and risks of so-called tight glucose control utilizing continuous or scheduled blood glucose measurements linked to titration of a continuous infusion of insulin. In this regard, carefully designed computerized decision support tools have been shown to be superior to simple paper protocols or clinician judgment in terms of achieving a target blood glucose value (accuracy) and reducing variation around this target (precision).

Similar computerized decision support tools have been designed for safe weaning of mechanical ventilation support among patients with acute lung injury, with goals of reducing duration of mechanical ventilation as well as ventilator-associated lung injury. Persistent need for mechanical ventilation represents the most common reason for prolonged ICU length of stay, and achieving both goals would have the effect of pulling the patient toward earlier ICU discharge.

Another common intensive care intervention involves infusion of various vasoactive and cardiotonic drugs to support cardiac output, blood pressure, and organ

Room	Room Status	Assigned Nurse	Assigned Resident	No Hemodynamic Instability	No Pulmonary Instability	Nonessential Catheters Removed	Discharge Criteria Met	Plan for Ward Analgesia/Anxiolysis	Nutritional Plan in Place	Family Education Complete	Floor Orders in Place	Attending to Attending Signout	Resident Signout	RT Signout	Care Coord/Social Work	Receiving Unit Ready	Date/Time Ready for Discharge	Notes
4134-1	Y	Claire	Frank	G	G	G	G	G	G	G	G	R	Y	G	G	R		
4134-2	Y	Betsy	Susan	G	R	R	R	Y	G	R	R	R	R	R	R	R		
4135	Y	Kelly	Susan	G	G	G	G	G	G	R	G	R	G	G	G	Y		
4136-1	Y	Vanessa	Frank	G	Y	R	R	Y	G	R	R	R	R	G	G	R		
4136-2	Y	Vanessa	Frank	R	R	R	R	R	R	R	R	R	R	R	R	R		
4137	Y	Denise	Elizabeth	G	G	G	G	G	G	G	G	G	G	G	G	G	12/15, 0730	
4138	Y	Annika	Susan	G	G	Y	G	G	G	Y	R	R	G	G	G	Y		
4139	Y	Teaessa	Susan	R	Y	R	R	Y	Y	Y	R	R	R	R	R	R		
4140-1	G																	
4140-2	Y	Claire	Ahmad	Y	R	R	R	R	R	R	R	R	R	R	R	R		
4141	Y	Denise	Elizabeth	G	G	G	G	G	G	G	G	R	G	G	G	G	12/14, 1900	
4142-1	R																	
4142-2	Y	Gloria	Ahmad	G	G	G	R	G	G	R	R	R	R	R	R	R		
4143	Y	Karen	Ahmad	G	Y	R	R	G	G	R	R	R	R	R	R	R		
4144	Y	Gloria	Elizabeth	Y	G	R	R	Y	R	Y	R	R	R	Y	R	R		

Figure 11.4 Trajectory andon summarizing individual and overall patient trajectory in the ICU. This simple visual tool permits rapid assessment of individual as well as total ICU patient status. Specifically, it identifies tasks that need to be completed in order to pull the patient toward ICU discharge. Red (R): incomplete or unresolved; yellow (Y): in progress or resolving; and green (G): complete or resolved. In general, more overall red hue indicates higher ICU illness intensity and slower patient flow toward ICU discharge, while more overall green hue indicates lower ICU illness intensity and faster flow toward ICU discharge.

perfusion. By continuously assessing a variety of input variables such as blood pressure, oxygen saturation of the blood, vascular volume status, and urine output, an algorithm can be derived to provide objective decisions regarding the escalation or weaning of such infusions. The complexity of such tools increases exponentially with the number of input variables.

It is easy to envision how such decision support tools could be implemented in a closed-loop fashion. For example, a device providing continuous monitoring of a patient's blood glucose can provide an electronic signal to a pump controlling an infusion of insulin. Similarly, devices continuously monitoring patients' exhaled carbon dioxide and blood oxygen saturation can provide electronic signaling to a mechanical ventilator to automatically adjust rate or depth of mechanical breaths or oxygen concentration being delivered. In the future, such approaches may not only facilitate patient flow in intensive care units but also allow for built-in error proofing.

Conclusions

The provision of critical care medicine naturally relates to a series of PDCA exercises all inexorably coupled with restoration of a patient's biochemical and physiologic homeostasis. When these cycles are delineated with standard work and longitudinally linked, a natural flow system is realized that pulls the patient toward steady recovery and more timely discharge from the ICU. This chapter discussed how such a system was designed and implemented to provide adequate but not excessive comfort for critically ill children. Similar approaches are being developed and tested to rectify other aberrations from homeostasis during critical illness, and include standard work, adequately explicit algorithms for the control of blood glucose, provision of mechanical ventilation, and delivery of vasoactive and cardiotonic drug infusions.

Eventually, an almost unimaginable amount of patient data will be captured from the complete electronic health record. These patient profile data related to specific conditions or diagnoses will be continuously updated to generate a graphical description of patient trajectory. Such systems will provide early identification of patient vulnerable periods per sophisticated programs designed to assess variance from expected trajectory and hence to avoid errors and to facilitate pull of the patient through his or her critical illness experience. Comparison of treatment effects and outcomes across healthcare systems will be possible and will drive iterative improvements in the specific standard work that will lead to precision in expected pulled patient trajectories.

Notes

1. J. R. Jacobs, J. G. Reves, and P. S. A. Glass, "Rationale and Technique for Continuous Infusions in Anesthesia," *International Anesthesiology Clinics* 29 (1991): 23–38.
2. J. P. Kress, A. S. Pohlman, and J. B. Hall, "Sedation and Analgesia in the Intensive Care Unit," *American Journal of Respiratory and Critical Care Medicine* 166 (2002): 1024–28.
3. J. D. Tobias, "Tolerance, Withdrawal, and Physical Dependency after Long-Term Sedation and Analgesia of Children in the Pediatric Intensive Care Unit," *Critical Care Medicine* 28 (2000): 2122–32.
4. E. Ista, M. de Hoog, D. Tibboel, and M. van Dijk, "Implementation of Standard Sedation Management in Pediatric Intensive Care: Effective and Feasible?" *Journal of Clinical Nursing* 18, no. 17 (September 2009): 2511–20.
5. A. D. Brook, T. S. Ahrens, R. Schaiff, D. Prentice, G. Sherman, W. Shannon, and M. H. Kollef, "Effect of a Nursing-Implemented Sedation Protocol on the Duration of Mechanical Ventilation," *Critical Care Medicine* 27 (1999): 2609–15.
6. T. D. Girard, J. P. Dress, B. D. Fuchs, J. W. Thaomaon, W. D. Schweickert, B. T. Pun, D. B. Taichman et al., "Efficacy and Safety of a Paired Sedation and Ventilator Weaning Protocol for Mechanically Ventilated Patients in Intensive Care (Awakening and Breathing Controlled Trial): A Randomised Controlled Trial," *Lancet* 371 (2008): 126–34.
7. S. Mehta, L. Burry, S. Fischer, J. C. Martinez-Motta, D. Hallett, D. Bowman, C. Wong, M. O. Meade, T. E. Stewart, and D. J. Cook, "Canadian Survey of the Use of Sedatives, Analgesic, and Neuromuscular Blocking Agents in Critically Ill Patients," *Critical Care Medicine* 34 (2006): 374–80.
8. M. D. Twite, A. Rashid, J. Zuk, and R. H. Friesen, "Sedation, Analgesia, and Neuromuscular Blockade in the Pediatric Intensive Care Unit: Survey of Fellowship Training Programs," *Pediatric Critical Care Medicine* 5, no. 6 (November 2004): 521–32.
9. W. B. Cannon, "Organization for Physiologic Homeostasis," *Physiological Reviews* 9 (1929): 399–431.
10. K. H. Deeter, D. A. Ridling, G. Linggi, M. A. King, L. Di Gennaro, A. M. Lynn, and J. J. Zimmerman, "Introduction of a Sedation Protocol in a Pediatric ICU," *Critical Care Medicine* 36, suppl. (2008): A181 (Abstract 701). SCCM 38th Critical Care Congress, Nashville, Tennessee, January 31–February 4, 2009.

Epilogue

Jerry J. Zimmerman

In the time since the publication of the first edition, we have continued to use clinical standard work (CSW) with embedded pull systems to reduce waiting and waste by cuing preemptive interventions. This epilogue describes three examples of the use of pull systems in the pediatric intensive care unit (PICU) at Seattle Children's Hospital: the use of comfort protocols, treatment of diabetic ketoacidosis, and weaning from mechanical ventilation.

During the resuscitation phase of critical illness, with an ever-present threat of patient death or disability, activation of care providers' own stress responses promotes continuous vigilance, heightened awareness, and timely escalation of critical care. However, the weaning phase of critical illness accounts for most of the length of stay in the PICU. In this less intense phase, critical care providers may favor the stable status quo and be reluctant to pursue de-escalation of therapy even when the patient's physiology dictates that it is appropriate to do so. Such a "safe" strategy decreases the value of critical care by exposing the patient to unnecessary risks and increasing costs of care. During this phase of critical illness, CSW with embedded pull systems may be particularly valuable, because they provide "overt encouragement signals" to care providers to continually advance recovery by steadily weaning patients from the accoutrements of critical care.

Comfort Protocol PDCA (Plan–Do–Check–Act)

Provision of analgesia and sedation are among the most common tools utilized by critical care providers. One of our earliest successes in using CSW to develop a pull system in the Seattle Children's Hospital PICU was the creation of a comfort protocol. In this case the pull system is a sustained target comfort score as established on daily rounds by the PICU care team. As previously reported, implementation of the comfort protocol CSW was associated with marked decreased administration of both opiates and benzodiazepines as well as reduction in duration of mechanical ventilation and PICU length of stay.[1] Our research suggests that empowering bedside nurses to continuously wean analgesia and sedation in the setting of a sustained target comfort score may be preferable to daily interruption of analgesics and sedatives.[2] Unfortunately early success of the comfort protocol CSW was short-lived: new drugs and new care staff in the absence of real-time run chart metrics, lack of an ongoing educational program, and dissolution of the CSW champion team resulted in loss of all previous gains in this clinical arena.[3]

With new knowledge of the risk of benzodiazepines, the importance of scheduled screening for delirium and the arrival of dexmedetomidine as a possible preferred sedative agent,[4,5] a revised comfort protocol was implemented and is currently under quantitative analysis. It seems clear that use of a sustained target comfort score pull system and active bedside weaning of analgesics and sedatives can reduce drug exposure and PICU resource utilization. This approach may also reduce the incidence of delirium that is known to be an antecedent of multiple adverse outcomes among patients in the PICU. Moving forward, the PICU team must respect and address the most difficult but ultimately most important characteristic of successful CPI, namely, a plan for CSW maintenance (the "check" and "act" of PDCA).

Diabetic Ketoacidosis Clinical Standard Work Development

Diabetic ketoacidosis (DKA) represents a common diagnosis in the PICU. Children with DKA frequently present critically ill, with hyperglycemia, ketotic metabolic acidosis, dehydration, and multiple electrolyte imbalances. The best available evidence suggests that a slow, deliberate correction of these abnormalities is preferable to rapid correction, to avoid the most lethal complication of DKA treatment, namely, cerebral edema, or brain swelling.[6] During design of CSW for DKA, care providers identified beta-hydroxybutyrate (BHOB) as a biomarker of DKA intensity. Monitoring BHOB provides a readily available, quantitative assessment of a biochemical pull system that can be used to guide DKA therapy.

We have learned that it is critically important to pay attention to the information that the BHOB pull system provides or risk hypoglycemia and potential neurologic complications. CSW for DKA typically involves multiple scheduled laboratory studies, and it is likely that value of the process could be enhanced with Lean methodology. However, employing BHOB as a biomarker of the DKA resolution pull system reduces duration of PICU stay and risk of hypoglycemia for children admitted with DKA.[7]

Since initial implementation of CSW for DKA, several iterative improvements have been incorporated, following real-time identification of emerging issues with run charts. In the course of this work, we have found it essential to have an interested, longitudinally engaged continuous process improvement team proactively select clinically meaningful metrics to track (e.g., hypoglycemia as discussed earlier). Two issues related to CSW for DKA remain challenging. First, as various contingencies for DKA care are addressed, the associated electronic medical record order set becomes increasingly complex and cumbersome. Second, although a wealth of reference information is available in the DKA order set for providers (essentially a systematic review of existing literature), use of the DKA order set may have resulted in "dumbing down" of novice providers. It would be preferable to have a forced-function electronic pull system that would engage the practitioner with just-in-time, state-of-the-art DKA education.

The Future: Clinical Standard Work for Mechanical Ventilation

Provision of mechanical ventilation represents the primary reason for prolonged PICU length of stay. Decreasing duration of mechanical ventilation can improve the value of PICU care by decreasing exposure to drugs, decreasing laboratory tests and associated risks of anemia and transfusion, decreasing the risk of ventilator-associated pneumonia, and decreasing respiratory care costs. CSW for mechanical ventilation is inexorably linked to the earlier discussion of analgesia and sedation, but deserves separate consideration.

Again, intensivists are quick to intervene with mechanical ventilation support when they encounter children with dyspnea but typically display a more laissez-faire attitude for weaning such support. At the time of this chapter revision, a computerized decision-support tool is being evaluated as a pull system to hasten weaning of mechanical ventilation in the Seattle Children's Hospital PICU.[8,9] Based on an algorithm originating with the Acute Respiratory Distress Syndrome (ARDS) Network,[10] and utilizing information about the patient's current mechanical ventilator support and oxygenation and ventilation status, the tool forces a potential weaning decision every four hours rather than the usual stuttered, haphazard approach. In the spirit of iterative CPI, following a rigorous safety evaluation, the tool will be implemented and compared to existing usual mechanical ventilation weaning practice.

Notes

1. K. H. Deeter, M. A. King, D. Ridling, G. L. Irby, A. M. Lynn, and J. J. Zimmerman, "Successful Implementation of a Pediatric Sedation Protocol for Mechanically Ventilated Patients," *Critical Care Medicine* 39 (2011): 683–88.
2. M. A. Curley, D. Wypij, R. S. Watson, M. J. Grant, L. A. Asaro, I. M. Cheifetz, B. L. Dodson et al., "Protocolized Sedation vs Usual Care in Pediatric Patients Mechanically Ventilated for Acute Respiratory Failure: A Randomized Clinical Trial," *JAMA* 313 (2015): 379–89.
3. B. Yaghmai, L. Di Gennaro, and J. J. Zimmerman, "50: A PICU Sedation Protocol for Mechanically Ventilated Patients Needs Sustenance beyond Implementation," *Critical Care Medicine* 42 (2014): A1381.
4. A. S. Czaja and J. J. Zimmerman, "The Use of Dexmedetomidine in Critically Ill Children," *Pediatric Critical Care Medicine* 10 (2009): 381–86.
5. L. D. Whalen, J. L. Di Gennaro, G. A. Irby, O. Yanay, and J. J. Zimmerman, "Long-Term Dexmedetomidine Use and Safety Profile Among Critically Ill Children and Neonates," *Pediatric Critical Care Medicine* 15 (2014): 706–14.
6. J. Wolfsdorf, M. E. Craig, D. Daneman, D. Dunger, J. Edge, W. Lee, A. Rosenbloom, M. Sperling, and R. Hanas, "Diabetic Ketoacidosis in Children and Adolescents with Diabetes," *Pediatric Diabetes* 10, suppl. 12 (2000): 118–33.
7. I. H. Koves, M. G. Leu, S. Spencer, J. C. Popalisky, K. Drummond, E. Beardsley, K. Klee, and J. J. Zimmerman, "Improving Care for Pediatric Diabetic Ketoacidosis," *Pediatrics* 134 (2014): e848–e856.
8. R. G. Khemani, K. Sward, A. Morris, J. M. Dean, and C. J. Newth, "Variability in Usual Care Mechanical Ventilation for Pediatric Acute Lung Injury: The Potential Benefit of a Lung Protective Computer Protocol," *Intensive Care Medicine* 37 (2011): 1840–48.
9. P. A. Jouvet, V. Payen, F. Gauvin, G. Emeriaud, and J. Lacroix, "Weaning Children from Mechanical Ventilation with a Computer-Driven Protocol: A Pilot Trial," *Intensive Care Medicine* 39 (2013): 919–25.
10. Acute Respiratory Distress Syndrome Network, "Ventilation with Lower Tidal Volumes as Compared with Traditional Tidal Volumes for Acute Lung Injury and the Acute Respiratory Distress Syndrome," *New England Journal of Medicine* 342 (2000): 1301–08.

Chapter 12

Patient Rounding: Delivering Compassionate Care through Clinical Standard Work

Glen Tamura and Darren Migita

Inpatient Rounding: Why Are We Doing This?

They arrive at the doors of our hospital afflicted by infection, tumor, and trauma. Often they come to us cradled in the arms of their parents, whose fear of what will occur next is surpassed only by their love for their child. Parents instinctively hope that within the walls of this hospital lie the expertise and medical machinery to cure; and when disease has exceeded their abilities as parents, they entrust that child to us. Yet a hospital remains an unfamiliar landscape replete with a new language, razor-sharp needles, pulsating magnetic resonance imaging (MRI) scanners, and hordes of white-coated personnel scurrying from here to there in a seemingly uninterpretable dance. A child's cure often lies at the end of a course difficult to navigate or endure. Tubes will be placed into their bodies, and difficult-to-pronounce medications will be injected into their bloodstream. We may further ask that radioactive tracer dye is swallowed, that blood be siphoned daily for testing, or that they be made temporarily unconscious for a painful procedure during which multiple sharp objects will be brought to bear.

Adding to the patient and family's challenge is the asymmetry that exists between medical professionals and the patient and family. The gap of knowledge between the two parties is generally wide and apparent. Without a means of communicating about each step of a child's care, a hospital stay can devolve into a frightening experience even absent an awful prognosis. Indeed, the application of medical interventions without proper explanation can appear as torture to the untrained eye. In the end, this series of events may lead to a cure, but if we fail to pause to inform, answer questions, acknowledge fears, explain the unexplained, and listen with the utmost humility, we have erred. The art of medicine is not merely the proper execution of applied science but the application of that science as art. Art in medicine is a combination of knowledge, partnership, compassion, transparency, and action. We seek to bring this art to the bedside for every patient every day by applying the principles of reliable methods and clinical standard work. Our story is about one aspect of clinical standard work, the creation of family-centered daily bedside rounds.

The Inpatient Medicine Service: The Players

The word "teaching" has special meaning at Seattle Children's Hospital (SCH). Graduates from medical school who choose a career in pediatrics come to us for an additional three years of intensive training, known as "residency," and these young physicians are known as "residents." Those in their first year are referred to as "interns," and those in their final two years are known as "senior residents." Attending physicians, or "attendings," are those who have completed their residency and have varying amounts of formal specialty training. Attending physicians have ultimate responsibility for all medical decisions and oversee the training of the residents. At SCH, patients on the inpatient medical service are divided among and cared for by three teams. Each team is composed of attendings, senior residents, and interns.

There are other players critical to the care of the patient. The bedside nurses log the greatest number of direct hours at the patient's bedside. They ensure that the plan for the day is executed and report any changes in clinical status to the MDs. Due to their nearly continuous presence at the patient's bedside, they are most likely to be privy to emotions in raw unfiltered form.

Pharmacists also play a critical role. They assess the patients' medications on a daily basis, look for potentially dangerous drug interactions, and, most important, ensure that dosages are correct. In short, they ensure that we do not harm our patients with the very drugs intended for cure.

Rounding: Where We've Been

"Rounding" is a long-standing tradition in medicine. Although definitions vary, it can be loosely viewed as a meeting in which the clinical problems of a particular patient are discussed by the care team. Prior to 2003, our system of rounding was highly variable. Each morning, attendings and interns would gather in conference rooms and discuss each patient on their service. Once this was accomplished, the team would then scatter to examine certain, but not all, patients and write the orders of the day. Depending on the day of the week, the preferences of the attending, and, perhaps, the nature of the patients, rounds were different every day. For this and other reasons, this system of rounding was fraught with difficulties.

Due to the day-to-day variability of this system, families and registered nurses (RNs) could not reliably predict which members of the care team would meet with them, if any at all. The daily plan formulated in the conference room was created without the input of RNs or family, who often held critical information about a patient's condition. As a result, plans were quite often changed as the day progressed, leading to significant rework and further confusion for the patient and family. Moreover, communication between the key players and patients was not reliable. Plans were often initiated without explanation. One could imagine the dissatisfaction of a parent whose child was whisked off for a computerized tomography (CT) scan without having met with the MDs who ordered the study! Without a deeper understanding of reliable methods and standard work, errors such as these were accepted by the care team as a regrettable part of the norm.

Sir William Osler, who many describe as the founder of modern medicine, pioneered the tradition of teaching in medicine at Johns Hopkins during the late 1800s. He disliked didactics and fervently insisted that physicians in training learned best at the patients' bedside—a principle that holds true to this day. In fact, his hope was that his epitaph would read, "He brought medical students into the wards for teaching." Osler stated, "I desire no other epitaph … than the statement that I taught medical students in the wards, as I regard this as by far the most useful and important work I have been called upon to do." Undoubtedly, rounds at SCH had evolved into something much less patient oriented than Olser envisioned.

Solution: Reliable Method for Rounds

Problems associated with rounds, including serious clinical errors related to poor communication, motivated SCH leaders to find ways to improve the process. SCH had begun to use continuous performance improvement (CPI) tools adapted from the Toyota Production System and had used this methodology on other projects with good success. Clinical and administrative leaders recognized that the complex multidisciplinary rounding process, which was neither capable nor efficient, could be improved using CPI tools. This decision to use CPI tools for this project was a major advancement in the hospital's use of CPI methodology, as it was the first time such a complex clinical and teaching process had been addressed using this approach.

Three process owners led the project: Georgeann Hagland, RN, director of the medical unit; Dr. Sterling Clarren, medical director of the inpatient medical unit; and Dr. Richard Shugerman, residency program director. In addition, one of the pediatric residents, Dr. Maneesh Batra, was also recruited to ensure that the resident perspective was heard and respected. Together, this group designed and planned a Rapid Process Improvement Workshop (RPIW) to fundamentally rework the rounding model. They collected data that the workshop team would use to redesign the rounding process, and recruited team members that included representatives from all the roles on rounds, including attending physicians, resident physicians, floor nurses, and discharge coordinators. The workshop was held over five days.

Prior to attending the RPIW, none of the staff involved had ever been involved in CPI processes, and so the first day was used to introduce and train staff in the fundamental principals of CPI and team dynamics.

The team then moved into a data collection and analysis phase highlighted by a "3 actuals walk." The team was broken into small groups that observed the "actual people" performing the "actual process" in the "actual location." During the three actuals walk, they recorded a variety of data, including process steps and the time required for each step. Although the observers were experienced clinicians who had participated in rounds for years, they learned many new things about the process of care. In particular, each observer became aware for the first time of many tasks that the various roles (interns, residents, attending physicians, nurses, care coordinators, et al.) were performing. By taking this broad and comprehensive view of the process, team members gained invaluable insights into the waste created by the current processes. When later describing their observations, there were many moments when team members laughed out loud at processes that were so convoluted with communication so poor that laughter or tears were the only reasonable responses. The team then analyzed the data they had collected with a focus on "value-added" and "non-value-added" steps from the patient's perspective. The team was shocked to find that few of the steps performed in rounds were truly of any value to the patient (see Table 12.1).

The team then brainstormed and designed a fundamentally new rounding process with the specific goals of eliminating 50 percent of the waste, while improving outcomes. The resulting process became and still remains the basic model by which rounds occur at Seattle Children's Hospital.

The most straightforward change was the creation of standard rounding times for each service. Each medical team cares for both general pediatric patients and subspecialty patients who are assigned to particular teams. Subspecialists had previously contacted the teams ad hoc and would expect the team to round whenever they called. Under the new system, each subspecialty was assigned a standard "rounding time."

The new process also redefined the participants on rounds. To the residents and attending physicians, who had previously been the sole participants, were added the bedside nurse, the discharge planner, and a new role, the "team coordinator." In order to allow the bedside nurse to participate, rounds were moved out of the conference room to the patient's room. It is worth noting that although the team discussed the possibility of including parents on rounds, in the initial rollout of the new system, the bedside nurse was tasked with voicing the concerns of families; families were subsequently included on rounds five months later as part of the plan–do–check–act (PDCA) process. This fundamental shift in rounds allowed all of the key stakeholders—physicians, trainees, nurses, discharge planners, and patients and their families—to discuss the case and to come to a consensus on the plan. Discharge coordinators had previously spent many hours in the afternoon trying to contact team members to discuss arrangements for discharge and frequently only identified those needs when the patient was ready to go home. The presence of discharge coordinators on rounds allowed them to communicate with the team much more easily, and to reliably identify home care and other needs and arrange for them to be ready on the day of discharge.

The team coordinator role has ultimately proven to be one of the most successful innovations of this workshop. Team coordinators have certain concrete duties on rounds, including calling nurses to let them know that the team will be arriving soon for rounds, shepherding the team through the most efficient route to see all of the patients, and acting as timekeeper by reminding the team when they need to meet with various subspecialists. In addition, during rounds they are able to identify tasks that do not need to be performed by clinicians, such as arranging primary care provider appointments after discharge, scheduling tests, and obtaining outside records, and complete those tasks, thus eliminating much of the nonclinical work from residents' and nurses' workload. Finally, team coordinators have proven to be a steady influence on rounds, helping to standardize a wide variety of new processes even as residents, interns, and attending staff change from week to week. For example, as part of an RPIW on communication with primary care providers at discharge, the team coordinators were charged with providing house staff with a

Table 12.1 Process Map Step Analysis

Analysis of Steps: Rounding on the Medical Service		*Current*	*New*
Analysis based on a three-year-old male with a lung infection transferred from an outside hospital, with a three-day length of stay	Number of steps	178	59
	Number of value-added steps	33	26
	Percentage of value-added steps	19%	44%
	Number of queues	23	4
	Number of delays	32	5
	Number of handoffs	17	10

daily list of patients whose primary care provider needs a discharge call, monitoring whether the discharge call is documented, and updating the list accordingly. Team coordinators have taken pride in this role, and discharge calls are now made on approximately 75 percent of patients, up from less than 50 percent before their involvement.

The sequence of work and content of rounds were also standardized, with specific tasks for all of those present. The primary intern presents the patient's history, assessment, and plan for the day. The bedside nurse and family then ask any questions they have, and provide input. The discharge coordinator then identifies any home care needs. The senior resident provides feedback and refines the plan, and the attending physician speaks last. During this process, the nonpresenting intern enters orders in the computer in real time as decisions are made, and reads them back to the presenting intern at the end of rounds to confirm those orders before submitting them. Finally, the senior resident and/or the attending physician make teaching points for the trainees.

Why Was This So Difficult?

Communication with key stakeholders was critical for successful implementation. Although stakeholders were represented on the team, and those team members were committed to a successful implementation, this alone was not enough. Care was taken to have separate meetings with each stakeholder group, with presentations by the stakeholder representatives. Feedback was elicited, and changes were made to the plan in response to the concerns expressed. After implementation, feedback was elicited from all team members. In retrospect, this communication was well worth the effort.

Perhaps the most difficult challenge in the implementation plan was that many subspecialists were reluctant to commit to attending rounds at scheduled times. Many subspecialists had other responsibilities, such as procedure block time and clinics, that created barriers to their attendance at the assigned times. Implementation required the direct and strong intervention of Dr. Bruder Stapleton, the chair of the Department of Pediatrics, to ensure that the required scheduling changes could be made and that the various subspecialty divisions would be held accountable for respecting the assigned rounding times. Without his leadership, implementation would have been impossible.

After the new rounding structure was implemented, it is not surprising given the global nature of the changes that further difficulties were encountered. In particular, the trainees were highly dissatisfied. Although they made a good faith attempt to implement the rounding plan, and several aspects of the plan met with their approval, there were serious consequences of the new rounding process. These problems were related to the smaller teams created in the new system, with only a single senior resident and two interns. These small teams were particularly vulnerable when both interns and senior residents frequently left for various training requirements. With loss of these personnel, these teams frequently became too small to function in the afternoons. In addition, frequently the team was forced to hand off patients to other teams in the afternoon—these cross-cover teams were then required to make important care decisions without the benefit of having been present on rounds.

These very real problems were ultimately addressed approximately two months after the initial implementation, again in the spirit of PDCA. The new rounding process and the scheduled times for rounds were maintained. The smaller teams were paired so that each team now consisted of two senior residents and four interns. This allowed the teams to function more effectively as various personnel left the hospital.

In retrospect, this response to the residents' concerns was much too slow. Enormous dissatisfaction built over the two months before the rounding system was revised, significantly impacting morale among both residents and interns as well as attending physicians and nursing staff. In subsequent process improvement projects, care has been taken to allow for much more rapid responses to concerns after implementation.

Measured Improvements

What effect did this intervention have on our patients? The NRC/Picker survey tool is a 27-question survey mailed to a randomly selected population of patients postdischarge. After implementation of the new rounding process in June 2004, survey responses ($n = 359$) revealed statistically significant results for questions regarding "overall rating of care" and "knew which doctor was in charge" based on chi-squared analysis. For the question "Overall, how would you rate the care your child received in the hospital?" the percentage of "excellent" responses increased from 44 percent (October–December 2003) to 67 percent (October–December 2004). Problem score ratings showed a downward trend (lower is better!) during the equivalent time frame ($p < 0.01$). For the question "Did you know which doctor was in charge of your care in the hospital?" the percentage of "yes" responses increased from 59 percent (October–December 2003) to 82 percent (July–August 2005). Problem score percentages fell from 41 to 19 percent during the same periods ($p < 0.016$). Though not statistically significant, for the question "Did you have confidence and trust in the doctors caring for your child?" the percentage of "yes, always" responses increased from 65 percent (October–December 2003) to 85 percent (July–August 2005). Problem score percentages fell from 34 to 14 percent during the same period.

A process map step analysis also revealed significant improvements. When a typical three-day stay of a medical patient was dissected, clear gains became evident.

The point that data speak powerfully should not be underestimated. Data appeal to our sense of logic, and because they are unemotional by nature, data have the unique ability to repel anecdotal resistance. All members of the design team immediately recognized what these data represented: better patient care. Concepts developed in industry had fused with medicine; manufacturing techniques and the art of medicine had been chimerized, and a new cadre of "true believers" in CPI had been born. Just as Toyota had propelled forward the Lexus brand by combining previously incongruent concepts of luxury and performance, the general medical service at SCH had now fused efficiency and the art of medicine. And the experience of our patients and families benefitted greatly.

Replication and PDCA (Plan–Do–Check–Act)

The general medical service represents only a portion of all the services at SCH. The logical next step was to attempt to spread these rounding techniques to other services. As of July 2009, the general surgery, hematology/oncology, bone marrow transplant, neurosurgery, orthopedics, cardiology, and cardiac surgery departments and the pediatric intensive care unit have completed RPIW events to operationalize standard rounding techniques. Replication has afforded us the opportunity to refine our reliable method for rounding and continuously improve based on the iterative experiences of the services. We have distilled our standardized elements of rounds into a single, easy-to-digest document that serves as the template for each replication event (see Figure 12.1). Moreover, we have standardized each team member's specific role in the rounding process so that their expertise contributes to the daily plan of care each day for every patient (see Figure 12.2).

For example, the bedside RN brings forth issues relating to barriers to discharge or any "hidden" family concerns that the MD team may not be aware of, pharmacists bring forth issues relating to drug safety, and nutritionists ensure that growth parameters are appropriate. The family is witness to all of this input from their team, and their understanding of the plan is confirmed on a daily basis. Questions are solicited and fears are allayed to the best of the team's ability. In the end, the product we seek to manufacture is not an automobile, but rather a daily plan of care that is created in partnership, transparent to all, instituted without delay, and executed with compassion—a fusion of art and medicine.

Epilogue

Since the publication of our chapter in the first edition, we have continued, and moved forward with, rounding as clinical standard work. A significant factor in the changes we have made was the building of a new facility to address two key

Seattle Children's

Elements of Standard Rounds

Create a work method for the rounding process with components 1-4 below. Demonstrate its reliability with component 5. A reliable method must be consciously developed and documented, always followed – by everyone performing the work, "owned" by someone and basis for improvement.

		Audit	Completion 25%	50%	75%	100%
1	**Create a standard rounding schedule (Mon-Sun)**					
	Establish a consistent start time					
	Communicate to families when they should expect to see you each day					
	Establish a consistent starting location					
	Track appropriate cycle time/takt time per patient	A				
	Round on every patient daily (if not, communicate with family about variation from standard)	A				
	Coordinate/sequence the rounds of different services on the same unit to avoid overlap of RN resource					
2	**Create a reliable method for rounding roles and team structure**					
	Define and standardize the roles involved in rounding (include role of the interpreter)					
	Define what the team needs to do					
	Assign one role to have ownership of rounds					
	Assign one role to have ownership of whiteboard to update the plan of care					
	Ensure RN is consistently present and an active participant	A				
	Ensure overnight care coordination data is presented					
	Introduce team to family by role at the start of rounds					
3	**Standardize whiteboards**					
	Ensure there is a whiteboard in every room (per patient)					
	Ensure each whiteboard has four distinct quadrants:					
	Upper left hand corner: Patient name, RN name, room #, etc.					
	Lower left hand corner: Family questions					
	Upper right hand corner: Plan of care (in a way the family can understand)	A				
	Lower right hand corner: Discharge criteria (in a way the family can understand)	A				
	Ensure whiteboard usage is the same across services					
4	**Involve families in rounds**					
	Track % of families participating in rounds, as partners in the care team	A				
	If families decline rounds, give them the opportunity to ask questions/provide feedback via other venues					
	Give families an idea of when rounds start and when you expect to arrive to their room					
	Utilize whiteboard with family during rounds:					
	Ensure questions from the lower left hand section have been answered					
	Discuss plan of care with family	A				
	Discuss discharge criteria with family	A				
	Standardize family communication handouts across services, and seek approval from Family Services					
	If you do not round with family, communicate with them about the variation from standard					
5	**Audit rounding process**					
	Use standard audit tool	A				
	Audit weekly until process is stable					
	Report audit results on standard spreadsheet (used by all services)					
	Task someone who is not involved in rounds to do the audit					
	Ensure process owners attend rounds periodically					

A = Included in Audit Plan

08-20-09

Figure 12.1 Elements of standard rounds template. Each service line deals with specific diagnoses; however, families value consistent, predictable interactions with clinicians, and standardizing rounding between services helps deliver that.

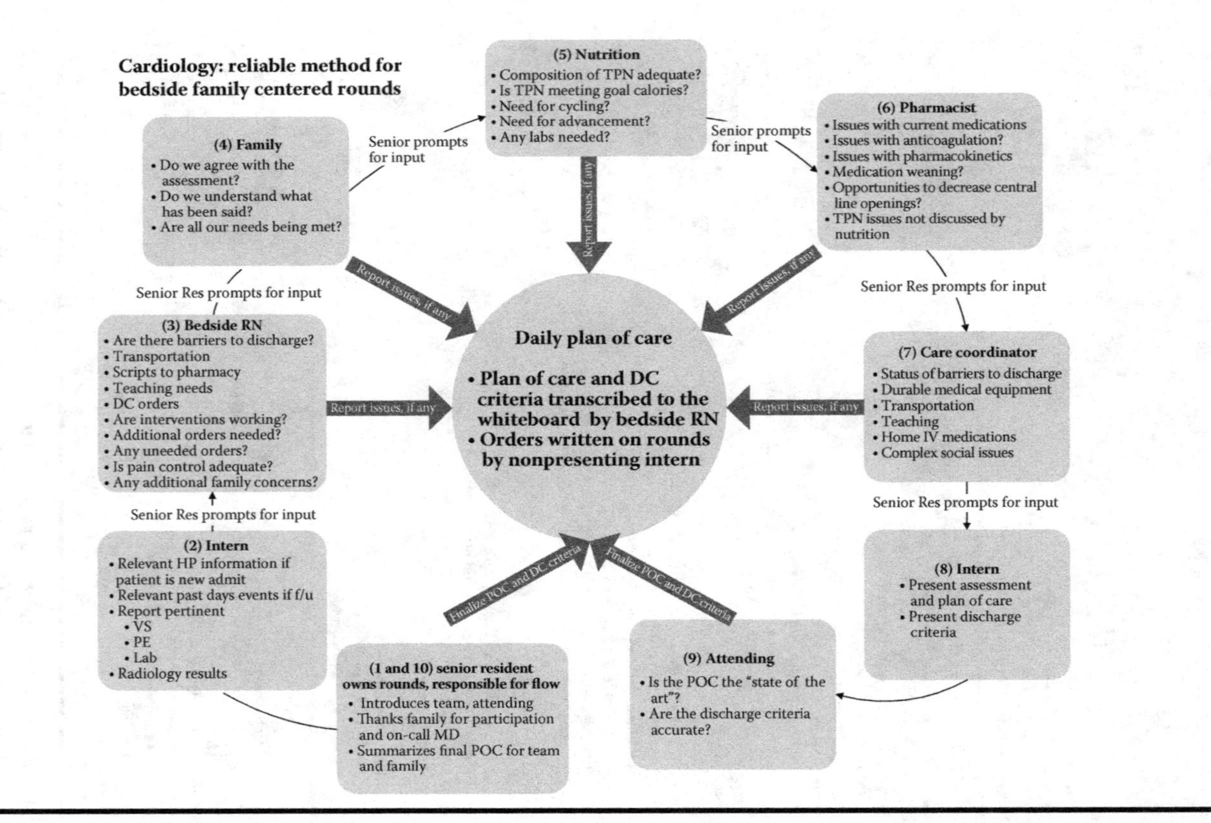

Figure 12.2 Daily plan of care for rounds. There are many roles represented during rounding. Defining those roles and the expectations for them reduces ambiguity, uncertainty, waste, and mistakes. HP, history and physical; VS, vital signs; TPN, total parental nutrition; DC, discharge; POC, plan of care.

problems that impeded more effective rounding: small, shared patient rooms and the distributed location of patient rooms.

In 2010, Seattle Children's Hospital recognized that the amount of physical space available was inadequate to serve the needs of its patients and their families. Nearly 50 percent of all inpatient medical beds were in double occupancy rooms, with patients separated only by a curtain. Patients and their families lacked desired privacy and were disturbed by care activity for the other patient. The overcrowding made a stressful hospital admission even worse. Caregivers were routinely apologizing for the crowded conditions and our staff was finding it increasingly difficult to explain how a world-class institution could offer such cramped quarters—less square footage per person than a college dormitory! Experienced families would sometimes vie for the few "single" rooms on the unit, leading to much consternation for all involved. In addition, the current "double" rooms did not allow care teams to round easily at the bedside, due to both privacy and space issues. As a result, care teams would round outside the rooms in narrow hallways. At peak rounding times, our wards resembled a congested freeway with teams crashing into each other—one fender bender after another.

In addition, due to the physical layout of the patient rooms, it was extremely difficult to ensure that individual teams cared for their patients within a manageable footprint. Instead, physicians cared for patients who were spread over all of the acute care units at the hospital and would routinely travel as much as an eighth of a mile between patients, with travel frequently involving climbing multiple flights of stairs. Rounding was at times a legitimate cardiovascular workout. The building itself created barriers to physicians' ability to rapidly respond to the changing needs of the patient. Such barriers frequently stymied the continuous advancement of care that allows a patient to be efficiently "pulled" through the system during their stay.

SCH used integrated facility design principles (see Chapter 19) while designing the addition, which opened for medical unit patients in August 2015. Explicit in the design was the vision of single-patient rooms and colocation of patients and their care teams, thereby reducing unnecessary travel. Projected patient volumes and length of stay determined the number of beds needed in each unit and rooms were designed with enough space so that all members of the team could fit inside comfortably during rounds. (See Figure 12.3.)

The new facility now supports improvements in rounds, which in turn has improved family-centered care. Daily patient rounds are the singular opportunity each day for the patient and family to meet with the entire care team. These rounds provide a critical "check step" to ensure that all participants are on the same page regarding the overall arc of the patient's care and allow all care team members to participate actively in a "pull system" to continuously advance care throughout the patient's stay.

As the addition was built, we began creating a new team structure, which we named "geographic ward teams." With the previous team structure, a team would care for patients located throughout the hospital, but with geographic ward teams, a

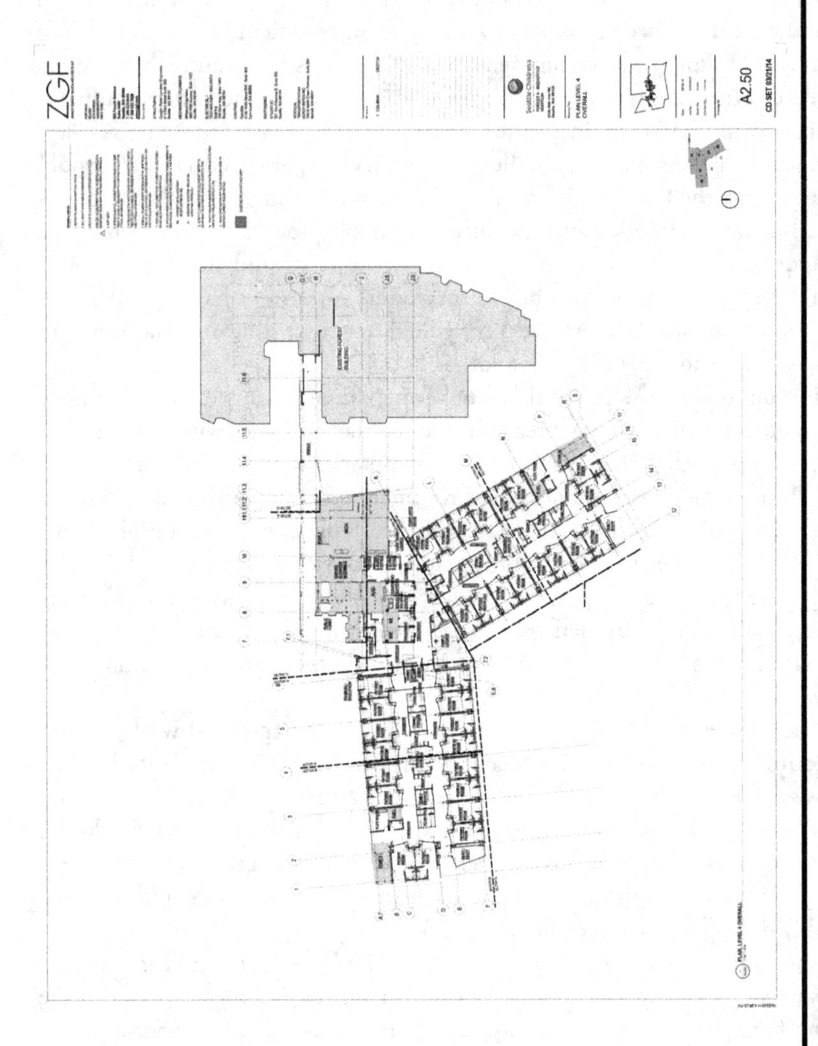

Figure 12.3 Blueprint of the new medical unit at Seattle Children's Hospital, opened August 2015. The new design includes single-occupancy rooms that are large enough to hold bedside rounds with the care team and family. Patients, physicians, and nurses are all located in the same physical space. This close working proximity decreases waste and provides opportunities to enhance teaching and advance care.

team now cares for patients in a specific set of rooms in a defined location. We also created a new rounding practice that takes advantage of the new space. Our work included redesigning three main processes: morning resident sign-out, teaching during family-centered rounds, and morning and afternoon interdisciplinary huddles.

Morning Resident Sign-Out

Morning resident sign-out is a time during which there is a critical handoff between the night team, which performs the initial evaluation and management of most admissions and provides ongoing care for all admitted patients at night, and the day team, which makes the final decisions on the plan for the entire stay. Handoffs are known to be a vulnerable time in part because the providers are distant from the patient care area. In addition, published studies have demonstrated that improving sign-outs can reduce patient harm.[1] Due to the small rooms and privacy issues in the old facility, the outgoing night teams needed to sign-out patients to the incoming day teams in the cafeteria or a secluded conference room.

In the new model, the teams perform morning handoff at the patient's bedside. This practice gives residents the opportunity to examine sick or recently admitted patients at the time of the sign-out. The new practice also simplifies and expedites prerounding workflow because patient exams are done at the time of the handoff. Furthermore, the new process improves the ability to recognize changes in the patient's condition and provides an opportunity to advance or change the care plan earlier in the morning. Finally, the face-to-face time during sign-out gives families a greater sense of security; they witness the handoff between the day and night teams and are able to meet the incoming care team more expediently than with the previous handoff process.

Teaching during Family-Centered Rounds

The old physical space often curtailed our ability to train residents effectively. As mentioned earlier in the chapter, Sir William Osler insisted that students learn best when brought to the bedside. We know from adult learning theory, as did Osler, that we learn best when learning in groups and when learning material that is closely tied to real-world experiences that support our professional proficiencies. Although we knew this teaching approach was best practice, double occupancy made it very difficult, if not impossible, to accomplish it. A teacher's description of a patient's condition and their physical findings or a discussion of their prognosis or care plan could be heard very clearly across the curtain, which was unacceptable from a privacy standpoint. Thus, delicate topics needed to be discussed outside of rounds at a separate time and place, interrupting continuous flow. Teaching was relegated to afternoon didactic sessions away from the bedside, which were often poorly attended.

The new facility layout allows the entire care team to meet with every family daily. This critical check step eliminates uncertainties about the care plan, thus allowing each individual team member to continuously advance care throughout the day. We believe strongly that the ability of teachers and trainees to round together at the bedside, which incorporates the key elements for the best adult learning, will enhance the residents' educational experience.

Morning and Afternoon Interdisciplinary Huddles

In addition to the new daily rounding process, we have added daily interdisciplinary huddles. Most patients on the medical unit have lengths of stay of only one or two days. A single daily rounding interaction does not allow for continuous advancement of care, because the status of patients on the unit changes so rapidly. The care teams now hold brief, five-minute huddles in the morning and afternoon. By augmenting team rounds with other opportunities to continually advance care and interface with our discharge coordinators and charge nurses, the huddles enhance the teams' ability to "pull" patients through the system.

Charge nurses play a critical role in the hospital; they oversee the distribution of beds and nursing resources so that patient care can occur seamlessly without delay. In the old facility, charge nurses were scattered throughout the physical space making their presence on rounds impossible. With the new system of geographic ward teams, charge nurses can participate in huddles. Their attendance allows care to be advanced by all members of the team and enables timely discharge planning and identification of potential barriers to discharge. Huddles represent additional opportunities to continually advance care and to efficiently and safely get our patients where they should be—at home, thriving without disease. To improve the efficiency of huddles, we use visual control boards in each unit. All of these processes would have been impossible without geographic ward teams.

As leaders, we took several steps to minimize the challenges inherent in the move and the shift to the new team structure and rounding practices: enabling and ensuring participation, coaching in the units, and freeing up needed resources. Prior to the move, we ensured the involvement of physicians and bedside nurses in designing the new process. Their collaboration was critical for several reasons. Involving the individuals with intimate knowledge of the work meant that the final design addressed their concerns. Their involvement also allowed for in-person negotiation when there were competing priorities. In addition, the workshop participants acted as ambassadors to their constituencies, advocating for the process change, addressing concerns, and providing informed and nuanced answers to their peers' questions. By ensuring the joint participation of physicians, nurses, and other caregivers, we maximized the opportunities for improvement afforded by the new space and design.

Coaching was another important element of leadership. After the move, clinicians found many points of difficulty with the new rounding process and new space. It was critically important that physician and nursing leaders were present daily in the units, listening to concerns, helping the clinicians manage situations that arose with the new design, and identifying leadership issues to address. Looking back, we can see how essential it has been for those of us leading this effort to hear and validate their concerns—no matter how small—and to take steps to address them.

As issues were identified, the clinical teams rapidly devised mitigation strategies. For example, the unit nurses recognized that there were too many supplies within the rooms, resulting in waste as extra supplies were discarded each time a room turned over. The clinical teams immediately created a task force of nurses to identify the degree of surplus and redesign the supply carts. Residents quickly noted that there was inadequate white board space in their team room for teaching. Leaders made available additional dry erase space on the doors of the team room. The rapid and continuous response to the concerns of staff helped them feel supported as they made the complex transition to the new process and space.

Identifying and accessing needed resources was another important leadership role. The most pressing resource limitation we faced was lack of protected time to work on the design process. We addressed this issue by communicating up the chain of leadership to get additional help. For example, we found that the participation of nursing shift administrators was critical, yet the volume of their administrative duties prevented them from focusing exclusively on our work during design events. By communicating the importance of their involvement and their lack of availability to executive leadership, we were able to garner the commitment of an executive nursing leader to participate in our design work.

As a result of the close involvement of staff in the process design, the rollout of the new team structure and the subsequent move to the new facility in August 2015 was a remarkably smooth transition. As our move was so recent, we have little data yet available. However, what we have observed so far suggests improvement. More than 85 percent of patients have been assigned to their targeted unit, which has allowed geographic ward teams to function as designed. With the new team structure, we have seen improvements in care team communication, which is reflected in our family experience scores. At baseline, 58 percent of families indicated that they were satisfied with doctor/nurse communication; after the restructuring 69 percent reported being satisfied. The residents' experience has also improved, as evident in their increased attendance at conferences. Whereas before restructuring an average of 41 residents attended the noon conferences, now attendance averages 54 residents, an increase of 33 percent. We believe that the increased attendance reflects a reduction in wasted time on the wards.

As we go forward, we will be assessing a number of metrics to measure the success of the changes we have implemented. We will track patient length of stay (LOS), an important cost and quality measure. (LOS is the single largest per day expense and it directly reflects time to recovery.) We will continue to track patient satisfaction through specific questions on our family experience survey. We will also be measuring residents' satisfaction with their educational experience and their logged hours on the wards. We anticipate that our residents will log fewer hours due to increased efficiency.

The physicians and nurses caring for medical patients had long-standing issues with inadequate time for rounds and the large geographic footprint over which patients were located. The opening of a new facility could have exacerbated both of these issues, with patients becoming even more widely separated. Instead, we took advantage of the opportunity to create new ways of working that could actually create significant improvements. As we go forward with our new team structure and rounding practice, we fully expect to see increased efficiency and the ability to be more responsive to our patients and families.

Note

1. P. Li, S. Ali, C. Tang, W. A. Ghali, and H. T. Stelfox, "Review of Computerized Physician Handoff Tools for Improving the Quality of Patient Care," *Journal of Hospital Medicine* 8 (2013): 456–63.

Chapter 13

Change That Nourishes the Organization: Making the Total Parenteral Nutrition (TPN) Process Safer

Polly Lenssen, Eric Harvey, and David L. Suskind

Dr. Rich Molteni, the medical director at Seattle Children's Hospital, was meeting with the directors of pharmacy and clinical nutrition in his office one morning.

The discussion centered on a recent event that was both seminal and scary. A toddler had received four times the intended dose of potassium in his bag of total parenteral nutrition (TPN). TPN is the nutrient-rich admixture with over 30 additives that is lifesaving in patients unable to eat or be fed through an intestinal feeding tube.

The child's kidneys were working just fine, and fortunately he was able to maintain his serum potassium level in a safe range. But if the error had occurred in the child with the damaged heart and sluggish kidneys in the next room, the outcome could have been lethal.

Dr. Molteni wanted to know if the dietitians and pharmacists could assume responsibility for TPN order writing. His reasoning was sound: dietitians and pharmacists have the training in nutrition and TPN admixtures, and yet we had medical residents, with no knowledge and no experience, writing these complex medical orders.

This question and proposal were hardly radical. Some hospitals in the community had already sought prescriptive authority for pharmacists to write TPN orders; and our dietitians at Children's Hospital were "ghost writing" orders for the residents and fellows to sign in the neonatal and bone marrow transplant services.

But the conversation with Dr. Molteni ended with the directors of pharmacy and clinical nutrition shaking their heads. Based on the way the hospital was currently structured, and the way it actually worked, they thought it would be impossible to implement TPN order writing by pharmacists and dietitians across 20 services at our academic medical center. They couldn't imagine convincing all the division chiefs and the resident education office to relinquish control of a medical order, or "teaching opportunity." Nor did they have the staff to gather the necessary clinical data to update prescriptions every day.

Several years passed, and numerous reports were published about fatal errors with TPN, especially in children, as well as safe practice standards that were under development.[1–4] And at Seattle Children's, the data were clear: the medication with the highest error rate was TPN.

Encouraged by Dr. Molteni's continuing conviction that we could implement a safer system, the pharmacy and nutrition leadership at our hospital kept emphasizing the high risk with our TPN process in our annual reports to the quality improvement steering committee. So, as the executive leadership at Seattle Children's considered early continuous performance improvement (CPI) projects, improving the TPN process surfaced as an obvious choice.

With executive support and a CPI consultant on board, the project was launched. As expected, the task was enormous. And, using a "value stream improvement" approach to the TPN process, we embarked on what was to become an eighteen-month journey to envision, design, and implement a standard TPN process throughout the hospital.

Today, we are doing much better in this area. We are linked together, and communication and flow are clear and efficient for the most part. But we still have breakdowns, although it's much easier for us to learn and improve because now we have a standard process in place.

Looking back, it's important and instructive to ask how we made this major—and difficult—transition in the TPN process.

It all started with bringing our leadership together in a three-day value stream alignment session. General medicine, nursing, pharmacy, nutrition, home care (where TPN was produced), and administration each attended the session and learned about one-piece flow, error proofing, check steps, queues, and the many types of waste in our processes. They also grasped how these principles from "Lean manufacturing" could touch every discipline in the TPN process and help detect errors earlier, before they reached the patient.

The alignment session inspired commitment across the disciplines, which helped sustain the passion and energy for such a large project. The leadership team then met weekly over the next 18 months to track progress and plan next steps. The team experienced continual recommitment as the methodology naturally broke down "the silos" and dismantled barriers that we faced daily in our work.

Three Rapid Process Improvement Workshops (RPIWs) were planned as weeklong events to design and implement each step in the TPN process: ordering, production, and administration. Baseline data were gathered; in addition to detailed error data on each step of the process, each discipline's satisfaction with the TPN process was measured. Pharmacists experienced intense frustration about the time wasted tracking down residents to clarify and correct TPN orders, and dietitians were equally discouraged to discover prescriptions for too many or too little calories, or inappropriate use of TPN when a feeding tube could have been inserted.

For staffing reasons, the administration RPIW occurred first, fortuitously as it turned out. Administration errors were the greatest in number. These errors included the inadvertent switching of rates for two components—the fat component, which ran at a slow rate, and the dextrose–protein and electrolyte component, which ran at a comparatively faster rate. The risk of an adverse outcome is considerable when electrolytes are not delivered as prescribed, and implementing an error-proofing method was reason enough to participate in this event. Error proofing for this risk included standardizing the labeling and placement of the tubing for the two components to greatly decrease the potential for mix-ups (see Figure 13.1).

Additional mistake proofing implemented as the result of the administration RPIW included matching the TPN label on the bag with the order form, and implementing pharmacy compounding software and an administration checklist.

A major shift also occurred in job assignment, since the process of administration was not standard in the hospital. Previously, the IV team nurse was designated to hang the TPN on the non-intensive care patients; and, after the event, the bedside nurse—regardless of site of care—was accountable for administration (see Figure 13.2).

The RPIW that was viewed as the most challenging—TPN ordering—took place six months into the process. Dr. Molteni believed that accurate calculation of TPN components was an extremely complex skill that was of little interest to most pediatric medical and surgical trainees. And, in most busy nurseries and on many pediatric floors, it's critical that the attending physician provide correct input when it comes to the patient's need for TPN; especially important is the articulation of any medical conditions that would dictate unusual preparations or ingredients.

The trick in the RPIW session on TPN ordering was convincing people, especially house staff and their leaders, that this was a "service" to them and their patients, and not a "takeaway" or intrusion on their authority.

The RPIW went well—better than expected—in part because the leadership team populated the management guidance team with senior physician leadership,

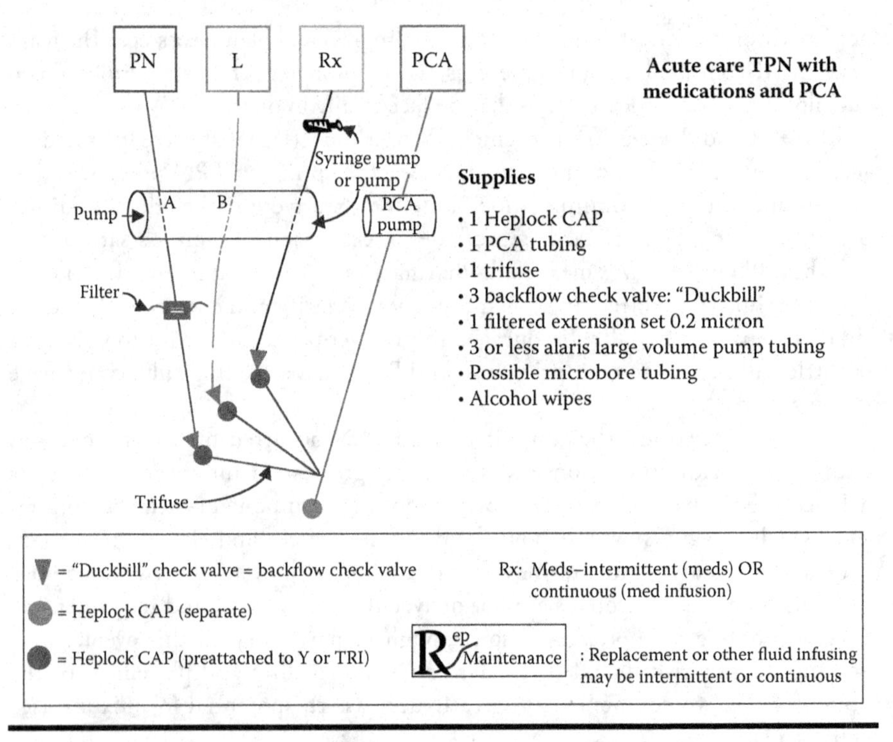

Figure 13.1 Acute care. TPN with medications and patient-controlled analgesia (PCA). A visual used to mistake-proof TPN delivery at the bedside.

including the surgical and medical chiefs, and extended invitations to staff pharmacists and dietitians, nurse practitioners, and our chief resident.

When the chief resident spoke, he immediately tore down some of the myths and barriers. He told us it was clear that TPN errors were among the most critical medication errors in the hospital. And, since residents were writing most TPN orders, he felt obligated to join the CPI team that was looking for a solution. He went further by saying that he wanted to not only contribute to designing a system that would minimize TPN ordering errors, but also ensure that resident education in nutrition and pharmaceutical topics wasn't compromised.

After the current state was mapped and all the waste was revealed, the ideal state quickly evolved with little controversy; the model was simple and clear (see Figure 13.3).

Still, there was persistent anxiety about whether resident training was rich enough without practical experience in writing the TPN. Because education is an explicit part of our organization's goals, it was important for some of the project work to develop a system where education was intertwined within the nutrition and TPN process. The model enabled nutrition to become a standard component of

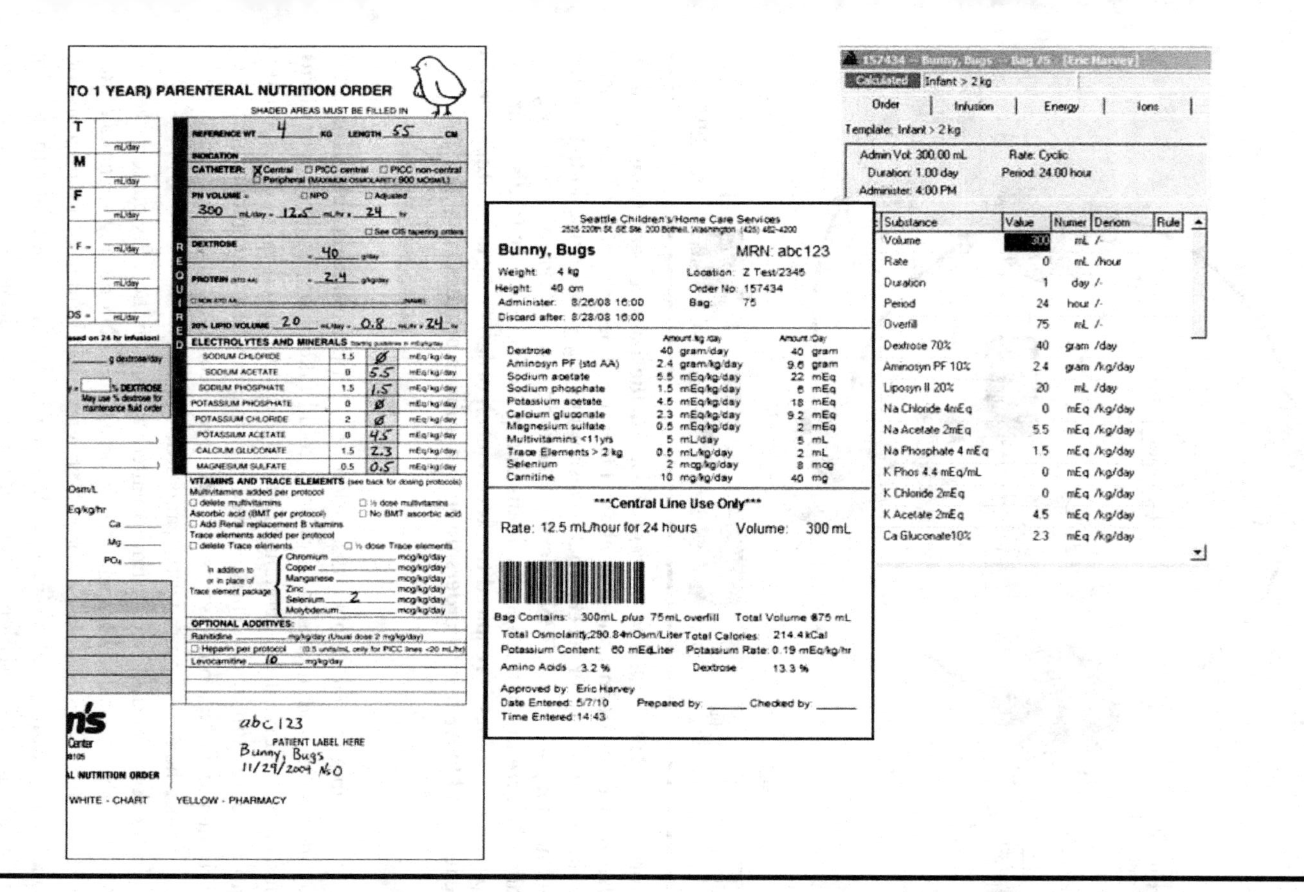

Figure 13.2 Order form, checklist, and software. Mistake proofing by validating the three TPN documents needed to deliver TPN.

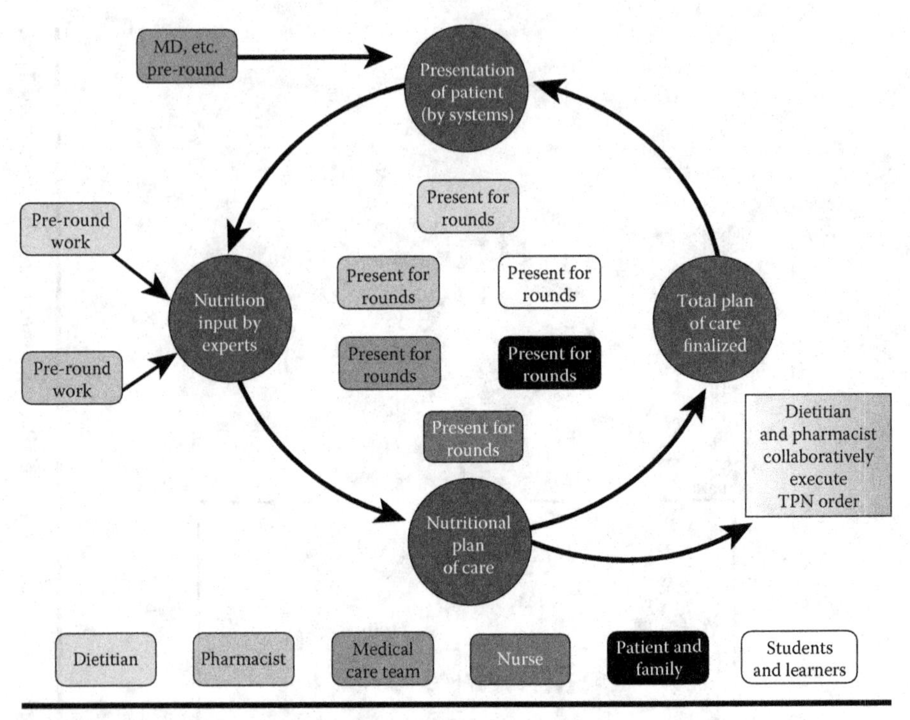

Figure 13.3 TPN ordering process flow. All the patient care team members (pharmacists, dietitians, and the medical team) will be present for TPN decision making seven days per week. That decision making will include initiation, discontinuation, and route. TPN orders will be executed by "TPN order-writing specialists," currently defined as dietitians and pharmacists. A specialist from two separate disciplines is required to execute each order. Over time, others can be credentialed to write TPN orders through a training process.

daily rounding so that an open discussion between the residents, dietitians, pharmacists, nurses, and attending physicians could take place. Within these discussions, enteral, TPN, and general nutrition education occurred. And, in conjunction with in-house rounds, residents received multiple lectures throughout the year on nutrition and TPN; a process was also set up to accommodate those residents who wanted specific education in writing and ordering TPN.

In the several years since we implemented changes to the TPN process, we have confirmed that skills and competencies in pediatric TPN ordering are not a critical area for pediatricians in their practice. We have worked hard to maintain a practice model that does not undermine the physician leadership—especially in decision making about TPN initiation, termination, and composition—but instead encourages continual dialogue between the physician, the nutritionist, and pharmacists to ensure best care practices for our patients.

Surprisingly, dietitians and pharmacists were a source of resistance when we rolled out the new TPN process model. Some of the pharmacists, for example, worried that the focus on TPN would make the rest of their job less safe. This anxiety dissipated over time as their competence and comfort level increased. For their part, the dietitians welcomed the opportunity to apply their skills, but they felt strong distrust from the pharmacists, who would only sign orders after they personally had a conversation with the physician. These feelings of distrust likewise diminished as staff learned about each other's competence, skill sets, and accountability.

To offset negative feelings and the very real anxieties about change and assuming new responsibilities, we reminded everyone that we did not want to return to the old way in which, on average, one TPN error occurred every day. And we met weekly for problem resolution and education. Some of the questions we raised were as follows: How do we standardize documentation? How do we hand off critical clinical information on weekends? How do you write TPN for a premature infant—if your expertise is in oncology? Our frontline staff members emerged as leaders and piloted the TPN order writing on the weekends, when resource levels within the hospital generally decrease. They also offered up teaching "pearls" about their specialties and relinquished their "exclusive" expertise in cross-training sessions with their colleagues.

The huge leadership commitment made at every level in our organization—initiated at the executive level, sustained over the years by midlevel management, and demonstrated in daily work improvements by the direct clinical staff—resulted in a significant cultural transformation. We were no longer willing or able to accept one TPN error a day.

Indeed, nurses, physicians, pharmacists, and dietitians across the board experienced greater satisfaction with the new TPN process (see Figures 13.4 and 13.5). Errors at each step dropped significantly, and this safety improvement rate has been sustained over time (see Figure 13.6).

Finally, cost avoidance, captured in a retrospective analysis, demonstrates that adding additional labor resources for this major patient safety initiative was a good economic decision (see Table 13.1).

In terms of our third RPIW on TPN production, the leadership team underestimated the length of time it would take to implement the TPN ordering model, and the team ended up canceling the third workshop because the production side already exhibited strong characteristics of one-piece flow (see Figure 13.7).

The two workshops we did complete, however, helped us move up the daily delivery of TPN from home care so that we are able to correct the electrolyte and nutritional status of patients one hour earlier.

But the ability to sustain one-piece flow in ordering to meet production and delivery deadlines remains difficult. As the hospital census has increased, and the organization has shifted to standard, family-centered rounding, team discussion has shifted later in the morning and challenged our production system.

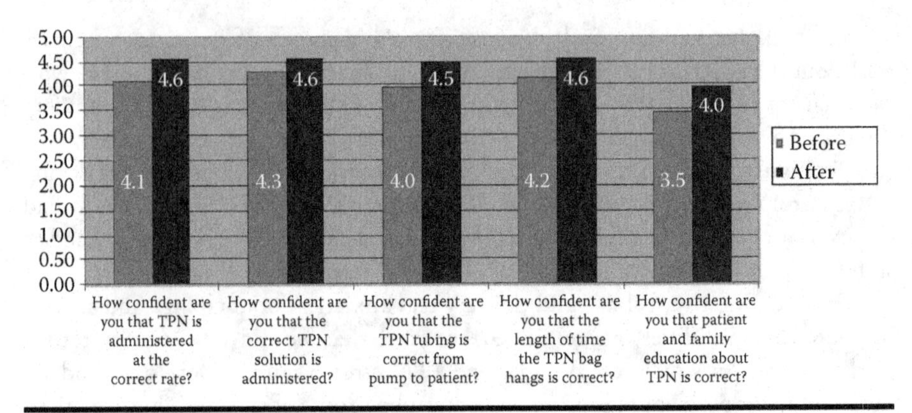

Figure 13.4 Nursing confidence in TPN process. Level of satisfaction among nurses before and after the implementation of the new TPN process.

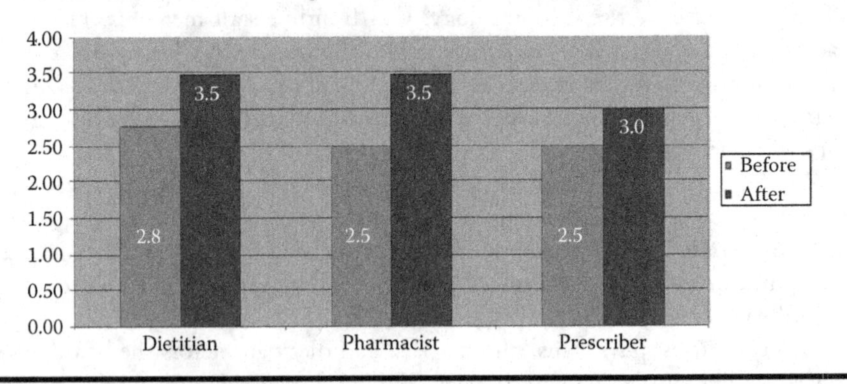

Figure 13.5 Comparative responses for overall level of satisfaction with the TPN process. Levels of satisfaction among various roles in the TPN process before and after the change.

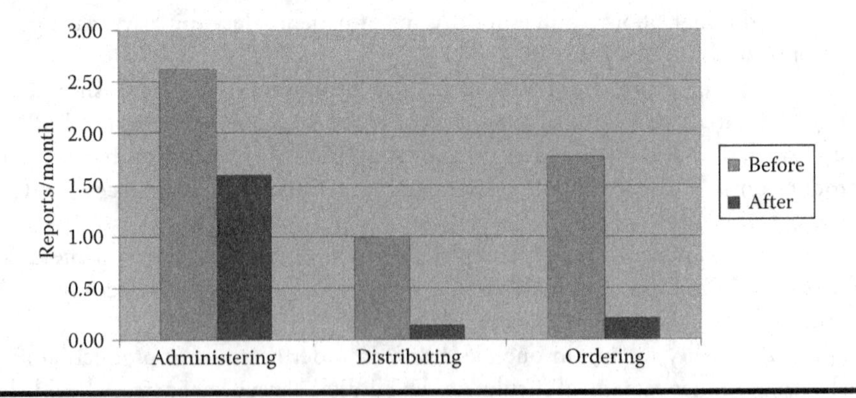

Figure 13.6 TPN incident reports per month reaching patients. Additional evidence validating the effectiveness of the mistake proofing.

Table 13.1 Cost Analysis

	2005 Preimplementation	*2009 Postimplementation*	*Difference*
Pharmacist Labor			
Hours spent on TPN	70 hours/week	124 hours/week	54 hours/week
Labor dollars spent on TPN[a]	$236,600/year	$419,120/year	$182,520/year
TPN Utilization			
% of patients receiving ≤ 3 days of TPN	23%	22%	1% (128 orders)
Utilization rate	0.2 TPNs/inpatient day	0.17 TPNs/inpatient day	0.03 TPNs/inpatient day (2,275 orders)
Cost avoided for unnecessary TPN[b]			$300,375/year
Error Avoidance			
TPN errors reaching patients	85/year	51/year	34/year
Cost avoided by reducing errors[c]			$186,422/year
Overall cost impact (–182,520 + 300,375 + 186,422) = $304,277 per year net cost avoidance.			

Sources: D. L. Kunac, J. Kennedy, N. Austin et al., "Incidence, Preventability, and Impact of Adverse Drug Events (ADEs) and Potential ADEs in Hospitalized Children in New Zealand: A Prospective Observational Cohort Study," *Paediatric Drugs* 11, no. 2 (2009): 153–60; and D. C. Suh, B. S. Woodall, S. K. Shin et al., "Clinical and Economic Impact of Adverse Drug Reactions in Hospitalized Patients," *Annals of Pharmacotherapy* 34, no. 12 (December 2000): 1373–79.

[a] Estimate $65 per hour as average salary plus benefits during this time frame.
[b] Estimate cost to pharmacy of $125 per order.
[c] Estimate cost per error of $5,483 (based on the most recent adult value and reported in 1999 dollars; most recent pediatric value reported in 2002 is approximately US$11,500).

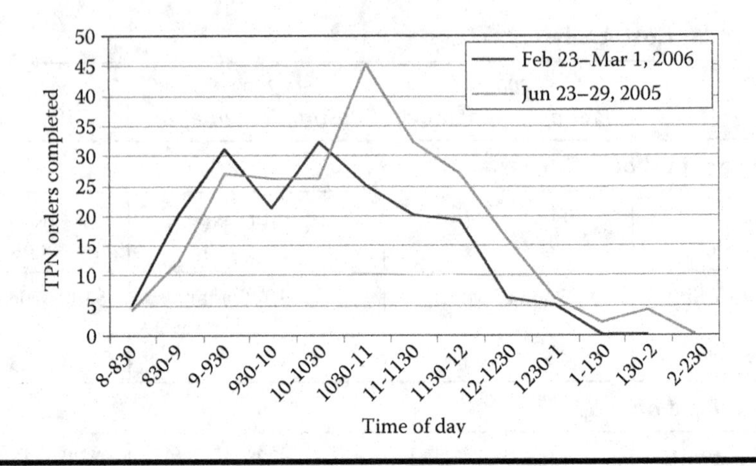

Figure 13.7 TPN order flow. Sustaining one-piece order flow remains difficult but efforts have resulted in reduction of the last minute rush of orders into the pharmacy prior to the noon deadline. Pharmacists can now enter orders without the stress associated with this last minute rush.

The final leadership lesson of the TPN project is that the improvement work is never done. A change in staff behavior across every discipline and multiple sites in such a complex process as TPN requires significant ongoing effort to maintain the initial gains five years postimplementation and additional effort to drive the process toward zero errors. Because the organization has embedded CPI into our daily lives and empowered a more horizontal leadership model in which the voice of the frontline staff can influence the process as much as that of the division head, the doubt that we initially experienced in Rich Molteni's office doesn't ever have to get in the way of change again.

Notes

1. Task Force for the Revision of Safe Practices for Parenteral Nutrition: J. Mirtallo, T. Canada, D. Johnson et al., "Safe Practices for Parenteral Nutrition," *Journal of Parenteral and Enteral Nutrition* 28 (2004): S39–S70.
2. Johns Hopkins Medicine, "JHM Reports Untimely Death of Child Cancer Patient," http://www.hopkinsmedicine.org/Press_releases/2003/12_19_03.html (accessed July 15, 2010).
3. "Two Children Die after Receiving Infected TPN Solutions," *Pharmaceutical Journal* 3 (August 1994): 2.
4. A. Ali, C. Walentik, G. J. Mantych, H. F. Sadiq, W. J. Keenan, and A. Noguchi, "Iatrogenic Acute Hypermagnesemia after Total Parenteral Nutrition Infusion Mimicking Septic Shock Syndrome: Two Case Reports," *Pediatrics* 112, no. 1 pt. 1 (2003): e70–e72.

Epilogue

Polly Lenssen and Eric Harvey

Since we have put in place standard processes for TPN management within our hospital and shored up the collaborative relationship between the leadership team and frontline staff, we have been gratified with strong results over each successive year. Improving TPN safety has not been a perfect journey, yet it has been a journey that embodies the spirit of Lean leadership: staff problem-solve one step at a time and leaders help to remove barriers and to escalate problems as necessary to medical and executive leadership. We know that no amount of improvement work will eliminate TPN as a high-risk medication. Our focus remains on creating the safest possible environment for the use of this life-saving intervention for patients who are unable to eat or use their gastrointestinal tract normally.

The cycle of improvement is best demonstrated by our reduction in the overall usage of TPN. Our leaders committed to tracking, analyzing, and sharing data on usage by service with the pharmacists, dietitians, medical staff, and hospital quality leaders. These leaders used the data to generate hypotheses and improvement opportunities for the ultimate safety metric: exposure to TPN. Figure 13.8 illustrates the multiple interventions that we believe contributed to the decreased use of TPN, despite a 40-percent increase in the clinical acuity of the patients we treat (measured by the increase in the case-mix index—a standard measure of the degree of illness—from 2.23 to 3.12 over just the last six years).

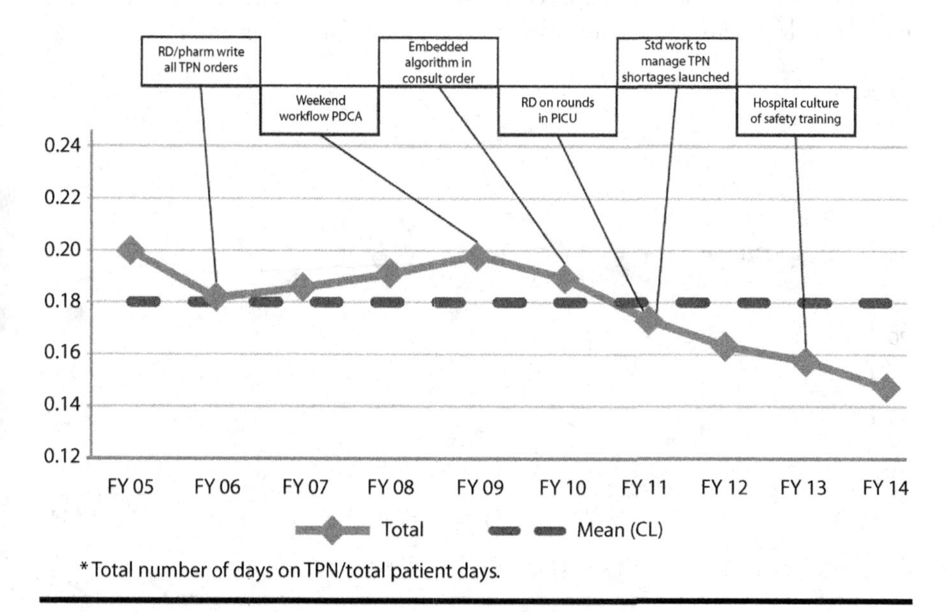

Figure 13.8 TPN utilization rate.

Our commitment to standard work, deference to the expertise of frontline staff, and reliance on evidence-based research made these interventions possible. For example, in our previous model, physicians ordered the TPN, sometimes resulting in decisions with which the dietitians and pharmacists did not agree. However, the pharmacists and dietitians were not always comfortable taking the steps to "stop the line," and sometimes did not have the time, especially on weekends, to win over the resident, or senior resident, or even attending physician, to their clinical viewpoint.

To address this issue, we married our improvement work with the goals of an informatics physician who understood that TPN contributed to bloodstream infections. This work led us to imbedding evidence-based criteria for initiating TPN into the electronic ordering system, requiring physicians to walk through a critical thinking process for each course of TPN they order. To track the effectiveness of this strategy and review it annually, we assess the percentage of very short courses of TPN (see Figure 13.9). Short courses of TPN may be a surrogate for inappropriate prescribing in which the risks for infections and errors outweigh any nutritional benefit.

Another example of how standard work and our shared mental model on Lean leadership have helped reduce TPN utilization is the process we implemented to navigate the ongoing and at times critical manufacturer shortages of TPN components. As the crisis with TPN shortages escalated, a small group of experts in neonatology and gastroenterology began meeting weekly with the hospital, home care, pharmacy, and nutrition leaders. The group determined a standard approach to each component shortage and communicated the approach to frontline staff, usually with recommendations to shorten courses of TPN. The group reported on

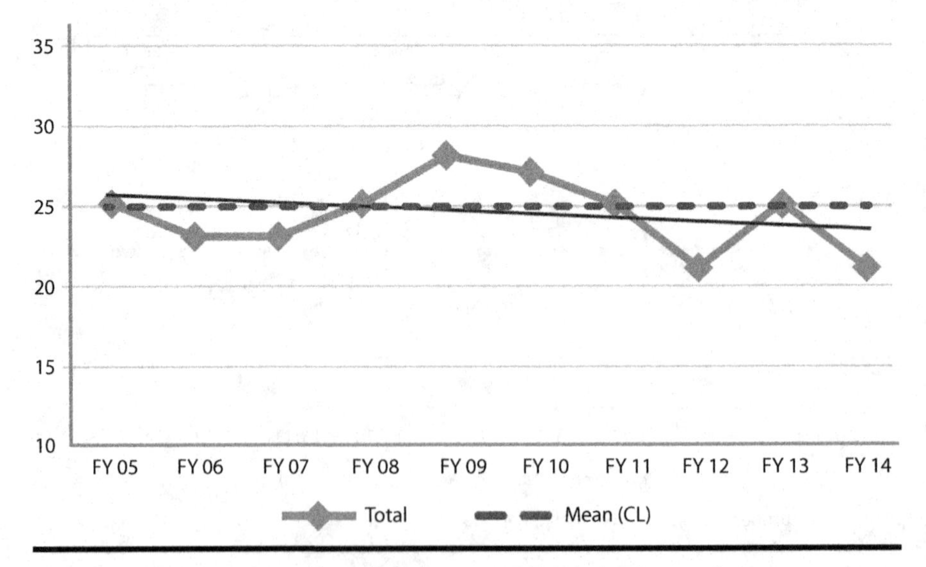

Figure 13.9 Percentage of total patients on TPN three days or less.

the status of shortages up through the established communication channels so that all necessary leaders in the organization were aware of the potential safety risks associated with the shortages.

During severe shortages of selected nutrients such as phosphate and potassium salts, we have involved medical and surgical leadership in the development and enforcement of recommendations across the hospital. Leaders and managers have devoted a considerable amount of time to managing the shortages, and yet those involved have not felt like they were working at cross purposes or wasting time, because we have cross-departmental standard work for managing this risk.

Figure 13.10 shows how we balance our workload on a daily basis using a visual management tool. When our model rolled out a decade ago, we often were in the red zone (the indicator of excessive workload) because of the limited capacity of the compounder, the machine located off-site that is used to mix TPN. We focused our efforts on maximizing one-piece flow: working with the clinical teams to round earlier in the day on patients receiving TPN whenever possible; removing technology barriers to getting orders to the compounding pharmacy; and directing additional staff support to services with higher volumes of TPN orders. With our lower TPN utilization, we are now usually in the green zone, with occasional days in

Service	#TPN
Bone Marrow Transplant	9
Cardiac ICU	8
Oncology	2
Medicine	1
Neonatal ICU	9
Pediatric ICU	1
Rehab	0
Transplant/Gastroenterology	3
Surgery	2
Total	**35**

15–35 (Good) **36–45** **>46 (Critical)**

When status is Critical:

- Strictly follow standard work using one piece flow and adhering to a Noon deadline for orders
- Rebalance workload amongst services to submit all orders before the Noon deadline

Figure 13.10 Visual management of daily TPN census.

the yellow zone. We no longer discuss leasing an expensive second compounder or increasing lead time by delaying deliveries from the off-site location. The visibility tool allows leaders to quickly assess the TPN work for the day, detect any abnormal conditions, and support the frontline staff in real time.

Empowering staff to own the improvement culture has been an essential element of our success in sustaining our gains. Every year over the last decade the dietitians have collaborated with pharmacists on various projects, including enhancing the safety and communication of orders for patients on home TPN; capturing only the essential elements in documentation; and improving the weekend routines and handoffs as our hospital census and footprint have grown. Leaders act as sponsors for these projects to ensure that they are truly actionable and within the scope of the staff's work. The frontline ownership of daily work has allowed leaders to focus their efforts on overall staffing as well as energizing the larger organization around breakthrough improvement, such as integrating the TPN order (still on paper) into our electronic medical record—a veritable challenge due to the complexity of the order.

A final note on Lean leadership: We have learned that we need to coach and empower our successors. To do so, we have developed several dietitian and pharmacist "owners" for the annual updates of our hospital TPN guidelines. These individuals are becoming experts in assessing competency for maintaining ordering privileges and conducting audits on our standard processes. As one of our leadership team has stepped into other responsibilities, these intentional development opportunities have allowed a new leader to emerge and "see with new eyes" the next steps on our journey. Practicing Lean leadership with our breakthrough and daily improvement work has been a very enriching experience and has produced outcomes that create a safer TPN environment for our patients.

Chapter 14

Hand Hygiene at Seattle Children's Hospital: A Call to Action

Thérèse Mirisola and Karin Rogers

Decreasing the number of central line-associated blood stream infections (CLABSI) has been an organization-wide goal at Seattle Children's Hospital (SCH) for many years. About a decade ago, SCH began to apply continuous performance improvement (CPI) to reducing these infections, and we were gratified to see the CLABSI rate drop in our Cancer Care Unit (CAN Unit) from 4.5 per 1000 central line catheter days in 2006 to 3.4 per 1000 central line catheter days in 2011. In terms of absolute numbers, 8 fewer patients developed CLABSI in our CAN Unit in 2011 than in 2006 (34 patients compared with 42 patients). In our 48-bed CAN Unit, we have had a special focus on reducing the CLABSI rate because of the number of patients in the unit who have indwelling central lines and the special risks associated with immunosuppression, which is common among patients with cancer.

CLABSIs are associated with a host of potential negative consequences, including increased stress for the patient and family, increased length of stay, the need for antibiotics with the risk of associated side effects, and possible transfer to the pediatric intensive care unit (PICU), which incurs a greater mortality risk. We knew that reducing the number of these infections was essential to improving care for our pediatric patients. But after application of a number of CPI tools, including maintenance bundles and compliance auditing, we found that our improvement had plateaued. We had documented observed compliance levels that were consistently more than 90 percent with hand hygiene protocols as healthcare workers entered and exited patient rooms, so we knew that additional work in this area would not likely translate into a substantial reduction in the CLABSI rate. We needed to look for other opportunities for improvement.

As care providers, we know that we need to clean our hands before and after patient contact. Nevertheless, many factors conspire to prevent our best intentions, including responding to a patient emergency, becoming distracted by an unexpected event, or rushing to complete our next task. Sometimes the supplies we need for hand hygiene are not readily available, we are carrying bulky equipment, or we simply forget to stop to clean our hands. Plus, hand hygiene involves more than simply washing our hands with soap and water or applying sanitizing gel. It requires an awareness of the situations in which hand contamination is possible.

In April 2013 the CAN Unit moved into a new building. The driving force in the design of the new CAN Unit was standardization, a shift to private rooms, and bringing more care to the bedside. Standardizing rooms was a response to both staff and family needs. In the older unit, staff wasted time looking for supplies and adjusting care practices to different room configurations. They were often frustrated by the inconsistent availability of supplies, as some rooms had plenty of space for storage and others did not. Families, many of whom were in and out of the hospital frequently, were never sure if they would have a private or semiprivate room, how the room would be configured, or whether they would have access to a shower.

All of the patient rooms in the new unit are private. Every patient room is identical by intention, to facilitate standard work and support CPI. We have computers on wheels in every patient room and a process by which medications are delivered directly to the patient rooms. Patient rooms in the new unit are equipped with a rolling storage cart stocked with the specific supplies necessary to perform day-to-day care for our patients. The cart rolls out from under the sink and provides an ideal work surface for clean or sterile procedures.

Once we moved into the new unit, nurses began completing documentation and preparing medication inside patient rooms for the first time. What became very clear was that staff were doing so much in the patient room that they occasionally missed opportunities for hand hygiene. Also, the storage carts added new complexity related to potential hand contamination during patient care.

Occasionally, executive leaders received feedback from the parents of CAN Unit patients that staff were failing to practice recommended aspects of infection control at the bedside. Given that the audits for hand hygiene were based on observations outside the patient rooms, improving hand hygiene practices at the bedside was a logical next step.

Leaders of the CAN Unit, staff nurses who were members of the unit's shared governance quality council and infection prevention, had discussed hand hygiene at the point of care (HHPOC) a great deal over the course of several months after the move. It became evident that there was a lack of clarity about when to perform in-room hand hygiene in the course of performing multiple patient-care tasks. Executive leaders saw HHPOC as an opportunity to reduce healthcare-associated infections (HAIs) to an even greater degree than previously possible. In July 2013, leadership set an organizational goal of 2.72 CLABSI per 1000 central line catheter days in the CAN Unit for fiscal year 2014.

As a first step in achieving this goal, in October 2013, SCH executives enlisted us (an infection preventionist and a cancer care clinical nurse specialist) to focus on improving HHPOC with patients in the CAN Unit who have central line devices. We were tasked with the completion of an A3 tool on HHPOC and leading a rapid process design event to implement identified countermeasures.

Using Continuous Performance Improvement to Implement Hand Hygiene at the Point of Care

Soon after we were identified as process owners for the HHPOC event, we attended a daylong course on the use of A3 thinking. This Lean approach, named for the size of the paper used to format the tool on a single page, helps the user follow a logical path when problem solving. It includes sections for defining the opportunity (issue, background, current condition), goal, root cause analysis, target condition, countermeasures, implementation plan, cost analysis, testing and follow-up actions.

Immediately after completing the course, we began using the A3 tool to prepare for a rapid design event. We recorded current state observations, conducted a pre-event staff survey on attitudes and practices related to HHPOC, and worked with staff to complete a root cause analysis. As part of this work, the two of us performed simulations using the existing infection control policies. This step turned out to be very enlightening. As we walked through the protocols, we found several errors, for example, the policy on central line blood drawing instructed the staff to place the pump on pause just before drawing blood (to maximize silent time), but this would necessitate touching a contaminated surface. We included this error on the list of problems for which staff would develop countermeasures during the rapid design event.

By January 2014, we had completed and received executive sign off on the left side of the A3 document, which included our issue statement, our goal, a description of the current condition (determined by our pre-event observations), and our root cause analysis (see Figure 14.1). We moved quickly to scheduling the rapid design event, which we held in February. To ensure the success of the event and to foster engagement in HHPOC, we enlisted the involvement of all relevant care providers. These included not only the nurses in the CAN Unit, but also those from home care, the intensive care unit, and the acute care float pool. We also included the vascular access nurse and the nurse educator from the CAN Unit, who is responsible for supporting preceptors and staff orientation on the unit. In addition, we invited leadership from clinical departments of the hospital to provide management guidance for the event. Two project managers and a CPI consultant helped run the event and monitor our progress in completing the A3 work.

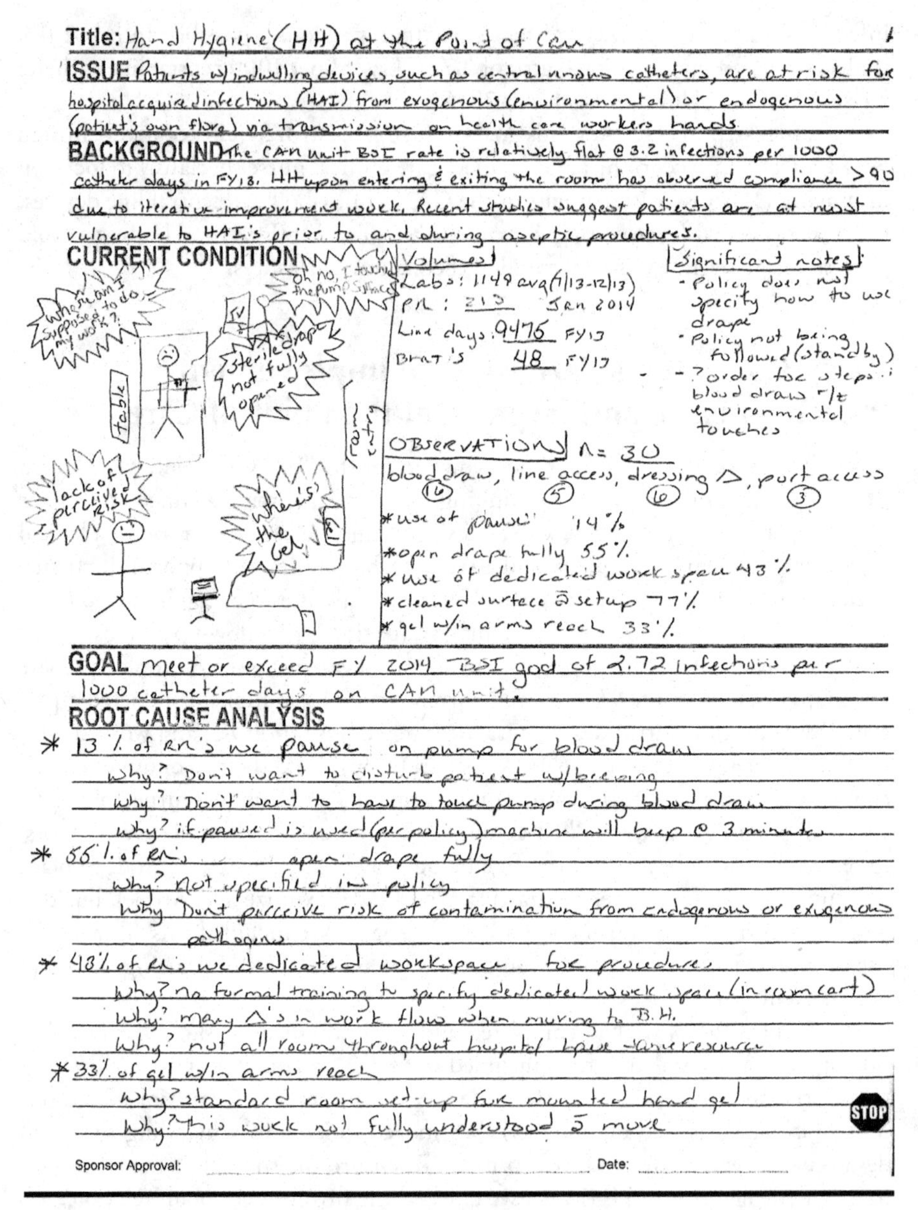

Title: Hand Hygiene (HH) at the Point of Care

ISSUE Patients w/ indwelling devices, such as central venous catheters, are at risk for hospital acquired infections (HAI) from exogenous (environmental) or endogenous (patient's own flora) via transmission on health care workers hands.

BACKGROUND The CAN unit BSI rate is relatively flat @ 3.2 infections per 1000 catheter days in FY13. HH upon entering & exiting the room has observed compliance >90 due to iterative improvement work. Recent studies suggest patients are at most vulnerable to HAI's prior to and during aseptic procedures.

CURRENT CONDITION

Volumes:
Labs: 1149 avg (7/13-12/13)
PR: 213 Jan 2014
Line days: 9476 FY13
Brat's 48 FY13

Significant notes:
- Policy does not specify how to use drape
- Policy not being followed (standby)
- ? order for steps: blood draw r/t environmental touches

OBSERVATIONS n = 30
blood draw (16), line access (5), dressing Δ (6), port access (3)
*use of pause 14%
*open drape fully 55%
*use of dedicated work space 43%
*cleaned surface ā setup 77%
*gel w/in arms reach 33%

GOAL meet or exceed FY 2014 BSI goal of 2.72 infections per 1000 catheter days on CAN unit.

ROOT CAUSE ANALYSIS

* 13% of RN's use pause on pump for blood draw
  why? Don't want to disturb patient w/ beeping
  why? Don't want to have to touch pump during blood draw
  why? if paused is used (per policy) machine will beep @ 3 minutes
* 55% of RN's open drape fully
  why? Not specified in policy
  why Don't perceive risk of contamination from endogenous or exogenous pathogens
* 48% of RN's use dedicated workspace for procedures
  Why? no formal training to specify dedicated work space (in room cart)
  Why? many Δ's in work flow when moving to B.H.
  Why? not all rooms throughout hospital have same resources
* 33% of gel w/in arms reach
  Why? standard room set-up for mounted hand gel
  Why? this work not fully understood ō move

STOP

Sponsor Approval: Date:

Figure 14.1 Left side of A3. Our team used the left side of the A3 document to record our issue statement, goal, a description of the current condition, and root cause analysis in preparation for a rapid improvement event on hand hygiene at the point of care (HHPOC). We completed the right side of the A3 document in the several months following the event.

As process owners of the event, it was our job to present the current state and the identified problems. The rapid design event team then focused on identifying and testing countermeasures, which they listed on the right side of the A3 tool. We ran simulations in an empty patient room with participants trying out the various potential practices (see Figure 14.2). As leaders of the event, we were gratified by the number of "aha" moments that participants experienced. For example, one nurse said, "I didn't realize that I always pull the side rail down at this point in the blood draw and am contaminating my hands when I do."

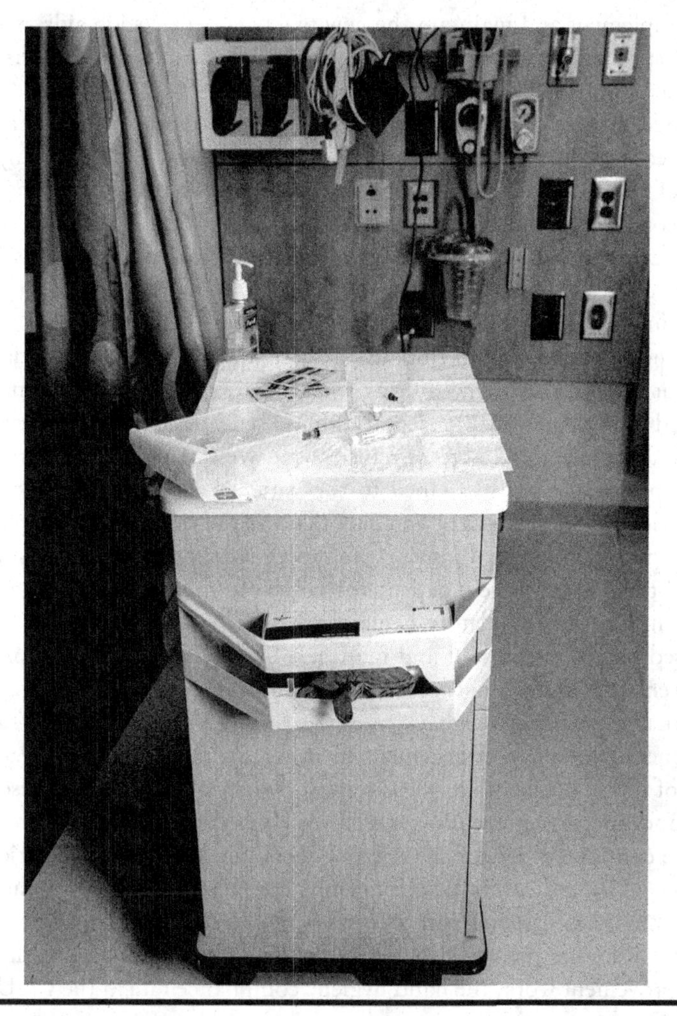

Figure 14.2 Mock-up used for simulation during rapid design event. Running simulations with mocked up storage carts allowed our team to identify HHPOC practices that would work during day-to-day care for our patients.

We helped participants identify two guiding principles from the design event, which were used to shape the new policies and procedures for HHPOC. These principles were

- Make sure you have what you need where you need it (e.g., gel, gloves, supplies)
- Put nothing on the bed; the bed is not a clean workspace

As part of the event, participants considered and then created the tools they would need to implement and maintain the new practices, such as job aids, written policies, and specified procedures. These tools included both photographs and electronic text to support different learning styles.

As leaders, we addressed several logistical obstacles to trying out the proposed countermeasures during the design event. Because of the fire hazard, only a limited amount of alcohol-based hand sanitizers is permitted in each patient room, which initially constrained the simulations. We consulted with the director of building and engineering and the fire marshal about safe amounts and locations within the rooms.

The number and location of trash receptacles in the patient rooms was also an issue during the design event. Initially the design called for an additional can near the patient care area. After consulting with the director of environmental services we learned that an additional receptacle would be at odds with the green initiative at SCH and significantly increase refuse costs. We interceded by offering bedside another option: a paper bag taped to the patient tray. Given these choices, the nurses decided to create a set of practices that use the existing trash receptacle.

In the month following the event, we supervised a two-week trial using the new HHPOC tools within a few patient rooms before rolling them out to the entire CAN Unit and the ambulatory hematology-oncology clinic. During this month we focused on educating staff and managers by presenting information from the design event at staff meetings, providing one-on-one coaching, and auditing standard work and providing feedback.

We encouraged staff engagement in using the new HHPOC practices in a number of ways. The fact that we, as process owners of the event, represented both nursing and infection prevention was extremely helpful in ensuring both perspectives were considered. Use of the A3 tool encouraged active participation in various aspects of the endeavor. Including an issue statement on the A3 that resonated with the nurses—"Patients with central venous catheters and other indwelling devices are at higher risk for HAI via transmission on health care workers' hands. With improvement work, the hand hygiene compliance rate in the CCU is >90%; recent research suggests risk around aseptic procedures"—focused nurses on a single common goal: patient safety. Breaking into small groups during the rapid design event to work through specific problems and find creative solutions fostered more active participation in design and ownership of the new HHPOC practices.

Finally, ensuring that staff members were backfilled in their patient care duties in order to participate in the rapid design event and given time to participate in the supportive activities before and afterward were important in enabling their engagement.

By proactively addressing challenges and taking steps to foster engagement, we found that nursing staff was very receptive to creating and adopting new practices. In fact, we experienced no real pushback. Instead of dealing with resistance or conflict, when issues arose during implementation we had conversations with the staff and found ways to make the necessary changes. For example, nurses identified an unnecessary glove change in the new policy. We reviewed the issue, amended the procedure, and communicated the revised policy to all staff.

The Results: Achieving Momentum for Greater Improvement

Using CPI tools we were able to achieve momentum and move off the improvement plateau on which we had been stalled. The attitudes and practices reported by staff are evidence of changed beliefs and behaviors. For example, prior to the design event, 63 percent reported using the bed as a work surface when changing the cap on the central line catheter. After the event, this figure dropped to 9 percent (see Figure 14.3). The survey results are supported by our daily audits, which have demonstrated compliance with hand hygiene at point of care practices of more than 90 percent in the CAN Unit.

These improvements in infection-control practices have translated into clinical improvements for our patients. The rate of CLABSI in the CAN Unit dropped to 2.6 for fiscal year 2014, surpassing the goal we had set for the unit (see Figure 14.4).

In addition to outcome improvements, we have seen an amazing shift in understanding about infection risk among our staff. The awareness and perception of risk is completely different today and extends well beyond the practices related to central line catheters. Conversations are now peppered with concerns about potential sites and circumstances for contamination. For example, a staff nurse observed a nurse instructor use a practice that could introduce contamination when teaching how to perform a procedure. The staff nurse recognized the risk based on what she had learned from the HHPOC event. She approached the instructor later and explained the hand hygiene protocol used for central line access and asked that the instructor incorporate the change in her teaching.

Perception of risk has increased among our patients' families as well. As one parent told us, "We love the use of the cart for the blood draws. It signals to our five-year-old that his brother's central line is going to be touched. He knows now to go sit on the couch during the procedure." The parents were appreciative of the cues that signaled the importance of line safety not only to staff but also to family members.

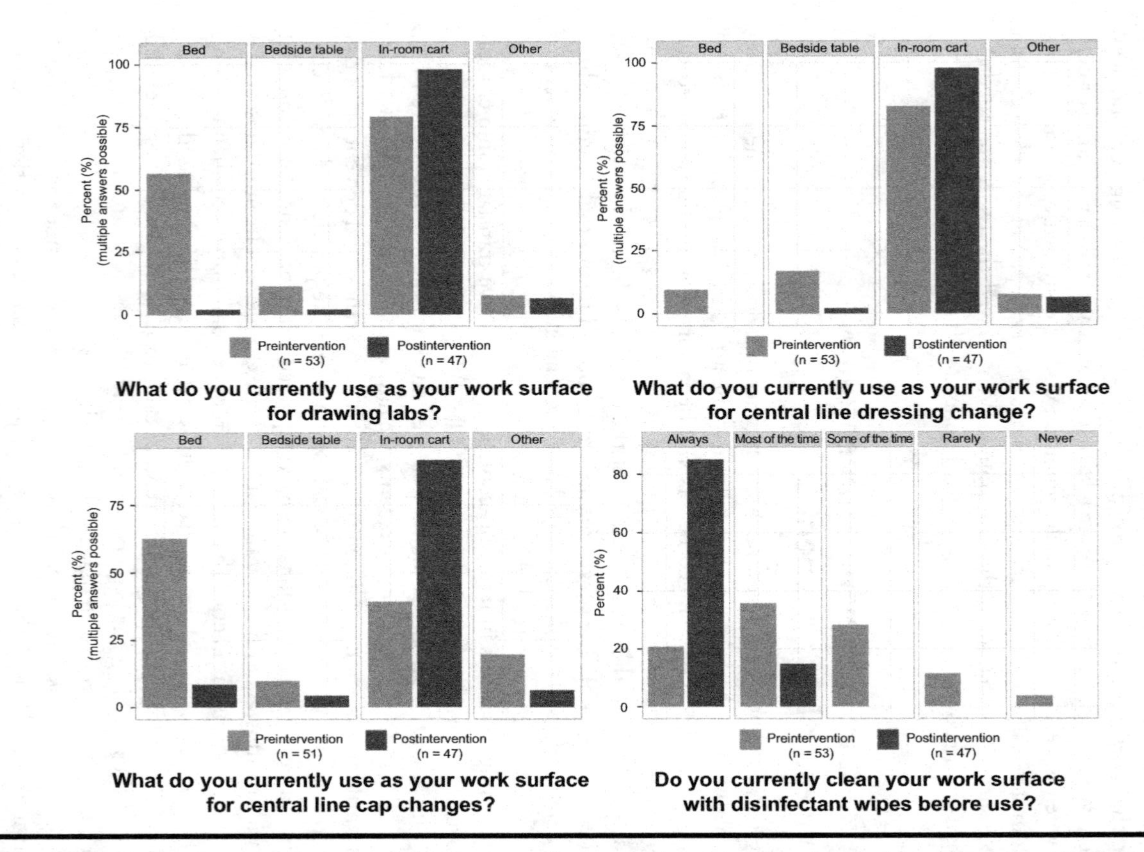

Figure 14.3 Data from pre- and postevent staff survey. Staff-reported attitudes and practices related to HHPOC changed after the rapid improvement event.

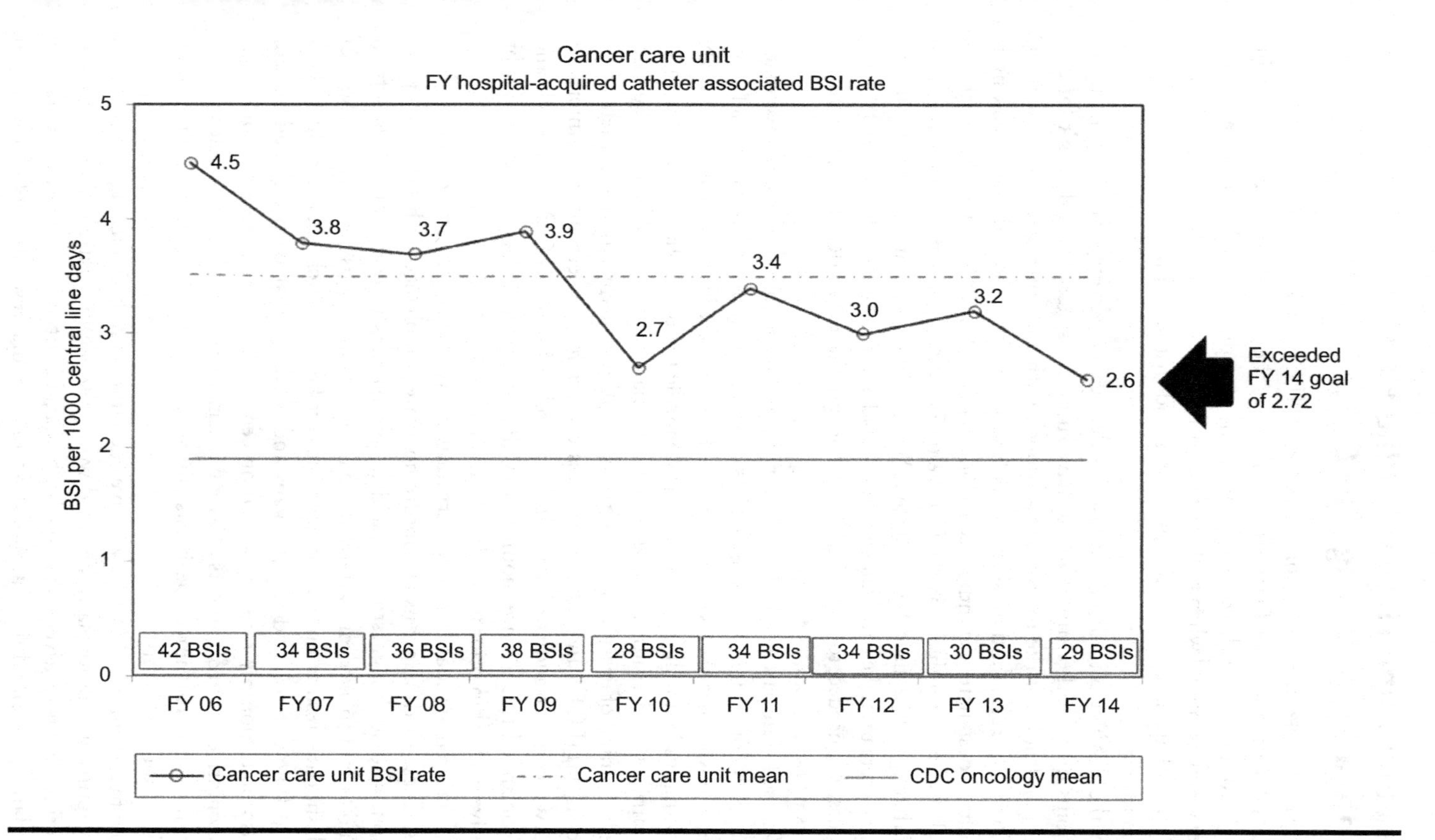

Figure 14.4 Catheter-acquired blood stream infections at SCH Cancer Care Unit. The CLABSI rate in the CAN Unit decreased from 4.5 in 2006 per 1000 central line days to 2.6 per 1000 catheter days in 2014.

Spreading Hand Hygiene at the Point of Care and Sustaining Our Gains

We began our planning work for spreading HHPOC to other units in April 2014. We ran education sessions for nursing staff across the entire hospital during the following two months. In July, we rolled out the new practices. The most significant barrier we encountered when replicating to other care areas was lack of standardization in the shape and size of patient rooms and in the equipment stocked within the rooms.

In the CAN Unit, all 48 rooms are identical by design. However, many of the rooms on the other units did not have sufficient space under the sink for cart storage, and none of the rooms was equipped with the same cart as the rooms in the CAN Unit. In addition, some units had a variety of room designs, making it difficult to designate a standardized work plan for HHPOC. We addressed this obstacle by ensuring that managers of the units identified the work surface in each room that would be used for HHPOC. We had multiple conversations with staff and managers to make sure that each room had a designated work surface. In some instances, we needed to requisition funds to purchase additional mayo stands to serve as work surfaces.

We used transparency and daily management to maintain the gains we made and support continuous improvement. We made sure to share our data widely. We created a poster that shows the number of days since the last CLABSI in the CAN Unit. It hangs in a well-trafficked area just outside the unit, where it is visible to all staff, families, and visitors. As part of daily management, we hold regular huddles at the beginning of every shift during which staff report any barriers to their work, including HHPOC, and identify process owners for implementing countermeasures. We conduct audits of standard work related to HHPOC every week and have continued this intense monitoring well beyond the initial expectation set by executive leadership prior to implementation.

We created standard work observation cards, which we use to conduct the audits. These cards allow us to capture not only compliance with HHPOC practices but also staff suggestions related to any barriers to compliance. Data from the audits is displayed on our results dashboard. Managers place screenshots of the dashboard results on each unit's visibility board, which they use on a daily basis to follow trends and identify gaps and obstacles that need to be addressed. We also hold monthly rounds focused on central line catheter care and practices. Representatives from all aspects of care participate in these rounds, including bedside nurses, clinical nurse specialists, infection prevention staff, and the family members of our patients.

The most significant barrier we have encountered to maintaining our gains has been capturing data for daily standard work observations outside the CAN Unit. Collecting data is relatively easy within the CAN Unit, because most patients have a standard daily blood draw at 4 a.m. In other units, fewer patients have central line access, and there is no standard time for blood draws, making it difficult to conduct consistent standard work observations in these units. We are still working on finding a way to make this data collection more consistent.

What We've Learned and Where We're Going

In the course of our work on HHPOC, we have learned some important lessons about process design and implementation that are essential for success. First, we could not have succeeded without the active involvement of frontline nurses in every aspect of planning and design. Their involvement was critical in creating new practices that would actually work at the bedside. In the same vein, simulations were essential. We used empty patient rooms to try the new interventions, such as the use of the new carts for the designated work surface, then created and adjusted practices until we had developed standard work that met our requirements for HHPOC. We found that we did not need high-tech or expensive solutions to address the identified problems.

Extensive education of staff after the design event was absolutely necessary to achieve consistent standard work around HHPOC. We used e-mail, in-person conversations, and coaching at a skills station to ensure that all staff was well trained on the new practice. Finally, it was critical to the success that both staff and process owners had protected time to devote to the HHPOC work. Executive leadership's approval of this work time allowed us to intensely focus for several months on the development and implementation of HHPOC in the CAN Unit and to support the spread of HHPOC throughout the hospital.

Looking to the future, we plan to incorporate HHPOC principles into patient care involving other invasive devices (e.g., tracheostomy, Foley catheters). We will work to spread HHPOC to other disciplines at SCH. We will also continue standard work observations across the hospital, providing additional training where needed and removing barriers to "doing the right thing."

Using CPI has allowed SCH to make headway—after years of being stalled at an improvement plateau—on reducing bloodstream infections in our patients with central line catheters. Using HHPOC to make such improvement is an achievement that many leaders within SCH and in other institutions are interested in replicating. The high level of interest we see when presenting our work on HHPOC at quality meetings within SCH and elsewhere is evidence of how important the topic is today.

While understanding and implementing specific HHPOC practices is important, CPI has also enabled SCH to make a more subtle but wider-reaching change: increased perception of infection risk among staff within and beyond the CAN Unit. In the autumn of 2014, staff from across SCH helped select new infusion pumps for the hospital. We were gratified to hear staff query the equipment vendors about whether they would be able to place a pump on pause for long enough to perform blood draws without contaminating their hands during the procedure. Bedside nurses more frequently recognize when patients are potentially at risk for CLABSI due to central line contamination, issues with caps or tubing, or other causes, and they bring these potential risks to the attention of the team, where they can be addressed.

Leaders across the hospital have a greater awareness of the importance of HHPOC in reducing infection risk. The medical director of the CAN Unit recently stated at a monthly quality meeting, "All providers should know about HHPOC. We go into patient rooms and may not touch the central lines but we do procedures that should be aseptic. This is information we need!"

It is amazing to hear our clinicians talking about infection risk in a much more global way. For us, HHPOC has been a big win!

Chapter 15

Balancing the Line in Outpatient Pharmacy

Steven D. Wanaka and Barb Marquardt

Imagine you are a charge nurse in the emergency room (ER) trying to get a patient admitted to a bed in the hospital. You make multiple calls and find out that beds will be available "as soon as we can get the patient discharged." Meanwhile, the ER waiting room is filling up with worried parents and sick children. All exam rooms in the ER are occupied by patients currently being cared for, waiting for test results, or waiting for admission to a hospital bed. For you, it's "another day in the ER," but you know that for the children and parents coming to you for help, the situation is at best stressful and at worst unsafe. So you keep making phone calls, hoping that your calls will "speed things up."

Now imagine that you are a nurse in the hospital. You know the ER is full, so you have been trying your best to "expedite" the discharge of patients on your floor. Your patients with physician discharge orders are ready to go, except they have not received their discharge medications from the hospital's pharmacy. The best you can do is to continue to call the hospital's outpatient pharmacy, where discharge orders are filled, hoping that your call will "speed things up."

Further imagine that you are in the outpatient pharmacy filling the discharge prescriptions. Most of the workload for discharge medications came to you in a "bolus" between 10 a.m. and noon. Some of the orders are complicated, containing more than ten medications. You are working as fast as you can, but the phone keeps ringing!

This was the situation that Seattle Children's Hospital found itself in when it launched a discharge medication turnaround time initiative in 2005. To be fair, medications were only one of the many causes of discharge delays. Nonetheless, the outpatient pharmacy took the challenge seriously and began work on how to remove medications as a "constraint" in the discharge process.

When the discharge medication process improvement work started, the first logical question was "Who are the customers of the outpatient pharmacy?" Customers were identified as the following:

1. Inpatients who are going home from the hospital
2. Postoperative day surgery patients
3. Patients seen in ambulatory clinics
4. Emergency department patients

Pharmacy leadership and staff were concerned about prioritizing prescriptions for inpatient medicine patients at the expense of other patients. If pharmacy focused only on decreasing the turnaround time for inpatient medicine discharge prescriptions, the turnaround time for other patients might increase. After pharmacy leadership explained their concern to the continuous performance improvement (CPI) consultants and inpatient medicine group, all agreed that the focus of the work should be to decrease medication turnaround time for all patients.

During the assessment and planning phase of the work, the team determined that a Rapid Process Improvement Workshop (RPIW) on "outpatient pharmacy flow" was needed. This workshop would require close collaboration between the medical service and pharmacy, so a medical unit physician and the lead outpatient pharmacist were assigned as co-process owners. While it is usually best to assign one process owner to a project, in this case the collaboration between co-owners was a key to success. The co-owners shared information about their respective work flows and facilitated improvement opportunities across the system.

In preparation for the RPIW, the workshop team observed current processes and documented their findings. Observers stood in the pharmacy, timed each step of the process, and tracked the movement of people, information, and materials. The observers included pharmacy and nonpharmacy staff. Initially, the pharmacy staff found it difficult to conduct their usual work when people with clipboards and stopwatches watched their every move. For many, this was the first time their work had ever been timed or their footsteps charted. Pharmacy leaders, sensing uneasiness from the staff, took time to introduce the observers to the staff, explain their role in the project, and answer questions. Today you will find that observations are commonplace in the pharmacy and being observed is part of the job. The results of observations are shown in Figure 15.1.

Once observations were complete, a work balance form was created (see Figure 15.2). The data showed that the pharmacy staff was meeting an average cycle time that was less than the required takt time (rate of customer demand) and that the workloads (cycle times) for the three members of the outpatient "assembly line" appeared quite balanced. At first glance, this made it appear that the pharmacy must be able to meet customer demand. However, this was very far from the truth. The

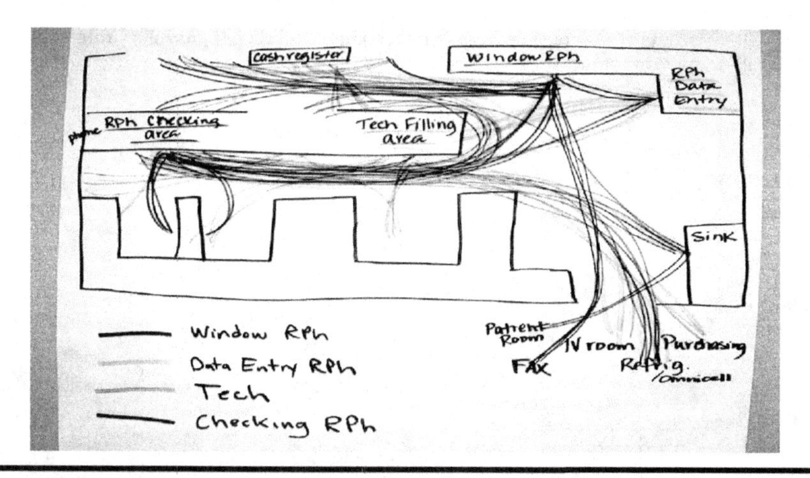

Figure 15.1 Spaghetti diagram. Mapping the "as-is" process and the roles supporting it. Although observation was uncomfortable for the staff at first, it was key to identifying waste in the process.

average cycle time did not reflect the reality of the wide-ranging variability in the time to perform each step. For example, the step done by the checking pharmacist could take anywhere from 42 seconds to 24 minutes. Whenever a step in the process exceeded the average, queues and backups would develop in the workflow, causing delays and lack of predictability. The Work Balance Form, which shows the takt time, average cycle time, and range of cycle times, was an especially helpful illustration of the need to achieve improved work balance between the three people working on the line: the order entry pharmacist, the fill tech, and the checking pharmacist.

The Work Balance Form emphasized the need for input from the RPIW team members and outpatient pharmacy staff on ways to remove waste and get the cycle time of each job at or below the required takt time. While gaining input from staff was critical for engagement and obtaining the best results, pharmacy managers grappled with the challenge of communicating with staff and obtaining their input while they were actively working on the line. Interruptions could lead to errors, jeopardize patient safety, and cause delays, but the production line needed to continue while the process improvement team did its work. Leaders and staff agreed that communication should occur with the least disruption of the process and maximal input from all participants. The group decided to communicate through frequent, brief meetings (less than 10 minutes); e-mail messages; and flyers posted in the pharmacy.

The team found that the spaghetti diagram was useful in quickly revealing work flow problems and in stimulating ideas to balance the work. The form showed that staff members traveled away from the pharmacy work area because they did not have the tools and materials they needed in their area. The RPIW team achieved quick wins by placing a fax machine and refrigerator in the outpatient pharmacy

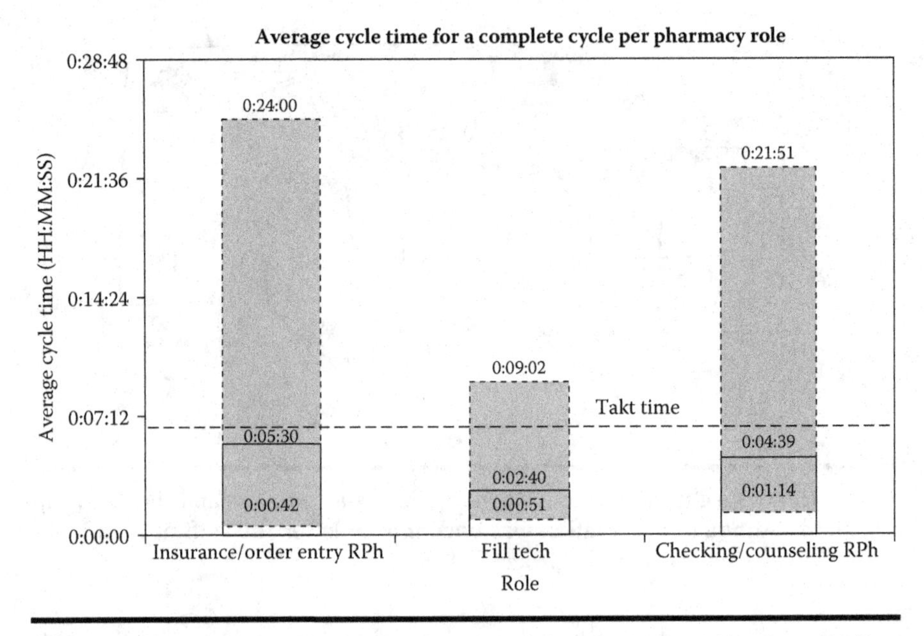

Figure 15.2 Work Balance Form. The mean cycle time is shown by the solid line. The gray shaded areas show the wide range in cycle times for each step of the operation.

area. These two small improvements eliminated wasted time and travel and, maybe more importantly, engaged the pharmacy staff, who saw immediate benefits from the RPIW. One reason for the checking pharmacist's wide-ranging cycle time was the need to leave the outpatient pharmacy area to deliver take-home medications to inpatients being discharged. A delivery could add more than 20 minutes to the cycle time. In a prior RPIW, feedback from families about the medication deliveries was generally positive, and the pharmacy staff had long thought the providers, nurses, and families viewed it as a value-added service. By 2005, however, it was clear that families and hospital staff valued timely completion of prescriptions over delivery to the patient's room. The data showed that the checking pharmacist's step was highly variable, and the team realized that variation could be eliminated if the pharmacist stayed in the pharmacy instead of making deliveries to patient rooms. The RPIW team members and the management guidance team decided to eliminate the deliveries in favor of a balanced work flow and more predictable turnaround time.

During the RPIW, the workshop leader introduced the concept of a service promise. The RPIW team calculated a takt time of six minutes, balanced the steps in the prescription-filling work flow, and reduced the variability of cycle times. They decided that the improvements should enable the staff to fill prescription orders of up to five medications per patient within 30 minutes of receipt in the pharmacy. This assumed that orders sent to the pharmacy did not require rework; orders with errors would be returned to the originating patient care unit for correction. Accurate, smaller order sets were named "speed scripts." Order sets of more than five prescriptions would take longer, and these order sets were named "complex orders." No turnaround time was defined for complex orders, but the team determined that the pharmacy would have time to work on these larger orders in the afternoon. The RPIW team publicized the 30-minute service promise and asked nurses not to call the pharmacy to ask if prescriptions were ready until 30 minutes had passed since sending them to the pharmacy.

Many improvements were made during the RPIW, and it was viewed as a success. While the work fell short of meeting the 30-minute service promise, the average turnaround time decreased by 40 percent (from 89 minutes pre-RPIW to 51 minutes 120 days post-RPIW).

While 40-percent improvement is impressive, Lean thinking in the organization led to the conclusion that this "wasn't good enough" and medications were still a cause for discharge delay. This conclusion led the pharmacy team into another period of analysis of the current situation and further improvements.

It became clear to pharmacy leadership and staff that there had to be a better way than working in a strict "first in, first out" system where the pharmacy worked on orders as they were received. The pharmacy needed to know when medications were needed and to ensure that work was completed by that time. It didn't matter if the turnaround time for a medication was 24 hours as long as it was ready when the patient needed it. Pharmacy leaders discussed the concept with pharmacy staff members and asked them to give suggestions for improvement. Based on staff input, the team decided to develop a prescription-scheduling system. The system was based on the concept of "heijunka," or load leveling. The staff created a scheduling board, which enabled them to schedule completion times for prescriptions in 5- to 10-minute intervals. The intervals reflected the current cycle times to fill prescriptions. The heijunka board helped level the workload in the pharmacy, and it enabled staff and pharmacy leaders to visually determine if the line was running behind or ahead of schedule. The staff has worked together to make continuous incremental improvements to the scheduling system, and it is still in use three years later.

Perhaps the biggest measure of success is that the phone in the outpatient pharmacy is no longer ringing off the hook because nurses can now count on predictable, timely delivery of discharge medications.

During the outpatient pharmacy's CPI journey, pharmacy leaders and staff have learned many valuable lessons. First, eliminating barriers to effective communication with frontline staff is key to achieving engagement and sustainable results. Second, the people who do the work provide the best ideas for improvement. And, last, while much can be achieved in a five-day rapid improvement workshop, using the plan, do, check, and act (PDCA) process to continue to improve after the RPIW event is critical. CPI truly is a never-ending journey with successes and failures along the way.

Epilogue

Barb Marquardt

Since the writing of the original chapter, the number of prescriptions processed by the outpatient pharmacy has increased by almost 50 percent and continues to increase at a rate of 5 to 8 percent per year. To handle this increased workload the pharmacy worked diligently to decrease waste and balance workload, while adapting to changes in hospital operations and collaborating with other departments.

Despite increases in capacity related to this work, it eventually became clear that we needed a second production line to meet the increased demand. Staff thought that our scheduling board, which is based on the heijunka concept of level loading, worked well and that the second line should also employ a scheduling board. What wasn't clear was how to split the work between the two lines.

The staff decided to run an experiment, diverting the processing of all the inpatient discharge prescriptions into the second or "back" line and leaving the processing of all other prescription to the first or front line (see Figures 15.3 and 15.4). The experiment was a success, and the staff liked the logical division. The back line had the added benefit of being located at a distance from the busy pick-up window, and staff there were freed of phone-answering responsibilities, so their work was less likely to be interrupted. The reduction in interruptions was important because discharge prescriptions are often more complex than other prescriptions and often require follow-up with providers. With the second line, which we operate only during the busiest times of the week, we have been able to meet the increased demand for prescription processing.

About two years ago, we used CPI to effectively adapt to another change. The outpatient pharmacy began receiving more phone calls from the nurses in the day surgery unit asking if the pharmacy had received prescriptions for a particular patient. They weren't asking whether the medications were ready, but rather whether the prescription order had been received. The additional phone calls translated into more interruptions for pharmacy staff, increasing the chance of errors and disrupting workflow. The outpatient pharmacy operations manager contacted the nurse manager of day surgery and learned that the increase in phone calls was due to a change in provider behavior.

In the past, providers wrote paper prescription orders and placed them in the patient's chart. When the patient was transferred to recovery, the prescription orders would be sent to the pharmacy. Nurses looked for the prescriptions in the chart and sent the orders to the pharmacy themselves. This process gave nurses an indication that the prescription order was being processed, thus avoiding potential delays at discharge. Some providers began writing the prescriptions earlier in the process, as early as at the pre-op appointment, and giving the prescriptions directly to the family or pharmacy. Also, with the ability

Figure 15.3 Outpatient pharmacy back line scheduling board.

to send prescription orders electronically to the pharmacy, a paper prescription was no longer needed for all medications. With these changes in provider prescribing behavior, nurses had no indication that discharge prescriptions were in queue.

After discussing the issue with staff in pharmacy and day surgery, the team agreed on a simple solution. Pharmacy staff would enter a communication order in the patient's electronic medical record (EMR) that indicates that the prescription order has been received and the estimated time that the medications will be ready. (Pharmacy staff use the scheduling board to predict an accurate completion time.) Both pharmacy staff and day surgery nurses are pleased with the new process and appreciated the opportunity to collaborate.

Because CPI philosophy, principles, tools, and methods have been incorporated into hospital operations for many years, the organization has a common language for improvement. When working with hospital leaders, other departments, nurses, providers, pharmacists, or pharmacy technicians, we all know that the aim is continuous performance improvement. Some improvements have been big, some small. Some would be viewed as successful and some not, but everyone is on the journey together with the common goal of providing safe and effective care for patients.

Figure 15.4 Outpatient pharmacy frontline scheduling board.

Chapter 16

Rapid Changeover in the Operating Room

Sean H. Flack and Lynn D. Martin

Healthcare processes require completion of a number of tasks in the delivery of care to patients. Sometimes, these tasks, or steps, directly involve the patient, but many times they are indirectly related and must be completed before or after direct patient care activities. While the patient might expect these tasks to occur, if we asked patients to pay for them, they would probably refuse. Patients come to us for procedures; that's what they think they are paying for.

Many of these indirect steps, though not "value added" for the patient, are necessary to prepare for the next patient. This preparatory work for the next patient encounter is defined as turnaround time or "changeover" steps. From the patient's perspective, these tasks are non-value-added steps (waste) in a process. Worse still, these steps are frequently completed serially, in one-at-a-time fashion; as a result, the total duration of this period of non-value-added activity is often longer than necessary. Examples of unnecessary steps can be seen with each clinic visit, radiology procedure, laboratory run, patient admission, or operating room (OR) procedure.

Time spent on non-value-added changeover tasks reduces the availability of critical resources (e.g., the clinic room, hospital bed, diagnostic equipment, or operating room). Reductions in changeover times will reduce waiting for both patients and staff, lower operating costs, and yield a better return on capital investment because institutional capacity is increased.

"Lean" manufacturing companies have focused for many years on reducing changeover times. Toyota, for example, has reduced the time required to change large body panel-forming presses from hours to minutes. In car-racing competitions, NASCAR crews are able to routinely change four car wheels in less than ten seconds.

Our efforts to improve patient experience while achieving significant reduction in room turnover times in the OR will be the focus of this chapter.

Starting with the Patient Experience

Imagine that you are the parent of a child about to undergo surgery. What are your fears? Most likely, pain after surgery will be at, or near, the top of your list. Unfortunately, the reality is that pain management after surgery is often poorly managed. This may surprise you. After all, aren't the doctors and nurses trained and skilled in the assessment and prevention of pain?

The reality, however, is that children frequently endure quite significant amounts of pain after surgery. There are many reasons for this, but two important reasons are an underappreciation of the amount of pain the surgery will cause, and a wish to avoid the many side effects of pain medicines such as nausea, vomiting, itching, bleeding, and excessive sedation.

Recognizing that this is a major problem, the anesthesiologists at Seattle Children's Hospital (SCH) routinely use procedures known as "nerve blocks" to reduce, and even eliminate, the need for traditional pain medications. These procedures help the children wake without pain and consequently help speed their recovery and discharge home. The reasons why these blocks are not more widely used are twofold: first, they require the acquisition of advanced skills not taught to many trainee anesthesiologists; and, second, these procedures are usually performed once the child is anesthetized in the operating room and, consequently, can delay the start of surgery, thereby extending the amount of time needed in the OR or reducing the amount of operating time available to surgeons. These delays might not be well received by either a busy surgeon with a heavy caseload or a hospital administrator looking to maximize operating room efficiency.

Leading Change, Encountering Tension

How, then, did the anesthesiologists convince their surgical and administrative colleagues to support the use of nerve blocks? Three words: passion, patience, and persistence. And two more: "rapid changeover." It required the passion of a leader who was absolutely convinced that this was the right thing to do for his patients. It took patience in recruiting skilled anesthesiologists who could offer these techniques. It took perseverance in not giving in to the stumbling blocks and boulders that occur with the introduction of any new process. And it required an approach—rapid changeover—that was capable of eliminating the stumbling blocks and boulders from this process.

Sidebar 16.1

The day before Dr. Lynn Martin planned to drop out of his anesthesia residency program at Johns Hopkins University, he arrived in the OR to find that his first case of the morning was a boy who had been seriously burned and was receiving a series of skin grafts.

During surgical preparation, Martin suggested to the attending anesthesiologist that, in addition to general anesthesia, the child receive regional anesthesia to block nerve sensation in the area of the painful graft. The attending anesthesiologist agreed.

Hours later, Martin accompanied the boy back to his room. When his mother saw her son sitting in bed contentedly holding a balloon, she burst into tears. Fearing that he had done something wrong, Martin went to comfort her and find out why she was so upset. To his surprise, the mother told Martin that this was the happiest she had seen her child since his admission to the hospital several weeks before.

In that moment, Martin realized the power of regional anesthesia to help children begin their recovery without the stress of postoperative pain. The event not only cemented Martin's career in anesthesia but also continues to inform his leadership in the field.

Dr. Martin believed in regional anesthesia and had a deep conviction that nerve blocks were the optimal way to treat pain after surgery. This is the critical first step. Without passion from the leaders, it is impossible to sustain the work of continuous performance improvement (CPI). But one physician can't take care of every patient or perform every nerve block. Therefore, Dr. Martin sought and recruited faculty that were skilled in these techniques. Importantly, he recruited a physician recognized as a world authority on regional anesthesia in children to spearhead the project. He assembled a team that supported his vision and could deliver the results he was after.

Next, the use of regional blocks was introduced gradually and incrementally. Simple blocks that took little time to perform were introduced first. Skills were honed, and surgeons were acclimated to the use of nerve blocks. Incrementally, more complex blocks, which required more time to place, were introduced. This is when things got interesting, and tensions between anesthesiologists and some surgeons surfaced. The causes were twofold: success rates and operating room delays.

Surgeons complained that too many of the blocks didn't work well and that the anesthesiologists were taking too long to perform blocks. These concerns—while seemingly disparate—were closely related. Anesthesiologists needed time to perform their blocks correctly and carefully without feeling rushed. However, they were well aware of the surgeons' concerns regarding delays, and so they were performing the blocks in a hurried manner or resorting to quicker, but less effective, techniques. The results were suboptimal pain relief for the patients, longer anesthesia and OR times, and considerable tension between physician colleagues.

This illustrates the importance of the plan, do, check, and act (PDCA) process. A great idea, once implemented, is unlikely to succeed without a rigorous and frequent audit of what is and isn't working. And something had to be done to rescue the vision for pain-free recoveries.

Continuous Performance Improvement Methods and the Realities of Change

With hospital support, Dr. Martin led a two-day CPI event focusing on the nerve block process and how to improve success rates while also reducing OR times. As with all our CPI events, the team included members from all affected disciplines. In this case, this meant representation from anesthesia, surgery, pharmacy, nursing, and engineering. The outcome was the creation of an external setup process akin to strategies to reduce changeover times employed by companies such as Toyota and Boeing.

Shigeo Shingo, who worked with Toyota to reduce the changeover time of its large stamping presses, first described the external setup process. Located on production lines, these presses were necessarily turned off for the duration of any changeover process. Shingo recognized that a great deal of the changeover process could be completed by the workers in advance, so that once the press was turned off, it could be retooled and ready for use again far more quickly than before.

In a similar fashion, rather than anesthetizing a child and placing the nerve block in the operating room after completion of the preceding case, a procedure room within the operating room suite was modified and equipped so that a child could be anesthetized and "blocked" while the preceding case was still underway. Additionally, the team mapped the steps, and standardized the roles and communication required to accomplish the new process.

As with all CPI projects, data were critical in designing the process and determining whether the work was ultimately successful. Primary outcomes for this project included the creation of standards (reliable methods), the reduction in nonoperative (nonop) time, and significant institutional cost savings. "Nonoperative time" refers to the time between cases when the surgeon is not operating (the time between completing the first patient's surgery and starting surgery on the next patient) and can be considered a form of waste. There will always be some nonoperative time, but the value of external setup is that it reduces this non-value-added portion of the process.

If we look at data from six patients, summarized in Table 16.1, we can see that our team's targets were admirably met. Indeed, the median nonoperative time was reduced from 74 minutes to 37 minutes.

Table 16.1 Focused Event Results

Process Measures	*Current Day 1*	*Trial Process Vision*	*60-Day Follow-Up*
Number of steps	19	14	16
Number of value-added steps	4	7	7
% of value-added steps	21%	50%	44%
Lead time	93 minutes	Scheduled: 75 minutes	Scheduled: 75 minutes
Number of handoffs	3	3	4
Number of checking steps	8	4	4
Number of queues	6	3	2
5S level	1	1	2.8
Staff travel distance	1,000 steps	300 steps	300 steps (↓66%)
Information and equipment travel distance	200 steps	50 steps	50 steps (↓75%)
Theme Measures	*Workshop Day 1*	*New Process Vision*	*60-Day Follow-Up*
Quality	0 reliable methods		5 reliable methods
Cost			206 × $36.88 = $7,597.28
Delivery	Median nonop time: 74 minutes	Median nonop time: 67 minutes (↓9%)	Median nonop time: 37 minutes (↓50%)

If quality improvement were simple, that would be the end of the story: problems are identified, solutions are implemented, and things run smoothly thereafter. In reality, this work is seldom easy and never finished. Despite the measurable successes of this project, bumps in the road inevitably emerged. This is predictable with any new process or venture, and is often compared with lowering the level of a hitherto smooth-flowing river. As the water level is lowered, hidden boulders break above the surface, creating ripples, currents, and even rapids.

Through PDCA, the team found that block room usage had deteriorated over time. The process surrounding its use was complicated, requiring multiple communication steps and considerable perseverance on the part of the anesthesiologist. Also, the room was seldom in a state ready for immediate use because no process had been established for ensuring its daily preparation. Consequently, an anesthesiologist with a shared interest in the project's success was asked to take charge of the block room and lead a fresh effort to maximize its use.

More difficult to address, however, were ongoing tensions between anesthesiologists and some surgeons, which threatened to severely limit the use of nerve blocks at SCH. Although most surgeons had come to appreciate the benefits of nerve blocks for their patients, a minority continued to perceive blocks as high-risk, low-reward procedures. Anesthesiologists also felt that their blocks were being unfairly targeted as the source of some postoperative complications. Once again, strong and resilient leadership was required so that we could persist in establishing nerve blocks as an integral part of anesthesia practice at SCH.

At this point, Dr. Martin took advantage of his close and collegial relationship with surgical leaders to help enlist their support. This led to the development of two groups: an oversight team composed of leaders from anesthesia and surgery that provided guidance and set the tone for collegial interactions, and a working group that used CPI tools to improve all aspects of the nerve block process.

The results? In 2009, regional blocks were used for 2,220 of 18,771 OR cases (11.8 percent). Random manual data collection after the implementation of the block room showed a reduction in nonop time from an average of 74 minutes to 37 minutes (a 50-percent reduction). And in follow-up data collection (n = 10), nonop time was 36 minutes for that sample (sustained improvement).

This case study demonstrates the central role that leadership plays in ensuring that great ideas get translated into established practice. Leaders provide the critical momentum to persist with CPI when challenges inevitably arise. They understand that this work is challenging and takes time. Tenacity is required with colleagues and coworkers who resist change, and patience is needed when initial efforts fail. And data are critical in demonstrating the benefits achieved by CPI work.

Addressing Long Turnovers in Otolaryngology

Over 60 percent of our surgical patients each day present for ambulatory surgery, meaning that they are admitted and discharged on the same day as their surgical procedures. The majority of ambulatory cases come for surgeries (ear tubes, adenoidectomy, tonsillectomy, etc.) by our otolaryngology (oto) staff. However, in studying our processes, we realized that only about 4.5 hours of the 10 hours available each day in our oto rooms were being used by the surgeons to perform procedures. Each of the ten to twelve cases completed daily included approximately 30 minutes of turnover time. Thus, over half of the available surgery time was actually used turning over the OR. The long turnovers allowed fewer patients into our ORs each day, creating a backlog of cases for our surgeons. As the backlog and associated wait time for the patients and families grew, the OR value stream leaders resolved to focus on reducing long turnover times for ambulatory oto cases. Our hope was to take these learnings from oto and replicate them for all other ambulatory cases in the OR.

A multidisciplinary team of anesthesiologists, surgeons, nurses, technicians, and other support staff was pulled together to focus on changeovers for ambulatory oto surgeries. Targets the team hoped to achieve through the development of standards in the turnover process included a 50-percent reduction in turnover time, an increase in operative time, and a reduction in the time between patients' clinic visits and their surgical procedures.

The first task in changeover improvement is to observe the changeover process and record each step, the roles completing the step, the distance traveled for each role, the time required for each role, and any variations in the completion of the steps. Next, each step must be reviewed to see if it is an internal or external changeover step. Internal steps are tasks that can only be completed while the resource in question is not in use. For example, cleaning the OR floor can only occur when the patient and instrument tables are cleared. External steps are those that can be completed while the resource is in use (e.g., preparation of the instrument trays for the next case). With this more complete understanding and documentation of the changeover process, the team is then ready to begin the improvement process (see Figure 16.1).

Having first 5Sed the work area, the team began by converting internal steps to external steps whenever possible. For example, surgical case trays now routinely

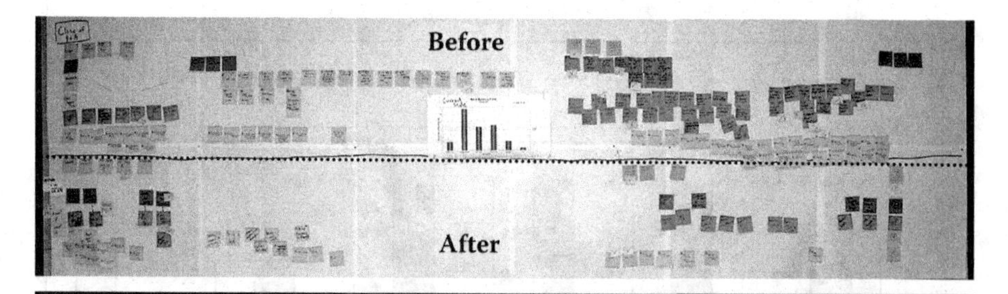

Figure 16.1 Process map before and after. The after model reflects Hirano's rules for rapid changeover in his *JIT Implementation Manual.* These seven rules are (1) begin and end with 5S; (2) change internal tasks to external tasks, then improve the remaining internal tasks; (3) anything that can't be easily moved is the enemy; (4) if you use your hands, make sure you do not use your feet; (5) don't reply on special fine-tuning skills; (6) standards are standards—they are not flexible; and (7) standardize all changeover operations. (From H. Hirano, *JIT Implementation Manual: The Complete Guide to Just-in-Time Manufacturing,* 2nd ed., 6 vols., Florence, KY: Productivity Press, 2009.)

included anesthesia supplies added prior to the case and brought to the anesthesia workspace to shorten anesthesia preparation time. Next, the team focused on the remaining internal steps and time required (cycle time) for each role and identified possible areas for improvement.

One major change was the conversion from serial family interactions by the circulating nurse followed by the anesthesiologist, to a single simultaneous encounter with the patient and family. This change eliminated duplication in communication with the patients and families and led to a significant increase in parental perceptions of effective teamwork.

Our observations also clearly documented significant differences in the number of tasks and cycle time by role. Our takt time for room turns was 14.5 minutes. Three of the six roles had cycle times in excess of the takt time, and the anesthesiologists had a cycle time twice as long as the takt time. Through teamwork and experimentation, tasks were balanced among other providers and staff in order to spread the total workload as evenly as possible and meet the takt time. It is important to note that tasks were shifted from the anesthesiologists to the circulating nurse and surgery and support technicians. In addition, the role of the anesthesia technician was completely eliminated; this allowed reallocation of this role to support more complex inpatient surgeries. These changes reduced the maximal cycle time by 37 percent to 18.5 minutes (short of the takt time of 14.5 minutes). This represented good progress, with more incremental improvement to come (see Figure 16.2).

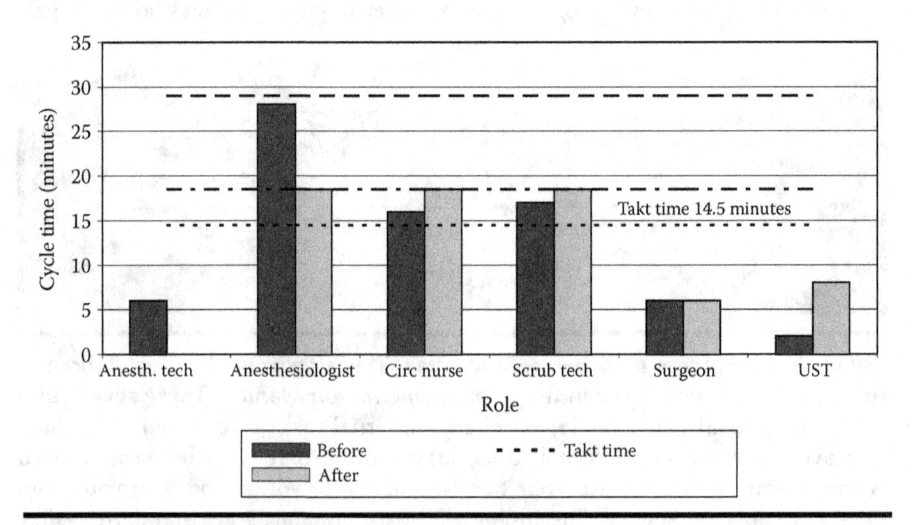

Figure 16.2 Work balance before and after. Rebalancing the workload among staff resulted in a reduction in cycle times. New working relationships among the various roles involved were key. UST, unit support tech.

At the end of the workshop week, this team had successfully developed a new turnover process in the oto ORs using iterative improvements via experimentation in the actual workplace.

The new process was significantly more efficient and radically different from our prior practice. Improvements noted from Day 1 (baseline) to the end of the workshop included a 47-percent reduction in steps, a 62-percent reduction in travel distance and handoffs, and a 59-percent reduction in turnover time (see Table 16.2). The key learning from this effort was the building of the team concept with shared roles across typical boundaries, as well as effective communication.

As with all change efforts, one of the most significant challenges is the ability to sustain the changes in the system. And not all of the changes implemented in this effort were sustained. The reliable methods for each role had evolved, but they were no longer being strictly followed by everyone. And turnover times were longer,

Table 16.2 Process Data

Process Measures	*Baseline*	*Day 5*	*% Change*	*Day 60*	*% Change*
Number of steps	108	57	–47%	57	–47%
Number of value-added steps	6	6	0%	6	0%
% of value-added steps	6%	11%	+50%	11%	+50%
Lead time (minutes):					
Turnover	45	18.5	–59%	27	–40%
Total (admit to discharge)	236	171	–27%	182	–23%
Number of handoffs	8	3	–62%	3	–62%
Number of checking steps	10	3	–70%	3	–70%
Staff travel distance (feet)	4,202	1,560	–62%	1560	–62%
Theme Measures	*Baseline*	*Day 5*	*% Change*	*Day 60*	*% Change*
Quality (reliable method)	0	5	100%	Not available	Not available
Delivery (number of days from clinic to OR)	50.2	50.2	0%	34.3	–32%

but they were still significantly shorter than what was seen on the first day of the workshop. The shorter turnover times did produce shorter total lead times (time from admit to discharge) and improved access to the operating suites (reduction in the surgery lead time from clinic to OR from 50 to 34 days). But the process was unique in many of its steps, and this made it very challenging to replicate for nonambulatory surgeries. This was particularly difficult in our hybrid or combined ambulatory and inpatient surgery suite.

Despite the slippage in desired outcomes, the leadership team was still pleased with overall reductions in turnover and lead times. Furthermore, the learnings from this event were helpful, because they provided very useful experience for the development and opening of our dedicated ambulatory surgery center. In fact, many of the processes designed in this workshop will be incorporated into our new "ambulatory-only" process in our new facility.

Epilogue

In the years since publication of our chapter, we have continued to refine our practices in regional anesthesia and otolaryngologic anesthesia, and have applied the knowledge gained from our work to design an innovative ambulatory surgical center. With more efficient workflow in our new space, we have improved both care quality and efficiency for our surgical patients.

A key to our success in redesigning these services was paying close attention to Hirano's *7 Rules for Improving Changeover*, which are[1]

1. Set-up begins and ends with 5S.
2. Change internal tasks to external tasks, then improve remaining internal tasks.
3. Anything that can't be easily moved is an enemy.
4. If you use your hands, make sure your feet stay put.
5. Don't rely on special fine-tuning skills.
6. Standards are standards; they are not flexible.
7. Standardize all set-up operations.

Rule 2 was instrumental in designing our new practice of external setup for regional anesthesia. As leaders, we made sure to involve our anesthesiologists in the design process. By making it clear that we heard their concerns and by involving them in looking for ways to improve processes, we encouraged their active involvement in identifying, refining, and implementing practice changes. However, applying rule 6 meant that we needed to consider ways to decrease the variability in the provision of regional anesthesia. Within our department, all anesthesiologists performed these procedures, and they wanted to maintain these clinical skills. However, a handful of physicians were very experienced with these techniques, while others performed a relatively low volume of procedures each month. We saw that reducing variability was essential.

In addition, we saw that optimal use of external setup only works if staff members are free of competing demands that limit their availability to reliably perform the work. Otherwise, creating the space and new processes to perform the work in parallel is a wasted effort. Often anesthesiologists were busy supervising the preceding case and unable to perform nerve blocks for the next patient.

To solve these issues, we created a five-member team of anesthesiologists with expert skills in regional anesthesia. Each day one member of the team is assigned to exclusively perform nerve blocks. An important part of their daily work is to be available to place the nerve blocks in the block room, while their anesthesia, surgery, and nursing colleagues are busy in the OR with the preceding patient.

One of our jobs as leaders was to hold difficult conversations with the physicians who would no longer be performing regional anesthesia. To move forward, we needed to listen to and acknowledge their concerns and feelings about this decision and remind them of our ultimate goal. We recognized that the decision had downsides, such as increased handoffs and that it was not what individual providers would prefer. We asked them to consider two questions: What would be best for our patients? What would I want as a patient or parent? Working through the conflict was challenging. The physicians were averse to letting go of this clinical skill. This difficult decision was vindicated by the improvements we have since achieved with complication rates, which have decreased year upon year, and by the fact that other organizations have followed our example in expanding the use of regional anesthesia yet limiting the procedure to a small number of experienced providers.

This practice change raised three principal concerns that we needed to address. First, the new workflow increased the number of handoffs between clinicians, increasing the opportunity for miscommunication. Second, the need to move an anesthetized patient from the block room to the OR posed safety concerns. We addressed these two concerns by developing a communication checklist to ensure that the child is moved from the block room to the OR only when all required equipment, supplies, documentation and medications are readily available (see Figure 16.3).

Third, the change required an increase in staffing. As leaders we decided that the anticipated improvements in OR efficiency and quality of care (i.e., because a few expert anesthesiologists place the nerve blocks) justified the increase in salary costs. That said, by changing our staffing model in another clinical area, we were ultimately able to implement this change without increased cost.

By identifying and addressing these issues using CPI, we have improved the quality and efficiency of the care we provide. The improvement in quality of care is evident in the substantial reduction in complications related to regional anesthesia (see Figure 16.4).

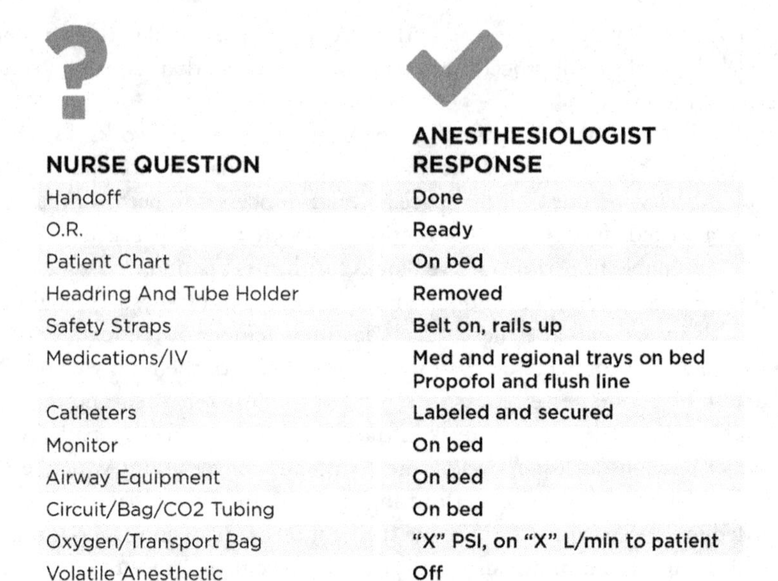

NURSE QUESTION	ANESTHESIOLOGIST RESPONSE
Handoff	Done
O.R.	Ready
Patient Chart	On bed
Headring And Tube Holder	Removed
Safety Straps	Belt on, rails up
Medications/IV	Med and regional trays on bed Propofol and flush line
Catheters	Labeled and secured
Monitor	On bed
Airway Equipment	On bed
Circuit/Bag/CO2 Tubing	On bed
Oxygen/Transport Bag	"X" PSI, on "X" L/min to patient
Volatile Anesthetic	Off

Figure 16.3 Block room departure checklist.

Regional anesthesia complication rate

Percentage

50
45
40
35
30
25
20
15
10
5
0

0 1 2 3

Year

Figure 16.4 Nerve block complication rate at SCH. Year 0 = baseline. Years 1 to 3 demonstrate sustained reduction in complication rate following introduction of an expert team.

Our success in improving the efficiency of care delivery is demonstrated in Figure 16.5, which shows the median nonoperative time for a surgeon whose patients are anesthetized in the block room. Nonoperative time starts when surgical dressing on patient A is completed and ends with surgical incision for patient B. This includes anesthesia emergence for patient A, room turnover, plus anesthesia induction, surgical positioning, and preparation for patient B. In operative services, nonoperative time equates to changeover time. These data clearly demonstrate that we have been able to sustain the time savings we initially achieved when the process was introduced.

Another key role we have played as leaders has been spreading lessons learned in one value stream across the organization. For example, a key aha moment during our redesign work in otolaryngologic anesthesia was the observation that the surgeon's cycle time was less than half of the cycle time for patient admission and anesthesia induction. This realization strongly influenced our design work for the new ambulatory surgery center, which opened in 2010.

Some hospitals and surgical centers minimize downtime for their surgeons by providing two operating rooms with two teams, with the surgeon moving from one OR to the other. This setup requires two teams of anesthesia providers and nurses

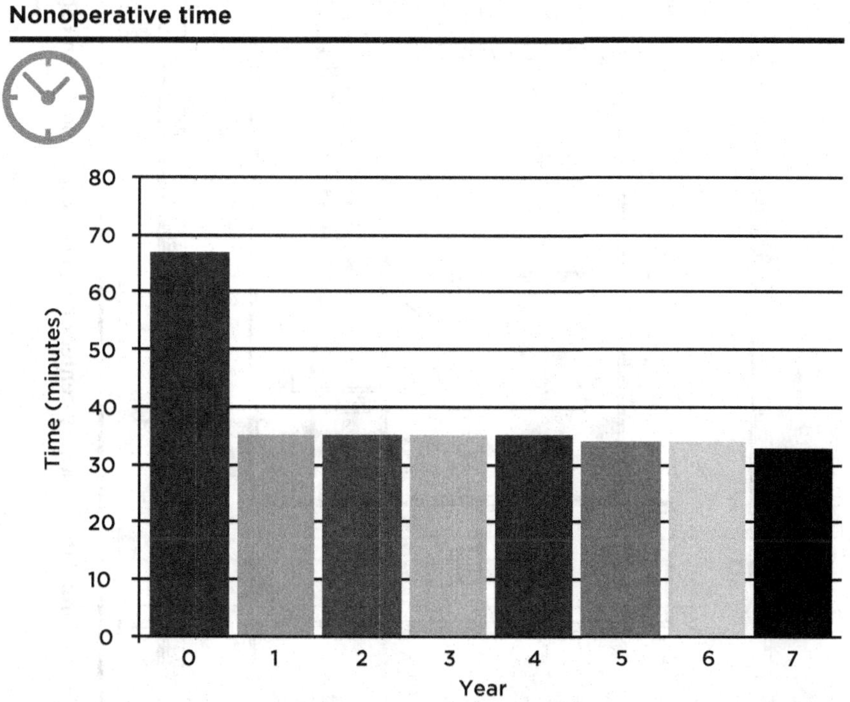

Nonoperative time

Figure 16.5 Nonoperative time for one operating room before (year 0) and after introduction of the block room.

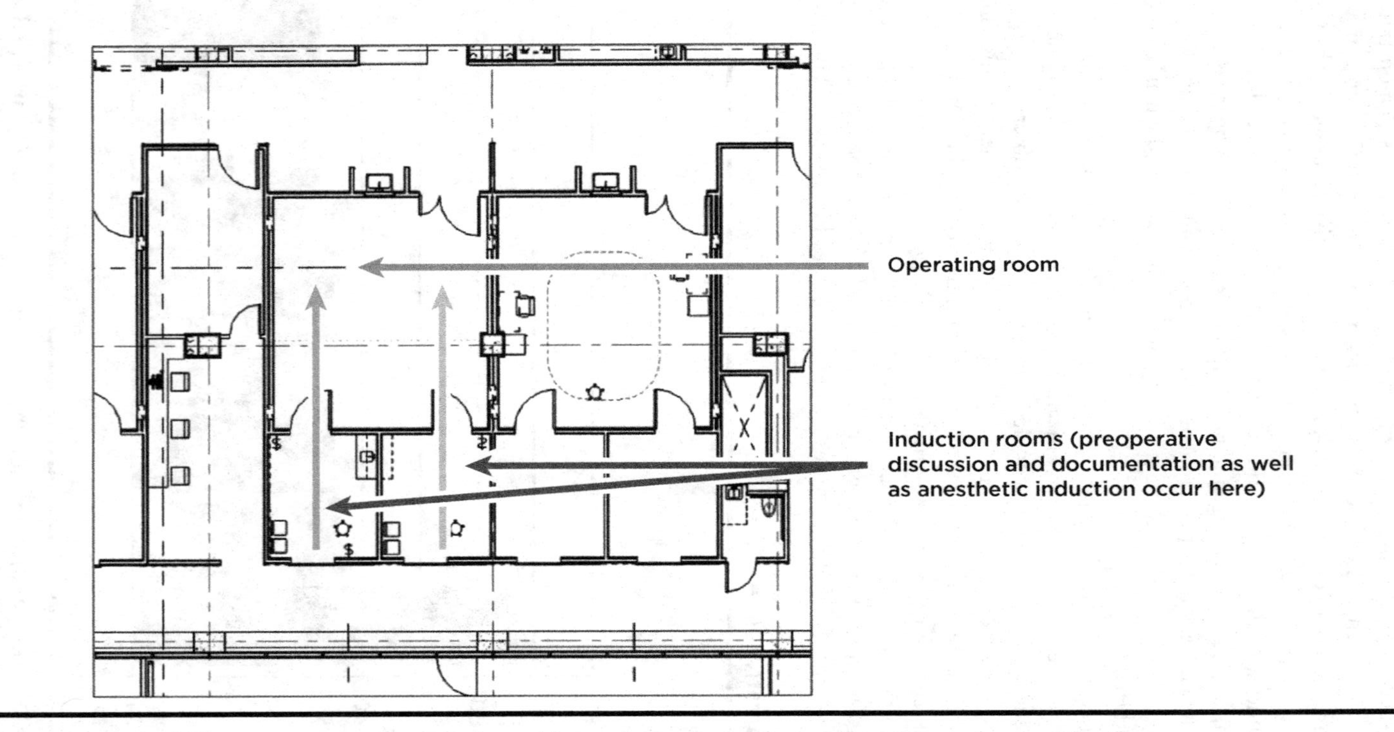

Figure 16.6 Ambulatory surgery center design with two induction rooms supporting each operating room.

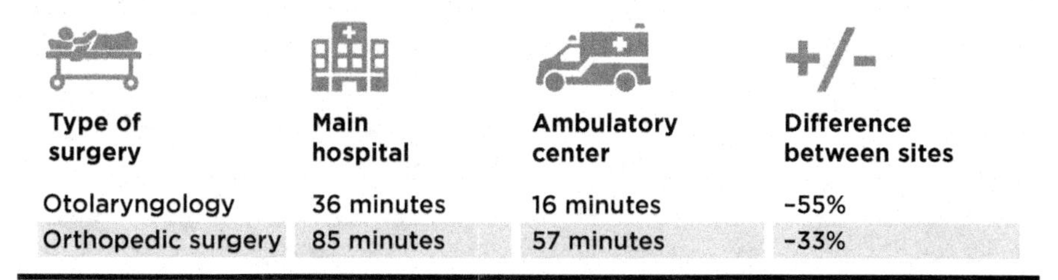

Type of surgery	Main hospital	Ambulatory center	Difference between sites
Otolaryngology	36 minutes	16 minutes	-55%
Orthopedic surgery	85 minutes	57 minutes	-33%

Figure 16.7 Median nonoperative (changeover) times.

to ensure that an anesthetized patient is "prepped and draped" when the surgeon arrives. However, this traditionally used approach results in inefficient use of the operative suites and anesthesia personnel.

Rather than building and staffing two very expensive ORs for each surgeon, our team decided, based on our experience in otolaryngologic anesthesia, to build and staff two anesthesia rooms to feed each OR (see Figure 16.6). Patients are admitted to these rooms and receive induction here before being transferred to the OR.

The lessons we learned from our initial work in otolaryngologic anesthesia have led to facility and workflow changes that have improved care and efficiency in other specialties such as orthopedics. The success of this design in reducing nonoperative time is evident in the comparison between surgical procedures performed in the ambulatory center and those performed in the main hospital (see Figure 16.7).

At Seattle Children's Hospital, we recognize that CPI is never-ending and that there are many untapped opportunities within operative services to improve the quality and efficiency of care. We are now looking to apply the lessons learned in our ambulatory surgical center to improving care quality and efficiency in the ORs of our main hospital. In the hospital, we have seen increasing pressure for OR time, yet a variety of constraints prevent the building of additional ORs. To address this demand, we need to use the available OR space and time more efficiently by reducing the proportion that is nonoperative, now about 50 percent of OR time.

To decrease nonoperative time, we will expand the use of external setup and improve changeover, with the ultimate goal of increasing patient access to our surgeons, reducing wait times, and maximizing value-added time in our operating rooms—without hiring more surgeons or building new operating rooms. Given our experience with improving efficiency in two anesthesia value streams, we have every reason to believe we will be successful in our quest to continually add value for our patients and their families.

Note

1. H. Hirano, *JIT Implementation Manual: The Complete Guide to Just-in-Time Manufacturing*, 2nd ed., 6 vols. (Florence, KY: Productivity Press), 2009.

Chapter 17

Lean in the Lab: No Culture Left Behind

Joe C. Rutledge and Xuan Qin

The Seattle Children's Hospital (SCH) Department of Laboratories is a comprehensive, multidimensional clinical laboratory serving SCH patients, performing testing for the region, and offering certain rare assays nationally. Eighteen faculty and 160 full time equivalents (FTEs) perform over one million annual tests in all clinical laboratory disciplines. This chapter illustrates the power of Lean when viewed over a decade, and how one round of improvements can catalyze new thinking and lead naturally to the next round of improvements.

In 2004 an expansion in inpatient beds resulted in increased demand for lab services. Before starting continuous performance improvement (CPI), we would have assumed that increased capacity would require more instrumentation, automation, space, and personnel. Using CPI methodology, we looked for other ways to respond to the increased patient activity, rather than defaulting to adding space and hiring more staff. We met the demand without additional resources by eliminating waste and ultimately reducing turnaround times (TATs) for many test results.

We began applying CPI in our core laboratory, which processes chemistry, hematology, coagulation, and urinalysis tests. This six-month project, which also involved streamlining phlebotomy, was successful beyond expectations. Our average TATs for routine tests decreased from several hours to less than 60 minutes—and produced an unexpected by-product: complete elimination of stat testing.[1] Over the past decade, we have sustained these gains. We have also used CPI to address nagging problems throughout the department, which have translated into further improvements, enabling us to provide test results for new critical needs and to absorb additional volume increase as the hospital expanded.

Initial Successes in Autopsy Testing and Cytogenetics

Several of our pathologists applied CPI tools to TATs for pediatric autopsy tests. At more than 60 days, the TAT was longer than national standards and caused parents to wait for important information about their child's death. To design a new process, we divided the work into tasks that take less than an hour and can be scheduled at the time of the autopsy. A visibility board and weekly reinforcement were key to keeping pathologists and trainees on track with the tasks. The board also enabled us to tell clinicians exactly when they could schedule a conversation with the parents to review the findings. With rare exception, our TATs for autopsy results have been less than 30 days since we implemented this new process.

In the cytogenetics laboratory, we were plagued with slow and variable throughput for our fluorescent in situ hybridization assays. We determined that the delays were frequently due to assay failures that required repeating a test that has a 48-hour processing time. We ran a CPI workshop to establish standard work for the assay process. Once implemented, the new processes resulted in a 50-percent reduction in queues, forms, and travel distances; a 28-percent reduction in work in process; and improvement in the lab's 5S assessment score (from 1 to 4). Most important, complaints from the cytogeneticists about failed assays disappeared with the establishment of standard work.

Applying Continuous Performance Improvement to Microbiology

The initial successes in autopsy testing and cytogenetics were foundational to subsequent improvement in other laboratory sections. We believed that microbiology, which had the longest average TATs of the department, was the section that would most benefit from CPI.

In 2004, the SCH microbiology laboratory was similar to those at other pediatric facilities at the time. The low-volume lab operated only from 6 a.m. to 11 p.m. When technologists arrived each morning they removed all the cultures in the incubators, some of which might only be a few hours old (and therefore not yet growing), while others had been plated on petri dishes more than 36 hours before. Most assays to identify organisms require hours of, if not overnight, incubation. If any microbe colonies were present, technologists used more than forty different procedures to identify the species and the antibiotic susceptibilities; if no colonies were present, the technologists returned the petri dishes to the incubator to be examined the next day. Once 48 hours had passed without colony growth, the technologist would mark the sample as negative. The entire process was complicated, including the use of many different assays in the identification step (see Figure 17.1).

Starting with Blood Cultures

The processing of blood cultures involves continuous incubation. When the incubation technology detects growth, it triggered an alert. The technologists, who were in the lab from 6 a.m. to 11 p.m., would respond by beginning the identification process. Although the timeframe for identification was similar to that of other laboratories, we knew we could improve TATs with process redesign.

The hospital supported our improvement work by providing a weeklong value stream mapping workshop. In addition, three representatives from our lab were included in the hospital's first trip to Japan to see flow in manufacturing. The flow that we observed in these factories was completely foreign to the batching process used in a traditional microbiology lab, but trying to apply the concept of flow to our work has been instrumental to our subsequent iterative improvements.

We proceeded to produce a value stream map (see Figure 17.2). What is key about the map is that it begins with the doctor's order for the patient and ends with the results affecting patient care. The value stream map made us think outside of the laboratory.

Asking the Key Question: What Does the Patient Want?

Early on in the microbiology journey, we brought a respected, experienced clinician to present the patient view of what faster turnaround times for infectious disease results would mean to them. This session was embraced by the technologists, who began to see their work from the patient perspective for the first time. The technologists invented the mantra of "No culture left behind" as a guiding principle to their work.

A positive blood culture result is indicative of bacteremia, a potentially life-threatening condition. When creating our value stream map, we used blood cultures as one product line. Through designing the map we developed a new understanding of flow for the processing of blood cultures. We saw that between 11 p.m. and 6 a.m. when the lab was not staffed, culture results were "being left behind." That is, they

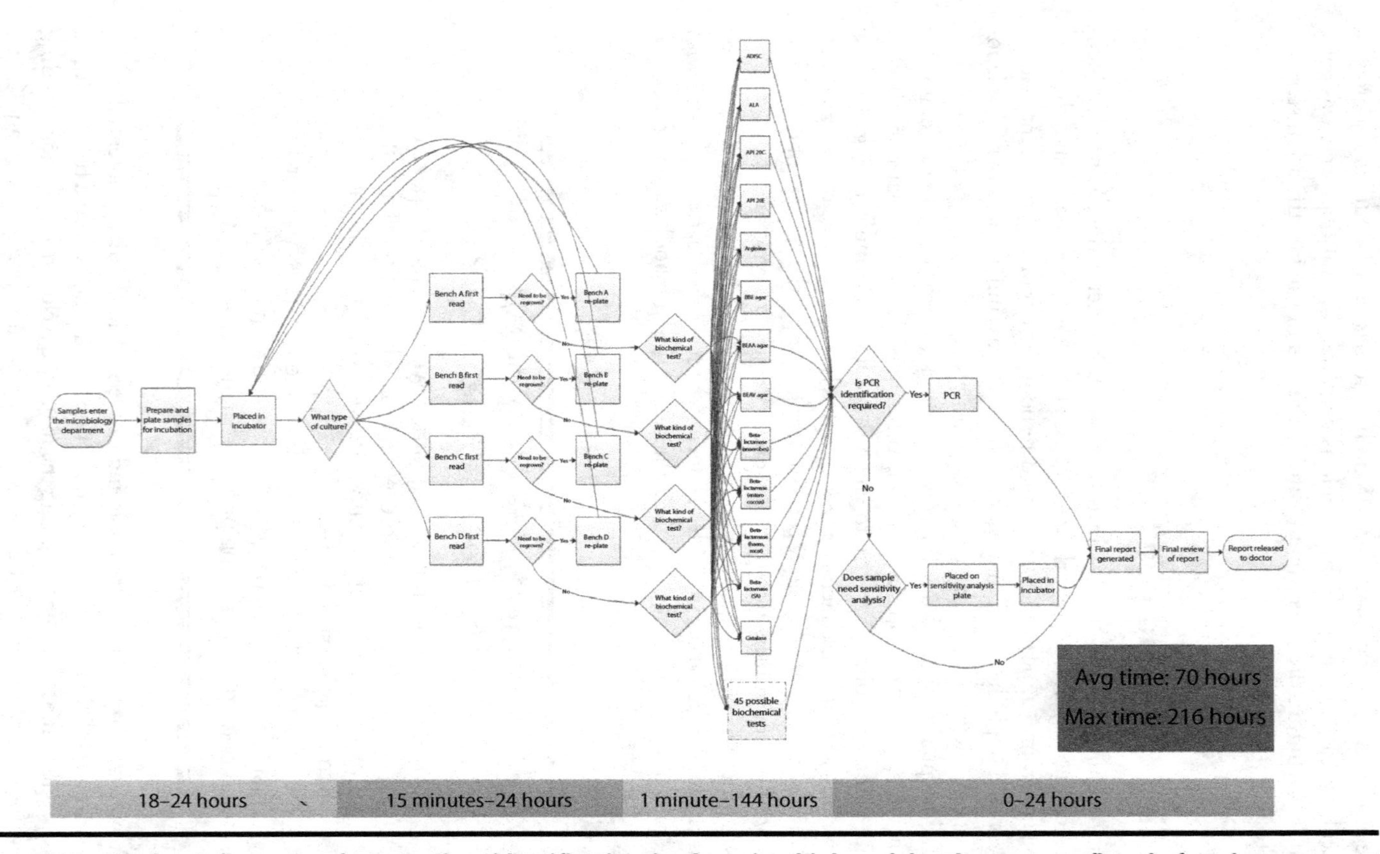

Figure 17.1 "Before" flow map for organism identification in the microbiology lab. The process flow before improvement included many different assays in the identification process, resulting in an average turnaround time of 70 hours.

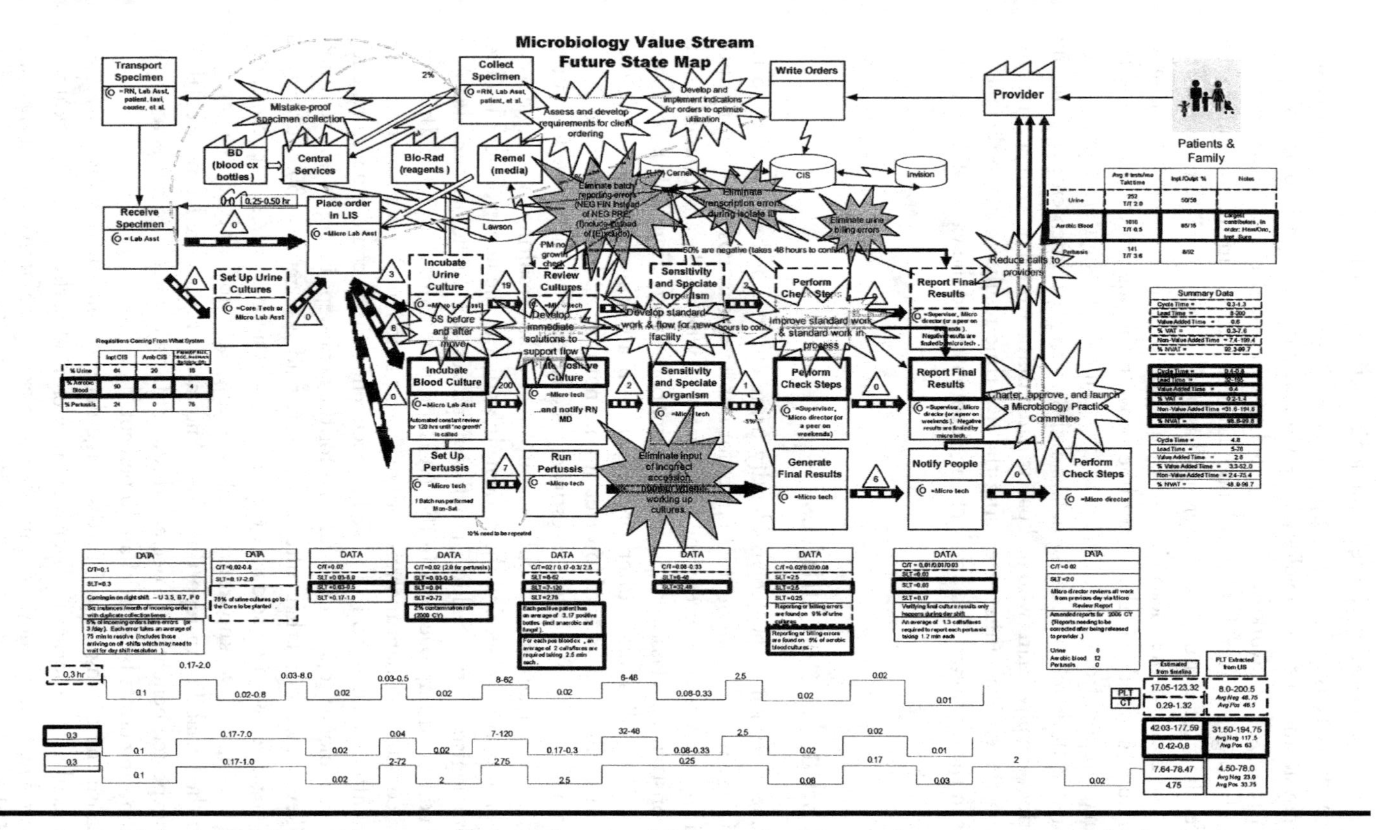

Figure 17.2 Initial microbiology value stream map. The microbiology value stream that we created at the beginning of our CPI work included steps inside and outside the lab. As we made improvements in our processes, we collaborated with other units to reduce waste in the steps located outside the lab.

were left to be processed until the technologists arrived for the day. To address this gap we conducted a Rapid Process Improvement Workshop and included infectious disease physicians, our microbiology supervisor, and frontline technologists.

As a result of the workshop we decided to cross-train the core lab technologists on the night shift to load new blood cultures into the incubator and to telephone results when culture results were read as positive between 11 p.m. and 6 a.m. Overall, we reduced the mean time to incubation of cultures from 130 minutes to 18 minutes and reduced the mean time between the postgrowth alarm and the preliminary report from 150 minutes to 55 minutes. Through error-proofing we eliminated 1300 batch processing delays and 8 wrong specimen entries annually. In addition, the physicians who had participated in the workshop verified that physicians on the clinical units were using the real-time results to make therapeutic changes in the off-hours. This small change demonstrated the value of 24/7 operation for the patient.

Next Step: Urine Cultures

Our value stream map helped us identify urine cultures as being critical to the microbiology work and a potential target for improvement. Positive urine cultures can confirm the source of fever in pediatric patients, who unlike adult patients, may not demonstrate the classic symptoms of a urinary tract infection (UTI). For febrile neonates, hospitalization is often prolonged until all urine cultures are deemed negative, usually at 72 hours. However, it does not take 72 hours for organisms to grow from the urine. When we investigated the cause of the delay, we found that technicians were reading these cultures only once a day, resulting in a single batch that was not optimally serving the patient. In addition, the nonlevel work load for the technologists contributed to an inefficient process and higher labor costs.

We addressed improvement in the TATs for urine culture in 2008. This work required considerable data analysis prior to process redesign. We determined that by 16 hours after a technician had plated a specimen, bacteria could grow sufficiently for the technologist to select the colonies for the next steps in organism identification. Likewise, we found that cultures that were read as negative at 30 hours would remain negative. With these data we were able to design a process that accelerated culture reading and workup from a single morning batch to four batches a day. This reduced the variability in reporting time. And, as with the core lab project, there were unexpected benefits. We decreased rework from 8 percent to 3.4 percent and reduced billing errors by more than 50 percent.

Because the timing of patient discharge depends on when clinicians receive culture results, the shorter TATs enabled new clinical pathways for the treatment of UTI and fever of unknown origin. This is an example of improvements at a subassembly level (i.e., urine culture processing) enabling improvements on the main assembly line (i.e., patient care).

Improving Viral Testing

Respiratory viruses tend to produce large swings in inpatient admissions and emergency department (ED) visits in pediatric healthcare facilities during the winter months, making the efficient use of bed capacity a necessity. Differentiating viral from bacterial infection and identifying the exact infectious organism are essential for effective treatment. Prior to our CPI work, the virology lab provided such specialized diagnostic testing in batches performed two to four times a day. Batching often meant that patients could wait hours to be discharged from the ED or moved to an appropriate inpatient bed.

The acquisition in 2011 of a nucleic acid detection system for a respiratory viral testing panel (FilmArray® from BioFire) partially solved this problem, because the system surveyed more organisms than previous technology and provided individual results in about 70 minutes. A design workshop validated that with this new technology virology testing could be performed in our 24/7 core laboratory.[2] However, offering this service would mean crossing traditional roles within the lab, now possible because the new system did not require an experienced microbiology technologist to interpret the results. By coupling new technology with Lean thinking, we reduced the average TATs for viral testing from 7 to 1.6 hours. Positive feedback from both the ED and inpatient clinical staff provided reinforcement for continuing our improvement work in the lab.

Further Improvements in the Microbiology Lab: Faster Organism Identification

Based on data we had collected, we knew that the most time-intensive step in the processing of samples in the microbiology lab was organism identification (see Figure 17.3). This step became the focus of our next work.

We adopted a new technology to accelerate organism identification in the microbiology lab: mass spectroscopy. The application of this powerful analytical chemistry technique to the identification of microorganisms began in the early 2000s. This technology is capable of identifying organisms with a high degree of certainty in an hour. With the new technology the process steps are unchanged, but the time required for identification is substantially shorter (see Figures 17.4 and 17.5). We then addressed redesigning the analytic process.

We leveraged several resources in this redesign work. First, we divided the technologists into three workgroups: analytical validation of the instrument, process redesign, and communications. Second, we brought in a group of industrial engineering students from the University of Washington to develop the prestate measures and project the poststate measures with flow optimization. Third, because our lab was an early adopter of mass spectroscopy for use in the microbiology lab, U.S. Food and Drug Administration (FDA) certification was not yet completed, so

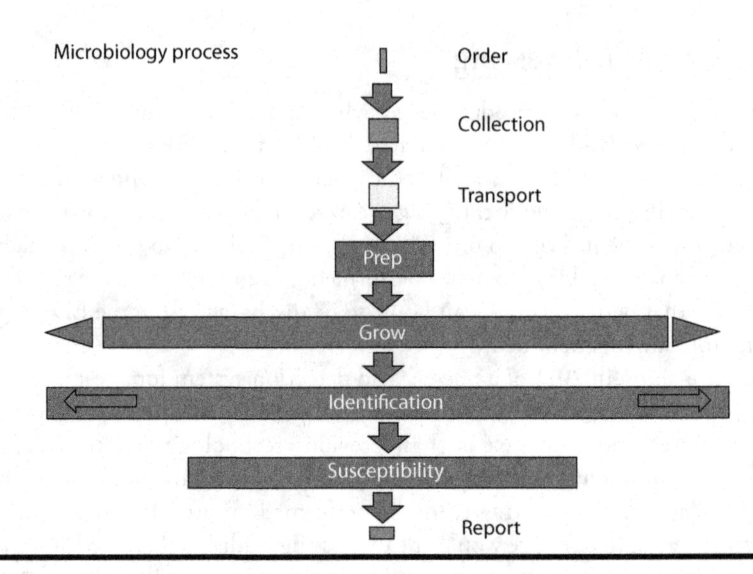

Figure 17.3 Our original microbiology process is depicted in relative length of time for each step. The most complex and unpredictable step was identification. Given its length there was little reason to work on shortening the other steps.

we had to validate the analytic method for the organisms that are typically seen in pediatric patients. We developed a close relationship with the vendor (Bruker) to ensure that our results matched theirs and those of other early users.

The technologists themselves recognized that to achieve the best flow, we would need to operate the process 24/7. Because of new efficiencies, however, the expanded hours did not require hiring additional staff. Instead, we reallocated work hours to include 11 p.m. to 6 a.m. This was a clear example of our frontline staff putting the patient first and ensuring that "no culture is left behind."

The analytical methodology was completely new with little literature to support it in the pediatric setting. Our validation of hundreds of organisms gave us confidence to switch to the new technology and to retire many of our individual assays. Not only was the new mass spectroscopy assay faster, but it also enabled us to simplify and reduce the overhead of training, maintaining, and troubleshooting a large volume of assays. In spite of the complexities of the mass spectroscopy instrumentation, our overall organism identification process is easier to deploy than with previous technology and minimizes variation among technologists in the workup process.

Using mass spectroscopy to shrink identification time and CPI process redesign to remove the waste of waiting to read cultures has completely changed our microbiology lab. We reduced the time from plating to organism identification in specimens from all sources. For example, identification of organisms from blood cultures within 12 hours increased from 31 percent to 100 percent with these

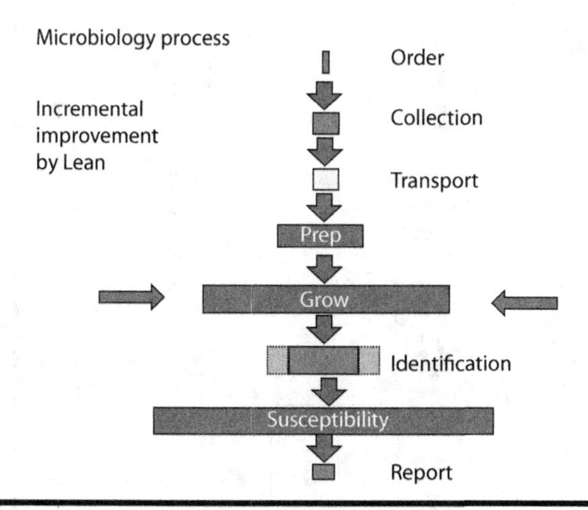

Figure 17.4 After our combined technological and Lean work, the grow step became predictable and the identification step was much shorter and had less variability.

changes; 80 percent are now identified in less than four hours. The improvement also allows cultures to be deemed negative much faster than before.

Lean Is Change Management

During our core lab redesign, which included a team heavy on supervisors, we encountered resistance from staff early in implementation that necessitated a remediation. Because change impacts employees, they needed to be part of the process to ensure that desired changes will be instituted. More important, frontline workers have in-depth insights into the work and what precisely needs to be changed. Involving frontline workers captures their expertise and celebrates their value.

Increasing Capacity by Investing in Staff

With CPI principles and the involvement of our people, we were able to spread the work to three shifts, consolidate many procedures into one, and simplify tasks. This decreased the number of staff required to complete the work; but rather than laying off personnel, we followed another new principle invented by the technologists—"No technologist left behind"—and viewed the savings in labor as a capacity opportunity. We decided to cross-train our microbiology staff in molecular virology. This decision replaced repetitive, sometimes nonstandard work with opportunities for professional growth. By training our technologists in the new emerging

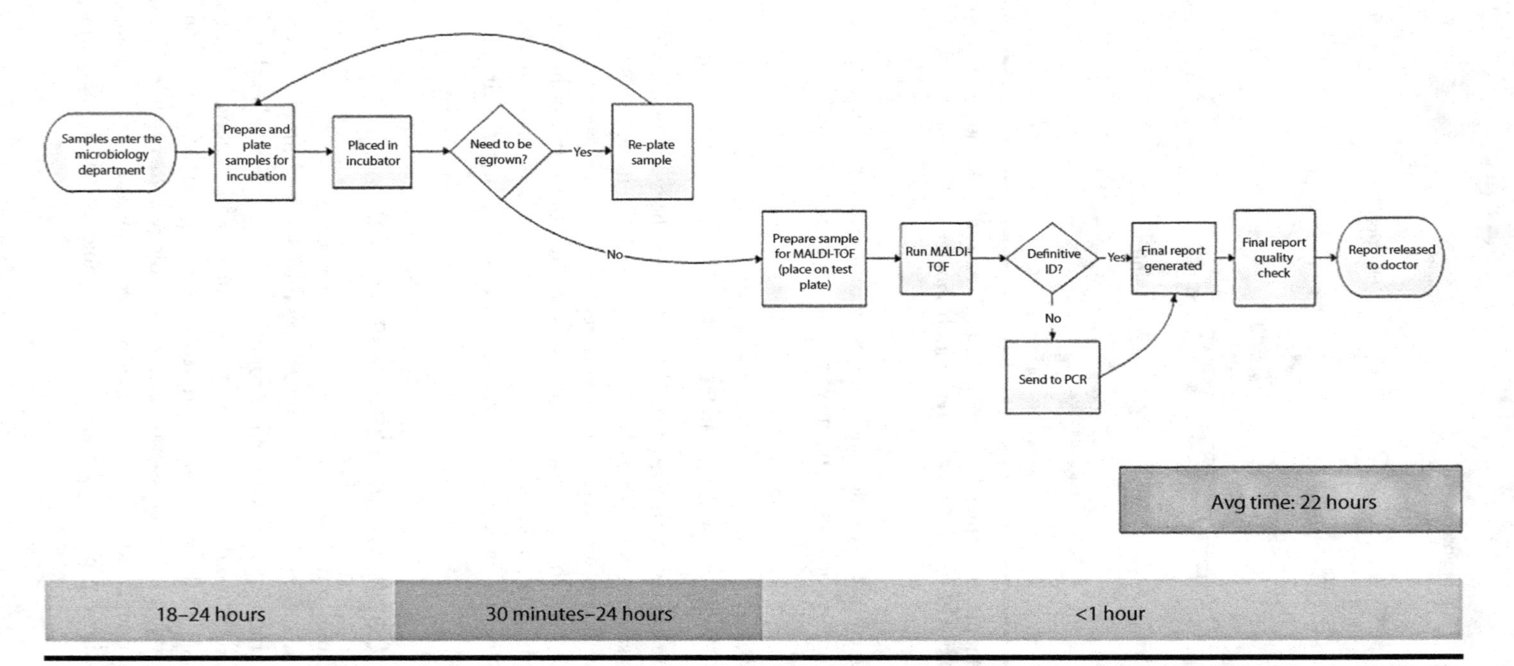

Figure 17.5 "After" flow map for organism identification in the microbiology lab. Our simplified process produced consistency and reduced the overhead associated with maintaining and training staff to perform a diverse group of assays. With the new process, our average turnaround time dropped to 26 hours.

technologies, they continue to learn, grow, develop, and ensure the future of the modern clinical laboratory.

The additional training allowed us to bring in house more than 5000 virology tests that we previously sent to a reference lab at an annual cost of more than half a million dollars. Had we chosen to lay off staff, the savings in staffing costs would have been less than one-tenth the annual cost of these reference lab tests.

The progression to becoming a Lean organization is incremental. It is difficult to determine when we reached the "tipping point." We certainly needed a critical mass of converts to achieve breakthrough thinking about improvement, which would have been difficult without the experience of prior projects. Certainly, as more of the faculty and staff have become directly involved in improvement projects, we are able to initiate and sustain improvements with less involvement from managerial staff. The journey has been long, but the rewards have been great. All of those involved have felt a sense of pride in knowing that they now apply new ways of thinking and operating to the lab services. Each person in our lab has benefitted from the improvements, as have our ultimate customers, our patients and their caregivers. Collaborative improvement work that benefits all involved is truly the soul of Lean.

Notes

1. J. Rutledge, M. Xu, J. Simpson, "Application of the Toyota Production System Improves Core Laboratory Operations," *American Journal of Clinical Pathology* 133 (2010): 24–31.
2. M. Xu, X. Qin, M. L. Astion, J. C. Rutledge, J. Simpson, K. R. Jerome, J. A. Englund et al., "Implementation of Filmarray Respiratory Viral Panel in a Core Laboratory Improves Testing Turnaround Time and Patient Care," *American Journal of Clinical Pathology* 139 (2013): 118–23.

Chapter 18

Registration to Cash Value Stream: Making the Right Call at the Everett Clinic

Janeen Lambert and Iwalani Paquette

The Lean transformation of the Everett Clinic business services unit began in November 2005. There was great anticipation among the participants, leadership, staff, and consultants; and surrounding staff members were anxious, excited, and curious. We didn't see it then, but in the wake of this experience, no situation, task, or process has ever been quite the same again.

We started with the registration to cash value stream. Once complete, this value stream would span the life of a patient request for service through payment. Over the next four years, the team would improve lead time, remove waste, create flow, and combine work teams to incrementally meet many of the value stream stretch goals (see Table 18.1). The anticipated annual savings of $2 million to $3 million would be realized, and the total resource reduction would climb to an unprecedented 30 full-time equivalents (FTEs) within business services. Administration promised that those engaged in Lean work would not lose employment, though their jobs would change. This FTE reduction would be achieved solely from the natural attrition of staff due to moves, job changes, and retirement.

Table 18.1 Event Summary for the Value Stream from Registration to Cash at the Everett Clinic

	Team Topic	*Measurements of Results*	*Before*	*After*	*Change*
1	Registration to cash value stream mapping	Total touch time	712 minutes	141 minutes	80%
		Total flow time (including claim time)	64,000 minutes	238 minutes	99.6%
		Total distance traveled	2,074 feet	1,672 feet	19.4%
2	Lean metrics	First pass yield	13.5%	53%	4x improvement

Sidebar 18.1

Payback: Assuming 50 percent of the resources in this value stream are dedicated to this work, there is an 80-percent reduction in touch time. Based on numbers from the accounting department, this will translate into between $2.25 million and $4.5 million in annual savings. In addition, at 6 percent cost of money, an additional one-time savings of $1 million will be realized due to higher turns.

- Completed current-state and future-state maps
- Performed gap analysis for action plans and used a possible, implement, challenge, or kill (PICK) chart to rank "Just Do Its," projects, and events
- Prioritized events and assigned ownership to all open items
- Calculated all Lean metrics and converted them to business metrics; achieved significant opportunities for labor savings and quality improvement

Lessons learned by participants:

- Hard to let go of the "ugly"
- Struggling to see the steps
- A lot behind the scenes
- We see many opportunities
- Empowered to make change

The targets that have been achieved provide compelling evidence of what a novice team can do with Lean tools, proper coaching, and administrative support. And, during a time of healthcare crisis and reform, this may well prove to be a key method for taking significant costs out of healthcare by raising the bar on overall customer service and quality.

Mapping the Value Stream

Staff began by learning about the tools that they would be using and the fundamentals of Lean transformation. As the mapping process progressed, the participants were amazed that such a simple process like using sticky notes to map out the work could be so revealing.

The picture that was initially painted of work flow was not pretty. The way the business unit had always done things—and done them well—was clearly not the best way, and the value stream map led the participants to this stark and honest conclusion.

There was no arm-twisting, no one-person idea; there was just a map leading us through the current process and helping us to envision better outcomes. Our goal was to create a new way of doing things that was much simpler; and we wanted a process that would move continuously and encourage staff members to work together seamlessly in providing value to our customers.

One of the challenges of improvement work is how to best communicate with, and involve, those who are part of the larger work group but not present in the room during the improvement process. Not surprisingly, it can be quite confusing for these people.

Choices need to be made by leadership when anxiety surfaces; there is a more passive approach, which allows staff members to work through their discomfort on their own, or the active approach, which draws people in. Our business office leadership recognized the potential for resistance and understood that the future success of this process required action. As a result, communications were made constantly through e-mail, informal meetings, and casual walking around to let staff know what was happening.

Team staff members were also invited to the improvement events to share their experiences, expertise, and observations about the work they performed and the process changes being considered, and to offer suggestions and give input.

Updates were posted throughout work areas, and team members, as well as clinic leadership, could monitor progress or participate in a daily huddle.

Management used a positive tone to remind staff that everyone would benefit from the findings. Keeping false rumors from circulating was a priority, especially because process change and the new improvement system being introduced were of interest to staff clinic-wide. Rumors were not unexpected; business services was one of the first units to put this new Lean process to the test, and a number of people expressed the belief that this was just another fad that someone had read about and now wanted to try for a few months. These naysayers thought the whole notion of Lean would die a quiet death rather than take hold as an emerging new trend.

Figure 18.1 Team value stream mapping process. The Everett Clinic's initial registration to cash value stream. Participants map the value stream from patient request for service to payment to improve lead time, remove waste, create flow, and combine work teams in pursuit of an anticipated $2 million to $3 million in annual savings.

It became evident, as the initial weeklong session progressed, that this first mapping was just the beginning of what would become the Everett Clinic business services improvement process (see Figure 18.1).

The first aha moment from the group was in discovering how the simple task of mapping could provide us with such a clear picture of what we were doing, and just how difficult we had made the process for our customers—the patients.

After this recognition, we realized—once again—just how critical communication and reassurance were to implementing change. There were many questions, and much anxiety and fear, as a sense of what we were doing became increasingly clear. Daily communications, in the form of dashboards and "just do-its," were a must; and we had to advise the larger group outside the room as progress was made and findings were uncovered during the initial event.

People are the most important element of a Lean transformation; if you are able to reach people, you will succeed in driving change.

Engaging Your People

Preparing staff members for a process improvement event includes educating them about Lean terms and tools, and providing them with the opportunity to learn through exercises and experiential training. Staff buy-in is a must, and the old saying "it takes a village" is applicable here. Without staff buy-in, an improvement system cannot succeed.

It's also important to remember that the event transformation and the transformation of people occur at different times. By the end of the initial event, staff members are believers; after a week passes, however, the belief begins to fade, given the day-to-day bog-down of work. Staff will slowly begin to slide back to the "old ways," and you have to work on auditing the new standard work to catch the subtle shift.

The principle of improving the work flow for the customer is positive and nonthreatening, and it produces results that inspire. Indeed, staff members found the tools and scientific data gathering clear-cut and easy to use; and once they learned more, it was obvious that improvement would result in a reduction of rework. New process designs, most specifically using a work cell approach, meant the elimination of steps and, as a result, less work for them.

Still, while they were acutely aware of the fact that the new process supported the Everett Clinic's guiding principles—"Doing what is right for each patient"; "Providing an enriching and supportive workplace"; and "Our team focuses on value: service, quality, and cost"—the reality of change was harsh.

To be sure, change is hard; but change that eliminates the very work someone is performing is very frightening, even if the work itself is not satisfying or does not add value. This is where process change becomes personal.

To sustain change in any organization, leadership needs to be present for the people who count on them for direction, guidance, and security. A strong communication feed must occur. Strong staff retention and reeducation programs must be in place. Staff members need to be reminded constantly that the process is about improvement and not a reduction in team members. This is a very challenging message to communicate.

At first, there were the nonbelievers, who knew that jobs would change and that work would be eliminated as defects were fixed. This type of awareness anxiety can create resistance. The Everett Clinic has always been a supportive workplace where our employees are valued and open communication is encouraged. And the Everett Clinic leadership reiterated throughout the value stream work that no one would lose employment, although jobs would change. It was very rewarding to see the clinic live up to that promise, and the staff savings to date have been accomplished without any layoffs.

Work Cell Design

The first opportunity for rapid change came when the initial Registration to Cash event was rolled out in March 2006. The goal was to establish flow for incoming calls and to resolve issues in a timely manner. Two separate departments came together to brainstorm this problem. They made breakthrough progress when two front-level staff members asked, "Why can't phone people from both insurance and customer service answer patient calls?" This idea would require a team approach that engaged two different areas and two different managers.

Quite frankly, this idea may have been more difficult for the managers to fathom than it was for the staff members who suggested it. But from that revolutionary idea came the mapping of a single flow process for incoming patient calls. The team came prepared to announce to its peers the following morning that we would be wiring all insurance and customer service phones so that they would be able to answer calls as a collective unit.

Despite the fears of peer reprisal, the team members successfully implemented the beginnings of a work cell design that would bring together nearly every skill needed to answer patient questions in a single call. This work trial would begin to eliminate the long-standing tradition of specialization in the Everett Clinic business services unit.

The goal of this one-phone program was to reduce waste, the average speed to answer phones, handoffs, and processing time for patient billing and insurance inquiries. And the results were strong. We doubled the number of staff answering calls by combining the insurance phone staff with customer services. We eliminated the phone menu so that patients spoke with a live person. And we cross-trained insurance and customer service staff members to answer any question (see Table 18.2).

In the wake of this success, we began to see just how important the leadership connection is in the Lean process. The Everett Clinic business services staff had a relationship of trust with immediate area leadership. Staff members spoke often and openly about their fears of change and work elimination. The trust for the Everett Clinic business services unit only grew stronger as the various process improvement events continued; all that had been explained and promised became reality.

Table 18.2 Business Office Event Results in a Scorecard

Business Office Phones Scorecard			
	Pre–March 2006	*March 2007*	*Results*
Phone speed to answer	1:21	0:17	–1:04
Handoff turned around	85 hours	1 hour	–84 hours
Same-day resolution	93%	99%	+06%
Days revenue outstanding	42.62	38.99	–3.63
Hours of operation	9:00 a.m. to 4:00 p.m.	7:00 a.m. to 8:00 p.m.	+6 hours
Business office FTEs	113.34	102.86	–10.48

Today's Work Today

The second improvement phase saved seven FTEs' worth of staff hours. Leadership and the team decided to use these hours to unburden their leads so they could mentor; the rest of the hours helped create a float group that could work in other areas of business services as needed. As people left the organization to take other positions or retire, these float staff members were moved into permanent positions.

The purpose of this second phase of improvement was to understand work flow throughout customer services and account services and to staff flexibly by hourly demand. To achieve this goal, we redesigned the physical work space, combining account services and customer services (see Figure 18.2). This allowed the merged staff to meet fluctuating demand and answer all questions in an efficient and informed way.

A new mantra was created during this event: "Today's Work Today." And we fulfilled the spirit of the slogan by meeting the demand of work on a daily basis through flexible staffing resources. Figure 18.3 shows our simple chart for tracking call volumes, task times, and staffing requirements per hour.

After working on the phone processes, we next turned to the cash collection process. The cash collection process included staff from two separate departments located on two different floors—3 FTEs from business services and 2.5 FTEs from accounting. Our goal was to decrease turnaround time, increase efficiencies in workflow, and reduce cycle time through replicating our previous experience by creating

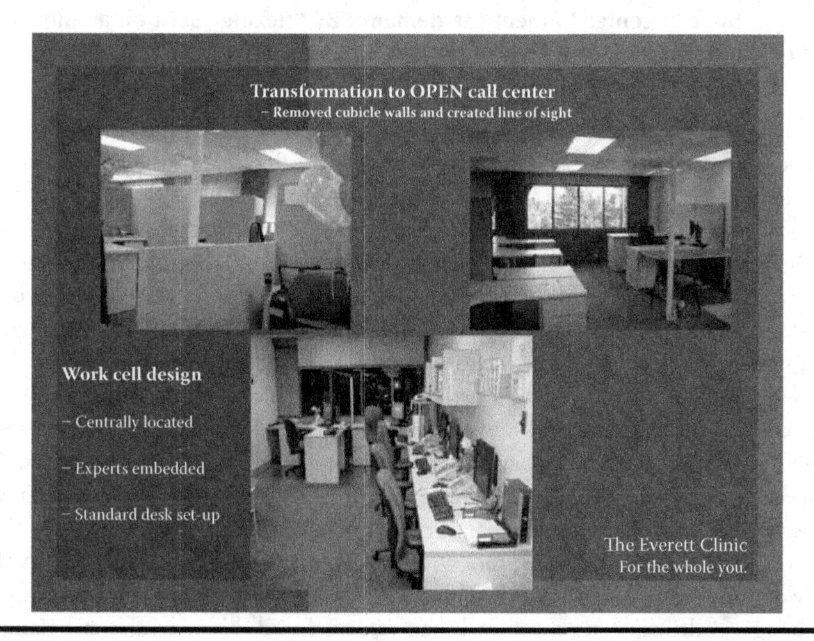

Figure 18.2 Transformation process to an open call center. An open call center created many advantages, chief among them being colocated staff leading to synergy, camaraderie, and easy access to each other and their leads.

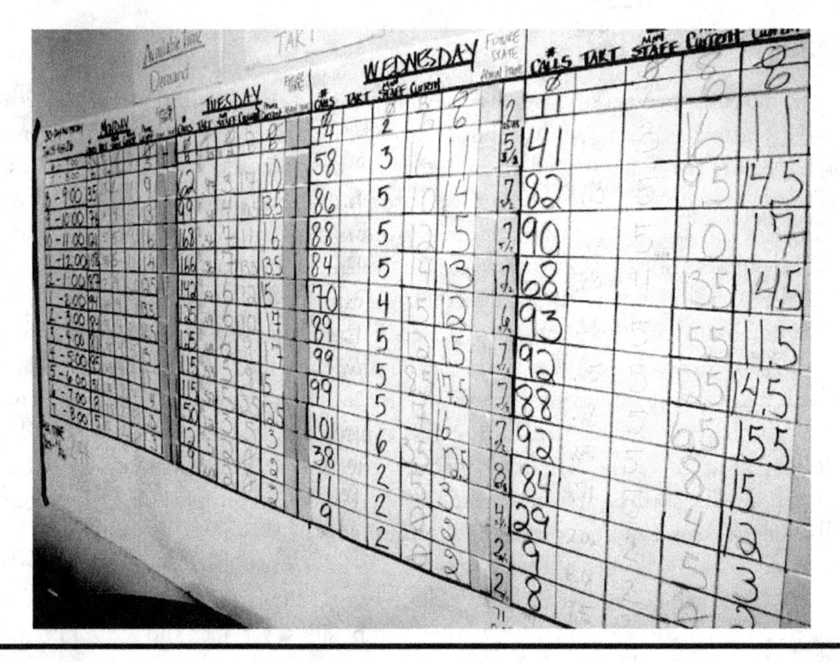

Figure 18.3 Charting of call volumes by day and hour. The hourly call counts were tracked and charted for a few months. Cross-trained staff were assigned hours in the call center to meet the demand. By "flexing" staff on a daily basis, call demand was met with fewer FTEs.

a work cell to potentially unite a new team and generate synergy. Management was quick to realize that this change would create a different set of anxieties; it also required a physical move and a different reporting structure.

Knowing the importance of communication, a meeting was organized with the accounting staff to provide an opportunity for those feeling the most ill at ease to share their concerns. The group was open and honest, and presented a list of 20 concerns that included everything from the space it would occupy to the unknown of a new management. As the meeting progressed and the team members worked through each item, some of the worries dissipated. This meeting set an example of true commitment to staff and was a turning point that made this a more successful event for all. Discussing the changes helped reiterate the value that the organization placed on each individual's contribution to the process and provided a forum that validated each person's opinions.

This was a big win for us, too. We were able to streamline the work so that only deposit monies were routed to business services, and there was now a one-way exchange of deposit—no more cash bag return. In addition, errors on balancing were now reported to reception daily (see Table 18.3).

We decided to move into the insurance area after this.

Table 18.3 Summary of the Cash Collection Event Work

Cash Collection Process Location: The Everett Clinic (October 8–13, 2006)						
Team Topic		*Measurements of Results*	*Before*	*After*	*% Improvement*	*Comments*
Business office cash collection processes	*1*	*Cash bag processing time*	*7:46*	*2:30*	*68%*	*Minutes*
	2	*Transfer of unused cash bags*	*30*	*0*	*100%*	*Bags transferred daily*
	3	*Achieve same-day turnaround on incoming funds*	*$48,731*	*TBD*	*100%*	*Expect $0 cash left at end of day*
	4	*FTEs*	*4.65*	*3.65*	*22%*	*FTE reduction through attrition*

Aim: Decrease turnaround time and increase efficiency in payment room workflow, resulting in reduced cycle time.

The Value of Standard Work

Further improvement opportunities awaited us when a diverse group from insurance, accounting, reception, and customer service assembled to examine the process for working unpaid insurance claims. Unfortunately, with a variety of carriers and a multitude of rules, staff members were skeptical about the possibility of establishing any standard work for this ever-changing process. But after observing and mapping a wide variety of ways that staff did the same work, the team came up with a standard process. Experienced and new staff could easily follow this guideline and end up with effective results.

The basic vision was to have standard daily one-touch resolution and standard work for processing all claims. We fulfilled this vision by changing the schedules for staff members so they aligned with those of the insurance carriers; we implemented daily huddles for good news and target setting; we created a toolbox for access to basic appeal guidelines; we made sure the claims in the worklist were worked on as they were assigned; and we saw to it that claims were no longer sorted by denial or carrier type—there was now one queue for all staff to pull from daily. The event results were favorable, as showed by the scorecard in Table 18.4.

Table 18.4 Insurance Worklist Event Results in a Scorecard

Worklist Event (May 2008)	*Pre-Event (February–May 2008)*	*June 2008*	*90 Days Postevent (May–July 2008)*
Staff satisfaction	67% positive	Goal: 75%	78% positive
Productivity (worklist claims per FTE)	170 per week per FTE	385 per week per FTE	299 per week per FTE
Days revenue outstanding	42.42	43.61	40.22
% Weekly worklist claims complete	25%	100%	100% of weekly worklist claims
Touches per claim—rework	6.5	Goal: 3.5	

Six months later, the work list claim count had dropped from 34,000 to 17,000 claims. Improvement continues for us in this area; and our staff members recognize and report opportunities for up-front claim issue resolution that will further reduce the need for manual intervention and work queues.

The Role of Leaders

Lean improvement from a human workforce perspective is much like any behavioral modification, and it requires constant focus and attention. It's imperative that leaders make themselves available, communicate at every level, and coach through obstacles and setbacks. Leaders must always share improvements using understandable data that are made visible with dashboards, messages, rewards, and constant encouragement.

Four years after starting the Lean initiative, the Everett Clinic business services staff is better able to adapt to any industry change. Many people in our organization are still finding ways to improve their processes to better meet the work demand of our customers. And defective processes can now be redesigned by the people doing the work; they use their own ingenuity and tools that have become part of our Everett Clinic Improvement System.

We have learned many things about change, but perhaps the most important lesson of the last four years has been that Lean transformation efforts are most powerful when they are deployed by frontline staff everyday in the workplace, not just "imagined" in a conference room. This lesson, combined with the knowledge that our managers, administrators, and CEO stand behind us as we transform our culture and our work methods, will continue to drive our success as we move forward.

Chapter 19

Integrated Facility Design at Seattle Children's Hospital

Michael D. Boyer, Lisa Brandenburg, and Joan Wellman

Strategic analysis of Seattle Children's Hospital's (SCH) market position and patient access challenges in early 2006 pointed out the need to expand accessibility and services offered to the rapidly growing "Eastside" of the Seattle metro area. The board approved the building of a clinic and surgery center off of the main campus in Bellevue, Washington, in order to improve access to pediatric subspecialty services, create additional capacity for the main Seattle campus by shifting outpatient clinic volume and procedures to the new building, increase SCH's presence for Eastside growth, and improve inpatient referral volume. The facility would be designed to support urgent care, specialty clinics, outpatient surgery and recovery, infusion, imaging (including MRI), a lab, and a pharmacy, with a 240-space parking garage.

Lisa Brandenburg arrived on the scene at SCH shortly after the board's decision and was handed the assignment to "get Bellevue built." Shortly thereafter, Lisa had a conversation with Pat Hagan, SCH's COO, which went something like this: "We've done continuous performance improvement (CPI) in almost every area of our enterprise, except facilities. Let's design and build this facility using Toyota methods. When can you go to Japan?" Before she knew it, Lisa was bound for Japan with SCH's CEO and other members of the senior team to participate in a factory production preparation process (3P).

Upon returning from Japan, Lisa and her executive leadership colleagues agreed to approach the design and construction of this new facility in a new way, staying true to the CPI philosophies and building on what the team had learned in Japan. Lisa laid down the challenge: deliver a facility that meets customer demands, occupies a smaller footprint, uses fewer design and build resources, is constructed in less time, and reduces the total ownership cost. To achieve these results, a very different process was needed.

Early estimates for the Bellevue project indicated the facility would need 110,000 square feet at a cost of $100 million to meet the desired program needs. The response to that estimate was simple: cut the square footage by 30 percent, reduce costs to $75 million, but keep the program requirements the same. As if the challenge was not great enough, the board of directors subsequently asked for an additional reduction to a $70 million total cost level or the project would be put on hold.

In the end, the 75,000-square foot (a 32-percent reduction) Seattle Children's Bellevue Clinic and Surgery Center opened on time (July 20, 2010) and under the $70 million budget by $3.5 million. This is the story of how this was accomplished by SCH and its partners.

The Approach

As a new space design for an efficient facility was envisioned, so was the supporting design process. The traditional approach of industry benchmarking, parametric sizing, protracted user group input, and the separation or siloing of the owner, project manager, architect, general contractor, and subcontractors was purged and replaced with a concurrent set of design activities through a sponsor and project management (PM) group, a facilities team, and a core team. The sponsor and PM group maintained strategic direction and removed barriers. Included in this group was SCH (owner), Joan Wellman & Associates (Lean counsel), the Seneca Group (design manager), NBBJ (architect), and Sellen Construction (general contractor). The facilities team provided guidance on specific design and construction issues and connected the owner, architect, and contractor throughout the project. The core team acted as stewards of the Lean principles, assured alignment as decisions were made, and defined the intersection between the functional work design and the physical construction. The core team integrated strategic plans and daily operations by blending user and designer desires from inception to delivery. Core team members acted as advocates and champions, subject matter experts, and inspired designers responsible for meeting project targets and ensuring success.

The process of design for the core team spanned four phases that included (1) a project management and governance phase, (2) a conceptual design phase, (3) a functional design phase, and (4) a detailed design phase. The overall core team project phasing is shown in Figure 19.1.

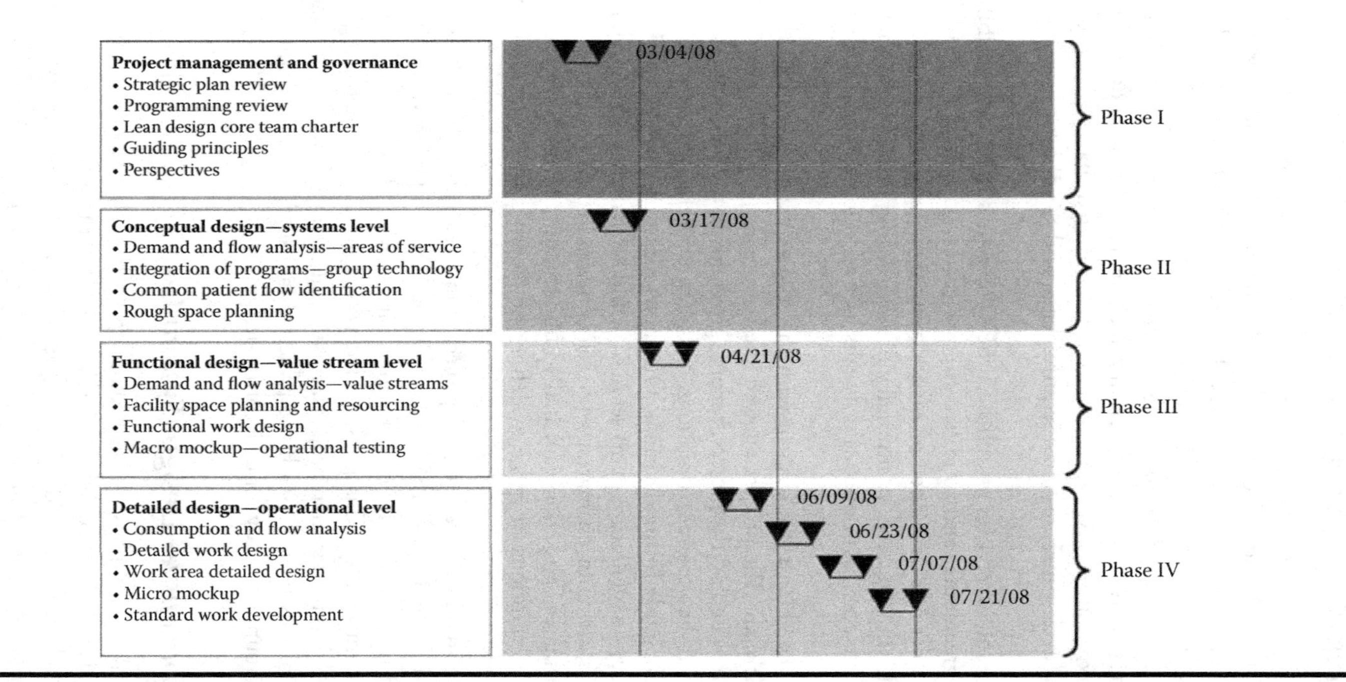

Figure 19.1 Core team process. The design phases and milestones where the core team worked to represent all stakeholders in the design process and ensure Lean principles were applied throughout.

Phase 1: Project Management and Governance

The purpose of the project management and governance phase was to ensure alignment on time frame, select the core team membership, and develop solutions or countermeasures for the issues that would impact core team launch. A key element was the interview and selection of the architect and the general contractor. Joan Wellman & Associates (JWA) collaborated with SCH in the selection of the core team and the internal project manager, charter development, and sponsor expectations. An initial data set was gathered that included process lead times and cycle times, resource requirements, and specific medical specialty requirements.

The governance activities established the core team's roles, responsibilities, norms, and agreements, and solidified the project expectations. A set of Lean guiding principles was developed to ensure core team alignment in project purpose, method, and outcome. A summary of the guiding principles is shown in Figure 19.2. The core team operating norms and agreements and metrics were set.

Next, considerable time was spent with the core team to understand the hospital's strategic plan. The process allowed the core team to fully understand the corporate strategy behind the project; become grounded in the data, logic, and policies that formed the project assumptions; and align with the performance parameters that would guide future decisions. Questions regarding the project timeline, whether primary or ancillary support services would be shared or dedicated, initial space estimates, demand estimates, and facility performance requirements were answered. Ultimately, the core team had to understand and buy into the strategic planning assumptions in order to define the facility's 10-year programming requirements.

In addition to strategy review, the project team conducted an analysis of the current operating conditions. The voices of the patient, family, provider, and staff were recorded through a series of structured interviews and gemba walks in the current outpatient facility. This phase ended with core team feedback regarding what had worked well on similar projects, what should be avoided, and what should be improved for this project. With the project established and governance issues resolved, the group was ready for conceptual design.

Phase 2: Conceptual Design (System Level)

The conceptual design phase was accomplished through a five-day integrated design event (IDE) that delivered a conceptual design or theoretical description of a facility that achieved the guiding principles. This overarching conceptual model provided a consistent vision from the strategic plan through to construction. The core team's involvement in this five-day event ensured that its members were the

Values/Beliefs/Philosophies

- The design is Patient/Family/Staff/Provider centered.
- The facility is organic and adapts with the future—it is not obsolete upon opening.
- Environmental Sustainability is considered and permeates all design and construction decisions.
- The facility creates a unique experience as a healing environment.
- Children's is an academic medical center with Bellevue in support of this intent.
- Patient safety is paramount.
- "Customers" include patients, families first. Our design must also support staff, providers, and the Bellevue community.

Assumptions

- The space/structure is designed with future flexibility in mind. Facility barriers to change are minimal.
- The multiple usage of available space is maximized and all spaces are considered candidates for multiuse. The exam rooms are universal and are designed for rapid reconfiguration and multiuse.
- Space is a function of need and is owned by the Common Patient Flow.
- The design maximizes the multidisciplinary model of care and supports the clinical research and teaching mission. Each service will determine the academic model that is appropriate.
- The facility is designed for high throughput (capacity and process meets demand).
- The clinical space is maximized and the office space is minimized utilizing a Lean perspective.

Principles

- The Value Stream contains multiple services and processes to drive effectiveness and efficiency. The clinical services are physically embedded within the flows.
- Standardization is the source of efficiency and flexibility and is the foundation of improvement.
- Simple designs with fewer components make for reliable service. The larger the system scope, the less reliable the system. Simple is always better, processes must be intuitive, complexity is a veiled type of waste.
- The space is right sized to the task (monuments are avoided) recognizing that too much space is an enemy and drives waste.
- Build tents, not castles—flexibility is built in to allow for rapid reconfigurations.
- There is a line of sight and visual management created that promotes flow and identifies abnormal conditions at a glance.
- 5S principles and infection prevention are high considerations in design—an ounce of prevention is worth a pound of cure (detection).

Concepts

- Continuous Flow Theory with the management of variability is used to achieve high throughput service. A pull system is fundamental to continuous flow and is used to minimize blocked or congested patient flow through the facility.
- The work cell concept is utilized and promotes single piece flow and dedicated services.
- The concept of subassembly production is used as it improves flow and throughput.
- The facility utilizes the modularization of internal components and the placement of modular components for future flexibility.
- The flow has "one way in/one way out" at the system level and the "same exit and entrance" at the work cell level. Materials enter from outside of the cell and handoffs are minimal. Location of services to entrance / exit must consider the process, service provided and hours of operation.
- Supplies, tools and equipment are at point of use and move from the dock to fingertips without storage.
- Flexible walls/partitions can be used so that exam rooms and team rooms can be created as required.
- Wayfinding is clear and apparent.
- There is point of care testing within the surgical suites.
- There are open area clinics with line of sight to exam rooms. Documentation / dictation will occur in the exam room. There are multiuse conference huddle spaces available for the Team Room function. There are Simple Cells / Complex Cells with Huddle Space.
- Pre-op and Phase I and II recovery are the same space. Families are in this space.

Figure 19.2 Bellevue Project guiding principles developed by the core team.

"keepers of the design concept" from early inception to the operation of the facility on move-in day.

During conceptual design, a work flow analysis was performed that considered the type of service demanded; the patient, family, staff, and provider routings; the lead time and cycle time of each process; and the associated resource requirements. Utilizing group technology (a methodology that balances cycle time, customer demand characteristics, and resource use similarities), the integration of programs yielded common routings and the logical grouping of similar services with shared resource solutions. From this work, common patient flows or value streams were identified and confirmed against the facility's program requirements. For example, the procedure-centric clinic specialties of ophthalmology, otolaryngology, dermatology, urology, and plastics would share space, while the longer cycle time and consulting nature of pulmonary, neurology, psychology, and adolescent medicine would be colocated. Likewise, the shorter cycle time clinic visits of urgent care, general surgery, gastroenterology (GI), nephrology, and cardiology led to the grouping of these specialties. These services would traditionally occupy separate and larger spaces. The conceptual design is shown in Figure 19.3.

Participants in the conceptual design IDE were asked to think "out of the box," without the square footage or building footprint constraints. The IDE outcomes from this phase included (1) a definition of patient flows that addressed the performance needs of the facility, (2) a performance specification and capacity analysis for each identified common patient flow or value stream, (3) a conceptual space design with room allocations in support of the value streams, and (4) a rough space plan with block diagrams and a schematic of the "seven healthcare flows." An example of the conceptual design with multiple flows is shown in Figure 19.4.

Phase 3: Functional Design (Value Stream Level)

During the functional design phase, the overall utility of the facility was defined. The constraints and requirements established adjacencies and necessary connections between value streams, resulting in an overall stacking and space plan. Through the construction of and experimentation with macro mockups, the group demonstrated how the value streams would operate, resources would be utilized, and people would interact in the proposed space. The realities of the structural and mechanical limitations were introduced at this point to ensure that the realities of the site, code, and other constraints were recognized.

During a five-day functional design IDE, the core team physically modeled seven healthcare flows in action so that a descriptive text of the functionality or operational composition of each value stream could be generated. The seven healthcare flows were patients, families, staff, supplies, equipment, medications, and information.

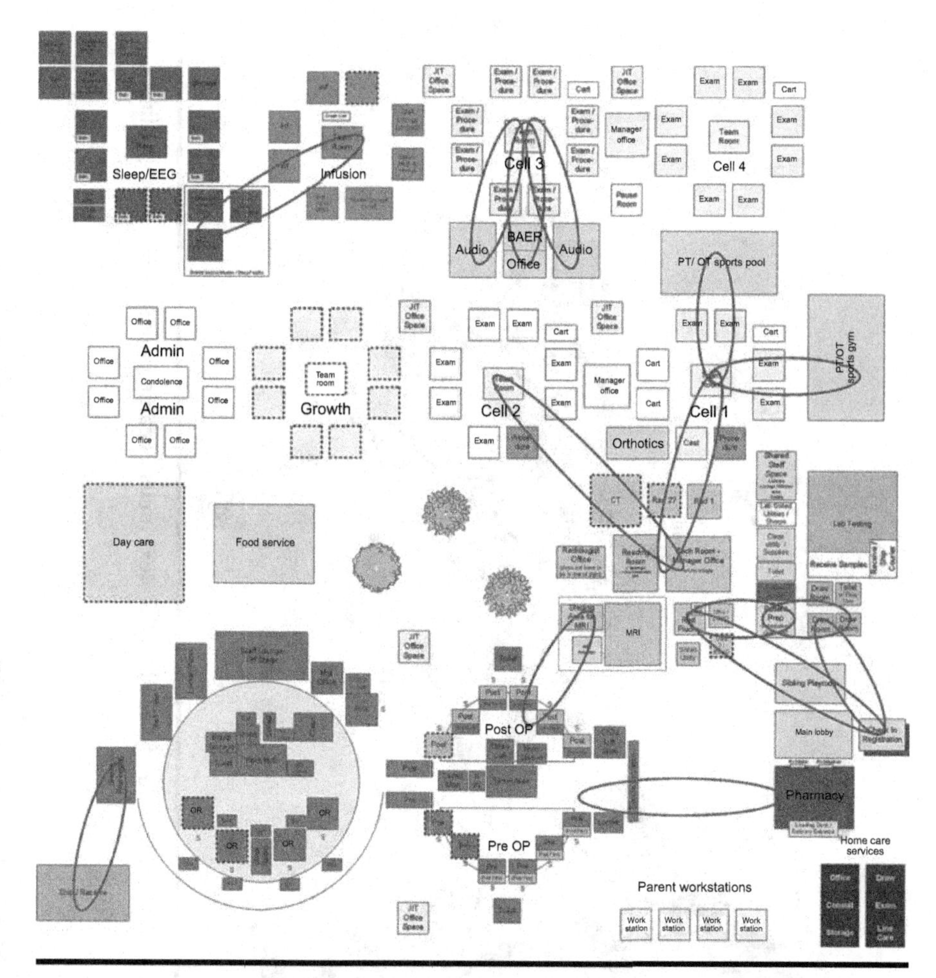

Figure 19.3 Conceptual design. Lean concepts were used to analyze and recommend floor layout to minimize space.

A full-scale "macro" mockup allowed the team to test space shape, size, and adjacencies. The mockup walls were easily repositioned to test new ideas within seconds. For example, the core team mocked up virtually all of the surgery space as part of the macro-mockup functional design. After experiencing the full-scale mockup, the team substantially changed the initially accepted two-dimensional paper design. Repeated scenario testing of the seven healthcare flows with stopwatches and simulated patient, family, provider, and staff "actors" demonstrated the strengths and weaknesses of the design. In addition to the mockup, a discrete event computer simulation of the value streams supported decision making regarding space relationships, final adjacencies, and functional affinities. An example photo of one of the macro mockups is shown in Figure 19.5.

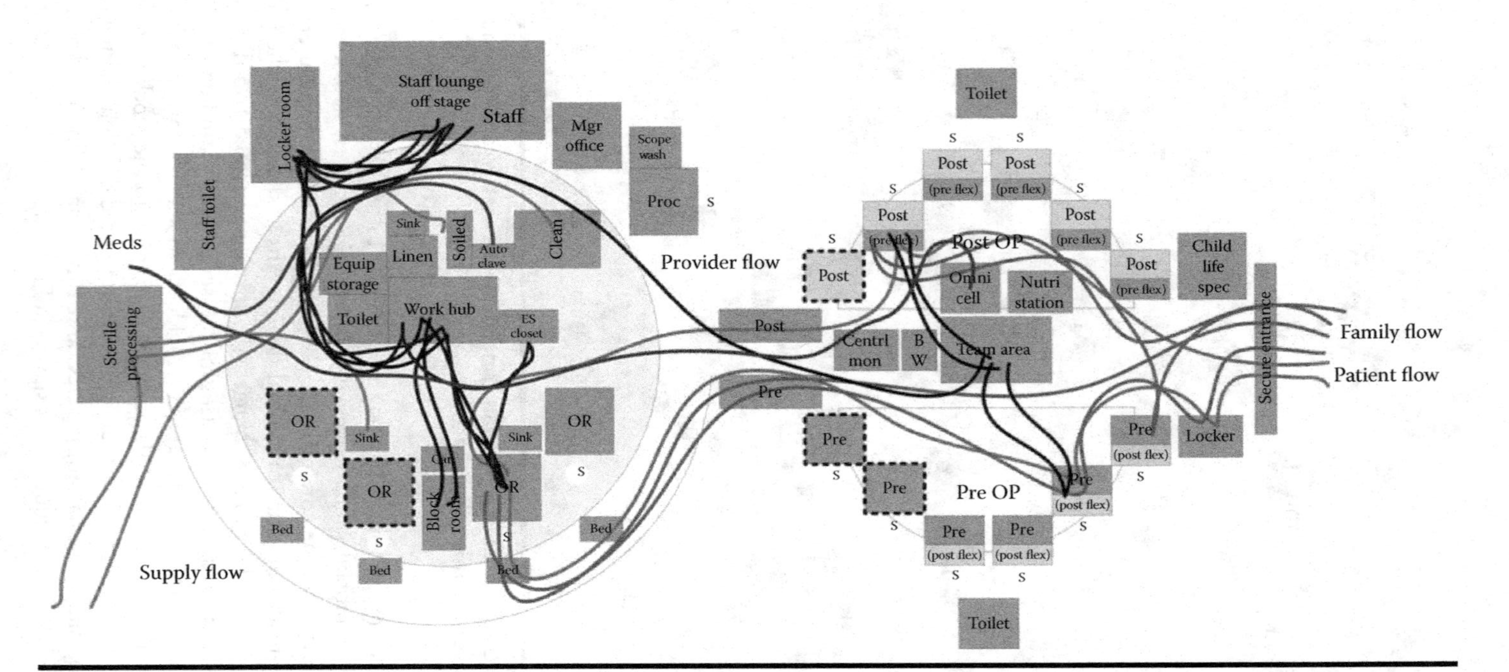

Figure 19.4 ASC conceptual design. With an efficient overall floor plan, the next focus became patient flow through clinics.

Figure 19.5 Macro-mockup example. Getting down to the details. Mockups allowed for various types of scenarios to be modeled where users could get a feel for what worked and what didn't before the design proceeded.

Phase 4: Detailed Design (Operational Level)

The detailed design phase was completed through a series of highly focused IDEs, combining the best thinking of staff, patient families, and designers. The purpose of these micro-IDE sessions was to define the working-level detail (e.g., interior equipment, services, work surfaces, storage, and utilities) for each area. Using "7 Flows of Medicine" and waste analysis, the IDE participants generated interior room details. Figure 19.6 shows the output of the detailed design event for a clinical floor. An example photo of a room interior is shown in Figure 19.7.

From Integrated Design Events to Construction

The use of Lean thinking did not stop when the IDEs were completed. Far from it! For example, when it came time to do construction detailing, three-dimensional modeling and further mockups and test fits were used along with weekly design workshops with experienced leaders from all disciplines. During construction, offsite prefab of facility components improved cost and schedule performance. A

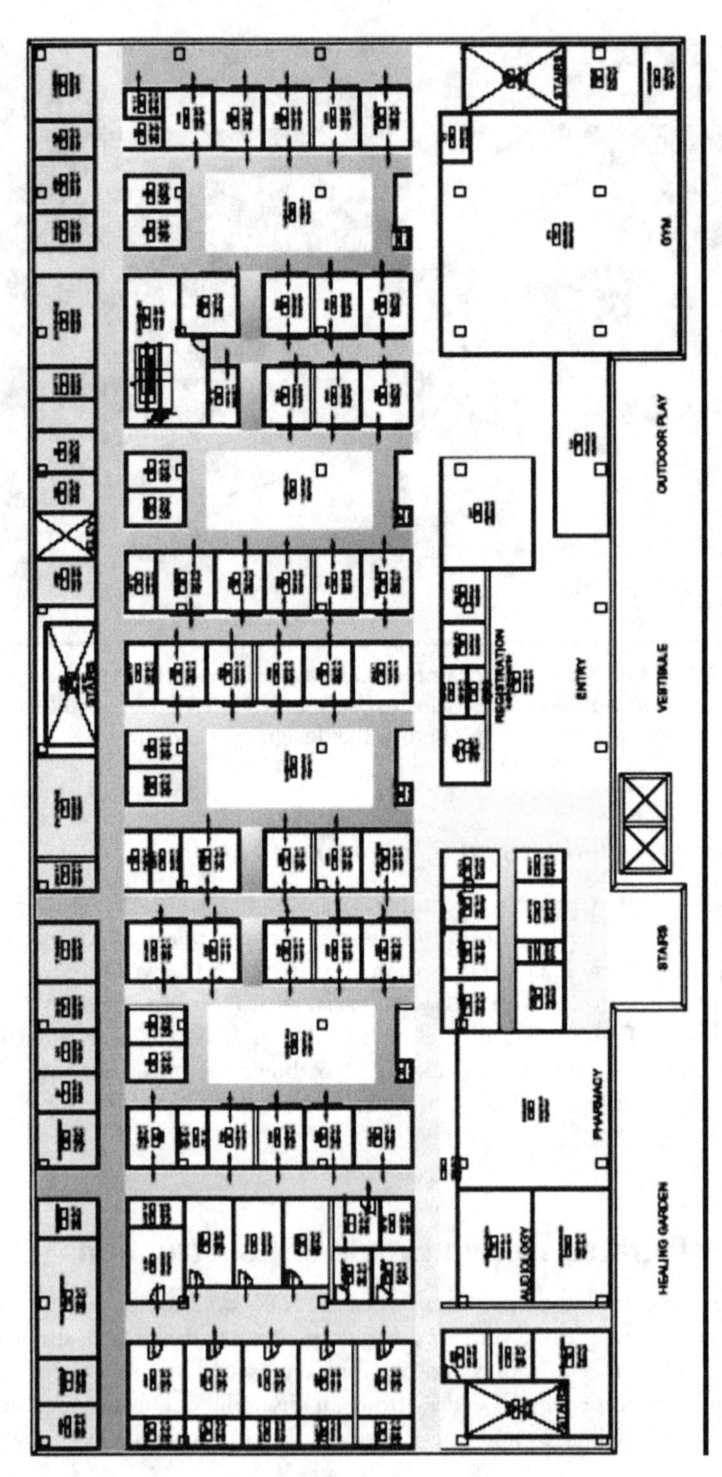

Figure 19.6 Detailed design of clinical floor. Finally, the team knows where everything goes.

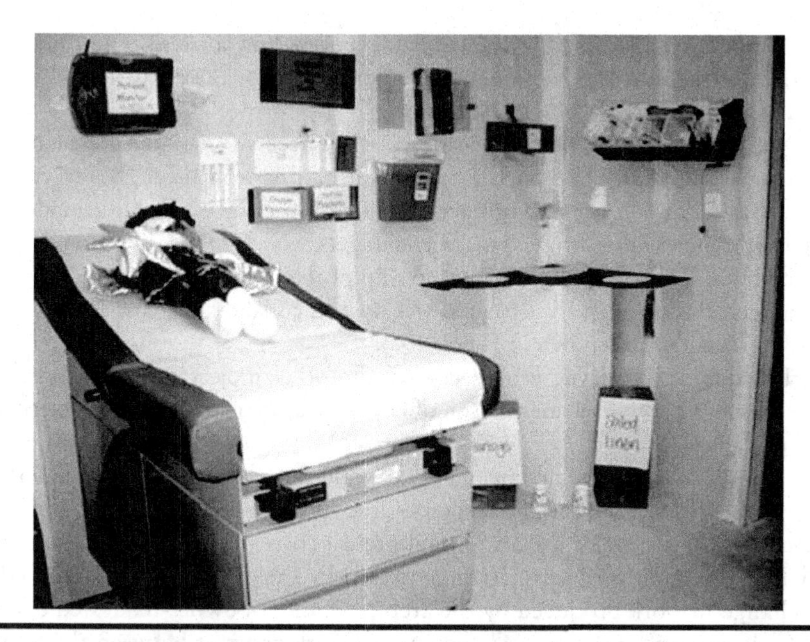

Figure 19.7 Exam room interior. As detailed design concludes, Lean principles are part of the design and nearly every detail has been considered. There should be little uncertainty or surprises at this point.

triparty contract agreement was used to align the owner, architect, and general contractor with a mutually beneficial common goal and shared "risk pool." This arrangement promoted teamwork and alignment in a way that traditional contracting had not and set the tone from the beginning that infighting and poor cooperation would only lead to everyone's misfortune. Lean construction principles were applied throughout the construction period, including the use of "pull planning" with subcontractors. The cumulative results of these innovations are described next.

The Payoff

The Bellevue project met the organizational goals for cost reduction, space reduction, and on-time delivery. The space reduction from 110,000 square feet to 75,000 square feet was achieved primarily by (1) the successive review of the mocked-up physical space by the core team, and the core team's agreement to minimize space requirements through multipurpose use; (2) data-driven capacity analysis based on Lean processes, not current practice; and (3) physical mockup and computer simulation of patient, provider, and staff flows to strip unnecessary square footage and travel distances that did not support efficient activities. The traditional approach of using industry benchmarks was rejected, and a zero-based methodology challenged all current-state baselines. The volume data, process flow analysis, and functional descriptions justified the requested space, not the personal or experiential preferences of the users.

One of the key validation measures of the success of the integrated project delivery or Lean design and build project is the cost performance. The target value design was set at $45 million and performed at $40 million. The cost model was based on benchmarks, while the target budgets were established through team collaboration. Each discipline had ownership of the costs and tracked its individual budget. Budget status was shared weekly and collaborative cost management caused a reduction, as shown in Figure 19.8.

How does the Bellevue project compare to other projects of similar size and scope? Table 19.1 shows a comparison of key metrics to demonstrate the success of the Lean approach.

It is well known in the design and build world that the amount of change activity over the life of a project and response time for the acknowledgment and resolution of issues are major drivers to total project costs. In reference to Table 19.1, an RFI is a request for information generated by the general contractor, a CIW is a change in work produced by the architect, and an owner-requested change (ORC) is written by the owner. There was a stark contrast between the Seattle Children's Bellevue Clinic's (SCBC) change activity and that of the comparison project. Also, the number of submittals (confirmation by the contractors to the architect's specs) is shown in Figure 19.9. The submittals indicate the relative ambiguity of the design and incompleteness of the information as each stage on construction progresses. The low number of submittals received (primarily at the front of the project) was a demonstration of the high quality of the design. This had a strong positive effect on lowering the cost. The rapid turnaround of the submittals also helped maintain excellent schedule performance.

The RFIs are requests from the general contractor and indicate the level of project rework. The RFI performance shown in Figure 19.10 was startling because of the low quantity, which further demonstrates the robustness and collaboration of the design and build processes.

The coordination of the design and build groups from the very beginning of the project, with fewer change requests occurring early in the process, helped keep the project plan well within schedule. Figure 19.11 shows the days ahead of schedule resulting from the integrated facility design approach.

Opening day of July 20, 2010, could have been accelerated further if required by the owner. Again, this metric was another indicator of a successful process and solid leadership.

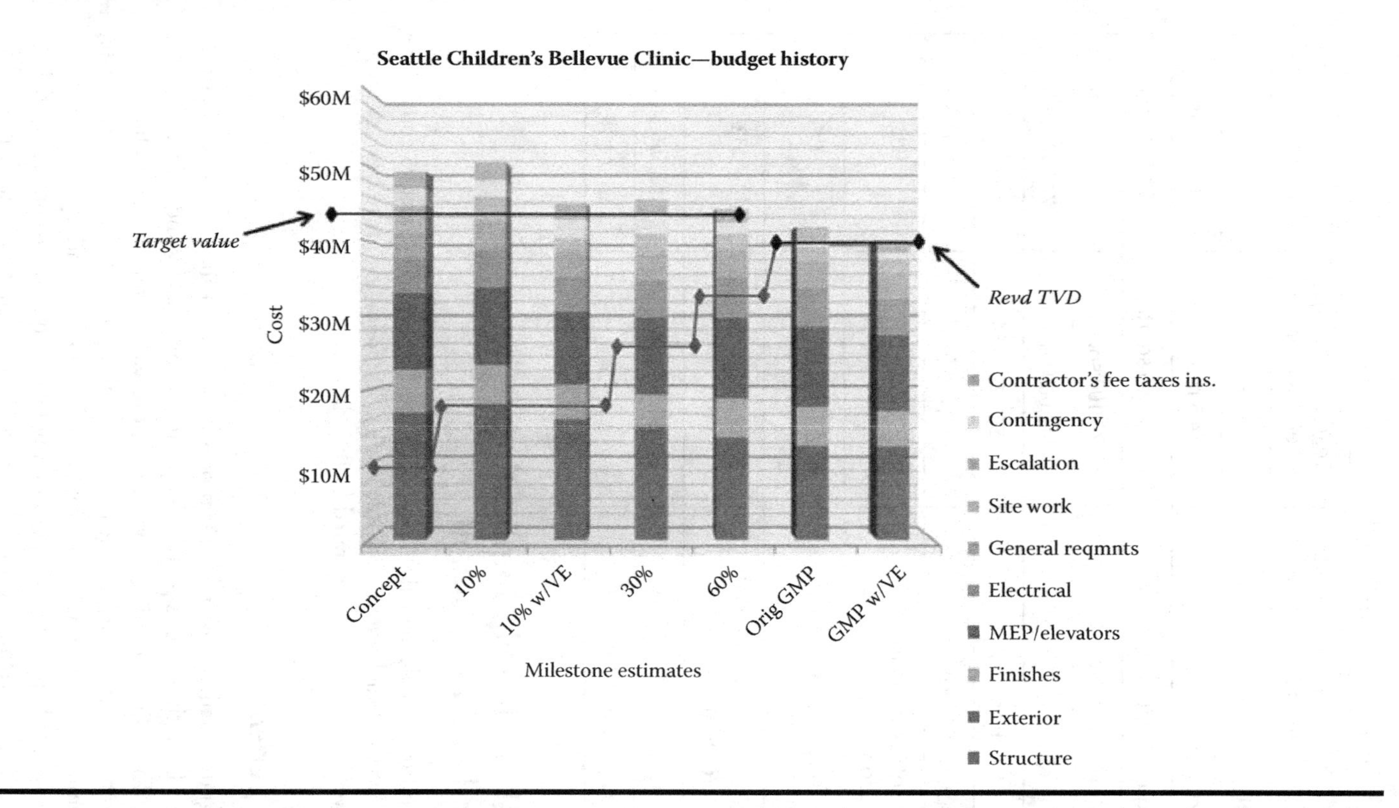

Figure 19.8 Cost target achievement. Estimating categories of cost at various points in the design process. Lean principles drove down cost. VE, valve engineering; GMP, guaranteed maximum price; TVD, target value design; MEP, mechanical, electrical, and plumbing. (Courtesy of Jeff Giuzio, partner, Seneca Group.)

Table 19.1 Metrics Comparison to Similar Project

Metric Description	*Seattle Children's Bellevue Clinic*	*Similar Project*
Completion date	June 2010	June 2004
Project duration	14.5 months	18 months
Gross square feet	186,000 sq. ft.	152,362 sq. ft.
Ambulatory surgery center	73,100 sq. ft.	78,065 sq. ft.
Parking garage	112,000 sq. ft.	74,297 sq. ft.
Total construction cost	$40,273,684	$33,544,682
Cost per square foot	$216.53	$220.16
Quantity of requests for information (RFIs)	78	608
Quantity of changes in work (CIWs)	37	39
Quantity of owner-requested changes (ORCs)	18	102
Total change order (CO) amount ($)	$1,500,000	$2,566,160
Total CO amount (% of total)	4%	7.6%

Critical Leadership Implications for Facility Development

Seattle Children's Bellevue Clinic gave the partners an opportunity to collaborate in very new ways to achieve remarkable results. The following are reflections on the "must haves" for successful integrated facility design.

Lean Experience

The integrated facility design (IFD) process is best used in an organization that already has Lean thinking as part of its operational philosophy and a natural way of thinking. The belief that much of what the processes contain is waste; that single-piece continuous flow of work is the goal; that waiting and idle resources are waste; that too much space is waste; and that travel, multiple handoffs, and searching should be reduced are foundational building blocks for an IFD process to deliver significant results. Attempting to do IFD and Lean design in an organization without prior experience with Lean would likely fail.

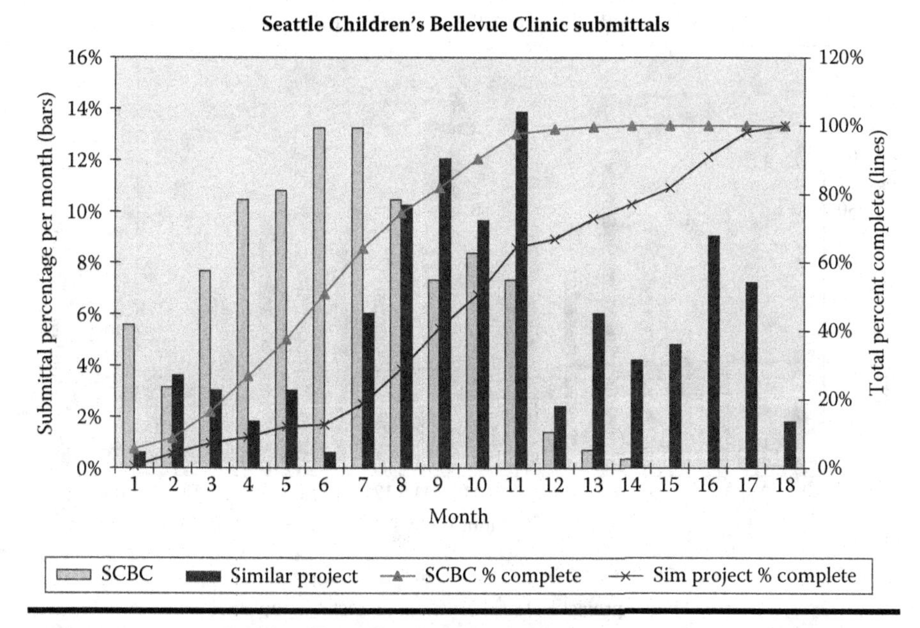

Figure 19.9 Submittal frequency. Lean design principles reduced the ambiguity in later months of design and drove the design to be completed sooner than by traditional methods. (Courtesy of Jeff Giuzio, partner, Seneca Group.)

SCH's CPI experience and knowledge helped resolve many design issues. Any of the issues could have been resolved differently if thinking had not been guided by a number of key Lean concepts. For example, the principle that all of the space should be flexible and usable for multiple purposes helped the core team break down the traditional departmental thinking and generated designs with more standard and shared spaces. The idea of "building tents, not castles" (a phrase coined by chapter author and book editor Joan Wellman for Lean facility design and adapted from the work of Hedberg, Nystrom, and Starbuck[1]) brought in a deeper understanding of flexibility and rapid reconfiguration in contrast to hunkering down into one's own space. Initially, few believed that too much space was an enemy until they saw how it promoted excess travel time and impaired "line of sight." The Lean principles permeated the mind-set of the participants from concept to construction so much so that waste was equally attacked in the design process and in the physical product.

Project Leadership

It is crucial to have strong, experienced leadership guiding the project. This process changes how people perform their work. The leader needs to continually bring the team back to their guiding principles and objectives over and over again and not allow the work groups to slip back into "traditional" facility design or decision-making practices.

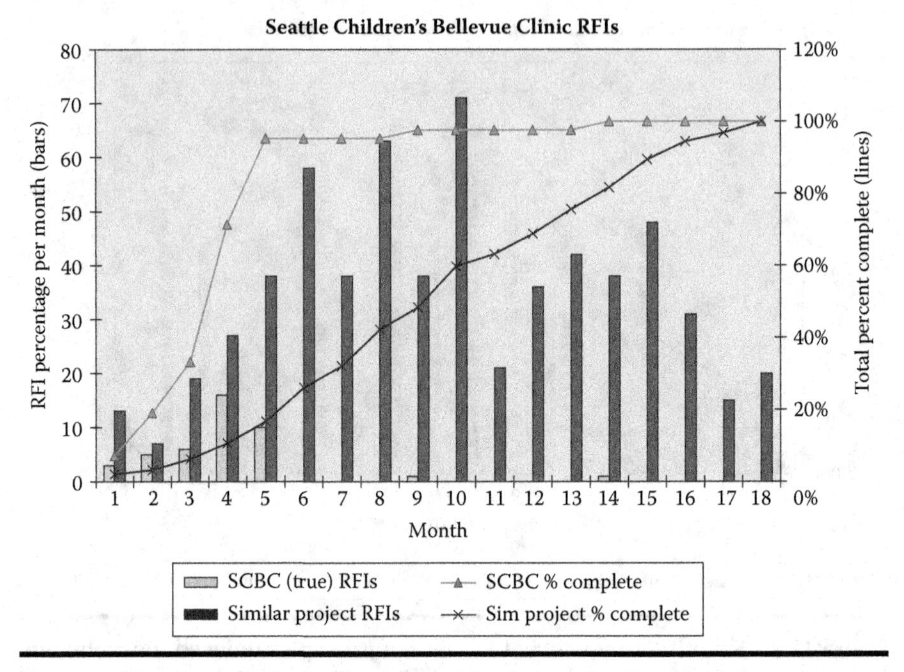

Figure 19.10 Request for information (RFI) frequency. Do you know what you want? With Lean design principles, you do, and rework required during design is vastly reduced. (Courtesy of Jeff Giuzio, partner, Seneca Group.)

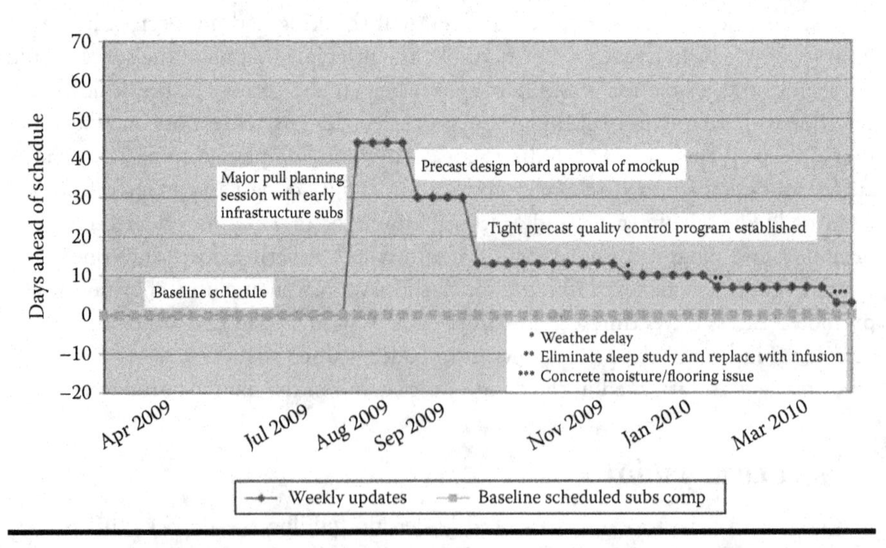

Figure 19.11 Days ahead of schedule. Less rework and less uncertainty mean faster results and a favorable schedule variance. (Courtesy of Jeff Giuzio, partner, Seneca Group. Unpublished intellectual property of the Seneca Real Estate Group Inc.)

For example, it was a foundational principle that the determination of the number of clinic rooms required for various specialties should be based on verifiable data (i.e., expected volumes, cycle times, and work-in-progress [WIP] calculations). There was a tendency to make the room decision based on personal beliefs ("I think this is how many I need" or "I need more than I have") or on architectural planning calculations guided by industry benchmarks. This tendency requires leaders to rely on quantitative analysis and computer simulation models when demonstrating that the building is "big enough." Strong and experienced operational leadership paired with strong facility-building leadership are critical in order to stay the course with Lean thinking.

Core Team

The core team should be composed of the organization's best Lean thinkers rather than populating the team with the "usual suspects" needed for political acceptance. The core team must "own" the design rather than simply react to the architect's design. In the Bellevue project, the core team lived the project from concept to becoming members of the operations team. Team members knew that they were accountable as stewards of the design from beginning to end. The core team needs to include all key parties from the start, including the architect, the general contractor, and other key construction partners.

Logical Sequence

It is common for groups to rush to a detailed layout prematurely. Applying a logical sequence for the development of the end user space meant moving from an abstract, unconstrained perspective to a detailed design by progressively adding constraints. Understanding the clinical and surgery center functional requirements, establishing critical adjacencies, and defining operational workflows before bringing in the constraints of the building and building site allowed the core team to design the building to fit the work rather than fit the work into a preconceived notion of the building. This may not always be feasible, but when building a new site it is an optimal approach.

The Value of Mockups

Mockups are frequently used during the design process, but rarely at the scale done for this project. The importance of mocking up not only individual spaces but also the relationship between spaces is critical to Lean design and can lead to considerable breakthroughs. In the Bellevue project, mockups promoted early rapid prototyping, and participants often made their spaces smaller, changed traditional adjacencies, or completely changed their design thinking after "seeing and using" their paper design brought to life. Renting empty warehouse space for large-scale mockups was worth the investment, resulting in an improved design, reduced change order activity, and minimal friction between owners and architects. In the traditional design

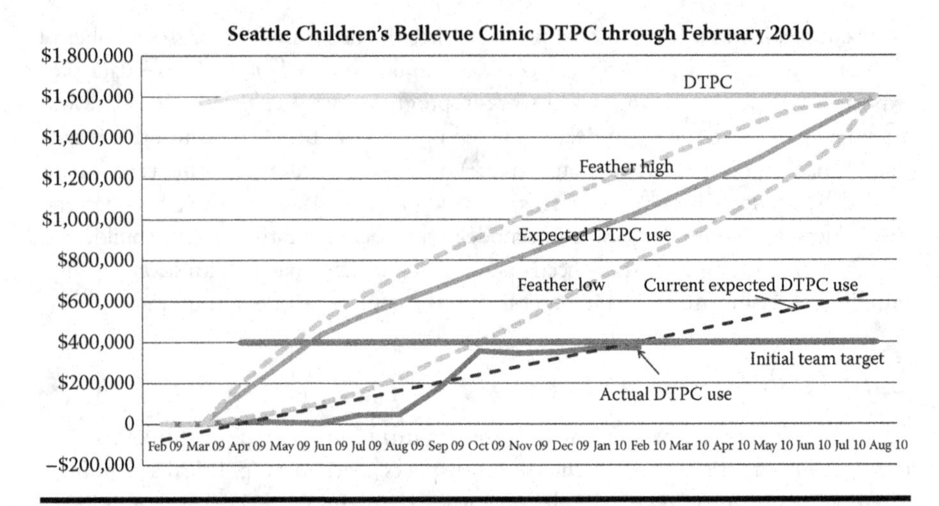

Figure 19.12 Triparty agreement pool. Sharing the risk and sharing the reward. Owner, architect, and general contractor all benefited financially by participating in the Lean process. (Courtesy of Jeff Giuzio, partner, Seneca Group. Unpublished intellectual property of the Seneca Real Estate Group Inc.)

process, the parties would be looking at blueprints and attempting to resolve conflicts or downsize without truly understanding how the proposed space would function.

Alignment of Incentives

As discussed earlier, a triparty contract agreement was used to align the owner, architect, and general contractor with a mutually beneficial common goal. A contingency fund was established so that if common goals were met, the pool would be split three ways. As shown in Figure 19.12, the design team performance contingency (DTPC) line represents an acceptable project but without the distribution of an award. The initial team target line represents the full incentive distributed. The "actual DTPC use" line shows that almost the entire contingency was received. It should be noted that there was also a risk element that balanced the reward. It was possible for the project to go above the DTPC line and for all parties to be required to fund the overage if costs were not controlled.

While an integrated form of agreement requires significant effort to develop, the payoffs in cost reductions resulting from collaborative decision making and integrated problem solving are considerable.

Conclusion

Not everything was perfect. It was said many times that "we learned as we progressed." The group did not "make it up as we went along" but rather traveled together on a project of new ideas and discovery as guided by a reliable process. The Lean, healthcare, project management, architectural, and construction expertise converged on new problems and solved them as they arose. For example, a traditional equipment-planning process was layered on top of the Lean design structure. In retrospect, equipment planning should have been integrated into the work early on. In the end the equipment budget was met, but it required more energy to complete than if integration had been comprehensive.

The project targets and methods were strategically driven from beginning to end. Traditionally, similar projects are viewed by many as a facilities responsibility and cost reduction expectations are expected to be generated well after the concept and functional decisions have been solidified. In this project, the new process changed the role of the facilities department, forcing much earlier and much deeper joint decision making with operational leaders in the room. While these were not uncomfortable changes, given SCH's history with CPI, they were nonetheless changes that required modifications to past practices.

SCH set the culture and expectation of excellence and the way work would be done. This approach changed the job for everyone, especially the architects and contractors in relationship to the owner's involvement. The core team became intimate with the design and "owned it," a role usually played primarily by the architect. The adjustments were not "drama-free," but when the team successfully emerged on the other side, there was agreement that the old way would never be used again.

Deeper education on the Lean principles was needed by all team members. For this project, the traditional sequential or "waterfall" model of design development was replaced by an integrated or iterative methodology. Concurrent engineering or the parallel and overlapping processing of conceptual, functional, detailed, construction, sustainability, and life cycle design activities was not understood by all and caused conflicts. Selecting a core team with Lean experience was not enough. Process experience with the Lean concepts was an insufficient replacement for specific Lean design and concurrent engineering knowledge. Also, there was the belief that the non-SCH team members could learn as the project progressed, but the mismatch in levels of Lean understanding caused friction and delay. The architects and contractors were selected because of their Lean experience, but as the project unfolded more education was needed than initially imagined.

"We Did It!"

The Achilles' heel of traditional facility design with user groups has been the inclusion of a select few, resulting in design disagreements by the eventual operational residents who were never asked. The process used throughout this project was very transparent. Great effort was made to solicit constant feedback at every decision point. With newsletters, daily updates, open houses, mockup tours, structured interviews, surveys, and countless tie-in meetings, every avenue of outreach was employed. The input was incredible. Patients, families, providers, and staff were involved every step of the way. The goal was to exhaust the users with requests for feedback and then ask them again. The results were worth the effort. Hundreds of people "touched" the design in some way. The outcome is truly the product of a shared vision.

Although the quantitative evidence demonstrates undeniable success, some of the emotional aspects spoke louder. The sense of accomplishment—"We did it!"—is palpable. Core team members frequently expressed their enthusiasm for being included in the project. Other non-SCH team members saw this as one of the best projects of their careers. Still others keep asking, "When are we going to do this again?" Such comments are the reward for the Lean leader.

Note

1. B. L. Hedberg, P. C. Nystrom, and W. H. Starbuck, "Camping on Seesaws: Prescriptions for a Self-Designing Organization," *Administrative Science Quarterly* 21 (March 1976): 41–65.

Epilogue

Mark A. Reed, Aaron Dipzinski, and Lynn D. Martin

On July 20, 2010, Bellevue Clinic and Surgery Center (BCSC) opened its doors to patients for the first time. Although there were a small number of flow and process issues that presented themselves on the first days and weeks, overall the opening was remarkably free of drama. BCSC was in business. By using its Lean tools to identify problems and by applying point improvements to address issues, we were able to improve flow daily. Daily management systems were employed to direct and sustain the improvements. Within a handful of months the center was moving past its startup phase and began taking on the characteristics of a functional Lean operation.

Implementation of a Lean Management System

This smooth startup did not occur by chance. Successful integrated facility design (IFD) requires implementing standard work in the new facility and a Lean management system for continuous improvement. So once the facility design and construction was underway, detailed value stream maps and standard work were immediately developed in order to be ready to go live. It was understood that the patient and provider processes enabled by the building design needed to be clearly documented and followed. Work was then begun on creating specific patient, family, and provider process maps as construction of the building was nearing completion. Multidisciplinary teams comprised of the significant stakeholders for a given process were brought into the yet to be occupied building so that all planning could be performed in the actual workplace. Each process map represented a highly detailed depiction of the work sequence and respective flow. An integral component in the process map/flow development was the trialing of the processes by iterative mock execution of the intended plan until the process was sound. It was then captured and documented as an operational standard. The processes thus designed were then iteratively trialed for each of the specialties that would be operating at BCSC. This allowed for the capture of the nuanced differences in flow that the patients of each specialty required while at the same time preserving the operational standards present in the process.

Daily Huddles

It was soon apparent that for the processes to be sustained and improved, a rigorous management system would need to be in place. To that end, standard work for daily huddles, visibility boards, and leader standard work were established. Daily unit huddles provided immediate advancements in establishing work unit readiness and in the identification of issues and opportunities for improvement. Ultimately, a facility-wide daily readiness huddle process was implemented. The addition of tiered huddles resulted in significant improvements in communication and collaboration. The facility huddles occur twice daily, one at 9:20 a.m. and the other 4 p.m. The entire team, 23 departments in total, participates in providing brief reports on the status of their operation. Each participant's contribution is brief and scripted resulting in huddles being completed within seven minutes. However, it is a very productive seven minutes. Building-wide abnormal conditions are captured and visual management is updated to capture the status of the facility. In addition, the facility huddles provided an unexpected but very important additional benefit. No one left. After the huddle participants lingered by the board engaging in discussions with their colleagues from other units and partnering on shared issues and the desired improvements. The teambuilding and sense of shared vision that arose out of the facility huddles established the foundation for the facility's daily management system and provided a pivotal advancement in the evolution of BCSC culture.

Continuous Improvement

Huddles are not the only element of the management system. Other important components include collection and review of both operational and success metrics, generation and capturing of improvement ideas, and the support of standardized operational and leader work. Visibility boards are posted throughout the center conveying information on important metrics and trends, capturing small and large issues, documentation of improvement work, updates of standard processes, and visual confirmation that standards are being followed.

The work of leaders in supporting the management system is also standardized and visible. Leaders regularly participate in both unit and facility huddles and provide structured improvement coaching to participants, supporting the connection between institutional goals and strategies and the unit work. Facility strategy deployment and review of progress are promoted through weekly leader "Hoshin" stand-up meetings held at the facility's strategy visibility wall.

Results

BCSC was Seattle Children's first effort to design and build a Lean facility. The hypothesis was that a facility designed upon Lean principles and using a comprehensive Lean management system would generate superior organizational outcomes. Through five years of operation that hypothesis has been supported by impressive success metrics.

- **Growth:** The clinic and surgery center have grown substantially since the opening of the facility. During the initial year of operations, the surgery center completed 2,446 cases and the clinic saw 26,179 patients. To date the clinic has grown 48 percent and the surgery center has increased the number of patients by 59 percent.
- **Patient satisfaction:** The patient and families have consistently rated the Bellevue Surgery Center as the highest patient surgical experience in the entire hospital system.
- **Cost:** The cost per unit of service, a measure of direct expense in relation to volume, has improved by 16 percent in the specialty clinics. More telling is that in the last nine months of operations over $80,000 of actual savings to the bottom line were identified and implemented by the teams. This does not include the savings in time, space, and other waste eliminated as a result of these small improvement efforts.
- **Engagement:** The Bellevue leadership team's employee satisfaction score is outstanding; scoring 4.89 out of 5.0 in the most recent survey. More important than the actual scores within the facility is the magnitude of improvement activity occurring throughout the building. In the first six months of the current fiscal year, 56 improvement presentations have occurred and this only measures a fraction of the actual improvements occurring throughout the facility.

These metrics demonstrate that a system founded on continuous performance improvement can lead to safe, effective clinical outcomes, improved patient satisfaction, high employee engagement, and significant cost savings.

That said, the need for improvement is never-ending. We have discovered our share of opportunities for further improvement (a good thing!), though some have been hidden in plain sight in spite of our best efforts. We can and will do better. We have confidence that as long as we continue to evolve as a problem-seeking, problem-reporting, and problem-solving organization, we will continue to improve, and produce an ever-more effective and satisfying experience for our patients and families, and for our staff.

Glossary

A-3 Report: A one-page form and storyboard based upon plan–do–check–act (PDCA). It is used for problem solving, proposal sharing, and information sharing. A-3 feedback and coaching is an important part of the management development process.

Abnormality: Any deviation from the expected standard process or standard work is considered an abnormality.

Andon: A visual and/or audible communication system indicating the current status of a process.

Batching: The mass-production practice of making large quantities of a part regardless of customer or process demand; causes excess inventory and process waits, and masks errors and their root cause.

Buffer resources: A small but sufficient amount of inventory (people, material, space) to meet customer demand when customer ordering patterns, or takt times, vary.

Cells: A process approach that uses groupings of equipment, tools, and people organized to perform an entire sequence of a process in one continuous physical location (cell). A well-designed cell can increase the flexibility of operations and produce a variety of products in smaller and smaller quantities. It reduces operating costs and improves the utilization of people as variation in volume and mix occur.

Changeover: The process of readying workspaces or machines for the next job. A component of "set up."

Continuous flow: The ideal process state where customers are provided what is needed, just when it is needed, and in the exact amounts needed. Continuous flow is synonymous with just-in-time (JIT).

Continuous improvement: A philosophy by which an organization looks for ways to always do things better. The gains made through continuous improvement activities are generally incremental, small-step improvements that lead to significant improvements over time in the quality, cost, delivery, and safety of an organization's products and processes, and the engagement of its employees in the work of the organization.

Continuous performance improvement (CPI): Seattle Children's Hospital's adaptation to healthcare of the Toyota Production System, CPI is a philosophical, long-term approach to continuous improvement. CPI focuses on improving results for the benefit of SCH patients and their families, and on supporting the people of SCH in their work.

Countermeasures: An action taken or planned that is intended to address the root cause of an abnormality.

Cycle time: The time that elapses from the beginning of a process to completion of that process. Cycle time is measured, not calculated.

Daily Management System (DMS): A system of day-to-day processes and activities that promotes the adherence to standards and process performance targets. DMS ensures rapid identification of problems needing immediate kaizen activity and often involves daily huddles, tiered problem escalation, visual displays of performance targets and actual performance (often case by case, hour by hour), leader standard work, accountability processes and boards, and standard work confirmation and coaching.

Defect: A defect in a product or process is an error that has moved beyond where the error occurred. Risk and cost increase as defects move further along in the process.

Error: Any deviation from a specified process or expected outcome.

Error proofing: A means of eliminating errors before they occur.

FIFO: First in, first out (FIFO) is a work-control method used to ensure that the oldest work (first in) is the first to be processed (first out).

5S system: A method for removing excess materials and tools from the workplace and organizing the required items, using visual controls, such that they are easy to find, use, and maintain. 5S stands for sort, simplify, sweep, standardize, and sustain (definitions follow).

Sort: The first activity in the 5S system. It involves sorting through and sorting out items, placing red tags on these items, and moving them to a temporary holding area. The items are disposed of, sold, moved, or given away by a predetermined time.

Simplify: The second activity of the 5S system. It involves identifying the best location for each item that remains in the area, relocating items that do not belong in the area, setting height and size limits, and installing temporary location indicators.

Sweep: The third activity of the 5S system, involving a regular physical and visual sweep of the area to identify potential problems. Keeps the area and equipment in good condition.

Standardize: The fourth activity in the 5S system. It involves creating the rules of maintaining and controlling the conditions established after implementing the first three Ss. Visual controls are used to make these conditions obvious.

Sustain: The fifth activity of the 5S system, where a person or team ensures adherence to 5S standards through communication, training, and self-discipline.

5 Whys: Ask "why" five times whenever a problem is encountered in order to identify the root cause of the problem and to avoid merely addressing the symptoms. By asking why and answering each time, the root cause becomes more evident.

Flow: The progressive achievement of tasks along the value stream so that a process or product proceeds one step at a time, timed to customer demand.

Flows of healthcare: Patients, families, staff, medications, information, supplies, equipment, revenue/cash, and the flow of improvements.

***Gemba*:** Japanese term that means the "actual place" where work is performed.

***Genchi Genbutsu*:** "Go and see for yourself" is a key principle of the Toyota System. Leaders at all levels go to gemba to directly observe the actual situation. Sometimes known as the "3 Actual Rule." Go to the actual place, see the actual "problem," talk to the actual people involved.

***Hansei*:** Deep "reflection." Management leads deep and comprehensive reflection about serious abnormalities or about past performance. When engaging in hansei, management leads a very candid discussion with participants from several levels of the organization, covering the many major and minor causes of an abnormality. This is also the first step in the hoshin kanri process (strategy deployment) and often takes up to 70 percent of the time with 30 percent dedicated to implementation planning.

***Heijunka*:** See *Load leveling.*

Just-in-time (JIT): A system that ensures customers receive only what is needed, just when it is needed, and in the exact amounts needed.

***Kaizen* (Continuous improvement):** Small daily improvements performed by everyone. *Kai* means "take apart" and *zen* means "make good." The goal of kaizen is the total elimination of waste.

***Kanban*:** *Kanban* means "to put away and to bring out" or "signal" and is a cornerstone of the just-in-time pull system. A kanban communicates upstream precisely what is required (in terms of work specifications and quantity) at the time it is required.

Lead time: Lead time is measured. It is the total time between customer order and customer receipt of a product or service.

Lean: A shorthand term for continuous improvement.

Load leveling: Balancing the amount of work to be done (the load) by time and by worker in balanced proportions based on customer demand and product or service variety. Also called *Heijunka.*

Monument: Any process or technology that necessitates batch processing.

***Muda*:** See *Waste.*

Plan–do–check–act (PDCA): Or plan–do–study–act; the Deming Cycle. The primary mechanism for a scientific approach used to sustain a mature

Lean organization. PDCA is the key referent for recognizing abnormal conditions and directly leads to rapid problem solving and improvements.

***Poka-yoke*:** A mistake-proofing device or procedure to prevent errors.

Process: A sequence of operations (consisting of people, materials, and methods) for the design, creation, and delivery of a product or service.

Processing time: The time a product is actually being worked on in design or production and the time an order is actually being processed. Typically, processing time is a small fraction of cycle time and lead time.

Pull: A system in which nothing is produced by the upstream supplier until the downstream user signals a need.

Push: Conventional work in which services or products are created based on schedules and availability of materials regardless of need downstream. It results in batching and the waste of inventory.

Quality, cost, delivery, safety, and engagement (QCDSE): The framework for continuous performance improvement at Seattle Children's Hospital. By removing waste from processes and systems, SCH seeks to improve the quality, delivery, and safety of its care and services. Through the elimination of waste, as quality, delivery, and safety improve, costs are reduced, and engagement of faculty and staff improves as barriers and obstacles in their work are removed.

Rapid Process Improvement Workshop (RPIW): An important tool of continuous improvement, particularly at the beginning of an organization's journey. The workshop consists of several days of focused learning, process mapping, waste removal, and process redesign with the intent to implement process changes by the end of the workshop. Multiple disciplines and multiple levels of faculty, staff, and management are involved in an RPIW, leading to enhanced engagement. PDCA is critical postworkshop to ensure continuous improvement.

Reliable methods: Reliable methods are consciously developed, consistently followed, and evaluated for capability. Reliable methods must have an identified owner to audit performance and uniformly maintain the methods as standard.

Respect for people: One of the two main pillars of the Toyota Way 2001 house, the other being continuous improvement. Lean philosophy includes the idea that if people are respected and treated well, then they will, with management's support, perform superbly. Toyota believes that people must be respected all the time.

Root cause: The ultimate reason for an event or condition.

***Sensei*:** A teacher with a mastery of a body of knowledge—in this case, CPI philosophy and methods.

Servant leadership: Servant leadership means that leaders must understand how they best serve, assist, and develop others at all levels of the organization so that everyone can continuously improve value-added service to patients and families.

Set-up time: The entire time it takes a process to switch from producing one part or service to another. Defined as the time from when the last step of process A is completed to the start of the first step of process B.

Single-piece flow: A process in which work proceeds one complete step at a time without interruptions, rework, or waste.

Spaghetti diagram: A map of the path taken by a specific product, person, or piece of information as it moves through the value stream, so-called because the route in an unimproved process typically looks like a plate of spaghetti.

Standard work: The application of time to reliable methods.

Standard work combination sheet: Defines the order of actions that each worker must perform within a given takt time. Illustrates the relationship between the processes manual time(s), automatic time(s), walking time(s), waiting time(s), and the takt time.

Standard work in process (SWIP): Minimum inventory that is necessary to perform the job safely and successfully within a given cycle time.

Standard work sheet: A visual control tool to help the worker, team leader, and manager maintain a standardized operation routine. It details the motion of the worker and the sequence of actions. Serves as a guideline for workers and supervisors to show where and in what sequence operations are completed in the work area.

***Takt* time:** The pace, or rhythm, of customer demand. Takt time determines how fast a process needs to run to meet customer demand. Takt time is calculated (not measured) and may be longer or shorter than cycle time. To calculate, divide the total operating time available by the total quantity required by the customer. Takt time is expressed in seconds, minutes, hours, or days.

Team charter: A document that describes the elements of an RPIW. It includes, but is not limited to, the following elements: (1) a clear definition of a team's mission, (2) a statement of team members' roles and responsibilities, (3) a description of the scope of the team's responsibility and authority, (4) project deadlines, (5) workshop metrics and targets, and (6) expected deliverables (outcomes).

U-shaped cells: A U-shaped, work area layout that allows one or more workers to process and transfer work units one piece—or one small group—at a time.

Value added: Defined from the perspective of the customer. An activity that transforms the fit, form, or function of a process or product. An activity that, if the customer knew you were doing it, they'd be willing to pay for it.

Value-added percentage: The percentage of the total lead time that is spent actually adding value to a product or service. To calculate value-added percentage, divide the total value-added time by the total lead time.

Value-added time: Time during which an action or process changes the fit, form, or function of the process, and a customer would be willing to pay for if they knew you did it.

Value stream: A collection of all the steps (both value-added and non-value added) involved between customer order and customer receipt of the product or service.

Value stream improvement plan: The key output of value steam mapping and analysis. It provides the roadmap to achieve the desired future state by certain dates with specific performance metrics.

Value stream leadership: Responsibility for the customer experience throughout the value stream, with an emphasis on relentless process improvements within and between the silos through which a product or service must transit.

Value stream map: Identification of all the specific activities (including waste), from the perspective of the customer, that occur along a value stream of a product or service.

Visual control: The placement in plain view of all tools, parts, work activities, and indicators of system performance, so the status of the system can be understood at a glance by everyone involved. This includes the use of color, signs, and clear lines of sight in a work area. Visual controls should clearly designate what things are and where they belong. They should provide immediate feedback as to the work being done and its pace.

Waste/*Muda*: The definition of muda has been expanding for the last 10 to 15 years. It simply means doing non-value-added work or activities that do not add value from the customers' perspective. In the current Lean literature, there are more than 25 descriptions of muda with variation driven primarily by organization type: manufacturing, service, healthcare, financial, military, administrative, and so on. In healthcare, common types of muda include processing, correction, search time, transportation, wait time, space, inventory, complexity, and underutilized people. Recent additions to the definition of muda include leadership wastes due to lack of focus and discipline or waste embedded in the organization or system structure.

Work in progress (WIP): Items (material or information) waiting between steps in a process.

***Yokoten*:** Spreading good ideas and improvements horizontally across the organization. When used systematically, yokoten becomes a great "force multiplier" of kaizen efforts.

Index

This index includes the glossary. Page numbers with f, s, and t refer to figures, sidebars, and tables, respectively.

D

M

N

O

P

Q

R

T

Printed in the United States
by Baker & Taylor Publisher Services